CURRENT ISSUES IN COMPARATIVE GRAMMAR

Studies in Natural Language and Linguistic Theory

VOLUME 35

The titles published in this series are listed at the end of this volume.

CURRENT ISSUES IN COMPARATIVE GRAMMAR

Edited by

ROBERT FREIDIN
Princeton University

KLUWER ACADEMIC PUBLISHERS
DORDRECHT / BOSTON / LONDON

Library of Congress Cataloging-in-Publication Data

Current issues in comparative grammar edited by Robert Freidin.
p. cm. -- (Studies in natural language and linguistic theory ; v. 35)
Includes index.
ISBN 0-7923-3778-6 (alk. paper)
1. Grammar, Comparative and general. I. Freidin, Robert.
II. Series.
P201.C87 1995
415--dc20 95-39852

ISBN 0-7923-3778-6

Published by Kluwer Academic Publishers,
P.O. Box 17, 3300 AA Dordrecht, The Netherlands.

Kluwer Academic Publishers incorporates
the publishing programmes of
D. Reidel, Martinus Nijhoff, Dr W. Junk and MTP Press.

Sold and distributed in the U.S.A. and Canada
by Kluwer Academic Publishers,
101 Philip Drive, Norwell, MA 02061, U.S.A.

In all other countries, sold and distributed
by Kluwer Academic Publishers Group,
P.O. Box 322, 3300 AH Dordrecht, The Netherlands.

02-0898-100 ts

Printed on acid-free paper

Printed in the Netherlands

CONTENTS

ACKNOWLEDGMENTS

This volume owes its existence to the Second Princeton Workshop on Comparative Grammar held April 27–29, 1989 and made possible through the generosity of the Andrew D. Mellon Foundation. The editor is indebted to Lorrie LeJeune for transforming a set of computer files into a book.

ROBERT FREIDIN

INTRODUCTION

The papers in this volume, based on work presented at the Second Princeton Workshop on Comparative Grammar held in April 1989, illustrate the diversity and productivity of research within the principles and parameters framework.[1] They take up a rich and varied set of issues, using strikingly different strategies. It is worth noting that even when researchers share fundamental assumptions of a common framework, quite substantial disagreements may arise—see especially the exchange between Uriagrereka and Otero, and the Aoun & Li and Williams papers. The following summary briefly sketches the contents of this volume.

The Burzio and Quicoli articles adopt complementary research strategies. Burzio's paper on binding theory is a model of the broad-ranging comparative analyses that have become possible under the principles and parameters framework. It employs binding data from an impressively broad range of languages to motivate a radical alternative to the standard binding theory. Quicoli's paper focuses primarily on parametric effects of inflection (an important topic in the Burzio paper as well) in infinitival constructions of Spanish and Portuguese. Quicoli demonstrates how the properties of these constructions in the two languages follow from the standard theories of Case and binding. Safir's comment elaborates on Quicoli's analysis and raises some objections to it, to which Quicoli responds.

The two articles by Torrego and Kornfilt also deal with the syntactic properties of infinitival constructions. Torrego's paper discusses the differential crosslinguistic behavior of the so-called raising verbs which take experiencer arguments (e.g. *seem* + *to*-phrase) in three closely related languages (Spanish, French and Italian). The research strategy of this paper is thus similar to that of Quicoli's. Kornfilt's article on NP movement and restructuring adopts yet another research strategy available to contemporary comparative grammar. Her investigation of the infinitival double passive construction in Turkish provides an fine example of how a deeper understanding of the details of the language faculty can be achieved by focusing on the analysis of constructions that appear to be rare among the world's languages. Harbert's commentary extends the discussion of constructions which appear to involve restructuring analyses by considering additional phenomena from a range of other languages, including the Norwegian complex passive, binding in German and Russian, and object agreement in Hindi and Hungarian. To the extent that the properties of such unusual constructions are predictable under current theories of UG, these constructions provide strong empirical support and may also be useful for fine tuning the theory.

The attempt to bring the analysis of what might at first glance seem like a recalcitrant phenomenon in line with the theory of UG often leads to new insights about the theory of grammar. Lasnik's article on the Case analysis of expletive constructions provides an excellent case study. It provides strong arguments against a mechanism of Case transmission and in favor of both Chomsky's visibility hypothesis linking Case assignment to the θ-Criterion and Belletti's (1988) partitive Case analysis, which it extends to account for parametric variation in the behavior of passives in English vs. Italian. Travis's comment elaborates on Lasnik's analysis of expletives and offers an alternative account for the behavior of the verbs *be* vs. *consider* and also for the contrasting behavior of English and Italian passives.

The articles by Browning, Cinque and Baltin address the theory of syntactic movement. Browning's article compares Rizzi's relativized minimality proposal for determining government (hence the proper formulation of the ECP (see Rizzi (1990))) with previous unrelativized formulations of the minimality condition on government and discusses potential problems for Rizzi's system. Cinque's article, which argues for Rizzi's government analysis (as opposed to that of Chomsky (1986)), explores the motivation for and consequences of a significant refinement to that analysis, i.e. restricting the class of elements that can undergo 'long' extraction to those "which refer to specific members of a preestablished set." Baltin's comment extends Cinque's discussion of the weakness of a notion of theta-government for licensing antecedent-trace relations across a barrier and argues against Cinque's analysis of referentiality as support for Pesetsky's D-linking analysis (1987).

Ideally the theory of UG should be so restrictive that it uniquely determines the analysis of any linguistic phenomenon, since by hypothesis this is how UG operates in the mind of the language learner. If our theory of UG were this perfect, the controversies in the remaining articles in this collection would not have arisen. The articles by Uriagereka and Otero address the analysis of determiner clitics in Galegan (Galician). Uriagereka's article proposes a syntactic movement analysis of these clitic constructions, while Otero's article argues against such analyses in favor of a phonological analysis. Those by Aoun & Li and Williams discuss the existence of LF as a distinct level of syntactic representation. Aoun & Li's article argues for the existence of LF based on an analysis of pronoun and anaphor binding in Chinese. Williams's comment raises two objections to this analysis. First he challenges the notion of linguistic scope assumed by Aoun & Li (and many others), and then offers a brief critique of two of their claims in support of a level of LF.

NOTES

[1] For discussion see Chomsky & Lasnik 1993 and Freidin 1994a. See also Freidin 1994b for some discussion of the evolution of this framework.

REFERENCES

Belletti, A. (1988) The Case of Unaccusatives. *Linguistic Inquiry* 19.1–34.

Chomsky, N. (1981) *Lectures on Government and Binding.* Dordrecht: Foris.

Chomsky, N. (1986) *Barriers.* Cambridge: MIT Press.

Freidin, R. (1994a) Generative grammar: principles and parameters framework. In R. E. Asher (ed.) *The Encyclopedia of Language and Linguistics.* Oxford: Pergamon Press, 1370–1385.

Freidin, R. (1994b) Conceptual Shifts in the Science of Grammar: 1951–1992*, In C.P.

Otero, C., (1994) *Noam Chomsky: Critical Assessments,* London: Routledge, vol. 1, 653–690.

Pesetsky, D. (1987) Wh-in-situ: movement and unselective binding. In A. ter Meulen and E. Reuland (eds.) *The Representation of (In)definiteness.* Cambridge: MIT Press 98–129.

Rizzi, L. (1990) *Relativized Minimality.* Cambridge: MIT Press.

LUIGI BURZIO

THE ROLE OF THE ANTECEDENT IN ANAPHORIC RELATIONS*

1. INTRODUCTION

In this article, I attempt to provide an account of the fact that the binding properties of subjects of NPs systematically distinguish two groups of languages. In languages like Chinese, Japanese, Malayalam, subjects of NPs seem to have a sufficient "proximity" to an NP external antecedent to allow a reflexive, and yet a sufficient "distance" from it to also allow a pronoun, as in (1).

(1) a. *Chinese* (Huang (1983))
Zhangsan$_i$ kanjian-le [{ziji$_i$ / ta$_i$} de shu]
Zhangsan see-aspect [self / him of book]
'Zhangsan$_i$ saw his$_i$ book'

b. *Malayalam* (Mohanan (1982))
moohan$_i$ [{tante$_i$ / awante$_i$} bhaaryaye] nulli
Mohan [self's / he's wife] pinched
'Mohan$_i$ pinched his$_i$ wife'

In contrast, in Indo-European languages, subjects of NPs seem to be sufficiently "near" an NP-external antecedent to both allow a reflexive and exclude a pronoun, as in (2).

(2) a. *Latin* (Bertocchi and Casadio (1980))
Ioannes$_i$ [sororem {suam$_i$ / *eius$_i$}] vidit
Ioannes [sister self's / *his] saw
'Ioannes$_i$ saw his$_i$ sister'

b. *Russian* (Timberlake (1979))
On$_i$ uze rasskazal mne o [{svoej$_i$ / *ego$_i$} zizni]
He already tell me about [self's / *his life]
'He$_i$ had already told me about his$_i$ life'

c. *Danish* (Pica (1984))
Jorgen$_i$ elsker [{sin$_i$ / *hans$_i$} kone]
Jorgen loves [{self's / *his} wife]
'Jorgen$_i$ loves his$_i$ wife'

This important fact is not accounted for by past analyses. In particular, the one of Chomsky (1986a: 170ff), following that of Huang (1983), accounts only for the Chinese-type facts of (1). It does so by relativizing the locality constraints to the type of bound element. In that analysis, if a subject is an anaphor, its binding domain is defined as the next higher phrasal level, while if it is a pronoun the binding domain is defined as the same structure of which the element is the subject. Under this elaboration, the facts in (1) are brought into line with the long-standing Binding Theory of (3) below, since the reflexives are "locally" bound in the main clause, while the pronouns are "locally" free in the bracketed NP. The problem, however, is that the pronouns in (2) should then also be permitted.

(3) A. An anaphor must be locally bound
B. A pronoun must be locally free
C. An R-expression must be free

In contrast to the Indo-European languages in (2), others, including English, permit bound pronouns as in (4), apparently siding with the "Chinese"-type languages.

(4) John_i read [his_i book]

This appearance is illusory, however, since the facts in (4) already fall under a different generalization to which I return shortly, which is that lack of a reflexive always licenses a locally bound pronoun. English and other Indo-European languages lack possessive reflexives, and for this reason they employ bound possessive pronouns instead, as in (4). Once we take account of this, the distinction between Indo-European languages and the languages of (1) is quite clear.

In what follows, I will argue that, in binding relations, an important role is played by the antecedent, which may be more or less "perspicuous", contributing to the well-formedness of the anaphor accordingly. I will argue specifically that the difference between (1) and (2) does not reflect different degrees of locality in the binding relation, but precisely a difference in the antecedent, which is more perspicuous in the Indo-European languages that in those of the other group. I will attempt to relate this fact to the different types of inflection that the subject antecedent is associated with, and propose in particular that in the languages of (1) the inflection is "weaker" because it does not manifest subject-verb agreement. I will argue that this results in a lesser prominence of the overall phrasal substructure containing the subject and the inflection, which, in a sense, is the true antecedent for the reflexive. I will then interpret the acceptability of the pronouns in (1) versus their exclusion in (2) by taking the availability of a pronoun as being always inversely proportional to the availability of the corresponding anaphor –the same mechanism that I take to be at work in (4). On this view, the different distribution of the pronouns follows from the non-optimality of the reflexive in (1), due to the weaker antecedent, versus its relative optimality in (2), where the antecedent is "stronger".

In discriminating among antecedents, binding of subjects of NPs appears to differ from local binding of objects, which exhibits no comparable discrimination, requiring the reflexive and excluding the pronoun in both groups of languages with all (subject) antecedents. We will see that this is due to the fact that binding of subjects of NPs is in fact not strictly "local", but rather more akin to long-distance anaphora. We will argue that it is that relative non-locality which, by placing an independent strain on the interpretation of reflexives, makes the role of the antecedent critical.

We will see that both main ingredients of this approach, namely the assumption that the antecedent makes a difference, and the assumption that possessive reflexivization is like long-distance anaphora, receive independent support from the very detailed discussion of Russian reflexives in Timberlake (1979), which, like the contrast between (1) and (2), poses serious challenges to past analyses.

The general approach I will propose departs from past ones in several respects beside assigning a role to the antecedent, and in particular by taking the choice between a reflexive and a pronoun to result from the compounded effects of several conditions, each of which defines gradient well-formedness, rather than outright grammaticality. Certain aspects of the analysis will necessarily be tentative due to the extent of the theoretical overhaul proposed. The latter, however, seems well-justified by the facts.

In the next few sections, we lay out our general premises for a the theory of binding, showing later on how they lead to the solution of the original problem. We begin by considering the relation between anaphors and pronouns in section 2. In section 3 we consider the locality conditions that anaphors must satisfy. In section 4 we see how antecedents contribute to the well-formedness of anaphors, and in section 5 we return to the possessives to formulate our solution.

2. THE STRUCTURE OF THE BINDING THEORY

In related work, I have argued that bound elements are not selected on the basis of the three principles in (3) above, but rather according to the hierarchy in (5).

(5) Binding hierarchy (anaphor first):
a. Anaphor > b. Pronoun > c. R-expression

The principle in (5) is taken to mean that a lower-ranked element, in particular a pronoun, can be used only to the extent that a higher-ranked one, namely an anaphor, cannot. This, in turn, depends on the locality and other conditions that the anaphor must satisfy. As argued in Burzio (1991), the principle in (1) has certain conceptual as well as empirical advantages compared with the formulation in (3). The former, because it is naturally interpretable as a principle of "referential economy", given that the progression "anaphor, pronoun, R-expression" is clearly one of increasing referentiality. Alternatively, given a general line-up of referential and morphological content to which we return, (5) can also be interpreted as a principle of "morphological economy", imposing minimal use of morphological information. In contrast, (3) seems to associate each class of NPs with arbitrary conditions. At the more empirical level, (5) directly accounts for the fact that, aside from some distributional overlaps (like that of (1)) to which we also return, pronouns and anaphors stand in a complementary distribution—an accident, if they fell under independent principles. In particular, (5) explains why a bound pronoun is always possible when the corresponding reflexive "defaults", regardless of the exact reason. This occurs not only in the better known case of (6a), where the "default" of the reflexive is due to violation of locality (Specified Subject Condition), but also in the cases illustrated in (6b-e).

(6) Bound pronouns:

a. John$_i$ wanted [Mary to see {*himself$_i$ / him$_i$}]

b. Ja emu$_i$ skazal vse o {*sebe$_i$ / nem$_i$} ... (Russian)
I him told everything about self / him
'I told him$_i$ everything about himself$_i$ ...'

c. Io$_i$ parlo di {*se$_i$ /me$_i$} (Italian)
I talk about self /me
'I talk about myself'

d. Jean$_i$ n'aime que {*soi$_i$ / lui$_i$} (French)
Jean not loves but self / him
'Jean only loves himself'

e. he$_i$ cladde hym$_i$ as a poure laborer (Middle English)
'He clad himself as a poor laborer'

The case in (6b) (Timberlake 1979: 115) illustrates the "subject-antecedent" restriction on a certain kind of reflexives, found in many languages. With object antecedents, as this restriction bars the reflexive, a bound pronoun always results. The cases in (6c,d) illustrate the workings of what I have referred to in Burzio (1991), (in press) as "Pseudo-Agreement". Certain reflexives, such as those represented in each of (6b-d), are morphologically invariant for all of gender, number, and person, a fact which I interpret as actual lack of morphological features (see Burzio (1992) for specific arguments). If correct, this means that these reflexives cannot truly agree with their antecedents in the sense of sharing identical features, but can only "pseudo" agree, in the sense of not bearing distinct features. However, different languages differ in their tolerance for pseudo-agreement (in fact, different items within the same language may differ, like clitics versus non-clitics, versus possessives). Many Western Indo-European languages draw a distinction between first-second and third person, permitting pseudo-agreement with the latter but not with the former, as in (6c) above, where a bound pronoun is again allowed under reflexive default. Other languages, like Russian and most of Eastern Indo-European, are more permissive, tolerating pseudo-agreement with all persons (and numbers), and hence reversing the facts of (6c) (see Timberlake (1979: 113, ex.14). But there are also languages which are even less permissive than the former (e.g. Italian), excluding pseudo-agreement with all persons, and tolerating it only with "impersonals", namely elements like "one" or "arbitrary" PRO. This is the case of French *soi* in (6d), where again a locally bound pronoun results. Finally, (6e) (Faltz (1977: 19) illustrates the case of languages (like Old and Middle English, and with some qualifications Frisian and West Flemish) which lack reflexives altogether, and which thus allow locally bound pronouns systematically. English possessives, which do not exist as reflexives, are simply a subcase of this kind as noted for (4) above.[1] The persistence of complementarity under such varied conditions as illustrated in (6) is a remarkable accident for a formulation that has independent principles. The problem is in fact even more specific. For consider that the presence of antecedent restrictions (requiring that the antecedent be a subject/third person/etc.) is coextensive with a specific type of reflexive morphology, precisely the one described above as being invariant–English-type reflexives, which vary in person and number (*myself*, *yourself*, etc.) never exhibit such restrictions. A characterization of such antecedent restrictions would therefore have to link them with the relevant morphological properties of the reflexives, hopefully in an explanatory, cause-and-effect manner. Now note that, in order to express the facts in (6), the formulation in (3) would have to build the antecedent restrictions not only into principle A, stating for example that the anaphor in (6b) must be *subject* bound, but also into principle B, stating that the pronoun must be *subject* free, hence allowed in (6b). The problem with this is that, while this kind of restriction is coextensive with a certain reflexive morphology as just noted, there is no correlation with *pronominal* morphology, so far as we know. That is, the pronouns of Russian, (/ Italian/ French/ Middle English/ etc.) do *not* appear to be any different from those of (Modern) English –only the reflexives are. Hence, a relevant extension of (3) ((3B) in particular) would be asserting that the morphology of reflexives determines the form of the binding principle for pronouns. And, while this state of affairs is not logically impossible, it seems highly unlikely. In particular, one cannot imagine that there could be a cause-and-effect relation between reflexive morphology and a principle for pronouns if the latter is independent, any more than there could be a cause-and-effect relation between reflexive morphology and, say, the principles controlling wh-movement.

In sum, the fact that a principle B turns out to have curious and accidental properties is the proof of its non-existence, and of the fact that the distribution of pronouns is rather just the residue of that of anaphors, or the "elsewhere" case (as had also been argued by Bouchard (1983), Pica (1984)).[2]

While accounting for the general complementarity, the formulation in (5) would, however, seem to incorrectly exclude well-known overlaps in the distribution of anaphors and pronouns, like that of (1) above. Yet, it is not the case that (5) excludes all overlaps in principle. Rather, certain specific circumstances make distributional overlaps quite consistent with the formulation in (5). One of these is structural ambiguity. For example, Chomsky (1986a: 170f) argues that apparent overlaps like *The children$_i$ heard stories about them$_i$ / each other$_i$* are due to the presence of "PRO" subject of NP in one case, thus excluding the anaphor via the "Specified Subject Condition" and licensing the pronoun, and to the absence of PRO in the other case, hence permitting the anaphor. Whether or not this is the correct account of the cases in question, the fact is that structural ambiguity is one possible source of (apparent) overlaps under (5), which must be considered.

Another possible source of overlaps is semantic non-equivalence, which is in some sense analogous to the "structural" non-equivalence just discussed. Thus, consider the cases in (7), where the underscored complex forms are often argued to be anaphoric, and yet occur in the same structural environments as the simple pronoun counterparts of (6).

(7) Complex forms:

a. ja ... stal rassprasivat' xudoznika$_i$ o *nem samom$_i$* (Russian)
I start question artist about him same
'I ... began to question the artist$_i$ about himself$_i$'

b. Io$_i$ parlo di *me-stesso$_i$* (Italian)
I talk about me-same
'I talk about myself'

c. Jean$_i$ n'aime que *lui-même*$_i$ (French)
Jean not loves but him-same
'Jean only loves himself'

d. *him self*$_i$ he$_i$ hynge (Middle English)
'He hanged himself'

There is reason to suppose that such complex forms, which combine a pronoun and an intensifying element meaning "self / same", have a special semantic function (Zribi-Hertz (1980), Kuno (1988, 2.5)). The same is true of their possessive counterparts like English *his-own* (Saxon (1990)). In essence, their function is that of "asserting" the coreferential relation, either for contrastive purposes, or to overcome an inherent semantic bias. The semantic distinctness of simple and complex forms is shown precisely by semantically biased contexts, which force a choice between them. For instance, in the context "x chatters with y", where the inherent semantics strongly disfavors identity of *x* and *y*, the complex form is required, e.g. French *lui-même*, and not *lui* (examples and further discussion in Burzio (1991), Zribi-Hertz (1980)). This result is analogous to that of English *John*$_i$ *was getting on *his*$_i$ */ his own*$_i$ *nerves*, where coreference must also overcome the inherent semantic bias of the expression. In contrast, in a context like "x had the whole team with y", where the semantics strongly favors identity of *x* and *y*, the simple form is required, e.g. French *lui* and not *lui-même*. This is analogous here to *John*$_i$ *lost his*$_i$ */ *his own*$_i$ *cool*, which is similarly biased *for* coreference. Distributional overlaps of pronouns and complex anaphors such as those of (6)-(7) are therefore not counterexamples to the anaphor-first principle in (5), since we need not suppose that the latter operates across semantically distinct structures, any more than we need suppose it operates across syntactically distinct ones.[3]

A third kind of overlap, more directly relevant to our main concern, is made possible by our specific interpretation of the anaphor-first principle (5), and of other relevant conditions. Our interpretation differs from more common views in two respects. The first is in taking conditions to define degrees of well-/ill-formedness, rather than absolute well-formedness. The second is in taking grammaticality to be well-formedness relative to alternatives, i.e. to consist of "best"-formedness, rather than just well-formedness as defined by the conditions. These two differences are partly related. In particular, it is clear that the second is contingent on the first since, unless well-formedness was graded, all well-formed structures would be on a par, and there would be no notion of "relative" well-formedness distinct from just "well-formedness". On the proposed view then, pronoun/anaphor overlaps may simply arise from an even tension between different conditions, which may sanction comparable degrees of well-formedness for both anaphor and pronoun. The conditions at play may be in particular the "anaphor-first" condition, which always favors the anaphor, and the locality conditions, which may sometimes weigh *against* the anaphor, and hence indirectly favor the pronoun, as in the cases we discuss in the next section.

3. LOCALITY CONDITIONS

3.1 The SSC and Long-distance Anaphora

Past research has featured many attempts to characterize the phenomenon of "long-distance" anaphora (LDA) illustrated in (8) below.

(8) *Icelandic* (Maling (1984)
Jón$_i$ segir [$_\alpha$ að María elski sig$_i$]
Jón says that María loves (subj.) self
'Jón$_i$ says that María loves him$_i$'

Such attempts have characteristically aimed to define the class of complements like "a" of (8) with which this phenomenon is possible. The factors most often cited as defining such a class of permissive complements in various languages are: lack of tense or agreement (Harbert (1982), Pica (1984), Everaert (1986), Freidin (1986), Timberlake (1979), Rappaport (1986), Vikner (1985)); and lack of an independent tense or mood (Anderson (1986), Giorgi (1984)). The former factor would draw a distinction between tensed and infinitival clauses; the latter, a distinction roughly between indicatives and subjunctive clauses, placing infinitives with subjunctives. Languages, however, differ considerably in this regard. For instance, Dutch permits LDA out of some non-finite clauses but not others (Everaert (1986), (1991)), while Faroese permits it even out of indicatives (Anderson (1986)). Characterizations focusing on the definition of the class of complements that behave as in (8) are therefore bound to remain language-specific. There is, however, one fact that seems invariant across languages, which we will attempt to focus on here. That is that LDA ranks complement types in a consistent fashion. Roughly speaking, uninflected structures like small clauses rank at the bottom of the scale, in the sense that they inhibit LDA the least compared with other complements, while indicative clauses rank at the top, inhibiting it the most. Subjunctives and infinitives come in between, with the latter closer to small clauses. This cross linguistically consistent ranking manifests itself by way of the implicational relations that hold among complement types, the possibility of LDA with a higher ranked complement (e.g. a subjunctive) always implying the same possibility with a lower ranked one (e.g. an infinitive). As a result of this, lower ranked complements will also permit LDA with greater cross linguistic frequency than higher ranked ones. This state of affairs would follow if we supposed that LDA was in fact *not* immune to the "Specified Subject Condition" (SSC) as assumed in most accounts, but only less sensitive to it than local anaphora, and furthermore if the SSC was not just one blocking effect, but a family of similar effects of different strengths, each obtaining with one specific type of complement. Then, the noted implicational relations would simply follow from the fact that a weaker blocking effect can be overcome any time a stronger one can.

The question then is how to go about multiplying the traditional SSC effect into several, spread over an appropriate scale of strength. The answer is clearly to assign a role to the inflection. For the "strength" of the SSC, and hence the ranking of complements seems to depend on the morpho-semantic content of the inflection, which plausibly goes from null in the case of some small clauses to a maximum in indicatives. In essence, we are thus proposing to reinterpret the intervention effect known as the Specified Subject Condition, first identified in Chomsky (1973), as due not to the subject alone, but rather to a larger substructure that includes the subject and its related inflection, when this intervenes between the anaphor and its antecedent in the manner illustrated in (9).

(9) Long Distance Anaphora/ SSC:

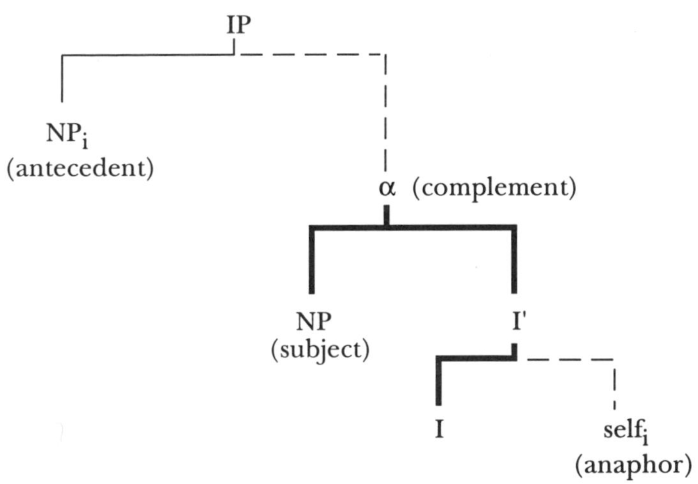

Several questions arise at this point. One remains of course the difference among languages, now cast in terms of the maximum blocking effect that each language can overcome (e.g. up to indicatives in Faroese, but limited to certain non-finite clauses in Dutch), which we will put aside, for the moment. A second question is why should the subject-I connection interfere with the anaphoric relation at all—a variant of the question that arises for any version of the SSC, which is why should a subject, rather than some other constituent, interfere with anaphora. We return to this question shortly below. A third question is why should the interference be tolerated only with some anaphors—the so-called "long-distance" ones, and not others. To answer this third question we first need to identify the distinguishing characteristic of "long-distance" anaphors like Icelandic *sig* of (8) above. Pica (1991), following Faltz (1977, 153ff) has suggested that long distance (LD) anaphors are systematically monomorphemic, in contrast to local ones, like English *himself*, which are *bi*-morphemic. Here, we will partially diverge from that characterization, which has gained wide acceptance, and suppose instead that LD anaphors are systematically uninflected, or morphological invariant in the sense discussed above, while the local ones are inflected, varying for some of the features of gender, person, number, as with English *MYself*, *YOURself*, etc. The different behavior of the two classes of anaphors in the structure (9) will now be expressed by the account that follows.

We suppose, as we will argue further below, that anaphora is essentially a relation of agreement, hence of the same kind as the subject-I relation in (9). We suppose further that all agreement utilizes the phrase-structure connections as paths. This view has the effect of (essentially) reducing the "SSC" to the prohibition in (10), that states that agreement paths connecting pairs of constituents cannot overlap.

(10) Avoid path overlap

The reason is that a path connecting antecedent and anaphor in (9) will always overlap with the path marked by the double line, connecting subject and inflection, thus generally rendering the structure ill-formed. This then answers the question of why should the subject-I connection (and not, say, an object) interfere with a more remote antecedent. The reason is that only subjects are related to inflection.[4] Note too that taking anaphora to be an agreement relation also accounts for the well-known fact that anaphors (unlike pronouns) require unique (and reject "split") antecedents. For it is independently clear that agreement mechanisms function only between *two* positions, in the sense that there is no agreement morpheme, in any language, which agrees with two different NPs simultaneously, as for instance with the conjunction of a subject and an object.

Thus, the prohibition against path overlap in (10) is our specific account of the "SSC". Just like SSC, that prohibition must now obviously be relaxed, however, given precisely LDA. But the relaxation must affect only "LD", i.e. uninflected anaphors, and not others, which must remain strictly local. In addition, even for LD anaphors, the relaxation must be made proportional to the "weakness" of the inflection I in (9), so as to appropriately "rank" the different types of complements. Both of these goals can be achieved by supposing that the computation of agreement relations is done by projecting the inherent features of the participants up the syntactic structure, rather than proceeding from one participant to the other by going up and down the tree. Then, in (9), subject and I will project their features up to a, while antecedent and anaphor will project theirs up to IP. We now only need to suppose further that path overlap is not excluded categorically, but only in a way commensurate to the amount of morpho-semantic information carried by the overlapping paths. That is, we treat phrase-structure links as being communication lines of sorts, which may "saturate" beyond capacity. Uninflected anaphors can now function long distance because they are inherently featureless, and as such project a null set of features (to IP in (9)), hence maximally satisfying the conditions for path overlap. At the same time, a "weak" I in (9) will also facilitate path overlap and hence LDA by projecting a lesser content, although we will not be able to characterize each inflection type beyond the intuitive level, in this regard. In contrast to uninflected anaphors, inflected ones will project a non-null set of I-features, hence more sharply violating the path overlap prohibition (10) ("saturating" the path), resulting in their exclusion from LD relations. This analysis correctly accounts for such minimal pairs as Turkish inflected reflexive *kendim* (/ *kendin*/ *kendi*/...), which is strictly local, versus its invariant counterpart *kendisi*, which can function long-distance (Faltz (1977, 133ff), while Pica's monomorphemic/ bimorphemic criterion would seem unable to make the distinction.[5] This advantage for our analysis seems offset by the fact that some (bimorphemic) anaphors like Norwegian *seg-selv* are not (obviously) inflected, and yet are confined to local relations (Hellan (1986)). There are two possibilities to bring this fact into line with our approach. One is to suppose that elements like Norwegian *-selv* do in fact have adjectival inflection, sometimes overtly realized (e.g. Icelandic *sjalfur*, Old English *self*), and sometimes not, as in Norwegian, and that even a non-overt inflectional element projects a (non-null) feature matrix. The other possibility is to suppose that, in complex forms, each subconstituent is independently linked with the antecedent, hence doubling the blocking effect due to path overlap (pace fn.5). We must leave this question open at this point, noting that the second approach would in effect partially subscribe to Pica's generalization, by taking bimorphemic structure as one of the factors behind strict locality.[6]

Note that the features of the anaphor and those of its antecedent meeting at IP in (9) (like those meeting at a) are required to agree, but recall also that agreement includes "pseudo"-agreement, parametrically set, as discussed above. Hence, the example in (8) above is well-formed because the combination of [3rd person, singular, masculine] and [no-person, no number, no gender] (as in *Jón...sig*) is an acceptable case of pseudo-agreement in Icelandic, as in many other languages.

On this analysis, the essential difference between anaphors and pronouns is that anaphors are linked by an agreement mechanism with their antecedents, while pronouns are not (although they may still agree, for independent reasons). In turn this difference follows from supposing that inherent reference is contingent on morphological content. Pronouns, which are systematically inflected for some of the I-features, "have" those I-features, and hence have (some) inherent reference. Uninflected elements correspondingly "lack" features, hence lack independent reference, and for this reason they are always "anaphoric", i.e. they need to be linked with an antecedent in order to refer. Inflected anaphors like English reflexives can be made consistent with this general view by supposing that the inflected element *my/your/him* is not in argument (/head) position and is for this reason irrelevant to the determination of reference. Rather, we take it to be in some peripheral, specifier-like position, which nonetheless plays a role in projecting its features up for linkage with an antecedent.[7] We must still note that the head itself also bears some inflection, as in *-self/ -selves*, but we may suppose that inflection for number alone is insufficient to provide referential content. Similar considerations apply to reflexives like Norwegian *seg selv*, Italian *se-stesso* and others, where the first morpheme is uninflected and in argument position, while the second, sometimes overtly inflected, is an adjunct. Again, the element with the I-features is here in a non-argument position and hence unable to determine referentiality.

The above characterization of the SSC is still inadequate in one respect, however, and that is that, unlike LDA, local anaphora is blocked by an intervening subject regardless of the presence of a corresponding inflection, as shown by (11) (from Faltz (1977: 2), structure ours).[8]

(11) John$_i$ saw [$_\alpha$ a snake near {him$_i$ /?*himself}]

We must thus extend the scope of the path-overlap prohibition (10) by supposing that subjects *always* project their features up the tree, regardless of an attendant inflection, and furthermore that overlap even at a single point (like a of (9)) suffices to pose a block for anaphoric relations. This is plainly stipulatory, but in fact just parallel to the stipulation that other theories need more generally to identify subjects as blocks, while excluding objects.

In sum, we have argued that the SSC effect obtains with variable strength, which depends on two factors: the strength of the inflection associated with the intervening subject, and the inflected versus uninflected character of the anaphor. We have proposed to account for both dimensions of variation by supposing that antecedent-anaphor relations are agreement relations, like subject-I relations, both established by using phrase structure links as paths, which must in general not overlap. We have then taken path overlap to be nonetheless permitted to the extent that the morphological (/semantic) content of each path is weak, hence only with morphologically featureless anaphors, and only with the weaker types of intervening inflections.

3.2 LDA AND PRONOUNS

In the light of the above discussion, we may now consider the data summarized in (12), relative to both LD reflexives and the corresponding pronouns in various languages, where a is the "complement" in (9). For ease of exposition we collect the relevant examples in the Appendix at the end.[9]

(12)

α	Icelandic	Italian	Russian	Danish	Dutch
a. Indicative	*refl pron	*refl pron	*refl pron	*refl pron	*refl pron
b. Subjunctive	refl pron	??refl pron	*refl pron	N/A	N/A
c. AP-sc Infin.	refl *pron	refl pron	refl pron	refl pron	*refl pron
d. PP-sc NP/PVC		refl ??pron	refl *pron	refl *pron	refl pron

(see Appendix)

Still aside from the differences among the various languages, the distribution of the reflexives in (12) will follow from attributing the appropriate role to the inflection in each case. In particular, we will suppose that the cases grouped in (12d), namely small clauses with PP predicates, NP's, and perception-verb complements (PVCs), are all inflectionless, taking the lack of *to* in e.g. *I saw [John (*to) leave]* to be indicative of this, and representative of the other languages as well.[10] The cases grouped in (12c), namely adjectival small clauses and infinitivals, are then taken to be cases with some inflection of a weak sort, while the inflection of the subjunctives of (12b) is stronger, perhaps because it involves person agreement, in contrast to the APs of (12c), which agree only in gender and number. Finally, we take the inflection of the indicatives of (12a) to be stronger still, plausibly for containing independent tense specifications (as generally argued in the literature), in contrast with the tense-dependency of subjunctives. This ranking thus accounts for the fact that, for each language, there is a point in (12) above which the reflexive is consistently possible, while being consistently impossible below it.

Turning now to the pronouns in (12), we note that their distribution stands in a fundamental complementarity to that of reflexives, just as it does in general, except for a small area of overlap in each language—the one enclosed by the double line, to which we return shortly.[11] This complementarity in LDA configurations is an important fact, which further confirms the correctness of the approach based on the "anaphor-first" condition of (5) above. For if pronouns were controlled by an independent principle "B", alongside of the mystery of why they can be locally bound exactly when the anaphors cannot as in (6) above, we would now also have the mystery of why they cannot be LD bound precisely when the anaphors can be, as in (12). As for the overlaps in (12), they also follow from our analysis, and in particular from the proposed interpretation of the relevant conditions as having a graded effect on overall well-formedness. Thus, if the blocking effect increases going from (12d to a), then, for each language, there will come a point at which the resulting inhibitory effect on the reflexive equals the (fixed) inhibitory effect on the pronoun imposed by the anaphor-first principle (5). That point, at the boundary between the "reflexive only" and "pronoun only" portions of the scale, should naturally allow both reflexive and pronoun to occur, indeed as in (12). Note here that, since we understand ungrammaticality to result from existence of a better-formed alternative, both anaphor and pronoun are correctly predicted grammatical when equally well-formed, and *not* equally marginal to reflect the respective partial violations of conditions. The non-existence of comparable overlaps with local anaphora follows from the fact that in that case there is no factor inhibiting the anaphor, which is thus directly imposed by the "anaphor-first" principle.

The correctness of this general perspective is confirmed by the fact that the anaphor-first principle does not only interact with the graded SSC effect to yield the facts of (12), but also with "pseudo-agreement", which itself has internal rankings, expressed by the implicational relations in (13).

(13) Pseudo-agreement Hierarchy
1st-2nd -> 3rd -> impersonal

The hierarchy in (13) states that if a language allows pseudo-agreement with first and second person antecedents (like Russian), then it will also allow it with third person and impersonal antecedents, while if a language allows pseudo-agreement with third person (like Italian), it will allow it with impersonals (like "PRO-arbitrary", or elements like "one"), but not necessarily with first and second person. The hierarchy in (13) can naturally be interpreted as one of increasing interpretive "cost", with first-second person being the most costly to use in pseudo-agreement, we presume because interpretively more distant from "zero features" than third person. This sheds light on the contrast between (14) and (15).[12]

(14) <u>Russian</u> (Timberlake (1979: 124))
a. Starik$_i$ ozivilsja i prosil [na kurort {ego$_i$/sebja$_i$} pokuda ne otpravljat']
old man enliven and ask [to resort him / self now not send off]
'The old man$_i$ came to life and asked (one) not to send him$_i$ off to a health resort just now'
b. On$_i$ dal [ej umyt' {sebja$_i$ / *ego$_i$} i vypil kruzku moloka]
he let [her wash self / him and drank mug milk]
'He$_i$ let her wash him$_i$ and drank down a mug of milk'

(15) <u>Russian</u> (Timberlake (1979: 127,fn.8))
a. Tetja Frosja, vy$_i$ razresite u {?(?)sebja$_i$ / vas$_i$} perenocevat'?
Aunt Frosja you allow by self / you stay overnight
'Aunt Frosja, will you$_i$ allow (us) to stay overnight with you$_i$?'
b. Tetja Frosja, vy$_i$ dadite u {sebja$_i$ / vas$_i$} perenocevat'?
Aunt Frosja you let by self / you stay overnight
'Aunt Frosja, will you$_i$ let (us) stay overnight with you$_i$?'

The facts in (14) are those reported in (12) above (and the Appendix). In (14a) the complement is a normal infinitival—the case of (12c), while in (14b) it is the complement of "causative" *let*, which we place in the same category as the PVC of (12d). The examples in (15a,b) are parallel to the ones in (14a,b) respectively, except for the fact that the antecedent to the reflexive is here second person singular "you", rather than third person. The differences are summarized in (16), where we can see that second-person pseudo-agreement consistently shifts relative well-formedness towards the pronoun, we presume by adding to the bias against the reflexive.

(16)

	Pseudo-agreement with:	
LDA into:	3rd	2nd
a. Infinitive	refl pron	(?)? refl pron
b. PVC	refl *pron	refl pron

There are thus (at least) three contending forces in the choice between a reflexive and a pronoun: the anaphor-first principle, the SSC, and pseudo-agreement. The chart in (12) above plots the interaction of the first two: anaphor first, which contributes a fixed bias in favor of the reflexive, and the SSC, which contributes a variable bias <u>against</u> the reflexive. The chart in (16) reveals a further dimension of variation due to the third factor, pseudo-agreement, which also contributes a variable bias <u>against</u> the reflexive. The choice between reflexive and pronoun is then determined by computing the overall bias, with ungrammaticality resulting when the alternative choice is better formed. We can see from both (12) and (16), however, that "worse-formedness" maps into ungrammaticality gradually, rather than sharply.

At this point it remains to account for the differences among languages illustrated by (12). On this we will not have much to say, comparing with past analyses in this respect. We will suggest, however, that the differences are not in the proposed system of conditions, which we regard as invariant, but rather in the reflexives themselves as individual lexical items. Note in this connection that it is clear that knowledge of the lexicon is not uniform, but somewhat stratified, some items being more prominent than others, in being more easily remembered or somehow more "accessible" than others. We then find it conceivable that LD reflexives in different languages may have different degrees of lexical prominence in some such sense, and furthermore that this latter factor may in fact constitute a further, fixed, bias for or against the reflexive, which will interact with the rest of the system accordingly. Different languages would then simply have different biases, resulting in different ranges of viability for the reflexive on the scale of (12). This proposal, locating the relevant "parameter" in the lexicon, while maintaining the syntax invariant, has at least the advantage of being maximally simple. Independent evidence for it, however, is admittedly limited at this point, and yet not totally lacking. Consider in particular that, as is well known (Everaert (1986), (1991)), Dutch reflexive *zich* is possible in the LD contexts described by (12), as well as in contexts of inherent reflexivity like

(17a), but not in other local contexts, which require the form *zichzelf* instead, as in (17b).

(17) Dutch (Everaert (1991))
  a. Jan_i schaamde {$zich_i$ / *$zichzelf_i$}
     Jan shamed self / self
     'Jan was ashamed'

  b. Jan_i verraste {*$zich_i$ / $zichzelf_i$}
     Jan surprised self / self
     'Jan_i surprised $himself_i$'

This state of affairs would follow if the item *zich* were assigned a certain negative bias in the sense just proposed, compared with *zichzelf*. Then, *zich* would be correctly expected to show up only in the contexts that exclude *zichzelf*. These are precisely the contexts of inherent reflexivity, where *zich* is plausibly required by the same principle that excludes the complex form in *John lost his/ *his own cool* and other such inherently coreferential contexts discussed earlier (see discussion of (7)), as well as the contexts of LDA of (12). However, in the latter contexts, we now correctly predict a lower cut-off point for the Dutch LD reflexive compared with that of other languages, such as for instance Icelandic, in which the contrast in (17b) does not obtain, hence implying that the LD reflexive in that language does *not* carry the same negative bias.

Beside thus possibly shedding light on the cross-linguistic variation in (12), this approach also leads to the welcome conclusion that there is no need to recognize, as a primitive class, a class of anaphors which may be bound only long-distance, like Dutch *zich*. For us, this is parallel to the fact that there is no need to recognize a class of pronouns which are only *subject* free (like Russian *nem* of (6b) above). In both cases the observed distribution follows as the "residue" of the distribution of some other element which lends itself to a straightforward characterization.[13]

This concludes our discussion of the Specified Subject Condition, accounting for the behavior of elements which are "in the domain of" a subject. To complete our discussion of locality conditions, we now need to turn to subjects themselves, which will take us closer to our initial concern—subjects of NPs.

3.3 THE NIC AND AGREEMENT

The ungrammaticality of anaphors in structures like (18), in which they occurs as the subject of a tensed clause, has received several accounts in the brief history of the theory of anaphora.

(18) John$_i$ believes [that {*himself$_i$ / he$_i$ } is intelligent]

In particular, the analysis of Chomsky (1980) proposed an inherent incompatibility between anaphoric status and nominative Case—the "Nominative Island Condition" (NIC), while that of Chomsky (1981) proposed that the agreement element (AGR) was itself capable of producing an SSC-type blocking effect. The analysis of Chomsky (1986a) relied instead on the "ECP", by supposing that anaphors move at LF to join their antecedents, leaving a tracc. Such a trace would then not be properly governed being the subject of a tensed clause, just as in the **that*-trace configurations produced by wh-movement.

In this work we will take the crucial factor in the ungrammaticality of (18) to be verb-agreement, though not in the same sense as Chomsky (1981). Rather, we will follow Rizzi (1989) in taking the relevant generalization to be that anaphors are ungrammatical in positions that trigger verb agreement, as stated in (19)—a condition which, however, must be independent of the "SSC".

(19) *anaphor-agreement

That the effects of agreement on a subject anaphor are not interpretable as a generalized SSC in the manner of Chomsky (1981) (where AGR was itself just another "SUBJECT"), is shown by asymmetries such as that of (20).

(20) <u>Icelandic</u> (Maling (1984), Everaert (1986))
a. Jón$_i$ segir [að María elski sig$_i$]
Jón says [that Maria loves self]
'Jón$_i$ says that Maria loves him$_i$'

b. *Jón$_i$ segir að sig$_i$ elski María
Jón says that self loves Maria

The facts in (20) show that, in languages that have verb-agreement, the "relaxation" of the SSC observed for LDA in (20a) is not paralleled by a corresponding relaxation of (19), as shown by (20b), leading to the conclusion that the two must be independent.[14] The condition in (19)-so far only a descriptive statement- correctly accounts for the fact that languages that do not have verb agreement, such as Chinese, Japanese and Korean, permit anaphors as subjects of tensed clauses, as we will see below. This is a clear advantage over the former "NIC" since, unlike agreement, nominative Case is found in both groups of languages. The condition in (19) also has important advantages over the ECP account of Chomsky (1986a), as shown by certain evidence discussed in Rizzi (1989), and other given in Kornfilt (1989), which we now consider.

It was argued in Rizzi (1982, IV), and has since been generally accepted, that in "null subject/ free inversion" languages like Italian, wh-movement of the subject involves not the pre-verbal, but rather the post-verbal/ "inverted" position of subjects. Assuming the ECP, this must mean that, unlike pre-verbal subjects, post verbal ones are "properly" governed. Yet post-verbal, agreement-triggering, subjects are just as ungrammatical as pre-verbal ones when they are anaphors, as shown by the minimal pairs in (21), (22) noted in Rizzi (1989).

(21) <u>Italian</u> (Rizzi (1989))

a. A $loro_i$ importa solo di $se\text{-}stessi_i$
to them matters only of self-same
'$They_i$ are only concerned about $themselves_i$'

b.*A $loro_i$ interessano solo $se\text{-}stessi_i$
to them matter only self-same
'$They_i$ are only interested in $themselves_i$'

(22) a. Quando si_i critica $se\text{-}stessi_i$ ...
when one criticizes self-same
'When we_i criticize $ourselves_i$...'

b.*Quando si_i criticano $se\text{-}stessi_i$...
when one criticize self-same

In (21), the dative *a loro* functions as a proper antecedent for the anaphor in (a), so that it ought to do the same in (b). Hence the only relevant difference is that in (21b) the anaphor *se-stessi* is linked with verb inflection, triggering verb agreement and receiving nominative Case, while in (21a) it is not. The same is true for the two variants of the impersonal-*si* construction in (22), the post verbal element triggering verb agreement in (b), but not in (a) (See also (25a) below, and for general discussion of this construction, Burzio (1986, 1.6)). Hence, provided that we take (19) not to refer to linear order, the latter condition will draw the right distinctions in (21)-(22), excluding all anaphors that trigger verb agreement. In contrast, the ECP would exclude only anaphors that occur pre-verbally, given the facts of wh-movement, hence permitting (21b), (22b) incorrectly.[15]

The discussion of Turkish nominals in Kornfilt (1989) further corroborates the above conclusion. Kornfilt notes that Turkish nominals permit two forms of agreement: a stronger one, exhibiting a full range of variation, and a weaker one, with fixed third person singular morphology. She then notes further that reciprocals are possible in subject position only in conjunction with the weaker agreement, as shown in (23) (agreement capitalized).

(23) Turkish (Kornfilt (1989), caps. ours)

a. ?Asker-ler$_i$ [birbir-lerin-in$_i$ öl-eceg-IN]-e inan-iyor-du
soldiers-pl each-other-3pl-gen die-fut-3sg-dat believe-progr-past
'The soldiers believed each other to be going to die'

b. *Asker-ler$_i$ [birbir-lerin-in$_i$ ölüm-den kork-tuk-LARIN]-a inan-iyor-du
soldiers-pl each-other-3pl-gen death-abl fear-ger-3pl-dat believe-progr-past
'The soldiers believed each other to be afraid of death'

In the main dialect of Turkish Kornfilt considers, there is no comparable difference with reflexives, which are uniformly excluded, even with weak agreement. However, another dialect she cites does exhibit the same distinction as (23) with reflexives, though no longer with reciprocals, now uniformly allowed. Hence, abstracting away from the noted difference between reflexives and reciprocals, as well as the one between the two dialects, we can say that both reflexive and reciprocal subjects are more strongly inhibited by a stronger agreement than by a weaker one. Abstracting away further from the residual extent to which (reflexive/ reciprocal) anaphors might be allowed even with weaker agreement in either dialect, which we will not attempt to account for, it is clear that the general effect observed by Kornfilt is of the type described by (19) and linked to agreement, and not one reducible to the ECP. For an ECP account would entail that stronger agreement (as in (23a)) is a weaker governor, and vice versa (as in (23b))—not an expected correlation under any circumstance.[16] We thus conclude that the "*anaphor-agreement" condition in (19) is indeed the correct cross-linguistic generalization, and now turn to ways to express it in our system.[17]

Note first that the very existence of the condition in (19) confirms our hypothesis that anaphora is a subcase of agreement. For, if it was a relation of some unrelated kind, there would be little reason why it should interfere with subject-verb agreement. Our system of agreement paths in fact provides a rather natural way to express that interference. Thus consider the configuration in question, as given in

(24)

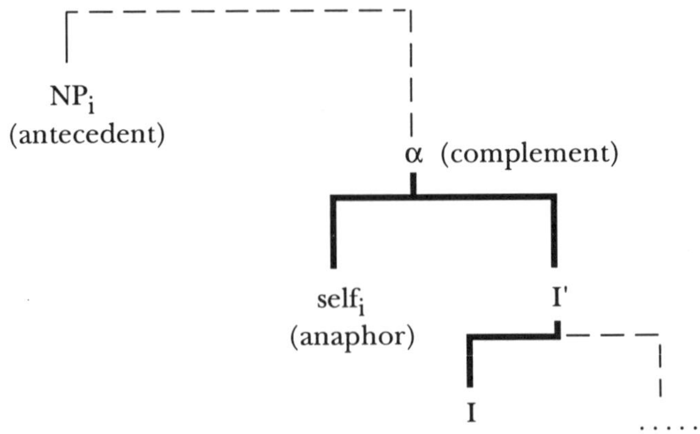

Following in part Rizzi and Roberts (1989, fn.3), Sportiche (1988), we will suppose that Case is never assigned under "m-command" (departing from Chomsky (1986b)), and that assignment of nominative Case to a subject by I in the structure of (24), is rather a form of agreement, which includes also agreement of I, specifically "AGR", with the subject. The "*anaphor agreement" effect of (19)/ (24) will now simply follow by supposing that these two aspects of subject-I agreement—Case agreement, and I-features agreement, must necessarily cluster, in the sense that neither one is permitted to proceed onto any path independent of the other. Then, if anaphora is agreement (in I-features) as we are supposing, a subject-anaphor in (24) would have to be linked for I-features with the antecedent while being linked for nominative Case to I –precisely what the clustering requirement excludes. This predicament has no escape, since it is clear that failing to link the subject to I so as to link it with the antecedent would leave the subject without Case in violation of Case requirements, while extending the subject's Case connection to the antecedent so as to provide the I-feature connection would also violate some fundamental principle of Case theory, which clearly must exclude assignment of the same Case (here by I) to two different arguments. As for the post-verbal subjects of (21b), (22b), we assume that the same account carries over, although some questions will remain. In particular, departing from Chomsky (1981), Burzio (1986) and others, we suppose that such post verbal subjects receive nominative Case directly from I via an agreement path, and that Case and I-features must cluster much as in the preverbal case, whence the identical results. Note, however, that the modalities of assignment of nominative Case post-verbally raise a number of theoretical questions (e.g., concerning the role of government, see fn.18) which we cannot fully address here (see, for example, Harbert and Toribio (1990), Sigurðsson (1991) for some discussion)). What is crucial to our account, however, is only that, with post-verbal nominatives, features and Case continue to cluster, as with pre-verbal ones, and this is independently established by the facts in (25).

(25) <u>Italian</u>

a. si legge / leggono <u>molti libri</u>
one reads / read many books
'One reads many books'

b. <u>li</u> si legge / *leggono
them one reads / read
'One reads them'

As discussed in Burzio (1986, 1.6), in the Italian impersonal *si* construction, the verb may or may not agree with an object NP, as in (25a), but agreement is excluded if the object is an accusative pronoun, as in (25b), showing that agreement and nominative Case must indeed cluster, targeting the same NP. While agreement with the underscored accusative pronoun in (25b) thus violates the clustering, both variants of (25a) are well-formed, simply because the underscored NP is ambiguously either nominative (yielding agreement), or accusative (yielding no agreement), unlike the pronoun of (25b).

Note that the system we are thus proposing in some sense reverses that of Chomsky (1981), which took the antecedent-anaphor relation and the anaphor-I relation in (24) to interfere with one-another because AGR (in I) is a closer antecedent. This view is near paradoxical, however, (as Chomsky (1986a:176) notes), since AGR is in fact not a viable antecedent, having no reference. Within our system, the antecedent-anaphor and the anaphor-AGR relations are also taken to be of the same kind, but not because they are both relations of antecedence, rather, because they are both relations of agreement. Unlike the approach of Chomsky (1981), this results in no paradox.

The case in (18)/ (24) above in which the anaphor is the subject of a tensed clause now contrasts with the one in (26), in which it is the subject of a small clause (equivalent to the case of ECM complements).

(26) John_i considers [{himself_i / *him_i} intelligent]

What for us makes the crucial difference in (26) is that the embedded subject is assigned Case by the verb under government, and not by an agreement mechanism. Because of this, there is no clustering requirement, so that Case and agreement (with the antecedent) will be free to operate independently.[18] Since the anaphor thus violates no constraints, the pronoun is categorically excluded (via "anaphor-first").

Let us now turn to subjects of tensed clauses in languages like Chinese, which seem "intermediate" between English tensed clauses and small clauses, in permitting *both* anaphor and bound pronoun in subject position, as in (27).

(27) a. Chinese
Zhangsan_i shuo [{ziji_i / ta_i} hui lai]
Zhangsan said [self / he will come]
'Zhangsan_i said that he_i will come'

b. Malayalam (Mohanan (1982))
kutti_i ammayoot [{taan_i/ awan_i} aanaye nulli enn] paraññu
child mother [self / he elephant pinched that] said
'The child_i told the mother that he_i pinched the elephant'

In these cases, even though the verb exhibits no agreement morphology, we take the (nominative) Case to still be assigned by an agreement mechanism, much as in English, as seems natural. This enables us to suppose that the clustering of Case and I-features is still in force. However, we will also suppose that such clustering is required more weakly here, since the I-features of the anaphor subject will remain "unmatched" by those of the nominative-assigning inflection, which has none (no AGR). In sum, we are suggesting that, in relation to spec-head agreement, Case and I-features strongly cluster if the head morphology has I-features, but cluster more weakly otherwise. On this view, verb agreement thus plays parallel roles with respect to two different conditions, as its absence yields weaker versions of both the above clustering principle, and the SSC, as shown by the pattern in (12) above, and also by the fact that languages without verb agreement, like those of (27), permit LD binding of objects out of tensed clauses quite generally. In (27a,b), then, the anaphor will be associated with a weak violation of the clustering principle, while the pronoun violates the anaphor-first principle (5) as always. The free variation/ overlap of (27a,b) can then be interpreted to mean that the two violations are of comparable degree. This account is quite parallel to the one we proposed for the overlaps in the LDA cases. Just as the latter involved a "weak" violation of the SSC on the part of the anaphor, so the former involve a weak violation of the clustering principle.[19]

The case of subjects of NPs in Chinese-type languages, exemplified in (28), is now correctly expected to be quite parallel to the case just discussed, allowing both anaphor and pronoun.

(28) a. Chinese (Huang (1983))
Zhangsan$_i$ kanjian-le [{ziji$_i$ / ta$_i$} de shu]
Zhangsan see-aspect [self / him of book]
'Zhangsan$_i$ saw his$_i$ book'

b. Malayalam (Mohanan (1982))
moohan$_i$ [{tante$_i$ / awante$_i$} bhaaryaye] *n*ulli
Mohan [self's / he's wife] pinched
'Mohan$_i$ pinched his$_i$ wife'

The reason is the exact structural parallelism of the two cases, both instantiating the abstract schema of (29), in which the head X assigns Case to the subject NP under spec-head agreement.

(29) $[_{XP}$ NP X ...]

With the clausal complements in (27), the head X is I, assigning nominative Case, while with the NPs of (28) it is the head noun, assigning genitive.

In both cases the head is equally uninflected for I-features, whence the identical behavior with respect to anaphora.[20]

The foregoing discussion of subjects has in a sense answered half of the original question of the difference in the behavior of subjects of NPs in two groups of languages, by characterizing subjects of NPs in the "Chinese" group. As mentioned in the introduction, we find the key to understanding that difference to be in the role played by the antecedent, which we thus consider in the next section.

4. ANTECEDENTS AS BLOCKS

4.1 Experiencers

In the previous section, we examined the two major blocking effects on anaphoric relations: the "SSC" effect on objects, and the "*anaphor-AGR" effect on subjects. We now consider the relation between blocks to anaphora and antecedents. We will argue that the two notions are very closely related, and in particular that, while blocks are not always antecedents, since AGR has a blocking effect on subject anaphors without being a possible antecedent as we saw, antecedents are generally also blocks, that is elements capable of excluding or inhibiting the use of a more remote antecedent. Aside from anaphors which are not subject-oriented, to which we return, this means that the "SSC" and the subject "orientation" of anaphors are in fact the same phenomenon.

There are two pieces of evidence that tie antecedents and blocks together in the above sense. The first is the identity of the two classes. Roughly speaking, each class includes subjects and excludes objects, whence the SSC on the one hand, and subject orientation on the other, as just noted. But what is more striking is that the two classes continue to be identical with respect to the "exceptions" to this classification. Thus, it is well-known that "subject oriented" anaphors, like all LD anaphors, can also take experiencers as antecedents (Bhat (1978), Timberlake (1979, fn.5), Bertocchi and Casadio (1980: 26), Giorgi (1984), Cole et.al. (1990), Huang and Tang (1991) among others). Less well-known is the fact demonstrated by Huang and Tang (1991) that experiencers also function as blocks. Huang and Tang note that, in Chinese, LD anaphora is blocked if an intervening subject differs in person from the intended antecedent, as shown in (30).

(30) <u>*Chinese*</u> (Huang and Tang (1991))
a. Zhangsan$_i$ renwei [Lisi$_j$ hai-le ziji$_{i/j}$]
Zhangsan think Lisi hurt-ASP self
'Zhangsan$_i$ thought that Lisi$_j$ hurt him$_i$ / himself$_j$'

b. $Zhangsan_i$ renwei [wo_j hai-le $ziji_{*i/j}$]
Zhangsan think I hurt-ASP self
'$Zhangsan_i$ thought that I_j hurt $*him_i$ / $myself_j$'

They note further that experiencers, which are possible antecedents as we know and as shown in (31a), give rise to the same blocking effect, as shown in (31b) (experiencers underscored).

(31) Chinese (Huang and Tang (1991))
a. [$ziji_i$ de xiaohai mei de jiang de xiaoxi] shi *Lisi*$_i$ hen nanguo
[self's child not get prize DE news] make Lisi very sad
'The news that his own_i child did not get a prize made $\underline{Lisi}_i$ very sad'

b. [[[$Zhangsan_i$ dui $ziji_{i/*j/*k}$ mei xinxin de shi] shi *wo*$_j$ hen nanguo de xiaoxi] shi $Lisi_k$ hen yiwai]
[[[Zhangsan to self no confidence's fact make] I very sad DE news] make Lisi very surprised]
'The news that I was saddened by the fact that $Zhangsan_i$ had no confidence in $himself_i/_{*j}/*me$ surprised Lisi'

While various questions now arise to which we return directly, the above evidence shows that, as noted by Huang and Tang, the classes of antecedents and blocks coincide in the manner illustrated by (32).[21]

(32)

	Antecedent	block
a. subject	yes	yes
b. experiencer	yes	yes
c. object	no	no

One obvious question will be how to capture the parallelism in (32). Another is how to express the "different person" blocking effect of (30)-(31). Beginning with the first, recall that, within our system, subjects are blocks because they project their features up to the nearest XP, thus inducing path overlap. For those subjects which are not associated with any inflection which would require upward projection independently, feature projection was stipulated. We now simply extend that stipulation and suppose that experiencers do the same, also projecting their features up, speculating that this may be a property of certain "semantically prominent" elements.[22] While the latter stipulation is obviously problematic, we note that other analyses fare no better on this point. In particular, accounts of subject orientation in terms of LF movement of the anaphor to inflection (Cole et al. (1990), Pica (1991) and others) face a more serious problem still. Since experiencers are not connected with inflection in any way, movement to I does not only not predict that experiencers may be antecedents, but in fact falsely predicts that they should not be (as also noted by Huang and Tang). Hence our stipulation has no viable alternative.

In order to account for the fact that certain kinds of anaphors are *not* subject oriented, we will now suppose that non-experiencer objects may also project their features up the syntactic structure. However, we suppose further that this optional step (not triggered by "semantic prominence") adds to the overall interpretive "cost". With uninflected anaphors like the LD ones, this cost will then compound with that of pseudo-agreement, correctly resulting in the exclusion of (non-experiencer) object antecedents. In contrast, with inflected anaphors like English reflexives, there is pseudo-agreement to deal with (since there is overt agreement), resulting in object antecedents as a viable option. Note here that the subject-orientation of anaphors is a relatively weak effect, as seems consistent with the above (cost-based) account (see Maling's (1986, ex. (1)), given in part below as (38a)), while a movement-to-I account would entail a sharper effect.[23]

Turning to the question of the identity of antecedents and blocks in (32), the latter follows directly from our system of feature-projection. That is, if anaphors merely project their features up the syntactic structure, they will only be able to link up with elements that, independently, also project their features, and which -by doing so- necessarily also act as blocks, inhibiting relations with more remote antecedents. Non-experiencer objects continue not to be blocks on this account, despite their being antecedents (to certain anaphors), because, while they may project their features, they are not required to do so.

Turning now to the "different person" blocking effect of (30)-(31) observed by Huang and Tang, it can be expresses within our system by simply supposing that overlapping paths must agree in person. Intuitively, this has a certain plausibility (Huang and Tang's solution is partially similar). Since we think of overlapping paths as different communications riding on the same line, it makes sense to suppose that partial sameness of the "signal" should be a precondition for sharing the line, with "person" being perhaps the most salient feature. There is one problem that we must leave unsolved, however, which is that—to our knowledge—this effect has not been reported for any of the (Indo-European) languages of (12) above.[24] This notwithstanding, the conclusion that, in anaphoric relations, antecedents and blocks are one and the same category, and our account of it, seem to stand.

4.2 WEAK ANTECEDENTS

A second piece of evidence for the identity of the notions of antecedent and of block is that the two categories are internally ranked in similar fashion. Thus, recall that blocks rank in strength as in (33), which repeats and slightly simplifies the ranking of (12) above.

(33) SSC effect ranked by complement type:
a. Tensed (strongest block)
b. Infinitival (AP-sc)
c. PVC (NPs, PP-sc) (weakest block)

Consider now that some of Timberlake's (1979) discussion of Russian reflexives reveals that antecedents rank quite analogously. As Timberlake notes, LDA discriminates among different antecedents in the manner illustrated in (34).

(34) Russian (Timberlake (1979))
a. I on_i ne prosil nikogo iz nix [provesti {$sebja_i$/ego_i} v nuznoe mesto...]
and he not ask any of them lead self / him to needed place...
'and he_i did not ask any of them to lead him_i to the necessary place...'

b. I on_i stydilsja poprosit' kogo-libo iz nix [provesti ?(?)$sebja_i$ / ego_i v nuznoe mesto]
and he embarassed ask any of them lead self / him to needed place
'and he_i was embarassed to ask any of them to lead him_i to the necessary place'

In (34a) the antecedent is the subject of a tensed clause, and the anaphor/pronoun overlap is as discussed in 3.2 above. In contrast, in (34b) the antecedent is the subject of an infinitival.[25] As the judgments indicate, the latter antecedent appears to favor the reflexive less than the subject of a tensed clause, and is thus a "weaker" antecedent in that sense. However, in contrast to LDA, local anaphora appears totally insensitive to differences among antecedents, always requiring the reflexive to the full exclusion of the pronoun, as shown by (35).

(35) Russian (Timberlake (1979))
a ... $menja_i$ poprosjat xotja v dvuk slovax rasskazat' o {$sebe_i$/*obo mne_i}
me ask if only in two words tell about self / about me
'...(they) would ask me_i to talk about $myself_i$ if only in two words'

b. Tixon Zaxarovic zastavil $rabocix_i$ ne scadit $sebja_i$ / *ix_i...
Tixon Zaxarovic make workers not spare self them
'Tixon Zaxarovic made the $workers_i$ not spare $themselves_i$...'

Let us then summarize the above facts as in (36).

(36)

Antecedent, subject of:	LDA into infinitival	local anaphora
a. Tensed	refl pron	refl *pron
b. Infinitival	?(?)refl pron	refl *pron
c. PVC		refl *pron

We can see that the hierarchy of antecedents in (36), ranking antecedents in LDA, mirrors the hierarchy of blocks of (33) except for the lack of evidence on subjects of PVCs in (36c) (not given in Timberlake's discussion). This, however, will be shown to fit the same pattern later on (see (44) below). This further parallelism of antecedents and blocks continues to follow from our system. For if anaphors can only link up with elements that intervene on the upward path and hence act as blocks, it seems natural that they should find stronger blocks to be more viable antecedents than weaker ones. The remaining question is of course why should the discriminating effect be present only in LDA and not in local anaphora. What this difference between the two cases suggests is that anaphoric relations simply treat blocks in a consistent fashion, in the sense that overcoming a block of a certain strength automatically makes all weaker blocks undetectable. We may state this as in (37).

(37) Blocking consistency: Once not a block, never a block

Such a principle seems natural. Its effects can be visualized by imagining a projectile traveling in a horizontal line, which will never be able to hit any obstacle lower than one it has already passed. The facts in (36) now follow from the principle in (37) since, in LDA out of infinitival complements, that principle will require that the antecedent be a stronger block than the subject of an infinitival, namely that it be the subject of a tensed clause, whence (36a). Subjects of other infinitivals will not be detectable, or -assuming a somewhat graded effect as for some of the other principles- only marginally detectable, whence (36b). In contrast, in local anaphora no block is being overcome, thus (37) is irrelevant, any block will be a viable antecedent, and the reflexive will be fully well-formed to the full exclusion of the pronoun.[26]

The principle in (37) accounts not only for the type of contrasts noted by Timberlake, but also for other striking ones never accounted for unitarily before. One, noted by Thráinsson (1979), and Maling (1986), is given in (38).

(38) Icelandic (Maling (1986))

a. Jón syndi Haraldi$_i$ föt á sig$_i$ / hann$_i$
Jón showed Harald clothes for self / him
'Jón showed Harald$_i$ clothes for himself$_i$'

b. Ég lofaði Haraldi$_i$ [að raka *sig$_i$ / hann$_i$]
I promised Harald to shave self / him
'I promised Harald$_i$ to shave him$_i$'

As Maling observes, LD reflexive *sig* can for many speakers also take an object antecedent, in partial consistency with our above account of subject orientation. This, however, is only possible when *sig* is locally bound as in (38a), and not in LD relations like that of (38b). This follows from our (37) since, to the extent that an object can be an antecedent and hence a block, it will surely be a block of the weakest kind (not being related to any inflection), and as such it will systematically be undetectable in any LD relation.

Another relevant contrast is the one in (39) noted by Maling (1984), as well as Giorgi (1984), and others.

(39) Icelandic (Maling (1984))

a. *Jón$_i$ kemur ekki [nema Sigga bjóði sér$_i$]
Jón comes not unless Sigga invites self
'Jón$_i$ does not come unless Sigga invites him$_i$'

b. Jón$_i$ segir að hann komi ekki [nema Sigga bjóði sér$_i$]
Jón says that he comes not unless Sigga invites self
'Jón$_i$ says that he will not come unless Sigga invites him$_i$'

The relevant generalization here is that LD anaphors contained in sentential adjuncts cannot take the subject of the most immediately dominating clause as their antecedent, as shown by (39a), while they can take the (more remote) subject of a higher clause, as in (39b). This follows from the principle in (37) if we take adjuncts like the one in (39) to be attached to IP (as Maling in fact argues), as in

(40)

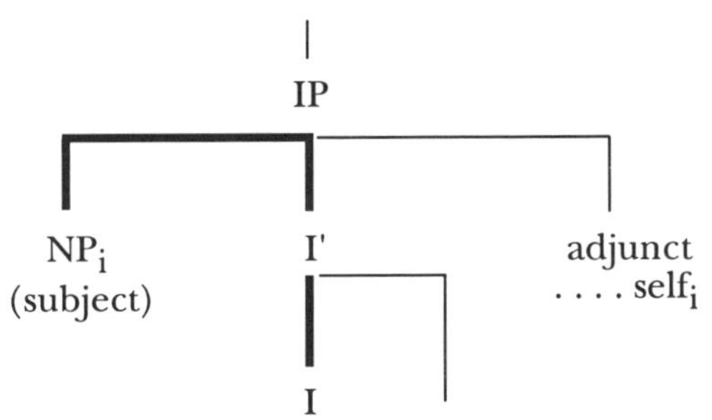

For then the path overlap relative to the nearest subject (the one in (40)) will be a "point" overlap (at IP), not implicating any path from inflection, and hence comparable to that due to subjects of *un*inflected clauses or objects. The resulting block, due to the subject alone, will thus again be one of the weaker variety and hence not detectable in (39a), where a stronger block— the subject-and-I in the adjunct, is being overcome.[27] In contrast, in (39b) the adjunct is *internal* to the VP of which the antecedent is the subject, so that path overlap will again implicate the connection between the subject and its inflection in full (as if the anaphor was within VP in (40)). In this case the subject will be a stronger block, and hence a viable antecedent under (37).

A third contrast accommodated under the principle in (37), albeit only to some approximation, is the one in (41), noted by Giorgi (1984), (1991).

(41) <u>Italian</u> (Giorgi (1984), (1991))

a. *Ho visto [$_{sc}$ il professore$_i$ accanto agli studenti [che seguivano il proprio$_i$ corso]]
I have seen the professor next to the students who were following the own course
'I saw the professor$_i$ next to the students who were following his$_i$ course'

b. ?Ho visto [$_{sc}$ il professore$_i$ contento del rendimento degli studenti [che seguono il proprio$_i$ corso]]
I have seen the professor pleased with the performance of the students who follow the own course
'I saw the professor$_i$ pleased with the performance of the students who follow his$_i$ course'

In (41a), the LD anaphor *proprio* is embedded in a tensed (relative) clause, and fails to take the subject of a PP small clause as its antecedent. This follows from (37), since PP small clauses rank lower than tensed clauses (and approximately like PVCs, as in (12) above).[28] The case in (41b) differs minimally, in that the antecedent is here the subject of an AP, rather than a PP, small clause. This configuration still violates (37), but now to a lesser degree, since AP small clauses rank higher than their PP counterparts (as in (12) above), because adjectives (at least in Italian), have an inflection. Hence at least the direction of the contrast is correctly predicted.

In conclusion, the principle in (37) will correctly draw the distinction between local and LD anaphora charted in (36), as well as account for a number of other significant facts.[29]

Once the role of the antecedent is thus defined in terms of (37), the solution of the original problem is close at hand, as we can now see by finally turning to the possessives.

5. POSSESSIVE ANAPHORA

The problem we began with is that languages like Chinese, that do not have verb-agreement, and Indo-European languages, that do, differ in the structure of (42) in the manner indicated.

(42)

	They$_i$ read [their$_i$ books$_i$]
a. Chinese type	refl pron
b. Indo-European type	refl *pron

In 3.3 above, we analyzed the pronoun/anaphor overlap of Chinese-type languages by arguing that possessive anaphora is not truly local, due to the weak interference of the spec-head relation with the antecedent-anaphor relation. If this is true, then possessive anaphora ought to exhibit a discriminatory effect with respect to antecedents similar to that of LDA, and unlike local anaphora. Indeed, this is the case, as shown in (43), again due to Timberlake (1979).

(43) Russian (Timberlake (1979))
a. ...on$_i$ ne mog najti [{svoju$_i$ / *ego$_i$} xatu]
he not able find [own / his hut]
'...he$_i$ was unable to find his$_i$ house'

b. Roditeli proposili Serezu$_i$ ne slusat' [{svoju$_i$ / ?ego$_i$} rakovinu]...
parents ask Sereza not listen [own / his shell]
'His parents asked Sereza$_i$ not to listen to his sea-shell...'

c. Roditeli zastavljali Serezu$_i$ ne slusat' [{?(?)svoju$_i$ / ego$_i$} rakovinu]...
parents make Sereza not listen [own / his shell]
'His parents tried to make Sereza$_i$ not to listen to his$_i$ sea-shell...'

The facts in (43) summarize as in (44), which thus complements the antecedent hierarchy of (36) above.[30]

(44)

Antecedent, subject of:	local anaphora
a. Tensed	refl *pron
b. Infinitival	refl ? pron
c. PVC	?(?) refl pron

We can now see that the "Chinese" facts in (42a) are virtually identical to the "Russian" ones in (44b), and in fact intermediate between (44b and c). Our original problem given in (42), is thus solved by simply assuming that subjects of Chinese tensed clauses rank on a par with Indo-European subjects of infinitivals/ PVCs as blocks, an assumption entirely consistent with our hypothesis that strength of block/antecedence is commensurate with the strength of the implicated inflection. Given the lack of verb-agreement, the inflection of Chinese-type tensed clauses will surely be "weaker" than that of Indo-European tensed clauses, in the same sense that the inflection of Indo-European infinitives is.[31]

Hence, no difference need be postulated with regards the internal structure of NPs, as the difference between the two groups of languages follows from the different roles of the respective antecedents, which we can independently predict.

Notice that, crucial to the above account, was the hypothesis that possessive anaphora is not strictly local. The latter assumption is in fact supported by several independent considerations beside the variation in (44). One of these is that, cross-linguistically, possessive anaphors are overwhelming of the LD rather than of the local variety (i.e. they are uninflected with respect to the features of the antecedent, although they may -irrelevantly- inflect for the features of the head. See below). This generalization in fact directly accounts for the non-existence of the series of English possessives like *himself's*, given the local character of *himself* series of reflexives. Another consideration that seems relevant is that, while some languages lack reflexive objects (like West Flemish, Frisian, Old English), many more (like Modern English and the Romance languages) lack reflexive possessives. This supports the view that reflexive possessives are more "costly", because systematically "long distance". Another relevant piece of evidence is provided by pseudo-agreement. Recall that in languages with a sufficiently broad range of pseudo-agreement, like Russian, LDA tends to exclude the more costly cases of pseudo-agreement, i.e. first-and-second person, as summarized in (16) above. The same is true of possessive anaphora, which contrasts with local anaphora in the manner of (45). For relevant examples see Timberlake (1979: 113).

(45) Russian

	Pseudo-agreement with:	
	3rd	1st–2nd
a. Local anaphora *(sebja)*	refl *pron	refl *pron
b. Possessive anaphora *(svoj)*	refl *pron	refl pron

That is, while local anaphora requires the reflexive *sebja* in all persons, possessive anaphora requires the reflexive *svoj* only in the third (a less costly case of pseudo-agreement), allowing both reflexive and pronoun in the first and second, hence roughly like LDA out of PVCs, as shown in (16b) above.[32] The conclusion that possessive anaphora is not strictly local, needed for our proposed solution to the contrast in (42), thus seems firmly established.

Our discussion has so far glossed over the fact that, in the Indo-European languages, reflexive possessives are generally adjectives, and not genitive NPs as in Chinese. Consider for example Latin *suus*, which we may plausibly analyze as having a nominal stem *su*, or perhaps the very same reflexive object *se*, and an adjectival morpheme *-us* (/-a/-um; -i/-æ/-a) agreeing in gender and number with the head. Our earlier discussion, which only considered genitive possessives, will plausibly carry over to this case as well, once we consider the parallelism illustrated by (46).

(46) a. se-us
b. NP-gen

If the genitive Case of (46b) (and, in general Case assigned to a specifier by a head) is a form of agreement, then it will be analogous to the agreement of the adjectival morpheme *-us* in (46a). As a result, in both (46a,b) there will be two agreements: one with the head (either in Case, or in I-features), and one with the antecedent (in I-features). In both cases the latter agreement is not overt, hence only a case of pseudo-agreement. For the case of genitives (46b), we supposed that the two relations, with the head and with the antecedent, partially interfered with one-another because of a clustering requirement peculiar to spec-head agreement. The exact nature of this clustering requirement, not completely clear for the earlier case, becomes admittedly even less clear in the case of adjectival possessives (46a), in which both relations involve I-features. Perhaps in the case of (46a) the interference in question is simply due to path overlap (analogous to that of fn.19), but we must leave this issue to further study. Recall in any event that the relative opacity of possessive anaphors including the adjectival ones is not in question, given the evidence discussed. Thus only the exact nature of it remains somewhat uncertain. Note in addition that the Chinese/ Indo-European contrast would fail to reduce to the difference between genitive and adjectival possessives just discussed, given for example the facts of Basque, illustrated in (47) below.

(47) <u>Basque</u> (Rebuschi (1987))
Peiok$_i$ [{bere$_i$ / *haren$_i$} txakurra] ikusi du
Peio-k [self's / his] dog seen Aux
'Peio$_i$ has seen his$_i$ dog'

According to Rebuschi (1987), reflexive *bere* in (47) is a genitive form (as is pronominal *haren*), yet the binding facts mirror those of Indo-European, not those of Chinese. From our point of view, this follow from the fact that Basque has a system of verb agreement (see Rebuschi (1986), (1987)) like the Indo-European languages, and unlike Chinese.[33]

6. CONCLUSION

This article has pursued two related goals. One, more specific, was to account for a certain cross-linguistic difference with respect to possessive anaphora. The other, more general, was to sketch out a general theory of anaphora. In essence, the connection between the two goals is provided by the two propositions in (48).

(48) a. In "long distance" anaphoric relations, antecedents which are subjects of inflected clauses provide a greater degree of well-formedness for the reflexive than antecedents that are subjects of uninflected clauses, while having the opposite effect on the pronoun.

b. Possessive anaphora is a subcase of long distance anaphora.

Most of our discussion was in fact aimed to showing that each of (48a,b) is true, and to providing a general framework that would account for them—our more general goal. Our more specific goal was then automatically achieved as the conjunction of the respective accounts of (48a,b), given the simple observation that, in languages like Chinese, tensed clauses are "uninflected", exhibiting no subject-verb agreement, unlike those of Indo-European.

We hope to have also shown in our discussion that anaphora is subject to a number of constraints related to the functioning of "agreement" or inflection, a fact which supports our general approach to anaphora as agreement. We list the relevant effects in (49) (where (49e) partially restates (48a)).

(49) a. The inflected versus uninflected morphology of the anaphor determines whether or not the anaphor may function "long distance".

b. The inflected versus uninflected character of a head determines whether or not an anaphor is allowed in "spec" (subject) position (the "* anaphor-AGR" effect).

c. In complement clauses, the character of the inflection that the subject is associated with determines the extent to which object anaphors may be bound long-distance (the variable "SSC" effect).

d. The character of the inflection that a subject is associated with determines the subject's viability as an antecedent in long-distance relations (the "blocking-consistency" effect).

e. The type of pseudo-agreement at work between antecedent and anaphor is a well-formedness of (long-distance) anaphoric relations.

APPENDIX (CHART (12))[34]

I. Icelandic

a. (Maling (1984)) (Ind)
Jón$_i$ upplysti hver hafði barið {*sig$_i$ / hann$_i$}
Jón revealed who had hit self / him
'Jón$_i$ revealed who had hit him$_i$'

b. (Maling (1984)) (Subj)
Jón$_i$ upplysti hver hefði barið {sig$_i$ / hann$_i$}
Jón revealed who had hit self / him
'Jón$_i$ revealed who had hit him$_i$'

c. (Anderson (1986)) (Inf)
Jón$_i$ skipaði mér að raka {sig$_i$ / *hann$_i$}
Jón ordered me that to-shave self / him
'Jón$_i$ ordered me to shave him$_i$'

c'. (Everaert (1986,301f)) (AP-sc)
Sálfræðingurinn$_i$ gerði Harald stoltan af {sér$_i$ / *honum$_i$}
psychiatrist made Harald proud of self/ him
'The psychiatrist$_i$ made Harald proud of him$_i$'

II. Italian

a. (Ind)
Gianni$_i$ diceva [che i giornali parlavano di {*sé$_i$ / lui$_i$}]
Gianni said [that the newspapers talked about self / him]
'Gianni$_i$ said that the newspapers talked about him$_i$'

b. (Subj)
Gianni$_i$ sperava [che i giornali parlassero di {??sé$_i$ / lui$_i$}]
Gianni hoped [that the newspapers would talk about self / him]
'Gianni$_i$ hoped that the newspapers would talk about him$_i$'

c. (Inf)
L'oratore$_i$ persuase la folla [a venire verso di {sé$_i$ / lui$_i$}]
the speaker persuaded the crowd to come towards of self / him
'The speaker$_i$ persuaded the crowd to come towards him$_i$'

c'. (AP-sc)
Maria$_i$ riteneva [ognuno innamorato di {sé$_i$ / lei$_i$}]
Maria believed each enamoured of self / her
'Maria$_i$ believed everyone in love with her$_i$'

d. (Giorgi (1991)) (PP-sc)
Gianni$_i$ ha aizzato [Maria contro di {sé$_i$ / ?lui$_i$}]
Gianni has incited Maria against of self / him
'Gianni$_i$ has turned Maria against him$_i$'

d'. (PP-sc)
Manuel$_i$ vide [il toro sopra di {sé$_i$ / ?*lui$_i$}]
Manuel saw the bull upon of self / him
'Manuel saw the bull upon him'

d". (PVC)
Maria$_i$ vide l'auto venire contro di {sé$_i$ / ?lei$_i$}
Maria saw the car come against of self / her
'Maria$_i$ saw the car come against her$_i$'

III. <u>Russian</u>
b. (Rappaport (1986)) (Subj)
Vanja$_i$ xocet, ctoby [vse ljiubili {ego$_i$ / *sebja$_i$}]
Vanja wants that [everybody love him / self]
'Vanja$_i$ wants that everybody love him$_i$'

c. (Timberlake (1979)) (Inf)
Starik$_i$ ozivilsja i prosil [na kurort ego$_i$/sebja$_i$}] pokuda ne otpravljat']
old man enliven and ask [to resort him / self] now not send off
'The old man$_i$ came to life and asked (one) not to send him$_i$ off to a health resort just now'

d. (Timberlake (1979)) (PVC)
On$_i$ dal [ej umyt' {sebja$_i$ / *ego$_i$} i vypil kruzku moloka]
he let [her wash self / him and drank mug milk]
'He$_i$ let her wash him$_i$ and drank down a mug of milk'

IV Danish

c. (Vikner (1985)) (Inf)
at Susan$_i$ overtalte Anne til [at hore på {sig$_i$ / ende$_i$}]
that Susan persuaded Anne to [that listen to self /her]
'that Susan$_i$ persuaded Anne to listen to her$_i$'

c'. (Pica (1986)) (AP-sc)
Larsen$_i$ betragter Jorgen some farlig for {sig$_i$ / ham$_i$}
Larsen considers Jorgen as dangerous for self / him
'Larsen$_i$ considers Jorgen dangerous for him$_i$'

d. (Jakubowicz and Olsen (1988), analysis ours) (PP-sc)
John bad Peter$_i$ [PRO$_i$ anbringe [bogerne bagved {sig$_i$ / *ham$_i$}]
John asked Peter [to put the books behind self / him]
'John asked Peter$_i$ to put the books behind him$_i$'

V. Dutch

c. (Everaert (1986)) (AP-sc)
Marie$_i$ maakte [mij jaloers op {*zich$_i$ / haar$_i$}]
Marie made me jealous of self / her
'Marie$_i$ made me jealous of her$_i$'

c'. (Everaert (1986)) (Inf)
Ria$_i$ vroeg ons [voor {*zich$_i$ / haar$_i$} te zorgen]
Ria asked us [for self / her to take care]
'Ria$_i$ asked us to take care of her$_i$'

d. (Everaert (1986)) (PVC)
Hij$_i$ hoorde [mij over {zich$_i$ / hem$_i$} praten]
he heard [me about self / him talk]
'He$_i$ heard me talk about him$_i$'

NOTES

[1] The cross-linguistic pattern of locally bound pronouns illustrated in (6) is very pervasive, and yet rarely noted in the literature. Locally bound pronouns were first drawn attention to in Zribi-Hertz' (1980) discussion of French.

[2] Additional arguments against principle B are given in Burzio (1989). The "asymmetry" in the acquisition of principles A and B often noted in the relevant literature is in fact a further argument against principle B. Everaert (1991: 113) summarizes the relevant observation as in (i), while the same children generally interpret anaphors correctly.

(i) ".. a sentence like *John washes him* is often interpreted by young children as meaning *John washes himself*"

From the point of view of two principles A and B with the same status, this asymmetry is extremely surprising. The facts are much less remarkable from our point of view: children to whom (i) applies have simply not yet acquired the "anaphor-first" principle in (5), while they may well be fully equipped to interpret anaphors —two rather different devices.

[3] In fact (5) is still relevant to the cases in (7) in selecting the first element of the complex. This is a pronoun only when there is no corresponding anaphor, just as in (6).

[4] This will raise obvious questions, which we are not in a position to answer at this point, about languages that have object agreement.

[5] There is also reason to believe that LD anaphor *proprio* "own", uninflected (for the features of the antecedent) is structurally complex, having the structure [e]-*proprio*, analogous to that of *suo-proprio* "his own", whence a further potential difficulty for Pica's criterion. Part of the evidence leading to that conclusion is the fact that *proprio* behaves like the complex anaphors in (7) with respect to the relevant semantic criteria, whence its ability to overlap with the pronoun in (i), contrasting with the complementarity in (2) above.

(i) Gianni_i legge {il suo_i / il proprio_i} libro
Gianni reads the his the own book
'Gianni reads his_i / his own_i book'

[6] There are other apparent exceptions to this generalization, for which we have no account, at the moment. One is the "long distance" use of English reflexives studied by Zribi-Hertz (1989) and others. We note that the latter phenomenon does *not*, to our knowledge, extend to inflected/ morphologically complex anaphors of other languages, and in this sense does not seriously challenge the proposed generalization. Another is represented by reciprocals, which are systematically local, cross linguistically, despite the fact that in some languages they are not obviously inflected (e.g. English *each other*). A third case is that of reflexive clitics, which are strictly local, cross-linguistically, regardless of their morphology.

[7] This is plausibly due to the fact that specifier, e.g. *my* and head, i.e. *self* are themselves linked by way of spec-head agreement, so that connecting a head to the antecedent implies connecting its spec as well.

[8] For ease of exposition, we take this and other complements to perception verbs to be clauses, rather than complex NPs as argued in Burzio (1986, 4.7), which would analyze a in (11) as in (i). The difference does not affect the issues at hand.

(i) $[_{NP}$ snakes_i $[_{IP}$ e_i near ....]]

[9] As indicated in (12), there is no subjunctive in Danish or Dutch.

[10] Despite the fact that in many languages (e.g. Romance) there is no overt difference between normal infinitivals and PVCs.

[11] The impression is rather widespread in the literature that LDA does not affect the distribution of pronouns, which is thought to remain constant, and as in English. The following quote from Koster and Reuland (1991: 2f) is indicative of that impression.

(i) "It is presently quite unclear why the opacity factor for pronominals does not vary, and why the complementarity between pronominals and anaphors, which is generally quite striking, breaks down in some constructions, especially in languages with long-distance anaphors."

On the other hand, the exclusion of pronouns in LDA contexts is attested by a variety of sources, like the ones listed in (ii).

(ii)	a.	Icelandic infin.:	Anderson (1986, ex.13)
			Maling (1986, ex.14b)
	b.	Icelandic AP-scs:	Maling (1986, ex.2)
			Everaert (1986, ex.128, p302)
	c.	Russian PVCs:	Timberlake (1979, ex.40-41)
	d.	Gothic infin.:	Harbert (1982, ex.12 and discuss. p7, top)
	e.	Latin infin.:	Bertocchi and Casadio (1980, p35)
	f.	German PP-scs:	Faltz (1977, ex.12, p2)
	g.	Yoruba tnsd claus.:	Mohanan (1982, ex.57-58 and discuss. p182f)

[12] Throughout the text and in the Appendix, Timberlake's diacritics ", ?, *" have been rendered as "?, ?(?), *", respectively.

[13] We thus differ here from Everaert (1991), who does postulate elements which are bound, but locally free, as a primitive category. Other languages which have been reported to analogously exclude the LD reflexive from local contexts and which we presume are also amenable to the text account are: Kannada (Bhat (1978)), Marathi, and Malayalam (Thráinsson (1991 and refs)).

[14] Anderson (1986) argues that the absence of nominative reflexives in Icelandic is a "morphological" gap. While Anderson's point seems quite correct, the gap cannot be accidental, since it is found systematically in language after language, calling for a syntactic account. For some related discussion see also Everaert (1991b).

[15] There are two important considerations that further bear on the issue. One is that (19) predicts that languages that have verb agreement with the object should exclude object reflexives. On this point we lack any direct evidence, except for that cited in fn. 33 below, relative to Basque. The second consideration is that, unlike the ECP-based account, an account based on (19) fails to relate the ability of languages like Chinese to have subject reflexives, to their known immunity to the "*that-trace" effect. To put it differently, an account of the anaphora facts based on verb-agreement would imply -given the correlation- that "**that*-trace" effects are also related to verb-agreement, a possibility that we leave to further study.

[16] Kornfilt's discussion also makes it abundantly clear that the blocking effect is in not related to nominative Case (as under the NIC), or any specific Case.

Her proposal for making agreement the relevant blocking element is essentially to reintroduce the notion of "SUBJECT" of Chomsky (1981), which, however, we have rejected on the basis of (20).

[17] Our account of (19) will be different from Rizzi's (1989) own, which is framed within a generally more conservative set of underlying assumptions than ours, and to which the reader is referred.

[18] Note that the distinction between post-verbal accusatives and post-verbal nominatives is then rather subtle. In particular, to the extent that post-verbal nominative may also be assigned under government (by I), we may expect clustering of

Case and I-features to no longer obtain, resulting in a nominative NP which does not trigger verb-agreement. This expectation is in fact fulfilled, at least in part, since there are languages in which post verbal nominatives can fail to trigger verb-agreement. Italian, however, is not one of them, raising the question of why clustering should obtain.

[19] Note that this approach predicts one further difference between the two groups of languages, and in particular that subject-internal anaphors should be blocked by path overlap in languages that have verb agreement, but not in those that do not, as in fact seems to be the case in (i).

(i) a. Danish (Vikner (1985))
   * at [Peter$_i$ troede at [[billederne af sig (selv)$_i$] aldrig ville blive til noget]]]
   that [Peter thought that pictures of refl (self)] never would become to anything
   'that Peter$_i$ thought that the pictures of him$_i$ would never come out'

b. Chinese (Cole et al. (1990))
   Zhangsan$_i$ shuo [Lisi$_j$ zhidao [ziji$_{i/j}$ de mama zai Taibei]]
   Zhangsan says Lisi knows self of mother at Taipei
   'Zhangsan$_i$ says that Lisij knows self's$_{i/j}$ mother is at Taipei'

In (ia) the subject "pictures of self" is connected with verb agreement, resulting in an overlap with the antecedent-anaphor connection. In contrast, in (ib) the subject "self's mother" is not connected with verb agreement since there is none, and hence there is no overlap. Note that while marginal English examples like (iia) are often reported as grammatical in the literature, the pattern of (ia) seems nonetheless general for the Indo-European languages, being attested also for those of (iib) as indicated. See also Freidin (1986: 157 and refs).

(ii) a. ??They$_i$ thought that pictures of each other$_i$ were on sale

b. Norwegian:	Everaert (1986, 253 fn.3)
Russian:	Rappaport (1986)
Hindi:	Harbert (1982)

[20] The parallelism would be maintained as well under the "DP hypothesis" (Abney (1987) and others), which would take the nominal structures in (28) to be "Determiner Phrases", their head X in (29) now being the genitive marker itself, assigning Case to the subject.

[21] Graffi (1987), (1988) also finds experiencers to act as blocks in the following kinds of English and Italian examples (experiencer underscored).

(i) a. ?I think it pleased them$_i$ that pictures of each other$_i$ are hanging on the wall
   b. ?*They$_i$ think it pleased me that pictures of each other$_i$ are hanging on the wall

(ii) a. ? Pietro$_i$ dice che sembra che i propri$_i$ antenati non siano stati degli eroi
   Pietro says that (it) seems that the own ancestors not have been some heroes
   'Pietro$_i$ says that it seems that his$_i$ ancestors may not have been heroes'
   b. ?*Pietro$_i$ dice che a Paolo sembra che i propri$_i$ antenati non siano stati degli eroi

Pietro says that to Paolo (it) seems that the own ancestors not have been some heroes
'Pietro$_i$ says that it seems to Paolo that his$_i$ ancestors may not have been heroes'

[22] However, the question will remain as how experiencer antecedents are to satisfy the C-command requirement. We will leave this question open, simply noting that two kinds of answers are possible in principle. One is that the C-command requirement, which is in any event not well understood, is simply relaxed with a certain class of prominent elements (see in this connection Huang and Tang's (1991) discussion of "subcommanders"). The other is that that requirement is in fact fulfilled, via the more abstract kind of D-structure and derivation proposed in Belletti and Rizzi (1988).

[23] Romance reflexive clitics, which *are* plausibly attached to inflection, do exhibit a strong subject-orientation, to the point of being quite uninterpretable with object antecedents.

[24] Note, however, that in the Western Indo-European languages this phenomenon may in fact not arise in quite the same fashion simply because first-and-second person NPs are *not* possible antecedents, due to the more restrictive pseudo-agreement. We note further that the French contrast in (i), from Pica (1986), may in fact fall within the same pattern as the Chinese facts, in that the intervening subject seems also required to agree with the antecedent, here in being (at least semantically) impersonal.

(i) a. *On$_i$ souhaterait toujours [que Paul dise du bien de soi$_i$]
one$_i$ would wish always [that Paul speak of well of self$_i$]
'One$_i$ would always wish that Paul speak well of oneself$_i$'

b. On$_i$ souhaterait toujours [que les gens disent du bien de soi$_i$]
one$_i$ would wish always that people speak of well of self$_i$
'One$_i$ would always wish that people speak well of oneself$_i$'

[25] Note that only in the English translation is there also a subject of a tensed clause "was embarassed". The corresponding Russian structure is an adjectival small clause. Its subject *on* "he" is therefore not a more viable antecedent for the reflexive than the "PRO" subject of the infinitival, and is thus irrelevant to the text discussion.

[26] Note that the effect of (37) is additional to that of the SSC, so that any block which is being overcome still introduces a cost for the reflexive, even if (37) is satisfied. This is why, in (36a), the LD reflexive is only possible and not obligatory.

[27] This, correctly predicts that the reflexive should be able to occur with the nearest subject as the antecedent when the adjunct is not sentential, as in (ia), contrasting with (ib), which is like (39a).

(i) Icelandic (Maling (1984))
a. Jón kemur ekki [án konu {sinnar / *hans}]
Jón comes not [without wife own / his]
'John$_i$ will not come without his$_i$ wife'

b. Jón kemur ekki [án þess að konan {*sinnar / hans} komi líka]
Jón comes not without it that wife own his comes too
'John$_i$ will not come unless his$_i$ wife comes too'

[28] Predictably, the result is grammatical when the anaphor is not contained in a tensed clause, as in (i).

(i) Ho visto [$_{sc}$ il professore$_i$ accanto ai propri$_i$ studenti]
I have seen the professor next to the own students
'I have seen the professor$_i$ next to his own$_i$ students'

[29] The same principle could perhaps shed light on the fact that Huang and Tang's (1991) "subcommanders" are proper antecedents for local relations, but not for LDA, and possibly also on the fact that intermediate subjects are not possible antecedents in Chinese LDA (Tang (1989, 109)).

[30] Where we may again note in passing how complementarity of anaphors and pronouns continues to be the primary generalization.

[31] Although of course Chinese tensed clauses cannot be fully equated with Indo-European infinitivals, with respect to phenomena like control and Exceptional Case Marking.

[32] This parallelism with PVCs is also consistent with the facts in (44), which show reversal of acceptability just around the "PVC" point. Sharp reversal is the indication that principle (37) is kicking in, and therefore that the chosen antecedent and the intervening block are approximately of the same strength.

[33] Rebuschi (1986, fn.6) observes that while *bere* is morphologically *be* plus genitive marker *re*, there is no object reflexive *be*. This is not problematic for our analysis, but would rather simply follow from (19) above and the fact that Basque has verb agreement with both subject and objects.

[34] The letters of the examples correspond to the letters in (12). We give no examples of LDA into NP's, which we have placed into (12d) somewhat tentatively. For relevant examples, see Manzini and Wexler (1986), Pica (1986), Vikner (1985), Hellan (1986), Rappaport (1986). The ungrammaticality of LDA into indicative complements in Russian, Danish and Dutch, for which we give no examples, is well known. Note that not all examples give both reflexive and pronominal variants in the original text. We have added the occasionally missing variant by relying for grammaticality judgments mostly on other relevant examples, and discussion, within the same source.

REFERENCES

Abney, S. (1987) "The English Noun Phrase in its Sentential Aspect," PhD Dissertation, MIT.

Anderson, S. R. (1986) "The Typology of Anaphoric Dependencies: Icelandic (and Other) Reflexives," in Hellan, L. and K. Koch Christensen, eds.

Belletti, A. and L. Rizzi (1988) "Psych-Verbs and θ-Theory," *Natural Language and Linguistic Theory*, 6.3.

Bertocchi, A., and C. Casadio (1980) "Conditions on Anaphora: An Analysis of Reflexive in Latin," *Papers on Grammar*, G. Calboli ed., CLUE, Bologna.

Bhat, D.N.S. (1978) *Pronominalization: A Cross Linguistic Study*. Decan College Post Graduate and Research Institute, Pune, India.

Bouchard, D. (1983) *On the Content of Empty Categories*, Foris, Dordrecht.

Burzio, L. (1986) *Italian Syntax: A Government-Binding Approach*, Reidel.

Burzio, L. (1989) "On the Non-Existence of Disjoint Reference Principles," *Rivista di Grammatica Generativa*, 14.

Burzio, L. (1991) "The Morphological Basis of Anaphora," *Journal of Linguistics* 27, 81-105.

Burzio, L. (1992) "On the Morphology od Reflexives and Impersonals," In *Theoretical Analyses of Romance Linguistics: selected papers from the nineteenth Linguistic Symposium on Romance languages (LSRL XIX)*, John Benjamins, Amsterdam.

Chomsky, N. (1973) "Conditions on Transformations," in S.R. Anderson and P. Kiparsky, eds. *A Festschrift for Morris Halle*, Holt, Rinehart and Winston, New York.

Chomsky, N. (1980) "On Binding," *Linguistic Inquiry*, 11.1.

Chomsky, N. (1981). *Lectures on government and binding*. Dordrecht: Foris.

Chomsky, N. (1982). On the representation of form and function, in Mehler et al., eds., 3-38.

Chomsky (1986a). *Knowledge of language*. New York: Praeger.

Chomsky (1986b). *Barriers*. The MIT Press.

Chomsky, N. (1989). Some notes on economy of derivation and representation. In Laka & Mahajan, eds., (1989), 43-74; also, edited, in Freidin, ed., (1991), 417-454.

Cole, P., G. Hermon, and L.-M. Sung (1990) "Principles and Parameters of Long-Distance Reflexives," *Linguistic Inquiry* 21,1. 1-22.

Everaert, M. (1986) *The Syntax of Reflexivization*. Foris, Dordrecht.

Everaert, M. (1991) "Contextual Determination of the Anaphor/Pronominal Distinction," in J. Koster and E. Reuland, eds. (1991).

Everaert, M. (1990) "Nominative Anaphors in Icelandic: Morphology or Syntax," in W. Abraham, W Kosmeijer and E. Reuland, eds., *Issues in Germanic Syntax*, Mouton-De Gruyter, Berlin.

Faltz, L. (1977) *Reflexivization: A Study in Universal Syntax*, Garland Publishing.

Freidin, R. (1986) "Fundamental Issues in the Theory of Binding," in B. Lust, ed. *Studies in the Acquisition of Anaphora*, vol. I, Reidel, Dordrecht.

Freidin, R., and W. Harbert (1982) "On the Fine Structure of the Binding Theory: Principle A and Reciprocals," in P. Sells and C. Jones, eds. *Proceedings of the Thirteenth Annual Meeting of the North Eastern Linguistic Society*, GLSA, U.Mass. Amherst.

Giorgi, A. (1984) "Towards a Theory of Long Distance Anaphors: a GB Approach," *The Linguistic Review*, 3.

Giorgi, A. (1991) "Prepositions, Binding and T-marking," in J. Koster and E. Reuland, eds. (1991).

Graffi, G. (1987) "Soggetto Strutturale e Soggetto Tematico," *Ipotesi e Applicazioni di Teoria Linguistica Dal XIII Incontro di Grammatica Generativa*, P. Cordin, ed., Università di Trento.

Graffi, G. (1988) "Structural Subject and Thematic Subject," *Linguisticae Investigationes*, 12, 2.

Harbert, W. (1982) "In Defense of Tense," *Linguistic Analysis*, 9.1.

Harbert, W. and J. Toribio (1990) "Nominative Objects," ms, Cornell University.

Hellan, L. (1986) "On Anaphora and Predication in Norwegian," in L. Hellan and K. Koch Christensen, eds., (1986).

Hellan, L. and K. Koch Christensen, eds., (1986) *Topics in Scandinavian Syntax*. Reidel, Dordrecht.

Huang, C.-T J. (1983) "A Note on the Binding Theory," *Linguistic Inquiry*, 14.3.

Huang, C.-T. J. and C.-C. J. Tang (1991) "The Local Nature of the Long-Distance in Chinese," in J. Koster and E. Reuland, eds. (1991).

Jakubowicz, C. and L. Olsen (1988) "Reflexive Anaphors and Pronouns in Danish. Syntax and Acquisition," ms, Laboratoire de Psychologie Expérimentale, C.N.R.S., Paris and Linguistics Department, University of Copenhagen.

Kornfilt, J. (1989) "A Typology of Morphological Agreement and its Syntactic Consequences," in *CLS 24-II: Papers from the parasession on Agreement in Grammatical Theory*: D. Brentari, G. Larson, and L. Mac Leold, eds.

Koster, J. and E. Reuland (1991) "Long-distance Anaphora: an Overview, in J. Koster and E. Reuland, eds. (1991).

Koster, J. and E. Reuland, eds. (1991) *Long Distance Anaphora*, Cambridge University Press.

Kuno, Susumu (1988) "Binding Conditions and Crossover Phenomena," ms, Harvard University.

Lebeaux, D. (1983) "A Distributional Difference between Reciprocals and Reflexives," *Linguistic Inquiry*, 14.4.

Maling, J. (1984) "Non-Clause-Bounded Reflexives in Modern Icelandic," *Linguistics and Philosophy*, 7.

Maling, J. (1986) "Clause-Bounded Reflexives in Modern Icelandic," in L. Hellan and K. Koch Christensen, eds., (1986).

Manzini, M. and K. Wexler (1987) "Parameters, Binding Theory and Learnability," *Linguistic Inquiry*, 18.3.

Mohanan, K.P. (1982) "Grammatical Relations and Anaphora in Malayalam, in A. Marantz and T. Stowell eds. *Papers in Syntax*, MIT Working Papers in Linguistics.

Pica, P. (1984) "Liage et Contiguité," in J.C. Milner ed., *Recherches sur L'Anaphore*, Paris VII.

Pica, P. (1986) "De Quelques Implications Théoriques de l'Etude des Relations à Longue Distance,"in M. Ronat and D. Couquaux eds., *La Grammaire Modulaire*, Minuit, Paris.

Pica, P. (1991) "On the Interaction between Antecedent- government and Binding: The Case of Long-distance Reflexivization," in J. Koster and Eric Reuland, eds. (1991).

Rappaport, G. (1986) "On Anaphor Binding in Russian," *Natural Language and Linguistic Theory*, 4.

Rebuschi, G. (1986) "Théorie du Liage, Diachronie et Enonciation: Sur les Anaphores Possessives du Basque," *Anuario del Seminario de Filología Vasca "Julio de Urquijo"*, 20, 2. Donostia, San Sebastian.

Rebuschi, G. (1987) "Defining the Three Binding Domains of Basque," in *Proceedings of the Conference on the Basque Language*, Donostia, San Sebastian.

Rizzi, L. (1982) *Issues in Italian Syntax*, Foris, Dordrecht.

Rizzi, L. (1989) "On the Anaphor-agreement effect," *Rivista di Linguistica*.

Rizzi, L. and I. Roberts (1989) "Complex Inversion in French," *Probus*, 1.1.

Saxon, L. (1990) "On One's Own: The Semantics and Pragmatics of Reflexives," in C. Georgopoulos and R. Ishihara, eds., *Essays in Honor of S.-Y. Kuroda*, Kluwer, Dordrecht.

Sigurðsson, H. (1991) "Icelandic Case-marked PRO and the Licensing of Lexical Arguments," *Natural Language and Linguistic Theory*, 9,2.

Sportiche, D. (1988) "Conditions on Silent Categories," ms, UCLA.

Tang, C.-C. J. (1989) "Chinese Reflexives," *Natural Language and Linguistic Theory* 7, 1.

Thráinsson, H. (1979) *On Complementation in Icelandic*, Garland, New York.
Thráinsson, H. (1991) "Long-distance Reflexives and the typology of NPs," in J. Koster and E. Reuland, eds., (1991).
Timberlake, A. (1979) "Reflexivization and the Cycle in Russian," *Linguistic Inquiry*, 10.1.
Vikner, S. (1985) "Parameters of Binder and of Binding Category in Danish," *Working Papers in Scandinavian Syntax*, no. 23, University of Trondheim.
Zribi-Hertz, A. (1980) "Coréférences et pronoms réflechis: notes sur le contraste *lui/ lui-même* en français," *Linguisticae Investigationes* IV:1.
Zribi-Hertz, A. (1989) "Anaphor Binding and Narrative Point of View: English Reflexive Pronouns in Sentence and Discourse," *Language*, 65.4.

A. CARLOS QUICOLI

INFLECTION AND PARAMETRIC VARIATION: PORTUGUESE VS. SPANISH*

1. INTRODUCTION

Under the Principles and Parameters approach to linguistic theory proposed in Chomsky (1981; 1986a) and related work, Universal Grammar (UG) consists of a system of principles, each with certain open parameters to be fixed on the basis experience with primary linguistic data. By appropriately fixing the parameters of UG, a particular (Core) Grammar is determined which, by hypothesis, correlates in some important aspects with the Real Grammar represented in some way in the mind/brain of the individual speaker. Ultimately, given an interesting theory of UG, by appropriately fixing the specific values of the parameters of UG, the facts of the particular (Core) Grammars should be deducible from the system of principles.

Assuming these goals, the study of the properties that differentiate among the various languages (i.e. Grammars) is of essential importance. Such studies not only may provide clues for the discovery and identification of the parameters of UG, but also provide interesting testing grounds to ascertain the predictions deducible from the principles tentatively attributed to UG.

In this article I will assume the Principles and Parameters approach and the characterization of UG provided by the principles of the theories of Government and Binding (GB Theory) developed in Chomsky (1981; 1982; 1986a, and related work). I then relate these assumptions to some of the phenomena associated with the presence of Infinitival Agreement ("inflected infinitives") as found in Portuguese[1] versus its absence in Spanish and other languages. In particular, I attempt to demonstrate how the principles of GB Theory interact with a parameter of UG (the "I-Parameter") to make correct predictions about a significant range of empirical situations and, thus, provides evidence in support of the Principles and Parameters approach.

2. THE I-PARAMETER

A first basic question that must be considered here is how to account for the linguistic variation involving subject-verb agreement morphology (i.e. AGR). More specifically, the problem that will be of central concern here is how to account for the fact that Portuguese allows AGR with finite verbal forms and also (as an option) with infinitives ("inflected infinitives"), whereas languages like Spanish, for example, allow AGR only with finite verbal forms.

Evidently, it does not seem plausible to suppose that UG comes equipped with a special module designed solely for inflected infinitives. What seems more likely is that inflected infinitives arise as the result of a choice among those permitted by the system of parameters of UG. Assuming this view to be correct, let us examine how it can be theoretically implemented.

Consider first the more common situation (i.e. the unmarked case) represented by languages in which only finite verbs contain agreement, whereas infinitives do not. This situation holds, for instance, in Spanish [S] and also (partially) in Portuguese [P]:

(1) [P] É correto que nos ignoramos isto.
[S] Es correcto que nosotros ignoramos eso.
'It is correct that we ignored this.'

(2) [P] É correto ignorar isso
[S] Es correcto ignorar eso
'It is right to ignore this'

In (1) the verb *ignoramos* in both Portuguese and Spanish is a finite form (present indicative) and it contains the subject-verb agreement morpheme -mos, which indicates first person plural, in agreement with its nominative subject (*nós/nosotros*). In (2) the form *ignorar* is a non-inflected infinitive in the sense that it contains no subject-verb agreement morpheme.

A straightforward account for these facts can be given as follows. Let us assume (with Chomsky 1981; 1986b) that the basic structure of the 'S-node' or Inflection Phrase (IP) is essentially as in (3):

(3) IP = [NP - INFL - VP]

Assuming further that INFL includes Tense and Agreement elements (cf. Chomsky 1981: 209; 1986: 9), the relevant portion of the INFL structure ('Modals' omitted for simplicity) is essentially:

(4) INFL = [[+/-TENSE], [+/-AGR] ....]

We may then interpret the INFL structure in (4) as a parameter of UG (what I will refer to as the "I-Parameter") containing values for Tense and Agreement (cf. Picallo, 1984; Raposo, 1987 for similar views).[2] In that case, finite embedded clauses such as in (1) would have INFL with the values [+Tense, +AGR], while non-inflected infinitival clauses such as those in (2) would have INFL with the values [-Tense, -AGR].[3]

This analysis can then be extended in a natural way to account for the inflected infinitive phenomenon (i.e. infinitives containing subject-verb agreement morphemes or AGR), which is found in Portuguese but not Spanish, as illustrated below:

(5) [P] É correto nós ignorarmos isto.
[S] *Es correcto nosotros ignorarmos eso.
'It is right for us to ignore-1pl. this'

The difference here, of course, is the presence of the agreement marker -mos in the infinitive, something which is possible in Portuguese but not in Spanish. This can be accounted for by assuming that INFL in inflected infinitives is [-Tense, +AGR]. Spanish and Portuguese would thus differ in that in Spanish infinitives INFL can only be [-AGR], while in Portuguese infinitives INFL can be [+/-AGR]. The [+AGR] element of inflected infinitives would then assign (nominative) Case (cf. the nominative *nós* [n s] 'we' in P(5) vs. the objective *nos* [nós] 'us'), thus avoiding the Case Filter (Chomsky 1981; Rouveret & Vergnaud 1980).

Viewed in this way, the I-Parameter (4) allows four logical possibilities:

(6) A. [+Tense, +AGR]
B. [-Tense, -AGR]
C. [-Tense, +AGR]
D. [+Tense, -AGR]

Of these four possibilities, we have discussed three. Case A would correspond to finite, tensed clauses; case B would correspond to tenseless, non-inflected infinitives (but see Stowell 1982 for an analysis which assumes that infinitives have tense); case C would correspond to inflected infinitives as found in Portuguese (and possibly also to Turkish inflected gerunds; cf. George & Kornfilt 1981), These are the three cases that will concern us here. Case D would be a language with Tense affixes but no subject-verb agreement affixes, a situation that seems to be exemplified by Japanese.[4]

An obvious—but independent—question that arises at this point has to do with 'markedness' considerations. In other words, if the I-Parameter allows inflected and non-inflected infinitives, how do we account for the fact that the former are rare while the latter are commonplace?[5]

An interesting hypothesis that can be invoked to account for this problem is suggested by Berwick's work on learning theory (Berwick 1982; Berwick & Weinberg 1984). Berwick gives evidence for a principle of learning—the Subset Principle—according to which children "hypothesize the narrowest possible grammar consistent with the evidence seen " (cf. Berwick & Weinberg 1984: 287). Only on the basis of positive evidence to the contrary will the child hypothesize a broader grammar. In terms of parameters, Berwick's Subset Principle states essentially that given two options for choosing the values of a parameter—say, options A and B—if option A generates a proper subset of the grammatical sentences generated under option B, then option A (the narrower grammar) would represent the "unmarked case", while option B (the broader grammar) would constitute the "marked case" (for relevant discussion, see also Chomsky 1986a: 146).

Now, it is clear that the set of (infinitival) sentences generated by the Grammar that allows only non-inflected infinitives is a (proper) subset of the language generated by the Grammar allowing both non-inflected and inflected infinitives. The Subset Principle would therefore make the correct prediction that the former would constitute the unmarked case, while the latter would represent the marked case. Under these assumptions, the marked nature of Grammars allowing infinitival agreement such as Portuguese can thus be explained in terms of a general principle, as is desirable.

Although the hypothesis concerning the I-Parameter above requires further investigation before anything more conclusive can be said, it does seem to provide at least a first approximation towards the characterization of the differences involving the distribution of AGR in finite and infinitival clauses in the languages under consideration. In view of this, I will tentatively adopt this hypothesis here.

3.0. PRINCIPLES OF GB THEORY: REVIEW

In the section above we argued that the presence of inflected infinitives cannot be plausibly attributed to a special feature of UG. What is more likely is that inflected infinitives result from a particular choice (albeit a marked one) among those choices provided by the parametric structure of UG (specifically, the "I-Parameter" suggested above). Similarly, it does not appear plausible to suppose that the empirical properties related to the presence vs. absence of inflected infinitives are due to any special set of principles of UG designed uniquely for this purpose. Rather, we should expect the properties in question to be determined by the general principles of UG.

In the discussion to follow I will attempt to show that, in fact, a significant range of the empirical properties of Portuguese and Spanish that appear to be related to the presence vs. absence of infinitival agreement are determined by the principles of GB theory, in interaction with the choices provided by the Inflection Parameter. So as to provide a background to the ensuing discussion, we shall briefly review the main concepts of Government-Binding theory that will be of relevance here.

Consider first Binding Theory. This theory contains essentially the following principles (based on Chomsky 1986a):

(7) Binding Theory
A. An anaphor is bound in a local domain.
B. A pronominal is free in a local domain.
C. An R-expression is free.

Binding Theory refers to two basic properties of NPs, 'anaphor' and 'pronominal'. By combination of these two properties the following basic NP-types (overt and null) are deducible (cf. Chomsky 1982: 78):

(8)	Overt	Null
a. [+anaphor, -pronominal]:	lexical anaphors	NP-traces
b. [-anaphor, +pronominal]:	pronouns	pro
c. [+anaphor, +pronominal]:	——	PRO
d. [-anaphor, -pronominal]:	names	wh-trace

The basic distribution of such elements is determined by the principles of Binding Theory: 'anaphors' are regulated by Principle A, 'pronouns' obey Principle B; while names and variables ('wh-traces') obey principle C. The 'pronominal-anaphor' PRO may not occur within a 'binding domain', otherwise a paradox would arise with respect to Principles A and B ('PRO theorem'; Chomsky 1981). Additional factors concerning the distribution of these elements are determined by other principles of GB theory as, for example, the Case Filter (reviewed below) and the ECP (cf. Chomsky 1981; 1986b; Lasnik & Saito 1984, among others).

For present purposes, the notion 'local domain' (cf. Chomsky 1986a: 166ff.) for an anaphor or pronominal (a) can be defined essentially as follows:

(9) Local Domain:
β is a local domain for α (α = anaphor or pronominal) iff β is the minimal maximal projection containing both a subject and a governor for α.

This notion corresponds to what Chomsky (1986a: 169ff) calls the 'minimal governing category'. A minimal governing category in Chomsky's sense is a minimal 'complete functional complex' in the sense that all grammatical functions compatible with the relevant head are realized within it. There are essentially two local domains. One is the domain of the closest c-commanding subject, which produces the so-called SSC effects. Within this domain , an anaphor must be bound while pronominals must be free. To illustrate, consider the structures below:

(10) a. [John_i believes [Mary_j to like herself_j/*her_j]]
b. [John_i believes [Mary_j to like *himself_i/him_i]]
c. [John_i believes [himself_i/*him_i to be smart]]

The possibilities of occurrence of anaphors and pronominals in such structures are determined by Binding Theory (Principles A, B). In (10a) and (10b) the local domain for the respective anaphors and pronominals is the embedded clause; the governor is the embedded verb *to like* and the embedded clause contains a subject (*Mary*). The only grammatical possibilities, as indicated, are those in which anaphors are bound and pronominals are free within this domain. In (10c), however, the relevant local domain is constituted by the full structure: the governor for the anaphor/pronominal in this structure is the main verb and the main clause contains a subject. Accordingly, anaphors must be bound and pronominals must be free in this domain, as indicated.

The other local domain is the position governed by INFL [+AGR]. In English and in many other languages this case is uniquely represented by the subject position of a tensed sentence, a position in which anaphors display the so-called NIC effects. Typical examples are:

(11) a. [*$Himself_i$/He_i AGR-swims]
b. [$John_i$ believes [*$himself_i$/he_i AGR-is rich]

In both cases here, the local domain is the clause containing the finite verb (i.e. AGR) since it contains both the governor (AGR) and a subject (*himself, he*). According to Binding Theory, the presence of an unbound anaphor in this domain is disallowed while the presence of a free pronominal is allowed, as indicated (see Chomsky 1986a; Freidin 1986 for further discussion).

Consider now Case Theory. Case Theory interacts in a crucial way with Government Theory since the principles of case assignment require reference to a governor (for discussion, see Chomsky 1981; 1986a; Rouveret & Vergnaud 1980). Among the principles of case assignment are the following (cf. Chomsky 1981:170):

(12) Case Assignment Principles
A. NP is nominative if governed by AGR.
B. NP is objective if governed by V.
C. NP is oblique if governed by P.

In addition, Case Theory contains a principle that is known as the Case Filter (Rouveret & Vergnaud 1980; Chomsky 1981;1986a). The formulation of this principle that I will adopt here is essentially:

(13) Case Filter
*NP, where NP has specified lexical content and lacks Case.

This formulation of the Case Filter differs from that given in the standard literature, which assumes that only "phonetically realized" NPs require Case.

Under the formulation above this is replaced by the notion "specified lexical content". NPs with "specified lexical content" are those lexically marked with feature specifications for properties such as person, number and gender. This class includes, of course, all phonetically realized NPs (R-expressions, pronouns, lexical anaphors) and, in addition, also the null pronominal pro typical of "null-subject languages". These are in contrast with 'traces', which are not lexical categories at all since they arise as the result of the operation of "move a", and the pronominal-anaphor PRO which I assume (contrary to Chomsky 1981:60) not to be lexically specified for person, number and gender (more on this later). An important consequence of the present formulation is that the Case Filter applies also to the null element pro, whereas in standard analyses it does not, a point that will be elaborated in the discussion to follow.

The principles of GB theory summarized above, associated with the I-Parameter suggested earlier, makes a number of reasonably clear predictions concerning contrasts between inflected vs. non-inflected infinitives. Thus, according to Binding Theory, inflected infinitives (unlike non-inflected infinitives) should constitute a local domain for anaphors and pronominals in subject position, since this position would be governed by [+AGR]. Similarly, according to Case Theory the [+AGR] feature of inflected infinitives (unlike the [-AGR] of non-inflected infinitives) should be able to assign (nominative) Case to its subject and, hence, should be able to license a lexically specified subject, thus avoiding the Case Filter. Suggestions to this effect have been made in the literature with varying degrees of precision and empirical support (cf. Rouveret 1980; Galves 1980; Zubizarreta 1980). The ensuing discussion seeks to provide further support to this view by adducing new facts and by exploring the matter in more detail.

4.0. INFINITIVAL AGREEMENT AND GB THEORY

In this section we examine some of the predictions that can be said to be deduced from the principles of GB theory related to presence vs. absence of infinitival agreement (assumed here to be determined by different choices of values for the I-Parameter).

4.1. Complex Adjectives and Factive Predicates

A non-inflected infinitive does not normally assign Case to its subject-position. Moreover, in the regular situation (excluding 'Exceptional Case Marking' verbs; cf. Chomsky 1981), a matrix verb cannot govern and assign Case to an embedded infinitival subject. Because of this, the subject-position of a non-inflected infinitive is normally ungoverned and Case-less. It follows from the principles of GB theory that PRO but not lexical NPs may occur in such environments.

In the languages under consideration, one such situation is provided by adjectival predicates which allow infinitival complements. Since both Spanish and Portuguese allow non-inflected infinitives, if the infinitive embedded under such a predicate is not-inflected, the facts of the two languages coincide:

(14) [P] É necessário [PRO terminar a tarefa]
[S] Es necessario [PRO terminar la tarea]
'It is necessary to finish the task'

(15) [P] *É necessário [nós terminar a tarefa]
[S] *Es necessario [nosotros terminar la tarea]
'It is necessary we to finish the task'

These contrasts can be explained by the Case Filter. The embedded subject in (15) has 'specified lexical content' but lacks Case, which is excluded by the Case Filter. On the other hand, PRO does not have specified lexical content and is exempted from the Case Filter, so that (14) is well-formed. However, since Portuguese (but not Spanish) allows inflected infinitives, we see that the inflected infinitive is sufficient to license the occurrence of a lexical NP as its subject, something which is not possible in Spanish:

(16) [P] a. É necessário nós terminarmos a tarefa.
b. É necessário [nós AGR-terminarmos a tarefa]
'It is necessary for us to finish-1pl. the task.'

This is allowed by the Case Filter since the AGR of the inflected infinitive assigns (nominative) Case to its subject.[6]

Furthermore, observe that the AGR element of the Portuguese inflected infinitive is also able to license the null-subject pro. Thus corresponding to (16), with an overt nominative pronominal subject, Portuguese (again unlike Spanish) also allows inflected infinitive structures with a pro subject:

(17) [P] a. É necessário terminarmos a tarefa
b. É necessário [pro AGR-terminarmos a tarefa]
'It is necessary (for us) to finish-1pl. the task'

The obvious assumption to make here is that the presence of (16) and (17) in Portuguese and the absence of similar sentences in Spanish are correlated. That is, both are possible in Portuguese (but not in Spanish) because the AGR of the Portuguese inflected infinitive may assign Case to its subject, thus avoiding the Case Filter. This would explain why Portuguese has both while Spanish has neither. However, this natural explanation can only be given if we assume that pro, like overt pronouns, is also subject to the Case Filter.

This view can be reinforced by comparing the facts pertaining to (14) with those illustrated by (16) and (17), which reveal a basic difference in the distribution of PRO vs. pro in infinitival complements. While PRO can only occur with non-inflected infinitives (a fact that follows from the 'PRO theorem' of Chomsky 1981), pro can only occur with inflected infinitives.[7] That is to say that while PRO must not occur in a Case-marked position and is exempt from the Case Filter, pro (like overt pronouns) must be assigned Case and be subject to the Case Filter. Notice that the points just made capitalize on the existence of inflected infinitives, since their inflection allows us to better ascertain the distribution of pro subjects.

The conclusion drawn from the facts just discussed—namely that pro must be Case-marked has interesting theoretical consequences. As is well known, standard formulations of the Case Filter assume that only categories that have "phonetic content" must be Case-marked (Rouveret & Vergnaud, 1980; Chomsky 1981; 1986a). However, since pro does not have phonetic content the standard formulation would not apply to it, leaving unexplained the facts under consideration. The problem can be corrected, however, if we adopt a formulation of the Case Filter which includes pro, such as the one given in (13). Under this alternative the Case Filter would apply to NPs with 'specified lexical content'—i.e. features for properties such as 'number' and 'person' (the 'phi-features' of Chomsky 1981). The filter would then apply to all overt NPs and to pro; but it would not apply to traces (which are not lexical items and hence lack 'specified lexical content') nor to PRO, which I assume not to have phi-features for person and number.[8] This proposal seems to me quite natural so I will adopt it here.

Consider now structures containing 'factive' verbs. In such structures the infinitival clause in also relatively 'insulated' from the main verb, so that the role played by the infinitive can be more clearly observed. Here too we find significant contrasts between Portuguese and Spanish, owing to the presence vs. absence of infinitival agreement. Thus, if the infinitive is not-inflected the facts of both languages coincide; PRO subject may occur but lexical subjects may not:

(18) [P] O fato [de PRO ter perdido o jogo] não os chocou.
[S] El hecho [de PRO haber perdido el partido] no les choco.
The fact of to-have lost the game did not shock them
'Loosing the game did not shock them.'

(19) [P] *O fato [de eles ter perdido o jogo] não os chocou.
[S] *El hecho [de ellos haber perdido el partido] no les choco.
The fact of to-have lost the game did not shock them.

However, in Portuguese (unlike Spanish) the presence of an inflected infinitive licenses a lexical subject in such environments[9]:

(20) [P] a. O fato [de eles terem perdido o jogo] não os chocou.
b. O fato [de terem eles perdido o jogo] não os chocou.
The fact of they have-AGR lost the game did not shock them
'The fact that they lost the game did not shock them.'

These are allowed since the inflected infinitive assigns Case to its subject. Notice, furthermore, that auxiliary-subject inversion (i.e. movement of the aspectual auxiliary to the head of CP; cf. Rizzi 1982; Raposo, 1987) is optional in such structures. This fact suggests that auxiliary movement into CP is not relevant for Case assignment in Portuguese since here the inflected infinitive appears to be able to assign Case to its subject in structures with or without such movement. Also, the possibility of the infinitival INFL receiving Case from the matrix INF as suggested by Raposo (p.95 ff) seems unlikely here since the complex NP structure of the complement should block this association.(More on this below).

In addition, as before, we see also that the Portuguese inflected infinitive licenses the null subject pro in such environments (which again is not possible in Spanish):

(21) [P] O fato de terem perdido o jogo não os preocupa
'The fact that they lost the game does not worry them.'

Such facts can also be explained in terms of the Case Filter in the manner already described if we assume, as argued here, that pro is subject to the Case Filter. Similar contrasts obtain with factives of the *lamentar* ' to regret' type in which the complement is post-verbal. If the infinitive is not inflected, lexical subjects cannot occur in either language:

(22) [P] *Lamento (o fato de) eles ter abandonado a equipe
[S] *Lamento (el hecho de) ellos haber abandonado el equipo
I regret (the fact of) they have abandoned the team
'I regret the fact that they abandoned the team'

But, as in the previous paradigm, Portuguese, but not Spanish, allows overt subjects and pro in such environments when the infinitive is inflected:

(23) [P] a. Lamento (o fato de) eles terem abandonado a equipe
b. Lamento (o fato de) terem eles abandonado a equipe

c. Lamento (o fato de) terem abandonado a equipe
I regret (the fact of) (they) have-3pl. abandoned the team
'I regret the fact that they abandoned the team'

These results are predictable. The inflected infinitive assigns Case to its own subject, thus by-passing the Case Filter.

Consider now extraction in the same structures. When such structures contain a head noun (corresponding to 'the fact' etc.), extraction is not possible since it yields familiar "subjacency effects" (probably explainable under ECP; cf. Chomsky 1986b). However, when the head-noun is not present extraction is sometimes possible. Thus, if the complement is finite, wh-extraction of the embedded subject is possible in both Spanish and Portuguese[10], as shown:

(24) [P] Que jogadores você lamenta que tenham abandonado a equipe?
[S] Que jugadores lamentas que hayan abandonado el equipo?
Lit: Which players do you regret that have left the team?

These are permitted.[11] The AGR of the finite verb assigns Case to its subject position, thus avoiding the Case Filter. In addition, the wh-trace in subject position would be properly governed either by AGR as suggested in Chomsky (1981) for null-subject languages, or by the wh-trace in the specifier position under CP (cf. Chomsky 1986b), so that ECP would also be satisfied.

Consider now the facts of wh-extraction with infinitives in the same construction. If the complement is a non-inflected infinitive, wh-extraction is not possible in either language:

(25) [P] *Que jogadores você lamenta ter abandonado a equipe?
[S] *Que jugadores lamentas haber abandonado el equipo?
'Which players do you regret to have abandoned the team?'

However, the presence of an inflected infinitive allow a further grammatical sentence in Portuguese (which is not paralleled by Spanish):

(26 [P] Que jogadores você lamenta terem abandonado a equipe?
'Which players do you regret to have-3pl. abandoned the team?'

These facts are also explainable by the Case Filter. The structures in (25) are excluded by the filter since the subject of the non-inflected infinitive is Case-less. Structure (26) is allowed, however, since the AGR of the inflected infinitive assigns Case to the wh-chain associated with the embedded subject. Also, the wh-trace in subject position would be properly governed, as in (24), so that ECP would also be satisfied.

4.2. Raising Construction

In this section we examine some contrasts between Portuguese and Spanish related to the presence vs. absence of infinitival agreement in raising structures.

As is well-known, in languages where infinitives do not have AGR (i.e. where infinitives are not-inflected) "raising" is normally possible out of infinitival clauses but not out of finite clauses. Thus, compare the facts of Spanish (S) and English (E) below:

(27) [S] Los embajadores parecen [*t* haber llegado a un acuerdo]
[E] The ambassadors seem [*t* to have reached an agreement]

(28) [S] *Los embajadores parecen [que *t* AGR-llegaron a un acuerdo]
[E] *The ambassadors seem [that *t* AGR-reached an agreement]

The structures in (27) are well-formed according to Binding Theory since the NP-trace (an anaphor) is bound within its binding domain (the full S). The structures in (28), however, display a "NIC effect"; they contain an unbound NP-trace in the binding domain created by the embedded AGR. Such structures are correctly ruled out by Binding Theory.

Similar facts obtain for Portuguese. NP-movement is possible in the case of non-inflected infinitives but is not possible in the case of finite structures:[12]

(29) [P] Os embaixadores parecem ter chegado a um acordo.
'The ambassadors seem to have reached an agreement'

(30) [P] *Os embaixadores parecem que chegaram a um acordo.
Lit: The ambassadors seem that reached an agreement

However, since Portuguese also has inflected infinitives a third situation must be considered. What happens when the subject of an inflected infinitive is raised? The answer is that this is not possible; examples like P(31) are not grammatical.[13]

(31) [P] a.*Os embaixadores parecem terem chegado a um acordo.
b. Os embaixadores$_1$ AGR parecem [[t$_1$ AGR-terem chegado a um acordo]]
'The ambassadors seem-3 pl to have-3pl. reached an agreement'

Under the assumption made here that inflected infinitives contain the feature [+AGR], these facts are predictable from Binding Theory. NP-movement has left an unbound anaphoric trace in the local domain created by the AGR of the inflected infinitive. Such structures would thus be excluded by Binding Theory in exactly the same way as the finite structures in P(30) (and its Spanish and English counterparts (28)).[14]

Let us turn now to a different empirical contrast related to the presence vs. absence of infinitival agreement in the same construction, this time related to a prediction deducible from Case Theory. In languages containing only non-inflected infinitives, raising of the embedded subject must take place for the sentence to be grammatical, as evidenced by the contrast between the grammaticality of the Spanish and English examples in (27) as opposed to the ungrammatical structures below (where e represents the empty subject position):

(32) [S] *e parece [los embajadores haber llegado a un acuerdo]
[E] *It seems [the ambassadors to have reached an agreement]

The standard GB account for such facts is as follows. In non-inflected infinitive languages, infinitives cannot assign Case to their subjects. Since intransitive verbs like *seem/parecer* cannot assign Case to an embedded subject either, if the embedded subject remains in its D-structure position, as in (32), the embedded subject would be Caseless and the resulting S-structures would be excluded by the Case Filter. This can be avoided however if the subject is raised, as in (27), so that it can be assigned Nominative Case by the AGR of the verb in the main clause (cf. Chomsky 1981; 1986a: 141).

Now given our assumptions concerning Portuguese infinitives we should expect the facts of Portuguese to differ from those of Spanish and English. In Portuguese (like Spanish and English) raising should be obligatory with non-inflected infinitives (due to the Case Filter). But with inflected infinitives raising should not be necessary since the infinitival AGR should be able to assign (nominative) Case to its D-structure subject. This observation is correct, as evidenced by the facts below (taken from Quicoli, 1982):

(33) a. *Parece ter os embaixadores chegado a um acordo
b. e parece [ter os embaixadores chegado a um acordo]
'(It) seems the ambassadors to have reached an agreement'

(34) a. Parece terem os embaixadores chegado a um acordo
b. e parece [terem-AGR os embaixadores chegado a um acordo]
'(It) seems the ambassadors to have-AGR reached an agreement'

To my knowledge, the implication of such facts have not been explored in the context of GB theory. Such examples display an interesting case of complementarity. When the infinitive is not inflected, the subject must undergo NP-movement to avoid the Case Filter, which accounts for the contrast between (29) and (33). On the other hand, when the infinitive is inflected, NP-movement not only is not necessary to avoid the Case Filter, but is actually excluded by Binding Theory since extraction of the embedded subject would leave a free anaphor in the local domain created by the infinitival AGR, which accounts for the contrast between (31) and (34).[15]

To proceed, consider a further difference between Spanish and Portuguese in the same construction. Both Spanish and Portuguese are null-subject languages, so that AGR in both languages is able to license the null-subject pro, an effect referred to as the "null-subject parameter" (see Chomsky 1981; Rizzi 1982; Adams 1986a,b, for relevant discussion). Finite structures present no special problem since they contain [+AGR] in both languages. However, since Portuguese allows infinitives with [+AGR] while Spanish does not, an additional difference concerning the distribution of pro is expected also here. This, in fact, happens. Thus while Spanish has only one possibility (with raising of pro):

35) a. Parecen tener razón
    b. pro AGR-parecen [*t* tener razón]
    '(They) seem to be right'

Portuguese has two possible sentences (cf. Dias 1918: 220, among others):

(36) a. Parecem ter razão
     b. pro AGR-parecem [*t* ter razão]
     '(They) seem to be right '

(37) a. Parece terem razão
     b. e parece [terem pro razão]
     '(It) seems they to be-AGR right'

Again, to my knowledge, such facts have not been discussed in the context of GB theory, yet they behave as expected. Since in Spanish only the finite AGR licenses pro, only the structure where pro is raised yields a grammatical result. In Portuguese, however, pro may be licensed either by the finite AGR as in (36), or by the infinitival AGR as in (37). Such rather interesting empirical results are entirely predictable given our present assumptions. Moreover, notice also that the facts, as analyzed, constitute further evidence to support the view advocated here that the Case Filter must be reformulated so as to apply also to pro.

Let us now examine some contrasts between Spanish and Portuguese related to the behavior of wh-movement in the same construction. In Spanish and English an infinitival structure containing a wh-subject can only produce a grammatical result if the embedded subject first undergoes NP movement and then wh-movement:

(38) [S] Qué hombres parecen tener razón?
     [E] Which men seem to be right?

(39) [S] $[_{CP}$ que hombres-Nom $[_{IP}$ *t* AGR-parecen [*t* tener razón]]]
[E] $[_{CP}$ which men-Nom $[_{IP}$ *t* AGR-seem [*t* to be right]]]

If the embedded subject undergoes wh-movement first within the embedded CP and is then moved to the matrix CP the result is ungrammatical:

(40) [S] *Qué hombres parece tener razón?
[E] *Which men does it seem to be right?

(41) [S] $[_{CP}$ que hombres $[_{IP}$ e AGR-parece $[_{CP}$ *t* $[_{IP}$ *t* tener razón]]]])
[E] $[_{CP}$ which men $[_{IP}$ it AGR-does seem $[_{CP}$ *t* $[_{IP}$ *t* to be right]]]]

These contrasts, again, are due to the Case Filter. Since infinitives in Spanish and English cannot assign Case to their subjects, the latter must be moved to the subject position of the main verb, as in (38) with the corresponding S-structures in (39). In examples such as (40), which are associated with the structures in (41), the embedded subject cannot receive Case and the structures are excluded by the Case Filter (cf. Chomsky 1981).

Consider now the facts of Portuguese. When the infinitive does not have AGR, the facts are parallel to those in Spanish and English:

(42) [P] a. Que homens parecem ter razão?
b. $[_{CP}$ que homens-Nom $[_{IP}$ *t* AGR-parecem [*t* ter razão]]]
'Which men seem to be right?'

(43) [P] a. *Que homens parece ter razão?
b. $[_{CP}$ que homens $[_{IP}$ e AGR-parece $[_{CP}$ *t* $[_{IP}$ *t* ter razão]]]]

These facts are of the common type and the same explanation above given for their Spanish and English counterparts applies. However, since the Portuguese inflected infinitive may assign Case, we should expect to find Portuguese grammatical sentences corresponding closely (except for the infinitival AGR) to the ungrammatical Spanish and English structures in (40). Surprisingly, this is indeed the case, as evidenced by the facts below:

(44) a. Que homens parece terem razão?
b. $[_{CP}$ que homens [e AGR-parece $[_{CP}$ *t* $[_{IP}$ *t* AGR-terem razão]]]]
Which men (does it) seem to be-AGR to be right?

These rather unusual facts, to my knowledge, have not been discussed in the literature of generative grammar. They can also be explained under our present assumptions. Unlike Spanish and English, which do not have infinitival AGR, the AGR of Portuguese inflected infinitives assigns Case to its own subject position, so that (44) is able to avoid the Case Filter.[16]

The judgments of grammaticality above are corroborated by the traditional literature dedicated to Portuguese infinitives. Among the examples noted by grammarians are the following:

(45) a. Os quais lhes pareceu dirigirem-se para o lado do célebre mosteiro. (A. Herculano; cited in Ali 1957: 74).
'Which ones (it) seemed to them to direct-AGR themselves towards the famous monastery.'
b. Referiu-me circunstâncias que parece justificarem o procedimento do soberano.
(L. Coelho; cited in Cegalla 1977: 305).
'(He) pointed out to me circumstances which (it) seems to justify-AGR the behavior of the sovereign.'

Under the analysis adopted here, such examples would be analyzed in the same way as (44).

A last set of facts pertaining to the raising construction that will be discussed here has to do with certain effects of 'topicalization' and 'raising' noted by various grammarians of Portuguese (cf. Góis 1958: ch. 22; Ali 1957: 74; Maurer 1968: 109) and analyzed originally in Quicoli (1976; 1980). Consider initially the situation in Portuguese and Spanish when the complement is finite:

(46) [P] As estrelas parecia que sorriam
[S] Las estrellas parecia que sonrian
'The stars it seemed that (they) smiled.'

(47) [P] *As estrelas pareciam que sorriam
[S] *Las estrellas parecian que sonrian
'The stars seemed that smiled'

Here, the facts of Portuguese and Spanish coincide, as expected, since both languages have finite AGR. The ungrammatical (47) are raising structures (as evidenced by the agreement between *parecer* and the surface subject) and are excluded by Binding Theory since the anaphoric subject-trace left by NP movement would be free in the local domain created by the embedded AGR. By contrast, the grammatical (46) (as originally argued in Quicoli, 1976; 1982) are not raised structures but, rather, topicalized structures (i.e. subcases of wh-movement according to Chomsky 1977). Extraction of the embedded subject by wh-movement is permitted here since the embedded subject would be case marked by the embedded finite AGR. In other words, 'topicalized' structures such as (46) are good for the same reason as (48):

(48) [P] Que homens parece que não estão contentes?
[S] Qué hombres parece que no están contentos?
'Which men (does it) seem that are not happy?'

This, of course, is expected since both cases are produced by wh-movement.

However, as a function of the Portuguese inflected infinitive, we observe again a significant contrast between Portuguese and Spanish when the complement is infinitive. Compare:

(49) [P] As estrelas pareciam sorrir
[S] Las estrellas parecian sonrir.
'The stars seemed to smile'

(50) [P] As estrelas parecia sorrirem
The stars seemed to smile-AGR
[S] *Las estrellas parecia sonrir
The stars (it) seemed to smile

The examples in (49) are raising structures, which are permitted in both languages, since the raised subject receives Case from the matrix AGR. However, Spanish does not allow the topicalized structure S(50); its non-inflected infinitive cannot assign case to the its subject, so that the structure is ruled out by the Case Filter. By contrast in Portuguese the topicalized structure P(50) is possible since the AGR of the inflected infinitive can assign Case to its subject.

For completeness, notice that it is really the presence of the inflected infinitive that is responsible for the occurrence of the topicalized structure in Portuguese. If the infinitive is not-inflected, the topicalized structure is ungrammatical (just like in Spanish):

(51) [P] *As estrelas parecia sorrir
The stars seemed to smile

Alternatively, as already pointed out earlier, if the inflected infinitive occurs, the raised structure is not possible:

(52) [P] *As estrelas pareciam sorrirem
The stars seemed-AGR to smile-AGR

Such structures would be excluded by Binding Theory since the anaphoric NP-trace would be free in the local domain created by the infinitival AGR, so that all possibilities are now accounted for.

4.3. Semi-Control Structures

In this section we consider effects of infinitival agreement in a class of verbs which I shall refer to as 'semi-control' verbs. In Romance (unlike English) this class includes verbs of the *believe/claim* type (for relevant discussion, see Kayne 1981; Rizzi 1982: ch. 3). Like 'raising verbs', such verbs cannot assign case to an embedded infinitival subject; however, unlike raising verbs, they do not allow NP extraction (raising) of the embedded subject (probably due to Projection Principle; cf. Chomsky 1982: 22) and, hence, have no way of avoiding the Case Filter by raising the subject.

Typically, such verbs do not allow government and case assignment to reach down to the subject position of an infinitival complement; as a result, overt subjects are normally excluded while PRO is allowed in this position.[17] This is true for non-inflected infinitive complements in both Spanish and Portuguese:

(53) [P] *Pedro crê $[_{CP}$ $[_{IP}$ eles ter cometido um erro]]
[S] *Pedro cre $[_{CP}$ $[_{IP}$ ellos haber cometido un error]]
'Peter believes them to have made a mistake'

(54) [P] Pedro$_i$ crê $[_{CP}$ $[_{IP}$ PRO$_i$ ter cometido um erro]]
[S] Pedro$_i$ cre $[_{CP}$ $[_{IP}$ PRO$_i$ haber cometido un error]]
'Peter believes to have made a mistake'

Such Romance facts are now well-known (cf. Kayne 1981b; Chomsky 1981). The contrasts in question follow from the Case Filter in the usual way (cf. Chomsky 1981; 1986: 189ff). The structures in (53) are excluded because the infinitival subject has lexical content but lacks case: non-inflected infinitives cannot assign case and the matrix subject cannot assign case across the CP-boundary (or CP and IP boundaries combined; cf. Chomsky 1986b). On the other hand, PRO which can only occur in non-governed position ('PRO-theorem'; Chomsky, 1981), is permitted.

The possibility of infinitival AGR in Portuguese, however, leads to further empirical consequences, which are unmatched in Spanish. Thus, the presence of infinitival AGR in Portuguese licenses an overt subject in such constructions (something which is not possible in Spanish):

(55) [P] Pedro crê terem eles cometido um erro
'Peter believes them to have-AGR made a mistake'

These are allowed because the infinitival AGR assigns case to its subject, thus avoiding the Case Filter.[18]

Similarly, the presence of infinitival AGR in Portuguese allows the occurrence of the null-subject pro with the infinitive (which again is not possible in Spanish):

(56) [P] Pedro crê terem cometido um erro.
'Peter believes (them) to have-AGR made a mistake'

As observed earlier, pro is also subject to the Case Filter. But since pro is case-marked by the infinitival AGR, sentence (56) is permitted.

Notice that under the present assumptions, in infinitival constructions pro must occur only with inflected infinitives (to avoid the Case Filter), while PRO must only occur with non-inflected infinitives (to avoid the PRO-theorem paradox). This has interesting consequences in the case of a problem noted in the traditional literature of Portuguese (see below) in connection with pairs such as (57):

(57) [P] a. Nós cremos estar preparados para a tarefa
We believe to be prepared for the task.
b. Nós cremos estarmos preparados para a tarefa
We believe to be-1pl. prepared for the task
'We believe that we are prepared for the task'

Under our analysis, these are associated with two different D-structures, one in which the embedded subject is PRO and another in which the subject is pro:

(58) a. Nós$_i$ - cremos [[PRO$_i$ estar preparados para a tarefa]]
b. Nós$_i$ - cremos [[pro$_i$ AGR-estarmos preparados para a tarefa]]

This is a natural proposal in view of the facts pertaining to the distribution of PRO vs. pro that we have considered so far.[19]

As noted, such facts were at the center of a time-honored controversy in the traditional literature of Portuguese infinitives. Some traditional grammarians (following Barbosa 1881) claimed that when the infinitival subject and the matrix subjects are identical the infinitive cannot be inflected. This hypothesis works for (57a) but not for (57b). Later scholars, notably Ali (1919) took examples such as (57b) to falsify the "Barbosa view". As an alternative, Ali proposes, instead, that the infinitive is inflected when it has a subject of its own and non-inflected when it does not (cf. Ali's dictum "infinitive without subject is the same as infinitive without inflection" p.61). Now, Ali's proposal works for (57b) but not for (57a), where it makes the implausible claim that the infinitive there is subjectless. So, although both proposals provide some insights, they are also seriously defective.

In light of the analysis advanced here the problems with the two traditional proposals above arise from the fact that neither can distinguish between PRO vs. pro. By contrast, the analysis given here makes this crucial distinction (which is deducible from the typology of empty categories determined by Binding Theory) and accounts for the facts related to the their complementary distribution in terms of general principles of grammar.

Let us now examine the behavior of anaphors in the structures under consideration. The lexical anaphors (i.e. reflexive pronouns) in both Spanish and Portuguese are clitics and behave like the other clitics. Thus, in Portuguese, anaphors cannot occur as D-structure subjects of infinitives (with or without AGR) in such constructions:[20]

(59) [P] a. *Eles se creem ser honestos
b. Eles se creem [[*t* ser honestos]
'They believe themselves to be honest'

(60) [P] a. *Eles se creem serem honestos
b. Eles se creem [[*t* AGR-serem honestos]]
'They believe themselves to be-AGR honest'
The situation is mirrored by non-reflexive clitics:

(61) [P] a. *Eles nos creem ser/sermos honestos
b. Eles nos creem [[*t* ser/AGR-sermos honestos]
'They believe us to be/to be-AGR honestos'

Leaving aside the facts pertaining to the inflected infinitive, which have no counterpart in Spanish, the facts of non-inflected infinitives of Portuguese above are paralleled by those in Spanish.

These facts can also be accounted for under our proposal. The ungrammatical examples with non-inflected infinitives (in both Portuguese and Spanish) are excluded by the Case Filter, since the clitics would be Caseless. On the other hand, assuming that the empty category associated with clitics is an trace-anaphor (Quicoli 1976;1986; Kayne 1975; Rouveret & Vergnaud 1980), although this is by no means an uncontroversial assumption (for discussion, see Borer 1987 and references cited there), the facts of inflected infinitives would be excluded by Binding Theory since the anaphoric clitic-trace in question would be free within the local domain created by the infinitival AGR.

The situation is quite different, however, when we examine the structures in which the embedded subject undergoes wh-movement. Here we observe, again, a contrast between Portuguese and Spanish, which can be traced to the presence vs. absence of infinitival AGR. When the infinitive is not-inflected, wh-extraction of the infinitival subject leads to ill-formed structures in both languages:[21]

(62) [P] *Os rapazes que o João afirmou estar doentes estão bem
[S] *Los muchachos que Juan afirmó estar enfermos estan bien
'The boys who John declared to be sick are well'

However, such structures are possible in Portuguese if the infinitive is inflected:

(63) [P] Os rapazes que o João afirmou estarem doentes estão bem
'The boys who John declared to be-AGR sick are well'

The Portuguese facts above were first noted by Raposo (1975: 158ff.). Under our proposal, the non-inflected infinitival structures of Spanish and Portuguese in (62) are excluded by the Case Filter since the wh-phrase has no case. The additional P(63), however, is possible since the wh-subject receives case from the AGR of the inflected infinitive.

A similar account can be given to contrasts involving Portuguese 'topicalized' structures such as the ones in (64) (due to Raposo 1975: 185):

(64) [P] a. Estas coisas eu considero terem grande importância
b. *Estas coisas eu considero ter grande importância.
'These things I consider to have-3pl./*to have great importance'

And, also, for contrasts such as:

(65) [P] a. Os ministros se sabia serem apenas serventuários (R. Barbosa, cited in Maurer 1968:182fn)
b. *Os ministros se sabia ser apenas serventuários
The ministers was-known to be-3pl./*to be servants
'The ministers were known to be mere servants.'

Our analysis predicts he existence of such sentences in Portuguese. They can be accounted for if we assume, as before, that such topicalized structures involve wh-extraction of the embedded subject. Under this assumption, the same explanation given to the wh-structures in P(62) and P(63) would also apply here. By contrast, similar examples are not found in Spanish, which is also predictable. Since Spanish lacks inflected infinitives, there would be no way of assigning Case to the underlying wh-subject and the structure in question would be ruled out by the Case Filter.

To complete the section, consider the complex Portuguese examples in (66), with their respective S-structures in (67) (the crucial example was taken from Sten 1952):

(66) a. Os versos que observamos <u>parecerem</u> interiorizar a paisagem. (cited in Sten 1952: 29)
The verses which-NOM we said to appear-3pl. to internalize the landscape.
b. *Os versos que observamos <u>parecer</u> interiorizar a paisagem .
The verses which-NOM we said *to appear to internalize the landscape.

(67) a. Os versos [que [pro observamos [*t''* [*t'* parecerem [*t* interiorizar a paisagem]]]
b. Os versos [que [pro observamos [*t''* [*t'* parecer [*t* interiorizar a paisagem]]]

Both S-structures are produced by NP-movement ('raising'), followed by double wh-movement of the raised subject. The difference is that in the grammatical (66a), the raising verb is an inflected infinitive (*parecerem*), whereas in the ill-formed (66b) the raising verb is a non-inflected infinitive (*parecer*). These facts, although rather unusual, can also be explained. In the well-formed S-structure (67a), corresponding to (66a), the AGR of the inflected infinite assigns Case to the trace of the raised subject (t'), which is then transmitted to the wh-phrase (*que*), so that the Case Filter is inoperative. On the other hand, in the ill-formed S-structure (67b), corresponding to (66b), the raising verb is a non-inflected infinitive and cannot assign Case to its trace subject (t''), so that the wh-phrase in question remains Caseless and the structure is correctly ruled out by the Case Filter.

By contrast, Spanish does not have sentences corresponding to either of the examples in P(66). Since Spanish has no inflected infinitives it cannot allow a counterpart to P(66a); the only possibility available in Spanish would be the counterpart of P(66b), with a non-inflected infinitive. But such structures would be excluded by the Case Filter, just like in Portuguese. The results are, thus, as predicted by our analysis.

4.4. Exceptional Case Marking (ECM) Verbs

The last type of construction that we shall consider is represented by the so-called Exceptional Case Marking verbs (ECM verbs). I assume that in Romance this class includes 'causative' and 'perception' verbs. Typically, such verbs in both Portuguese and Spanish allow overt subject with non-inflected infinitives:[22]

(68) [P] José via os problemas crescer entre os assessores
[S] José via los problemas crecer entre los asesores
'Jose saw the problems grow among his advisers'

Following familiar assumptions, this can be accounted for by assuming that ECM verbs are (optionally) subcategorized so as to allow IP complement (or, alternatively, as taking S'/CP and permitting S'/CP deletion, as in earlier analyses). Accordingly the S-structures corresponding to (68) would be as in (69):

(69) [P] José via $[_{IP}$ os problemas crescer entre os assessores]
[S] José via $[_{IP}$ los problemas crecer entre los asesores]

Since the clausal boundary in question would not be a 'barrier' to government (cf. Chomsky 1981; 1986b; Kayne 1984 for relevant discussion), the main verb can assign case to the embedded subject, thus avoiding the Case Filter.

In Portuguese (unlike Spanish) an additional possibility exists in which the infinitive is inflected (cf. Maurer 1968: 174 ff. for discussion of the data):

(70) [P] José via os problemas crescerem entre os assessores
'Jose saw the problems grow-AGR among his advisers'

Under our analysis, the S-structure corresponding to (70) is as in (71) (with either CP or IP as a complement):

(71) [P] José via [os problemas AGR-crescerem entre os assessores]]

In such structures, the embedded subject is assigned (Nominative) Case by the AGR of the inflected infinitive, regardless as to whether the complement is IP or CP. If we take the complement to be IP, the AGR would be the closest governor/case assigner in accordance with some version of the Minimality Condition (cf. Chomsky 1986b: 42ff. for relevant discussion), thus precluding Case assignment by the main verb. Alternatively, if we take the complement to be CP, CP would constitute a barrier to outside government and Case assignment.

Consider now cliticization facts in such structures. As expected, Portuguese and Spanish allow cliticization of the embedded subject of a noninflected infinitive in such constructions. Compare:

(72) [P] José nos viu sair da casa
[S] José nos vio salir de la casa
'Jose saw us leave the house'

(73) [P] José nos viu [$_{IP}$ *t* sair da casa]
[S] José nos vio [$_{IP}$ *t* salir de la casa]

These are allowed. The subject-position of the infinitive is Case-marked by the ECM-verb, thus rendering the Case Filter inapplicable; in addition the empty category associated with the clitic (an anaphor under our analysis) is bound within its local domain (the matrix CP structure, which contains the governor for the anaphoric empty category).

However, the presence of the inflected infinitive in Portuguese precludes cliticization of its subject (an observation made originally by Ali 1919):

(74) [P] a. *José nos viu sairmos da casa
b. José nos viu [*t* AGR-sairmos da casa]]
'Jose saw us leave-AGR the house'

This is, again, as expected. Although the embedded subject would be assigned Case, the structure is excluded by Binding Theory since the Clitic-trace in subject position of the infinitive is not bound within the local domain created by the infinitival AGR (cf. also Zubizarreta 1980).

A similar situation (though rare) arises in Portuguese when the embedded subject undergoes NP-movement:

(75) [P] a. Os soldados foram vistos cair (cf. Góis 1900: 175)
b. *Os soldados foram vistos cairem
'The soldiers were seen to fall/*to fall-AGR.'

(76) [P] a. Os soldados AGR-foram vistos [e cair]
b. Os soldados AGR-foram vistos [e AGR-cairem]

Facts similar to P(75a) obtain in Spanish (cf. Bello 1903:292 ff.). In the well-formed P(75a) the embedded subject cannot receive Case from the matrix ECM verb since the passive morphology absorbs Case (Chomsky 1981). But the embedded subject can still be assigned Case by the matrix AGR, which saves the structure from being excluded by the Case Filter. Moreover, the anaphoric NP-trace is properly bound, thus satisfying Binding Theory. In the ill-formed (75b) the embedded would also be assigned Case in the same way. However the structure is excluded by Binding Theory since the anaphoric trace is free within the local domain created by the infinitival AGR.

Consider now wh-extraction in the same construction. Again, as expected, Portuguese and Spanish allow wh-extraction of the subject of an non-inflected infinitive:

(77) [P] Os problemas que José via crescer entre os assessores o incomodavam muito.
[S] Los problemas que José via crecer entre los asesores lo incomodavam mucho.
'The problems that Jose saw grow among his advisers bothered him a lot.'

These are expected since the embedded subject position is Case-marked by the matrix ECM-verb across the IP, thus avoiding the Case Filter.

Consider now the predicted additional Portuguese example in which the infinitive is inflected:

(78) [P] Os problemas que José via crescerem entre os assessores o preocupavam muito.
'The problems that Jose saw grow-AGR among his advisers bothered him a lot.'

Given our present assumptions, such sentences should be possible since the wh-phrase would receive Case (via its trace) from the inflected infinitive. In my own judgment, P(78) is well-formed, co-occurring with P(77) in the dialect that we have been considering here. These judgments are also corroborated by facts cited in the traditional literature. Examples such as P(77), with non-inflected infinitive are common-place and need no elaboration.[23] More interesting are examples of inflected infinitives similar to P(78) such as the ones given below:

(79) a. Pilhas que via subir, decrescer, dissiparem-se consoante os ventos da fortuna.
(A. Ribeiro, cited in Sten 1952: 112).
'Piles that (he) saw rise, diminish, vanish-AGR according to the winds of fortune.'

b. Os mal-entendidos que ja sentia crescerem as sua volta.
(Regio, cited in Sten 1952: 112)
'The misunderstandings that (he) already felt grow-AGR around himself.'

c. Velhos guerreiros vi eu chorarem tambem ali. (G. Dias, cited in Góis 1958: 168)
'Old warriors did I see cry-AGR also there.'

Example (79a) is particularly interesting since wh-extraction of the subject co-occurs with non-inflected and inflected infinitives in coordinate structures. Example (79b) is similar to P(78), while (79c) is an instance of 'topicalized' structure (i.e. wh-structure) of the type already discussed.

Although some problems remain[24], if we assume that the well-formedness of such examples with inflected infinitives (alongside those with non-inflected infinitives) represents the general situation in the dialect in question, the facts can be given a plausible analysis in terms of Case Theory and Binding Theory, as argued here.

5. CONCLUSION

We have examined here a significant range of empirical distinctions between Portuguese and Spanish that can be plausibly attributed to the presence of infinitival agreement in Portuguese vs. its absence in Spanish. It was argued that the presence vs. absence of infinitival agreement results from different choices of values of a proposed universal parameter—the I-Parameter. The core grammar of Portuguese selects a marked option of this parameter and, as a result, allows inflected infinitives in addition to the common non-inflected infinitive, while the grammar of Spanish selects the unmarked option and only allows non-inflected infinitives. It was then shown that as a consequence of a different choice in the values of the I-Parameter the grammar of Portuguese allows a range of empirical results that are in sharp contrast to those allowed by even a closely related grammar such as Spanish.

More importantly, it was shown that once the values of the Inflection Parameter are appropriately fixed the empirical contrasts in question can be deduced—and, hence, explained—from the principles of the theories of Government and Binding.

In view of these results, it seems legitimate to conclude that the state of affairs represented by the facts of Portuguese and Spanish analyzed here provides further exemplification of the explanatory power of the principles of the theories of Government and Binding and, therefore, constitutes additional evidence in support of the conception of Universal Grammar provided by this theory.

NOTES

* Portions of the material covered in this article were presented in lectures at UCLA (Summer 1982), MIT (Fall 1983) and Princeton University (Spring 1987). I am indebted to Robert Freidin and Carlos Otero for comments and encouragement. Thanks are due also to Aryon D. Rodrigues and Mario Montalbetti for comments. The article was written while I was a Visiting Scholar in the Department of Anthropology at Dartmouth College, Summer 1987, and I would like to express my gratitude to the Department for a most pleasant working environment. The research was supported, in part, by a UCLA Academic Senate Research Grant, which I gratefully acknowledge.

[1] The term Portuguese in this article refers to a rather conservative system which we may call the "official dialect". In terms of the infinitive facts discussed here, this system is essentially the same for Brazil and Portugal. In Brazil, this official dialect is the system taught at school, used in scholarly lectures and writings, in the regular media, and spoken by educated speakers (particularly in formal situations). Although many Brazilians are native speakers of this dialect, it should be noted that many others are not; the latter speak Brazilian dialects, which are quite different—particularly with respect to verb-agreement morphology—from the official dialect. Some of these speakers learn the official dialect (with varying degrees of success) primarily at school. Because of this, care must be exercised in assessing informant's data. For an informal descriptive study dealing with infinitives in the "official dialect", see Maurer (1968).

[2] A grammatical parameter can be regarded as a set of values expressing systematic differences among languages such that selection of the possible values of the parameter corresponds to different distributions (i.e. different grammars). In some cases the parameter may be 'binary' (e.g. the null-overt subject values of the null subject parameter) with languages selecting one or the other value; but this is not necessarily so, as parameters may contain a larger set of values and more than one value can be selected by a grammar. Thus, in the well-known example of the parameter associated with the Subjacency Principle (Rizzi 1982; Chomsky 1981), the parameter in question includes three values {NP, S, S'}. English selects the values NP, S; Italian selects the values NP, S'; while Russian appears to select all three. The I-Parameter proposed here is of the latter type. Of course, under the Principles and Parameters

approach, systematic differences among grammars (such as the systematic differences involving inflected/uninflected infinitives discussed here) must be reduced to parameters.

3 This is in general agreement with Picallo's (1984) analysis, which also assumes that inflected infinitives are [-Tense, +AGR]. However, I am in disagreement with Picallo's claim that Portuguese inflected infinitives "are stylistic variants" of subjunctives (p. 88fn) (which she also assumes to be [-Tense, +AGR]). This claim seems incorrect; if we compare P(1) and P(5) we see that inflected infinitives alternate also with indicative finite complements in structures where no subjunctive can occur (cf. the ungrammaticality of * É correto que nós tenhamos ignorado isso 'It is correct that we have-subj. ignored this'). Also, as we show later, inflected infinitives occur in factive constructions with complex NPs (cf. P(23) *Lamento o fato de eles terem abandonado a equipe* 'I regret the fact that they have abandoned the team'), an environment where subjunctives can never occur. Picallo's analysis is of course more general and the specific issue raised here should not detract from the many merits of her overall analysis.

4 I am indebted to Gwen Yount (p.c.) for this information. Paul Schachter (p.c) informs me that a similar situation arises in Tagalog with 'aspect' (a fact that suggests that perhaps 'tense' is not exactly the correct category). Also, the existence of the so-called infinitives with tenses in Classical Greek (cf. Smith 1920: 417 ff.) suggests that further investigation is required. (I am indebted to Aryon D. Rodrigues for bringing the Greek facts to my attention).

5 It should be kept in mind, however, that the problem related to markedness here, though important on its own merit, is independent of the analysis of the facts of infinitives in terms of the principles of GB theory given here, which is the focus of this article. Evidently, both inflected and non-inflected infinitives must be allowed by UG and any linguistic analysis of infinitives must reflect this parametric difference. Contrary to the views expressed by some readers, the fact that one value occurs more often than another of course does not invalidate a theory which posits both values (like the analysis given here), though we may want to know—as a separate problem—why one value is favored over another, which is why we also addressed this problem here. The point ought to be obvious. Consider, for example, the well-known study concerning the distribution of light and black moths (Biston betularia) in England. Since both varieties occur, a genetic theory that postulates 'light' and 'black' as values for the color genes in English moths would be correct, even if it did not explain why light moths predominated at one point in time, while black moths predominated later. The latter problem, as it turned out, requires a separate explanation based on changes in the environment of the region.

6 This assumption is in disagreement with a recent proposal by Raposo (1987), according to which only infinitives marked for Case can assign Case. We return to this point later in connection with other examples.

7 Apart from the theoretical argument based on the 'PRO' theorem given above, the empirical evidence to support the claim that pro occurs with inflected infinitives while PRO occurs with non-inflected infinitives appears to me to be quite conclusive. Thus, independent of what is predicted by Case Theory, in examples such as (17) with inflected infinitive, we must assume that the subject is 'pro-1pl' (corresponding to (16) with the overt pronoun subject), otherwise the correct 'personal' interpretation of the sentence cannot be accounted for. By contrast, in (14) with non-inflected

infinitive the subject of the infinitive must be 'Arbitrary PRO' in order to account for the 'impersonal' interpretation of the sentence. Second, in structures of obligatory control (the typical environment where PRO is assumed to occur), inflected infinitives cannot occur:

(i) Eles tentaram sair/*sairem
'They tried to leave/to leave-3pl.'

Third, as shown later in section 3.3, in structures where the null embedded subject is clearly not controlled (which precludes the occurrence of PRO and where pro must be postulated) only the inflected infinitive may occur:

(ii) Creio estarem preparados
'I believe (them) to be-3pl ready-pl.

(iii) *Creio estar preparados
'I believed (them) to be-uninflected ready-pl

For further discussion of such examples, see section 3.3. For additional discussion, see Safir's comments and my response, both included in this volume.

[8] The best evidence for this, in my view, is the behavior of PRO with respect to Portuguese inflected infinitives. Suppose PRO had features for person and number (i.e. 'phi-features'; Chomsky 1981). Then in a language like Portuguese, which allows infinitives to agree in person and number with its subject, we should expect PRO to 'trigger' subject-verb agreement and always occur with inflected infinitives. However, just the opposite is true. In fact, in structures of 'obligatory control' (where PRO is the only option) the infinitive cannot be inflected at all. Compare (i) and (ii):

(i) Nós tentamos sair

(ii) *Nós tentamos sairmos
'We tried to leave/*to leave-1pl.'

Since the presence of PRO does not trigger person-number agreement with infinitives in Portuguese, it seems reasonable to conclude that PRO lacks features for person and number (a point originally made in Quicoli 1982: Ch.3).

[9] Similar effects are observed in adnominal infinitival complements. Thus sentences with PRO subjects are possible in both languages:

(i) [P] A possibilidade de PRO perder o jogo não os preocupa
(ii) [S] La posibilidad de PRO perder el partido no les preocupa.
'The possibility of loosing the game does not bother them'

But lexical subjects are possible only in Portuguese and when the infinitive is inflected:

(iii) [P] A possibilidade de eles perderem/*perder o jogo não os preocupa.
[S] *La posibilidad de ellos perder el partido no los preocupa.
The possibility of them losing the game does not bother them

For these, the same explanation given in the text also holds.

In Spanish, as Mario Montalbetti points out to me, it is sometimes possible for the infinitive to have its own (nominative) subject in examples such as (iv):

(iv) De ganar los brasilenos no me incomodaré.
'Were the Brazilians to win it would not bother me.'

In such cases, the inverted infinitive seems to be able to assign Nominative Case to its subject, which suggests that a different strategy (similar to the one found in Italian; Rizzi 1982) may be operative in Spanish, but I will not pursue this issue here.

[10] Since such constructions allow a subjunctive complement it does not seem appropriate to refer to them as 'factives' since 'factive predicates' normally presuppose the proposition expressed by their complements to be 'true' (something that is incompatible with the subjunctive mood). But this is not relevant to the analysis given here.

[11] Zubizarreta (1982) gives a different pattern which implies that Portuguese examples such as P(24) and P(26) are ill-formed, in contrast with Spanish examples such as S(24). She takes this to be evidence for a subject-verb asymmetry in (Brazilian) Portuguese. However, to my ear, P(24) and P(26) are quite normal (I am also indebted to Nancy Antello for verifying this with additional Brazilian informants) and I will take these to be well-formed in the relevant system under consideration. This of course does not preclude the possibility of variation in line with the paradigms given in Zubizarreta's article, a possibility that remains open.

[12] This observation is in agreement with traditional descriptions of the "official dialect" and seems to me correct. Thus Góis (1958: 99) points out that when the verb embedded by *parecer* is finite, *parecer*, as rule, must remain 'impersonal' (i.e. stays in the unmarked third person singular form), even when the embedded subject is preposed. Some of the examples that he gives are:

(i) O amor e a poesia parece que seriam o principal enlevo de Camões (L. Coelho)
'Love and poetry seems-unmarked that were-3 pl. the main concerns of Camoes'

(ii) As estrelas parecia que sorriam
'The stars seem-unmarked that smiled-3 pl.'

(iii) As horas parecia que voavam
'The hours seemed-unmarked that flew-3pl.'

Góis explicitly rejects examples such as P(30) as ill-formed (p.127). Most grammarians seem to agree on this and I take Góis's description to accurately reflect the facts of the "official dialect" (cf. also Spanish).

It is known, however, that some Brazilian speakers accept examples such as P(30). I assume that such speakers have a grammar that is different from that of the "official dialect" analyzed here (see note 2), and that such facts require a different analysis than the 'raising' analysis given in the text.

Silva (1983: Ch. 4) discusses one such non-oficial dialect, which he refers to as the "oral language". According to Silva, such speakers accept sentences such as

(i) As árvoress parecem que estão dormindo.
(Lit: The trees seem that are sleeping)

(Cf. his example (16) on p. 331). Silva proposes to analyze such examples as instances of raising (NP movement). However, this would violate Binding Theory and also would not account for the fact that speakers of the official dialect of Portuguese (as well as Spanish) reject these. Moreover, Silva's 'raising' analysis for such examples is undermined by his own observation that the same speakers also accept sentences like (ii):

(ii) As árvores parecem que elas estão dormindo.
(Lit: The trees seem that they are sleeping)

(Cf. Silva's example (15b) on p. 330.) In such examples clearly no NP-movement is possible. The analysis that suggests itself is that such examples come from D-structures where both *parecer* and the embedded verb have lexical subjects (i.e. *As árvores parecem que (elas/pro) estão dormindo*), somewhat reminiscent of English examples such as "These trees look as if they are sleeping." For relevant discussion based on similar facts in Rumanian, see Grosu & Horvath (1984).

13 Although grammarians generally agree on the ungrammaticality of P(31), some also claim that if there is a 'certain distance' between *parecer* and the infinitive (created by the insertion of intervening words), the infinitive may also be inflected (cf. Góis 1958: 98; Maurer 1968). As evidence, the same grammarians cite examples such as *As aves aquáticas ... pareciam nos seus vôos incertos, ora vagarosos, ora rápidos, folgarem...* (A. Herculano, cited in Góis, 1958:98), 'The water birds seemed-3pl. in their uncertain flights, sometimes slow, sometimes fast, to enjoy-3pl...'. However, such grammarians do not make any attempt to provide a principled way to determine the 'distance' in question, which seems a rather dubious notion in grammatical theory. On the other hand, it seems plausible to suppose that 'distance' (i.e. time elapsed between utterances) is a performance factor and that the occurrence of such ungrammatical examples are due to extra-grammatical (performance) factors, a view which I will adopt.

14 The explanation given in the text is based on Binding Theory. However, some analyses within the GB framework (following Chomsky 1981) assume that 'NIC effects' such as the above are excluded by the (Standard) ECP (cf. Silva 1983 for Portuguese and Grosu and Horvath 1984 for Rumanian). According to the Standard ECP requirement of proper government, traces must be either lexically-governed or antecedent-governed. Thus, for instance, ungrammatical examples such as E(28) would be excluded by the Standard ECP: neither the antecedent nor *seem* can properly govern the trace across the CP boundary in the structure in question and in English (which is not a 'null-subject language') AGR cannot be a proper governor for the trace either, so that E(28) would constitute an ECP violation.

However, the Standard ECP analysis, as described above, encounters problems when we add facts of 'null-subject' languages, such as Spanish and Portuguese examples S(28) and P(30). Since Spanish and Portuguese are null-subject languages the NP-trace would be properly governed (either by the embedded AGR or by the verb if we assume 'free inversion 'in the sense of Rizzi 1982). Given the standard ECP analysis, we should then expect English to differ from Spanish/Portuguese with respect to NP-traces just as it does with respect to wh-traces in (i):

(i) [P] Que embaixadores parece que chegaram a um acordo?
[S] Que embajadores parece que han llegado a un acuerdo?
[E] *Which ambassadors does it seem that have reached an agreement?

But this is not so. The raising structures E(28), S(28) and P(30) are all ill-formed, which is a problem for the standard ECP analysis.

An additional problem for the standard ECP analysis is posed by raising structures where an embedded object is incorrectly raised as in (ii):

(ii) [P] *Estes livros parecem [que Maria leu *t*]
[S] *Estos libros parecen [que Maria ha leido *t*]
[E] *These books seem [that Mary read *t*]

Under a Binding analysis of NP-traces, the explanation is straightforward. However, under the standard ECP analysis such facts are problematic; the NP-trace would be 'properly governed' since it is lexically governed by the embedded verb in such structures. Yet the examples are ill-formed.

A different approach, however, is suggested in Chomsky (1986b), who proposes a restricted version of ECP, according to which proper government for traces involves only antecedent-government. This restricted ECP approach overcomes the problems just noted (although it also invalidates some standard arguments for ECP such as subject-object asymmetry and the null-subject parameter). At issue is whether or not relation between a lexical anaphor and its antecedent is different from that between an NP and its trace (cf. Chomsky 1986b; Aoun 1985 for discussion). These are important empirical questions which constitute a focal area of current research and alternative approaches are being actively pursued. For presentation purposes here I will cast the analysis in terms of Binding Theory.

[15] To be sure, there is a further question of detail involved in connection with the structures above. Examples such as (34) are grammatical only if the aspectual auxiliary *ter* is 'fronted' (presumably moved into the head-position under CP; cf. Rizzi 1982; Raposo 1987). However, this inversion phenomenon (at least in Portuguese) seems to be a separate problem, apparently not related to Case assignment, contrary to a recent claim made in Raposo's 1987 (for a recent discussion of factors regulating inversion, see Carrano 1987). Notice that inversion by itself is not sufficient to assign Case since (33), even with inversion, is not grammatical. On the other hand, as mentioned earlier, examples such as (16) and (20) suggest that inflected infinitives can assign case irrespective of auxiliary inversion.

Notice also that Raposo's claim according to which only infinitives that are marked for Case may assign Case (p.94) appears to be inconsistent with examples such as (34). Raposo does not discuss such examples, but their relevance seems clear. Since *parecer* 'seem', an intransitive verb, cannot assign Case there would be nothing to assign Case to the inflected infinitive here; yet the infinitive clearly must assign Case to its subject. Raposo's analysis is of course more general and the specific issue raised here should in no way obscure the many merits of his important analysis.

[16] In addition, one might also argue that the wh-trace in subject position is 'properly governed', satisfying ECP (or, alternatively, the wh-trace in subject position is 'bound' by the trace in CP, so as to satisfy (Generalized) Binding Theory, as proposed by Aoun, 1985).

[17] 'Semi-control' verbs may allow lexical subjects or PRO with their infinitive complements and are, thus, in opposition to (obligatory) 'control verbs' (e.g. *try, promise*) which always require PRO, which I assume to be a lexical property of these verbs. Notice that inflected infinitives cannot license a lexical subject in such environments (cf. **José tentou os homens sairem*, 'Jose tried the men to leave-AGR'), which suggests that control phenomena requires a special theory and cannot be subsumed under Case Theory, as it is sometimes assumed. In addition, as already noted, such control verbs cannot occur with inflected infinitives (which is predictable from Binding Theory; cf. the 'PRO theorem' of Chomsky 1981).

18 Again, such examples are only grammatical with auxiliary-inversion, which we assume to be due to factors independent of Case Marking, possibly having to do with the requirement that subjects must be lexically governed, but I will not pursue this matter here.

19 The plausibility of the argument above becomes obvious when we consider examples such as

(i) Nós cremos estarem preparados para a tarefa.

(ii) Nós cremos estarem eles preparados para a tarefa.
'We believe (them) to be-3pl ready-pl. for the task'

which are parallel to P(55) and P956) in the text. Clearly, in (i) (which corresponds to (ii) with overt pronominal subject) the null subject of the inflected infinitive is not controlled. Hence, the subject of the inflected infinitive here cannot be PRO but must be analyzed as 'pro'. Likewise, P(57b) with inflected infinitive corresponds to

(iii) Cremos estarmos nós preparados para a tarefa.
'(we) believe-1pl us to be-1pl. ready-pl for the task'

and hence, its null subject must also be analyzed as 'pro'(cf. structure (58b)). Such sentences are unique to Portuguese and, hence, support the view that 'pro' can occur as subject of infinitives only when the infinitive is inflected. By contrast, sentences like P(57a) are not unique to Portuguese but correspond to control structures found in languages such as Spanish (cf. *Creemos estar preparados* 'We believe to be ready') and French where control is obligatory and, hence, require 'PRO' subjects as in (58a) rather than 'pro'. This of course supports the view that non-inflected infinitives normally require its subject to be PRO rather than 'pro'. I believe the facts in question provide strong support for the hypothesis concerning the distribution of PRO vs. pro advanced in the text.

20 Small clause structures such as

(i) Eles se creem [*t* honestos]

are, of course, possible. In such cases, as Chomsky (1981) suggests, the small clause boundary does not block government and Case assignment to the subject trace, so that the clitic is marked for case. Similarly, the clitic trace would be bound by the clitic within the relevant local domain, thus satisfying Binding Theory.

21 As noted by Kayne (1981b) French (unlike Portuguese and Spanish) allows sentences similar to the ungrammatical Portuguese and Spanish sentences in (62). Thus Kayne points out the grammaticality in French of examples such as *Quel garçon crois-tu être le plus intelligent de tous?* ('Which boy do you believe to be the most intelligent of all?'; p. 356). According to Kayne these are due to the fact that French allows Case assignment to the wh-trace in CP. In light of the facts in (50) this is apparently not possible in Portuguese and Spanish. The question arises as to how such contrasts are to be accounted for, a problem which I will not pursue here.

22 In the official dialect of Brazil there is a preference for the use of inflected infinitives in such environments, although it seems that both inflected and non-inflected infinitives are possible in such environments, the position that I adopt (for factual discussion, see Maurer 1968).

[23] Zubizarreta (1980) gives a different pattern in which examples such as P(78) are well-formed while examples such as P(77) are ill-formed, a situation that I was unable to verify.

[24] The findings reported here are in apparent conflict with previous observation made in judicious studies by Perlmutter (1972) and Perini (1974), who point out contrasts between examples of the type:

(i) Os cavalos que vimos correr eram lindos.

(ii) Os cavalos que vimos correrem eram lindos.
'The horses that we saw run/run-AGR were beautiful.'

According to both Perlmutter and Perini, (i) is grammatical while (ii) is not. While it is correct that there is a strong preference (at least among Brazilian speakers, myself included) for (i) over (ii), in view of the facts in the text (particularly the fact that P(78) is fully grammatical), it is not clear whether the preference here reflects grammaticality or stylistic preference. At any rate, it seems clear also that inflected infinitives must occur in such contexts; in fact, there are situations where only the inflected infinitive seems possible. Compare:

(iii) Os cavalos que se via correrem de um lado para outro eram lindos.

(iv) *?Os cavalos que se via correr de um lado para outro eram lindos.
'The horses that one saw run-AGR/*?run to and fro were beautiful'.

Here it could be suggested that the clitic *se* absorbs Case (cf. Jaeggli 1982) from the ECM verb, so that only when the inflected infinitive occurs can the embedded subject be assigned Case. However, because of the uncertainties concerning some of the data, the analysis given here must be tempered with a certain degree of caution.

REFERENCES

Ali, M. S. (1919) *Dificuldades da Lingua Portuguesa,* (5th edition, 1957), Livraria Academica, Rio de Janeiro.

Aoun, J. (1985) *A Grammar of Anaphora,* MIT Press, Cambridge, Mass.

Barbosa, J.S. (1881) *Gramatica Filosofica da Lingua Portuguesa,* Academia Real das Ciencias, Lisboa.

Bello, A. (1903) *Gramatica de la Lengua Castellana,* Roger and Chervoviz, Paris.

Berwick, R. (1982) *Locality Principles and the Acquisition of Syntactic Knowledge,* Ph. D. dissertation, MIT, Cambridge, Mass.

Berwick, R. and A. Weinberg (1983) *The Grammatical Basis of Linguistic Performance,* MIT Press, Cambridge, Mass.

Borer, H., (ed.) (1987) *The Syntax of Pronominal Clitics,* Academic Press, New York.

Carrano, M. L. (1987) *Subject Infinitival-Auxiliary Inversion in Portuguese,* M.A. thesis, UCLA, Los Angeles.

Cegalla, D. P. (1977) *Novissima Gramatica da Lingua Portuguesa,* Editora Nacional, Sao Paulo.

Chomsky, N. (1977 "On WH-Movement," in P. W. Culicover, T. Wasow, and A. Akmajian, eds., *Formal Syntax,* Academic Press, New York.

Chomsky, N. (1980) "On Binding", *Linguistic Inquiry* 11, 1-46.

Chomsky, N. (1981) *Lectures on Government and Binding*, Foris, Dordrecht.
Chomsky, N. (1982) *Some Concepts and Consequences of the Theory of Government and Binding*, MIT Press, Cambridge, Mass.
Chomsky, N. (1986a) *Knowledge of Language: Its Nature, Origin, and Use*, Praeger, New York.
Chomsky, N. (1986b) *Barriers*, MIT Press, Cambridge, Mass.
Dias, A.E.S. (1918) *Sintaxe Historica Portuguesa*, Livraria Classica Editora, Lisboa.
Freidin, R. (1986) "Fundamental Issues in the Theory of Binding," in B. Lust, ed., *Studies in the Acquisition of Anaphora*, D. Reidel, Dordrecht.
Galves, C. (1980) *Les Relations Anaphoriques en Portugais*, Doctoral dissertation, University of Paris IV, Paris.
George, L. and J. Kornfilt (1981) "Finiteness and Boundedness in Turkish," in F. Heny, ed., *Binding and Filtering*, MIT Press, Cambridge, Mass.
Góis, C. (1958) *Sintaxe de Concordancia*, 12nd edition, Livraria Francisco Alves, Rio de Janeiro.
Grosu, A. and J. Horvath (1984) "The GB Theory and Raising in Rumanian," *Linguistic Inquiry* 15, 348-353.
Jaeggli, O. (1982) *Topics in Romance Syntax*, Foris, Dordrecht.
Kayne, R. S. (1975) *French Syntax*, MIT Press, Cambridge, Mass.
Kayne, R. S. (1981a) "Binding, Quantifiers, Clitics, and Control," in F. Heny, ed., *Binding and Filtering*, MIT Press, Cambridge, Mass.
Kayne, R. S. (1981b) "On Certain Differences between French and English," *Linguistic Inquiry* 12, 349-371.
Lasnik, H. and M. Saito (1984) "On the Nature of Proper Government," *Linguistic Inquiry* 15, 235-289.
Maurer, T. H. (1968) *O Infinitivo Flexionado Portugues*, Editora Nacional, Sao Paulo.
Perini, M. A. (1974) *A Grammar of Portuguese Infinitives*, Ph.D. dissertation, University of Texas, Austin.
Perlmutter, D. M. (1972) "Evidence for Shadow Pronoun in French Relativization," in P.M. Peranteau et al., eds., *The Chicago Which Hunt: Papers from the Relative Clause Festival*, Chicago Linguistic Society, Chicago, Illinois.
Picallo, C. (1984) "The Infl Node and the Null Subject Parameter," *Linguistic Inquiry* 15, 75-102.
Quicoli, A. C. (1976a) "On Portuguese Impersonal Verbs," in J. Schmidt-Radefeldt, ed., *Readings in Portuguese Linguistics*, North-Holland, Dordrecht.
Quicoli, A.C. (1976b) "Conditions on Clitic Movement in Portuguese," *Linguistic Analysis* 2, 199-224.
Quicoli, A.C. (1982) *The Structure of Complementation*, Story-Scientia, Ghent.
Raposo, E. (1975) *Uma Restricao Derivacional Global sobre o Infinitivo em Portugues*, Boletim de Filologia 24, 75-293.
Raposo, E. (1987) "Case Theory and Infl-to-Comp: The Inflected Infinitive in European Portuguese", *Linguistic Inquiry* 18, 85-109.
Rizzi, L. (1982) *Issues in Italian Syntax*, Foris, Dordrecht.
Rouveret, A. (1980) "Sur la Notion de Proposition Finie: Gouvernment et Inversion," *Recherches Linguistiques* 9, 76-140.
Rouveret, A. and J.R. Vergnaud (1980) "Specifying Reference to the Subject: French Causatives and Conditions on Representations," *Linguistic Inquiry* 11, 75-107.

Silva, S. M. (1983) *Etudes sur la Symetrie et l'Asymetrie Sujet/Object dans le Portugais du Bresil*, Doctoral dissertation, University of Paris VIII.
Smyth, H. W. (1920) *Greek Grammar*, Harvard U. Press, Cambridge, Mass.
Sten, H. (1952) L'Infinitivo Impessoal et L'Infinitivo Pessoal en Portugais Moderne, *Boletim de Filologia* 13.
Stowell, T. (1982) "The Tense of Infinitives," *Linguistic Inquiry* 3, 561-570.
Zubizarreta, M. L. (1980) "Remarks on Inflected Infinitives in Portuguese", ms., MIT, Cambridge, Mass.
Zubizarreta, M. L. (1982) "Theoretical Implications of Subject Extraction in Portuguese," *The Linguistic Review* 2, 79-96.

KEN SAFIR

PRO AND pro: COMMENTS ON QUICOLI

Aside from word order perhaps, there are very few aspects of linguistic typology that have been as closely studied as the null subject property, especially from the perspective of recent theoretical work within the principles and parameters framework initiated by Chomsky (1981). The appeal of the parametric perspective is that a variety of language typological characteristics can be linked, if the account is successful, merely by selecting appropriate value settings (provided by Universal Grammar) for formal properties of grammar that are permitted to vary (parameters). Within a principled theory of grammar, the formal setting will have predictable effects which may then be examined in detail. In a wide variety of studies informed by this perspective (see Jaeggli and Safir (1989) for discussion and references) the null subject property has been linked to a range of other properties, or else the parametric perspective has provided a stimulus to distinguish the effects of a positive setting of Null Subject Parameter (i.e., a setting that results in null subjects) from independent sorts of linguistic variation.

Professor Quicoli's analysis of the European Portuguese inflected infinitive investigates the effects of the Null Subject Parameter by isolating a small portion of the grammar in which the introduction of a new variable smoothly adjusts to the positive setting for null subjects - with all of the accompanying predictable effects. The most salient empirical manifestation of the Null Subject Parameter is generally exemplified as a contrast between languages like French, on the one hand, which must have a subject in a finite sentence, and Spanish, on the other, which need not have a subject in the same context. In the case of the European Portuguese inflected infinitive, introducing person an number marking onto the infinitive, Quicoli argues, leads to behavior indistinguishable from the behavior of tensed sentences in the relevant respects.

There is, however a covert assumption here that is worth highlighting. The Null Subject Parameter will only extend in exactly the way expected to inflected infinitives in a null subject language. Although I do not know of any non-null subject language that has inflected infinitives (indeed the option may be limited to null subject languages), presumably the hypothetical infinitives in such a language would not show the null subject effect if the Null Subject Parameter is fixed for the language as a whole, rather than for a particular construction. Only under the latter non-trivial assumption is the extension of the null subject property to the inflected infinitive construction unsurprising.

This paper is divided into two parts. In the first part I will raise three objections to theoretical points raised in Quicoli's paper, while in the second part I will introduce three independent diagnostic tests that show that his overall analysis is correct.[1]

1.0 Three Objections

My first objection is to the conclusion that the apparent markedness of inflected infinitives can be derived from the Subset Principle proposed by Berwick (1986) and by Wexler and Manzini (1987). The latter works propose that for any option O (selected from those provided by UG) that results in a larger class of possible strings in a language, O is marked by comparison with options that do not extend the size of the class of possible strings. This reasoning is motivated as follows: If a child acquiring the language always assumes the smallest possible language compatible with the data, then it has a means of avoiding overgeneralizations that could not be corrected by subsequent data.

Quicoli contends that inflected infinitives are marked because having them in addition to uninflected infinitives means a larger language. This is true if it is the case there are instances where an inflected infinitive occurs where a normal uninflected infinitive could also occur.

The problem with this reasoning is that it says nothing specific about inflected infinitives. Given the markedness reasoning proposed, a language with inflected infinitives and no uninflected ones would be just as unmarked as Spanish, a language with infinitives, but without inflected ones. If inflected infinitives, in addition to being rare, are truly marked, then the subset reasoning does not yield the right result without further assumptions, e.g., that inflected infinitives are only possible in languages that have uninflected ones.[2]

My second objection is to Quicoli's claim that he has presented evidence to show that pro must be Casemarked. It seems to me that this evidence is weak, even if the conclusion may be right.

Quicoli shows that in every position where he hypothesizes that pro can occur, a lexical NP can appear and wh-extraction is possible. In English, a gerund can have a lexical subject or not, but it has been assumed that when the subject of a gerund is lexically empty, its subject is Caseless PRO, not pro. If Case assignment is optional in inflected infinitives, as it is in English gerunds, then whether or not pro (or PRO, for that matter) is Casemarked in inflected infinitives depends on showing that Casemarking is obligatory in these contexts. No such demonstration is made.

Rather Quicoli shows that, in addition to lexical subjects, wh-movement is possible from the subject position of an inflected infinitive. Following Chomsky (1981), the assumption that wh-trace must be Casemarked accounts for the failure of *who is it likely t to die, since the raising predicate likely is a proper governor of its infinitive complement subject (i.e., it is not ruled out by ECP). But if Case assignment is optional to inflected infinitive subject position, then the success of wh-extraction does not bear on the +/- Case status of PRO.

In fact it might be argued that Case is irrelevant for pro as long as pro is governed (and perhaps "identified" in one of the senses drawn from the literature by Safir and Jaeggli (1989; section 4)) by INFL/+agr.[3] Every example cited by Quicoli where pro is licit is compatible with this assumption, and so the question of whether or not pro needs Case remains open.[4]

My third objection is to Quicoli's claim that PRO does not have phi features since, as he points out, it does not agree with the infinitive verb (see also his fn. 5)[5]. But it appears that it is necessary to assume that PRO can be plural in predicative contexts, as pointed out by Chomsky (1981; 322) so it can have number, as illustrated in (1a). Moreover, as pointed out by Rizzi (cited by Chomsky (1981; 61), PRO_{arb} is plural in Italian (1b), and as the French example (1c) shows, it also can agree in gender in languages that mark predicative adjectives for gender. Finally in (1d) we see that the reflexive only has an appropriate antecedent within its binding domain if it is bound by PRO, so PRO must be capable of bearing person features as well.

(1) a. They tried PRO to be doctors
b. non e chiaro come essere allegri
not is clear how to-be happy (plural)
c. Les femmes veulent etre intelligente
the women want PRO to-be intelligent(fem-plural)
"The women want to be intelligent"
d. You shouldn't try to kill yourself

Furthermore, in some languages it appears that Case agreement with PRO is possible. As pointed out by Thrainsson (1979; 298-9) and those he cites, predicative adjectives in infinitives in Icelandic reflect either Nominative or the Case of the controller of PRO (updating Thrainsson's assumption of equi-NP deletion). Thus in (2a) ACC on the adjective is ungrammatical where the controller of PRO is Dative, while in (2b) Dative fails when the controller of PRO is Accusative.

(2) a. Maria skipaði honum að vera goðum/goður/*goðan
Maria ordered him/DAT [PRO to be good/DAT/NOM/ACC]

b. Maria bað hann að vera goðan/goður/*goðum
Maria asked him/ACC [PRO to be good/ACC/NOM/DAT]

Whether or not PRO can be assigned Case directly by a Case assigner we may leave as an open question, but it appears that it can facilitate agreement with a predicate adjective just as overt subjects in Icelandic do.

I conclude that the claim that PRO lacks phi-features is simply false.

2.0 PRO VS. PRO: SOME CONFIRMATION

The last two objections discussed above raise questions about how PRO and pro are to be distinguished. If they do not differ with respect to phi-features and they both can be Casemarked or not, then it is possible that every instance where Quicoli has argued that there is a pro, a PRO could be present without changing the predictions. To maintain such a view we would have to assume (A) that Casemarking by inflected infinitives is optional and (B) that PRO is not excluded when governed by the INFL/+agr of inflected infinitives. Both assumptions may be problematic theoretically, but they have not been shown so far to be false in so far as inflected infinitives are concerned.

I believe that Quicoli's analysis of the null inflected infinitive subject as pro, is correct, but to support his arguments I must have a means of distinguishing PRO from pro systematically. These tests will show that pro, distinct from PRO, must be at least available for for the subject position of inflected infinitives, although I will not attempt to show that PRO is an impossible option in this context. Three tests, two adapted from Safir and Jaeggli (1989), can be employed to establish the PRO/pro distinction.

2.1 The Resumption Test

As pointed out in Jaeggli and Safir (p.16-17), it is possible for pro to act as a resumptive pronoun, in the marginal (or in some languages, fully grammatical environments) where resumptive pronouns are permitted. The examples in (3a) show that both English and Spanish, respectively, permit a resumptive pronoun strategy for relative clauses, however marginal.

(3) a. That's the guy that we didn't know whether it was possible to talk to him
b. Ese es el tipo que no sabiamos si seria posible hablar con el

Yet no language with (uninflected) infinitives ever permits its PRO subject to be a resumptive pronoun, as is illustrated for English and Spanish in (4a,b), respectively.

(4) a. *That's the guy who we didn't know whether it was possible PRO to swim
b. *Ese es el tipo que no sabiamos si seria posible PRO nadar

English and Spanish differ in that the latter is a null subject language, and the null subject of tensed sentences in Spanish (5a) can be used as a resumptive pronoun in the same sort of relative clause context where an overt pronoun would be acceptable (in fact required) in English.

(5) a. That's the guy who Mary knows the woman who he/*Ø married
b. Ese es el tipo que Maria conoce a la mujer con quien ?el/Ø se caso

The distinction between (4a-b) and (5a-b) is quite sharp, even though the examples in (5) are marginal for some speakers or stylistically marked. Clearly if the null subject of an inflected infinitive is pro then it should be available for use as a resumptive pronoun. Although an overt pronoun is preferred as a resumptive in (6a,b), the null subject of an inflected infinitive (6b) can be used as a resumptive as easily as the null subject of a tensed sentence (6a), which clearly supports the availability of the pro analysis for inflected infinitives.

(6) a. Os linguistas [que eu li [o artigo [que tu disseste que ?eles/??Ø escreveram]]] estavam na conferencia
the linguists [that I read [the paper [that you said that they wrote]]] were at the conference
b. Os linguistas [que eu li [o artigo [que tu disseste ?eles/??Ø terem escrito]]] estavam na conferencia
the linguists that I read [the paper [that you said them/Ø to write]] were at the conference

2.2 *The Expletive Test*

Another Safir and Jaeggli diagnostic that distinguishes PRO from pro is based on the EMEX condition of Safir (1985), which simply requires (but does not explain why) expletive elements must be governed. With respect to what is at stake here, this means that PRO cannot be expletive. This judgement, like the resumptive test, is also robust, as illustrated by the English examples (7a) vs. (7b).

(7) a. It is unclear when it will be possible for John to leave
b. *It is unclear when to be possible for John to leave

The important distinction between pro and PRO is that pro, as in the standard null subject environment in (8a), permits an expletive, as it would under the assumption that it is governed by INFL/+agr. As shown in (8b), the infinitive empty subject in Spanish cannot be expletive, as we would expect if the infinitive subject in Spanish is exclusively PRO, never pro.

(8) a. No esta claro si es verdad que Juan es culpable
(pro) not is clear if (pro) is true that Juan is guilty

b. *No esta claro si ser verdad que Juan es culpable
(pro) not is clear if __ to-be true that Juan is guilty

By contrast, in European Portuguese inflected infinitives, where the structure permits government of the null subject by INFL/+agr (by assumption), it is predicted that it should be possible for the null subject to be expletive, since pro is available. This prediction is borne out.[6]

(9) a. __ surpreendeu-me __ ser tão obvio que ele estiveffe bebado
pro surprised-me pro to-be so obvious that he subj-pst-be drunk
"It surprised me for it to be so obvious that he would be drunk"
b. __ surpreendeu-me que __ fosse tão obvio que ele estivisse bebado
pro surprised-me that pro be-subj. so obvious that he subj-pst-be drunk
"It surprised me that it would be so obvious that he would be drunk"

2.3 linked arbitrary interpretation

A third argument that shows that the subject of the Portuguese inflected infinitive must permit pro, as opposed to normal infinitives which require PRO, is that a certain class of interpretations, interpretations associated with PRO in infinitives in other languages, are not required in Portuguese. The interpretations in question are "linked" interpretations, first pointed out by Lebeaux (1984), where the arbitrary subject of the first infinitive must be interpreted to be the same arbitrary agent as the subject of the second infinitive, not only in (10a), where this is plausible, but in (10b) where it is difficult (not impossible) to provide a plausible interpretation.[7] When pronouns are overt no such linked interpretation is required as in (10c) where the pronouns do not match, nor in (10d), where they do.

(10) a. To raise the rent is to irritate the tenants
b. To raise the rent means to leave the apartment immediately
c. For you to raise the rent means for us to leave the apartment immediately
d. For him to raise the rent means for him to leave the apartment immediately

If the obligatoriness of this linked interpretation is a property of PRO, then we may ask if the same obligatory interpretation is required of pro. Once again we can compare contexts in Spanish tensed sentences where pro is available, in fact contexts where an arbitrary interpretation is intended (see Jaeggli (1986; 59)), and see if the interpretation is obligatorily linked. The linked interpretation is optional in this context in Spanish (11a) (i.e., the fixer and the caller can be different or the same, the former being favored pragmatically). The English example in (11b) more closely resembles the appropriate translation of the linked interpretation, though the PRO infinitive subjects are obligatorily linked in English, as mentioned earlier. In (11c) (also from Jaeggli (1986)), Spanish infinitives also require the linked arbitrary interpretation, even where an unlinked interpretation would be favored.

(11) a. Para que pro vengan a arreglar la heladera, es necessario que pro llamen al tecnico por lo menos tres veces
for that come-3pl to to-fix the refrigerator is necessary that call-3pl to-the technician by the least three times
"In order for arb comes to fix the refrigerator, it is necessary that arb calls the technician at least three times"
b. In order to come to fix the refrigerator, it is necessary to call the technician at least three times
c. Para [PRO poder salir de compras] hay que [PRO abrir los negocios]
for [PRO to-can go-out of shopping] has that [PRO to-open the shops
"In order (for arb) to go out shopping, arb must open up the shops."

If European Portuguese inflected infinitives have pro subjects, then the linked interpretation should be optional, not obligatory. The inflected infinitive data are presented in (12) with contrasting finite examples presented in (13a,b) corresponding to (12a,c), respectively.

(12) a. Subir-em a renda significa sair-em do apartamento imediatamente
to-raise-3p the rent means to-leave-3p of-the apartments immediately
b. Subir-es a renda significa sair-mos do apartamento imediatamente
to-raise-2s the rent means to-leave-1p of-the apartments immediately
c. Para virem arranjar a maquina e necessario chamarem o tecnico pelo menos tres vezes
for to-come-3pl to-fix the refrigerator is necessary to-call-3pl the technician at least three times

(13) a. Que subam a renda significa que sairao do apartamento
that __ raise-subj the rent means that __ will-leave the apartment

b. Para que venham arranjar a maquina e necessario que chamem o tecnico pelo menos tres vezes
for that __ come-subj to-fix the refrigerator is necessary that __ call-subj the technician at least three times
"For that one/someone would come to fix the refrigerator, it is necessary that one/he call the technician three times"

As predicted, the linked interpretation is not required for (12a) (any more than it is required for tensed (13a)[8]), which permits either a linked interpretation or a (less favored) unlinked one (see (10d)), while (12b) corresponds to the non-arbitrary interpretation in (10c). Furthermore (12c) corresponds to the Spanish (11c) except the infinitive is inflected, and rather like the Spanish tensed (11a) and Portuguese (13b), (12c) permits, but does not require, the linked interpretation.[9]

Thus all three tests lead to the same conclusion: The null subject of the inflected infinitive in European Portuguese must at least permit a pro subject, although I have not established that a PRO subject could not be optional in these contexts.

3.0 SOME CONCLUDING THOUGHTS

Although I have disagreed with some of Quicoli's conclusions about Case, learnability, and the pro/PRO distinction, I have agreed with his more important claim that the inflected infinitive in a null subject language can be expected to behave just like a finite sentence with respect to null subjects. In the latter respect, the advantages of a parametric approach have been further illustrated, in that the licensing of pro in an uncommon context has an expected variety of very subtle effects (the possibility of permiting resumption, expletives, and unlinked arbitrary interpretations) which correlate with the assumption that agreement marking provides the key ingredient for the identification of pro.[10]

NOTES

[1] I would like to thank Eduardo Raposo, a very informed informant, for his invaluable assistance with the European Portuguese data.

[2] Raposo (1987), whose work addresses some of the same issues, assumes that inflected infinitives are marked because the setting of the null subject parameter for null subjects and the setting of the INFL parameter to allow +agr to choose freely between +/-tense is a rare combination. Beyond rarity, no other argument is made as to the markedness of the construction, though a crucial relation between the two parameters is assumed.

[3] Although the issue will not come up directly here, I assume, following Jaeggli and Safir (1989) and references cited there, that the licensing of null subjects and the identification of null subjects are distinct requirements which must be met for a thematic subject to be missing.

[4] As Luigi Rizzi pointed out during discussion at the conference, however, pro in object position appears to be sensitive to Case, in so far as verbs that license pro in English never do so if they are passivized (i.e., they do not assign ACC Case). See Rizzi (1986).

[5] The reasoning in Quicoli's note 5 is nearly circular - if there are no inflected infinitives how could PRO agree with uninflected ones? If the infinitive is inflected, then Quicoli assumes the inflected infinitive must have a pro subject, not PRO. Quicoli points out that infinitives may not be inflected in contexts of obligatory control, where he assumes that PRO is the only possible option for the infinitive subject. Perhaps so, but one would want to exclude the possibility that inflected infinitives are not excluded in these environments for independent reasons, such as aspect. I have in mind a parallel with subjunctives, which are not possible as complements to many verbs.

[6] Actually, (9b) is somewhat degraded, though not thoroughly unacceptable, perhaps because the tensed subjunctive restricts the class of pronouns that can be construed as its subject, as is well-known with respect to disjoint reference effects with a matrix subject. The exact nature of the restriction in this environment is not clear to me.

[7] If the same people both own the apartments and live in them, and these people are suddenly forced to depend on revenue from these apartments in order live, then it may be more lucrative for the owners to rent cheaper apartments elsewhere and charge the high rent on the apartments they own to newcomers.

[8] My principal informant finds (13a) awkward, apparently because predicates with both tensed sentential subjects and tensed sentential complements are disfavored for at least some speakers. When this factor is abstracted away from, both readings are available.

[9] When the infinitive is in the third person singular, which is not morphologically distinct from an uninflected infinitive, the linked interpretation appears to be required (the one who comes and the one who calls must be the same), which suggests that PRO must be used in this environment, contrary to the prediction born out with respect to expletives. This interpretation is doubly odd since the arbitrary interpretation normally requires plurals.

(i) Para vir arranjar a maquina e necessario chamar o tecnico pelo menos tres vezes
for to-come to-fix the refrigerator is necessary to-call the technician at least three times

I am not sure why this should be so, unless there is some principle that prefers the use of PRO rather than pro when the options are not morphologically distinct. Eduardo Raposo, personal communication, finds the third person singular in Portuguese always a little strange as pro (as opposed to an overt pronoun), suggesting perhaps another reason why PRO is preferred. If PRO is preferred, it will still not be preferred where an expletive is required, because if the PRO option is chosen, no sentence is possible.

Whatever the reason for this fact, it does not change the conclusion that the overtly inflected infinitives all behave as expected if their null subject is pro rather than PRO.

[10] Raposo (1989) points out that in European Portuguese there is also a prepositional inflected infinitival which does not permit pro, Even though the subject of the prepositional inflected infinitival can get Case from a higher verb, the construction still doesn't license pro. Raposo argues that pro cannot be identified by Case without AGR, or vice-versa.

REFERENCES

Berwick, R. (1986) *The Acquisition of Syntactic Knowledge*, MIT Press, Cambridge, MA.

Chomsky, N. (1981) *Lectures on Government and Binding*, Foris, Dordrecht.

Dell, F. (1981) "On the Learnability of Optional Rules," *Linguistic Inquiry* 12.1.

Jaeggli, O. (1986) "Arbitrary Plural Pronominals," *Natural Language and Linguistic Theory* 4; 43–76.

Jaeggli, O. and K. Safir, eds., (1989) *The Null Subject Parameter*, Kluwer, Dordrecht.

Lebeaux, D. (1984) "Anaphoric Binding and the Definition of PRO," in *The Proceedings of NELS 14*, U. of Massachusetts, Amherst.

Raposo, E. (1987) "Case Theory and Infl-to-Comp: The Inflected Infinitive in European Portuguese," *Linguistic Inquiry* 18;85–110.

Raposo, E. (1989) "Prepositional Infinitival Constructions in European Portuguese," in K. Safir and O. Jaeggli, eds., *The Null Subject Parameter*, Kluwer, Dordrecht.

Rizzi, L. (1986) "Null Objects in Italian and the Theory of *pro*," *Linguistic Inquiry* 17; 501–558.

Safir, K. (1985) *Syntactic Chains*, Cambridge University Press, Cambridge and New York.

Thrainsson, H. (1979) *On Complementation in Icelandic*, Ph. D. dissertation, Harvard University.

Wexler, K. and M.-R. Manzini (1987) "Parameters and Learnability," in T. Roeper and E. Williams, eds., *Parameter Setting*, Kluwer, Dordrecht.

A. CARLOS QUICOLI

INFLECTION AND EMPTY CATEGORIES: RESPONSE TO SAFIR'S COMMENTS

OPENING REMARKS

The comments on my article by Professor Safir are balanced and fair, and contribute a great deal to our understanding of the empirical problems investigated in my article. There is, as Safir notes, a substantial number of areas in which he is in agreement with my analysis—in particular, my overall analysis according to which the inflected infinitive in Portuguese (the standard Brazilian and European dialects having a similar pattern) behaves essentially like a finite clause with respect to null subjects. In addition, Safir has contributed three independent diagnostic tests of his own which provide additional empirical support to the view that the subject of inflected infinitives is pro and never PRO, giving additional support to the view advocated in my article.

In the areas where Safir raises objections to my analysis his commentary raises fair questions and legitimate empirical issues, though I disagree with some of his conclusions. Charles Peirce once remarked that the purpose of scientific investigation is to settle real problems according to evidence. In this spirit I would like to address Safir's objections to my analysis with the hope of contributing towards the settlement of the issues they raise.

1. LEARNABILITY AND THE SUBSET PRINCIPLE

One objection raised by Safir has to do with the role played by the Subset Principle. Safir questions the validity of assuming this principle to explain the marked character of inflected infinitives. But I think there are two separate problems involved and Safir's objection against my proposal does not actually apply.

In my analysis, the I-Parameter has four values:

(1) a. [+Tense, +AGR]
 b. [-Tense, -AGR]
 c. [+Tense, -AGR]
 d. [-Tense, +AGR]

From what we know, non-inflected infinitives can occur without inflected infinitives, while inflected infinitives can only occur in addition to non-inflected infinitives. Let us call the latter assumption the "AND-problem." Now, having inflected infinitives in addition to non-inflected infinitives would clearly lead to a larger language and the Subset Principle would correctly make this addition a marked one, as I claimed. So I think it is fair to claim that the Subset Principle gives a correct account of the AND-problem—an important part of the inflected infinitive puzzle.

The issue raised by Safir's is concerned with a different problem. Namely, since both inflected and non-inflected infinitives are obviously permitted by the language faculty, why is it that languages that have only one infinitive choose the non-inflected one? Let us call this the "OR-problem."

Clearly, the two problems are distinct. In one case we are dealing with the marked character of a language with both non- inflected infinitives and inflected infinitives. In the other case we are dealing with the bias in the choice between non- inflected infinitives or inflected infinitives (but not both).

The Subset Principle, in my view, provides a plausible explanation for the AND-problem, which is the problem I sought to resolve. As for the OR-problem, I simply assumed that this required independent principles (so far unknown), and Safir's comments serves to highlight the need for this additional assumption. Still, the point made in my article remains valid. The explanation given to the AND-problem in terms of the Subset Principle can still be maintained, even though the OR-problem remains unexplained.

Of course it would be nice if we could also account for the OR-problem: given that both inflected and non-inflected infinitives are permitted options, why is there no language with only inflected infinitives? The issue is often avoided in the literature (cf. Chomsky 1981: 52) and I did the same in my article, preferring to focus on the AND-problem. Safir also offers no suggestion in this regard. So, at this point, one can only speculate.

One suggestion that seems to me plausible, at this point, is that the symmetrical options [-Tense, -AGR] and [+ Tense, + AGR], with identical values for Tense and AGR, are perhaps unmarked due to a general principle of structural symmetry, which favors symmetrical systems over non-symmetrical ones (an idea somewhat reminiscent of Sapir's concept of congruity of the patterning). This would give a correct solution to the OR-problem in the case of infinitives. But it also makes the prediction that [+Tense, -AGR] languages are more marked than [+Tense, +AGR] languages, though the status of this prediction is not clear. At any rate, if such a hypothesis can be maintained it would provide a reasonable explanation for the OR-problem.

However, as already noted, whatever the explanation for the OR- problem may be, this problem seems independent of the AND-problem and the explanation given to the later in terms of the Subset Principle in my article, though limited, remains valid.

2. CASE FILTER AND PRO

A second objection raised by Safir has to do with my claim that pro must be Case-marked to satisfy the requirements of the Case Filter. Safir finds the evidence that I gave for this weak "even if the conclusion may be right". Although I find Safir's discussion of this point most interesting, I think his objection does not apply for the reasons given below.

In my article I argued that pro behaves like phonetic realized NP's with respect to the Case Filter in that pro must also occur in a Case-marked position in S-structure.

Consider for example the argument I gave for this based on the facts of the raising construction. In Portuguese (as in many other languages) a phonetic realized NP occurring as a subject of a non-inflected infinitive under a raising verb must be raised in order to receive Case (cf. Chomsky 1982):

(2) a. Os embaixadores parecem ter chegado a um acordo. (Q29)
b. Os embaixadores-NOM parecem AGR [*t* ter chegado a um acordo]
'The ambassadors seem to have reached an agreement'

But since Portuguese also has inflected infinitives, when an inflected infinitive occurs under a raising verb, a phonetically realized NP does not raise since it can be Case-marked by the AGR of the inflected infinitive (the problem of auxiliary inversion here is not germane to the issue at hand):

(3) a. Parece terem os embaixadores chegado a um acordo. (Q34)
b. ec parece [terem-AGR os embaixadores-NOM t_v chegado a um acordo]
'It seems that the ambassadors have reached an agreement'

Now, as argued in my article, the same patterns are observed with pro subjects. pro must raise when the infinitive is noninflected, but remains in the embedded clause when the infinitive is inflected:

(4) a. Parecem ter chegado a um acordo (cf. Q36)
b. pro-Nom parecem-AGR [*t* ter chegado a um acordo]
'(They) seem to have reached an agreement'

(5) a. parece terem chegado a um acordo (cf. Q37)
b. ec parece [pro-Nom terem-AGR chegado a um acordo]
'(It) seems that (they) have reached an agreement'

Since the behavior of phonetically realized NP's under standard assumptions (Chomsky 1982) is explained by the Case Filter I proposed that the behavior of pro can be explained in the same way by the Case Filter. Several other additional paradigms were then added to support the same view.

Safir raises two objections to my hypothesis. One objection is that I have not demonstrated that the AGR of inflected infinitives assigns Case "obligatorily" (he alludes to the behavior of English gerunds in this connection, though the facts do not seem quite parallel). The second objection is that the distribution of pro in the paradigms that I give can be given an alternative explanation in terms of some version of the Theory of Identification (cf. Jaeggli and Safir 1989), without the need to assume that pro must be Case-marked.

But notice the consequence of Safir's argument. According to Safir's argumentation one might say that the AGR of inflected infinitives assigns Case optionally and pro does not have to be Case-marked. In that case, one might say that the S-structure corresponding to (5a) is not (5b)—as I assumed—but, rather, (6):

(6) ec parece [pro[-Case] terem-AGR chegado a um acordo]

It would be only under such analytical assumptions that one could claim that the presence of pro can be accounted for only by the Theory of Identification, without the need to invoke the Case Filter.

However, it seems that (6) is an implausible analysis for (5), which serves to highlight the problems faced by any proposal that relied solely on the Theory of Identification to account for pro and did not assume that pro must also be Case Marked. So, rather than an argument against my proposal, I believe Safir's discussion helps to demonstrate the unwarranted consequences that arise if we were to assume that the Case Filter does not apply to pro. Here only by assuming that pro is subject to the Case Filter can we exclude the implausible (6) as a possible S- structure for (5).[1]

Moreover, there are empirical reasons for rejecting (6). As shown in (7), in (Brazilian) Portuguese when the inflected infinitive occurs in ECM structures the subject must be Nominative:

(7) a. Maria viu nós-nom sairmos ([nos])
b. *Maria viu nos-acc sairmos ([nós])
Maria saw we-nom/*us-acc leave-1 pl.

Clearly, the AGR of inflected infinitive assigns Nominative Case 'obligatorily' (just like the AGR of finite verbs), as evidenced by (7a). If inflected infinitives assigned Case optionally, in the situation where it failed to do so the subject should be able to receive Case from the ECM verb here. But, as we see, the corresponding sentence (7b) with an accusative subject is ill-formed, which shows that Nominative Case assignment by the inflected infinitive must be obligatory.

Fortunately, the two theories in question can be reconciled. Evidently, we need the Theory of Identification (in some version), as Safir contends, in order to account for the parametric difference between null-subject vs. non null-subject languages—an assumption that is only implicit in my article and which should have been made explicit. At the same time, it seems clear from the facts analyzed in my article that we must also assume that pro must be Case-marked, as I have argued in my article. Unless we assume the latter, the fact that pro behaves like phonetically realized NP's in the paradigms I discussed would be left unexplained, and undesirable analyses such as (6) would be permitted. I conclude then (pace Safir) that the claim made in my article that pro must be Case-marked remains valid.

3. DOES PRO HAVE PHI-FEATURES?

The third issue raised by Safir has to do with my hypothesis that PRO does not have lexical features, or 'phi-features' in the sense of Chomsky (1981). Here Safir's conclusion is that this part of my hypothesis is simply false. I disagree with Safir's conclusion for the reasons presented below.

Notice that the issue as to whether or not PRO has features arises in my article in connection with the behavior of pro with respect to the Case Filter discussed in the previous section. According to standard assumptions (cf. Chomsky 1982) four empty categories (EC's) are permitted: anaphors (e.g. NP-traces), variables (e.g. wh-traces), pronominal-anaphors (e.g. PRO) and pronominals (e.g. pro). If we assume that pro (like overt NP's) must be Case-marked in order to satisfy the Case Filter, as I have argued, then it is necessary to differentiate pro from the other three EC's—NP-traces, wh-traces, and PRO.

There appears to be, in fact, a basic difference between pro and the other three EC's in question. Thus, controlled PRO, NP-traces and wh-traces must be coindexed with a fully specified overt lexical category, so that lexical features required for agreement and anaphora can be "picked up" from their 'antecedents' in a chain. But this is not the case with pro, which does not enter into similar chain formations, and hence must contain its own lexical features (phi-features). Based on these (and other) considerations, I hypothesized that pro (like overt NP's) is "lexical" (i.e. contains inherent phi-features for person, number and gender), while traces and PRO are "nonlexical" (i.e. do not contain phi-features), with the consequence that the Case Filter applies to pro and phonetically realized NP's, but not to traces or PRO.

Traces, of course are "nonlexical" and, according to my hypothesis, should not be subject to the Case Filter. NP-traces do not pose problems for this assumption since they are generally assumed to be Caseless (cf. Chomsky 1981). But what about wh-traces? Here Safir objects to my hypothesis on the basis of a claim, first made in Chomsky (1981), according to which wh-traces must be Case-marked so as to exclude ill-formed English S-structures such as (8), which Safir cites :

(8) *Who is it likely [*t* to die] ?

Although this argument appears to be widely accepted in the literature, it seems to me that there is no compelling reason to assume that wh-traces must be Case-marked in order to exclude such structures. Notice that the wh-phrase (*who*—a phonetically realized element, hence "lexical")—is also Caseless in the structure in question, so that the Case Filter will already apply to the wh-phrase and correctly exclude such structures, without any need to refer to its trace. This is what I assumed in my article.

Now, given that the Case Filter normally checks lexical elements such as wh-phrases for Case, it seems superfluous to add a special condition requiring wh-traces to have Case. In fact, a more general formulation of the filter can be given if traces in general are exempted from the Case Filter, as argued in my article. Thus, I see no force to Safir's objection based on such facts and I conclude that the hypothesis that traces are not subject to the Case Filter remains valid.

Another complicated issue has to do with distinction between pro and PRO. My hypothesis is that pro contains inherent phi-features (i.e. is 'lexical') and is, thus, subject to the Case Filter, while PRO does not contain inherent phi-features (i.e. is 'nonlexical') and, hence, is not subject to the Case Filter.

The argument given in my article to support this claim is based on the crucial difference between pro and PRO with respect to inflected infinitives. Thus, arbitrary PRO interpretation can be imposed on (9) with noninflected infinitive, but not on (9) with the inflected infinitive, where the subject can only be interpreted as the first person plural null pronoun (pro):

(9) É correto ignorar isso (Q2)
'It is right to ignore this'

(10) É correto ignorarmos isso (cf Q5)
'It is right for us to ignore-1 pl. this'

Similarly, inflected infinitives cannot occur in obligatory control structures containing PRO:

(11) Nos tentamos sair/*sairmos.
'We tried to leave/*leave-1 pl.'

Since PRO (unlike pro) cannot occur with inflected infinitives– that is, PRO cannot undergo subject-verb agreement in person and number with its predicate—I concluded that PRO (unlike pro) does not have inherent phi-features, and I then went on to reformulate the Case Filter accordingly.

Safir strongly disagrees with my claim that PRO does not have phi-features, though it is unclear to me how the facts of Portuguese inflected infinitive such as the ones above can be accounted for if one assumed otherwise. Instead, Safir bases his objection on two different kinds of phenomena which, according to him, shows that PRO must have phi-features. One kind of evidence presented by Safir is the existence of facts such as the following:

(12) a. They tried [PRO to be doctors]
 b. Non e chiaro come essere allegri
 it is not clear how to-be happy-plural
 c. Les femmes veulent [PRO etre intelligentes]
 d. You shouldn't try [PRO to kill yourself]

According to Safir, such examples show that PRO must have phi-features. Allegedly, PRO must have must have number features because of (12a, b), gender-number features because of (12c), and person features because of (12d). So, Safir concludes that my claim that PRO lacks phi-features must be false. The matter is, or should be, controversial and Safir is entirely justified in raising the issue. However, I believe Safir's conclusions in this regard are incorrect, and his objection to my analysis does not hold. The reasons for this are as follows.

First, notice that, with the exclusion of (11b) which appears to be rather exceptional[2], in all examples PRO is coindexed with its controller. So the features that are required for the agreement relations in (12a,c,d) can be read off the controller, not necessarily off PRO. There is, thus, no compelling reason to assume that PRO must have inherent features based on such examples. Just as there is no compelling reason to suppose that traces must have phi-features to account for (13):

(13) a. They seemed [*t* to be doctors]
 b. Les femmes semblent [*t* etre intelligentes]
 c. You seem [*t* to admire yourself]

In the trace examples in (13) it is generally assumed that the agreement features are read off the antecedent of the trace, not off the trace itself. A similar analysis can be given to PRO in (12a,c,d), which I believe is the correct one.

Second, as shown in (14), the Portuguese counterparts of (12a,c,d) seem to require, in fact, an analysis in which the relevant features must be picked up from the controller rather than from PRO:

(14) a. Eles tentaram [PRO ser/*serem médicos]
They tried [PRO to be/*be-3pl doctors-masc. pl.]
b. Estas mulheres querem [PRO ser/*serem emancipadas]
These women want [PRO to be/to be-3 pl. liberated-fem. pl.]
c. Eles tentaram [PRO se lavar/*lavarem]
'They tried [PRO to wash/*wash-3 pl. themselves]

In (14a) and (14b) gender-number agreement is satisfied, and in (14c) the agreement in person and number between the anaphor and its antecedent is satisfied, just like in Safir's examples. However, if the features for person and number in such examples were inherent phi-features of PRO, then we should expect subject - verb agreement in person and number with the infinitive as well. But this is not the case. Subject-verb agreement (i.e. inflected infinitives) cannot take place in such structures. So under an analysis in which PRO is assumed to have phi-features to account for gender-number and anaphor-antecedent agreement, we would have a paradox with the inflected infinitive.

Notice, on the other hand, that the facts in question can be accounted for if we assume that PRO has no inherent phi-features, and agreement is assumed to be established by "matching rules." The analysis for such facts would then be as follows. Predicate adjectives and lexical anaphors contain phi-features, and the agreement rules require that the same features be found in an appropriate 'antecedent.' In the examples at hand, the predicate adjective and the anaphor would be associated with PRO and their features would be correctly matched by the controller of PRO through the process of chain formation.

Portuguese infinitives, on the other hand, may appear with or without agreement morphology (the bearer of phi-features). When agreement morphology is absent (non-inflected infinitives) there are no phi-features in the infinitive and, hence, there is no need for the subject-verb agreement rule to apply and 'look' for an 'antecedent' for such infinitives. This accounts for the correct structures with non-inflected infinitives in (14). Inflected infinitives, on the other hand, contain agreement morphology (and, hence, phi-features) and must therefore have an antecedent. However, when the inflected infinitive is associated with PRO, as a first step to satisfy the agreement rule through chain formation, the agreement morphology (AGR) also has the undesirable effect of marking PRO for Case (Nominative). As a result, the ungrammatical structures where PRO occurs with an inflected infinitive in (14) would all be ruled out by Binding Theory since PRO would be in a Binding Domain (cf. the 'PRO theorem' of Chomsky 1981).

The second type of evidence presented by Safir to show that PRO must have phi-features is the phenomenon of Case Agreement in Icelandic. Thus,

Safir points out examples such as the following:

(15) Maria skipaði honum að vera góðum/góður/*góðan
Maria ordered him/DAT [PRO to be good/DAT/NOM/ACC]

(16) Maria bað hann að vera góðan/góður/*góðum
Maria asked him/ACC [PRO to be good/ACC/NOM/DAT]

However, here it seems to me that the facts show the opposite of what Safir had intended to demonstrate. The generalization appears to be that the predicate adjective in Icelandic either agrees in Case with the controller of PRO or is Nominative (probably the unmarked Case). In neither instance is there evidence that PRO must have phi-features to account for Case Agreement. On the contrary, when the agreement is made with the controller of PRO it is clear that the relevant features are read off the controller and not off PRO. This undermines Safir's argument based on the facts in (12) and, at the same time, reinforces my claim that PRO does not have inherent phi-features, since they show that the features necessary for agreement are not contained in PRO itself but in its controller.

4. CONCLUDING REMARKS

To conclude, I am thankful to Professor Safir for his thought-provoking discussion of my article. I acknowledge with pleasure that there are many areas in which we are in agreement, though there are, of course, some important issues where we disagree. As for the areas in which we disagree—my hypotheses concerning the explanatory role of the Subset Principle in accounting for the marked character of inflected infinitive languages, the Case-marking requirement for pro (with the consequent reformulation of the Case Filter), and that PRO does not have inherent phi- features—I have discussed the evidence presented by Safir and I have concluded that Safir's objections to these aspects of my analysis do not hold and that the claims made in my article remain valid.

NOTES

[1] The point of course is of general theoretical consequence and can be put to further empirical test. Consider a language like Chinese where pro is not identified by agreement but rather by principles of discourse (Huang 1984). My analysis would predict that pro can occur as subject of finite verbs since it would be Case-marked (and identified) but not as subject of (non- inflected) infinitives, since pro would not be Case-marked in this position (though it would still be identified). However, an analysis which assumed that pro is licensed only by identification and does not

require Case would predict that pro may occur as subject of both finite verbs and (non-inflected) infinitives since pro would be identified by the discourse principles in both cases. Though systematic research is necessary to settle this, it appears to be a good bet that pro cannot occur as the subject of non-inflected infinitives in such languages either.

[2] Normally the adjective in such constructions appears in the unmarked form (which usually coincides with the masculine, singular form). Thus, the Portuguese equivalent is

(i) Não é claro como ser honesto
'It is not clear how to be honesto-masc. sing.'

Other possibilities are precluded:

(ii) *Não é claro como ser honesta
'It is not clear how to be honest-fem. sing.'

(iii) *Não é claro como ser honestos/honestas
'It is not clear how to be honest-masc.pl/fem.pl.'

So such examples appear to involve the unmarked gender-number form of the adjective, rather than agreement with PRO.

REFERENCES

Chomsky, N. (1981) *Lectures on Government and Binding*, Foris, Dordrecht.

Chomsky, N. (1982) *Some Concepts and Consequences of the Theory of Government and Binding*, MIT Press, Cambridge, Mass.

Huang, J. (1984) "On the Distribution and Reference of Empty Pronouns," *Linguistic Inquiry* 15, 531–74.

Jaeggli, O. and K. Safir, eds., (1989) *The Null Subject Parameter*, Kluwer, Dordrecht.

ESTHER TORREGO

EXPERIENCERS AND RAISING VERBS*

INTRODUCTION

In this article I address a number of questions concerning the syntax and semantics of 'seem'-class of verbs. These are all questions raised by the syntactic behavior of these verbs in the Romance languages.

English and Spanish differ in that (a) the inflectional system of these verbs exhibits important restrictions when the experiencer is unrealized; (b) the experiencer needs to be "doubled" by a dative clitic; (c) the experiencer prevents subject-to-subject raising. A large part of this article is devoted to accounting for these syntactic effects. The first domain of differences is tied to the restructuring phenomenon of Romance 'pro'-drop. The second is traced back to the particulars of Case licensing of 'to'-phrases in clitic-doubling Romance; the blocking affects of dative clitics in raising structures is considered to be a consequence of the expletive nature of dative clitics in these structures.

1. 'SEEM' VS 'SEEM' + 'TO'-PHRASE

It is commonly assumed that *seem* takes a clausal complement and an optional 'to'-phrase. In general, we do not expect to find that the absence of an optional argument has effects for Tense, Auxiliaries, and other properties of the inflectional system of the verb. This, however, is what we find with raising verbs in Spanish. The evidence appears to support the view that the 'to'-experiencer is not a true argument of raising verbs, and that raising verbs are restructuring verbs in the sense that they establish their syntactic and semantic properties at LF by combining their inflectional system with that of the embedded verb.

1.1 Asymmetries in the Inflectional System of parecer.

As *seem* in English, *parecer* in Spanish can occur with a clause and an experiencer:

(1) Les parecio que Maria estaba cansada.
To them-seemed that Mary was tired
It seemed to them that Mary was tired

Also as in English, *parecer* (also *resultar* 'turn out') appears in the two typical configurations of (2):[1]

(2) a. Este taxista parece [t estar cansado].
This taxi driver seems to be tired
b. Parece que [este taxista esta cansado].
It seems that this taxi driver is tired

In Spanish, the absence of the experiencer with *parecer* has consequences for the inflectional structure of the clause. These restrictions show up with Tense, Aspect, Mood, and auxiliary modification. Let us see which ones they are.

While both the present and the imperfect are allowed irrespective of the experiencer, *parecer* cannot be in the preterit unless there is an experiencer:

(3) a. Parece/parecia (IMP) que Juan estaba malo.
It seems/seemed that Juan was sick
b. *Parecio que (PRET) Juan estaba malo.
It seemed that Juan was sick
c. Nos parecio (PRET) que Juan estaba malo.
It to us-seemed that Juan was sick

The verb *resultar* does not behave in this way:[2]

(4) Resulto (PRET) que Juan estaba malo.
It turned out that Juan was sick

Similarly, *parecer* can be in the progressive when there is an experiencer, but not otherwise:

(5) a. *Esta pareciendo que Juan cocina muy bien.
It is seeming that Juan cooks very well
b. *Juan esta pareciendo cocinar muy bien.
Juan is seeming to cook very well
c. Me esta pareciendo que Juan cocina muy bien.
It is seeming to me that Juan cooks very well

In addition, *parecer*, contrary to *parecer* + experiencer and *resultar*, allows the subjunctive in the subordinate clause:[3]

(6) a. Parece que lloviera (SUBJ).
It seems that rained
b. *Me parece que lloviera (SUBJ).
It seems to me that it rained
c. *Resulta que lloviera.
It turned out that rained

It is characteristic of operator-like verbs to be subjunctive "triggers". In this respect, *parecer* acts like epistemic modals such as *poder*: *puede que llueva* (SUBJ) 'it may rain').[4] Furthermore, Spanish perfective auxiliary *haber* ('to have') is disallowed in these clauses:

(7) a. *Ha parecido que Juan los habia encontrado.
It has seemed that Juan had found them
b. *Juan ha parecido haberlos encontrado.
Juan has seemed to have found them

Neither *parecer*+experiencer nor *resultar* exhibit such a restriction:

(8) a. Me ha parecido que Juan los habia encontrado.
It has seemed to me that Juan had found them
b. Ha resultado que Juan los habia encontrado ya.
It has turned out that Juan had found them already

In sum, *parecer* behaves as a defective verb when the experiencer is unexpressed. The verb *parecer* is, to my knowledge, the only non-canonical modal that prevents perfective *haber* in Spanish.

The modal-like behavior of Spanish *parecer* can also be observed when associated with standard modals. In sequences of more than one modal, the second modal verb cannot be interpreted as epistemic (Picallo (1990)). *Parecer* imposes the same restriction on its adjacent modal:

(9) a. Rosario debe poder hablar quechua.
'Rosario must be able to speak Quechua'
b. Rosario parece poder hablar quechua.
'Rosario seems to be able to speak Quechua'

In neither (9a) nor (9b) *poder* can have an epistemic reading. Thus (9a) cannot mean: it must be the case that it is possible that Rosario speaks Quechua, and (9b) cannot mean 't seems to be the case that it is possible that Rosario speaks Quechua.'[5] Similarly, *parecer* causes the same effect on *deber* than *poder* does:[6]

(10) a. *Rosario puede deber hablar quechua.
Rosario may must speak Quechua
b. *Rosario parece deber hablar quechua.
Rosario seems must speak Quechua

The special properties of raising verbs have not passed unnoticed. Rothstein (1983) takes the position that raising verbs are not theta-role assigners, but copula-like verbs with different assertive force. For Rothstein, these verbs are inflectional operators taking sentential scope. In a similar vein, it is argued by Napoli (1989) that the *seem*-class of verbs are not predicates themselves, but parts of predicates. These ideas are appealing because a standard CP/IP-clause analysis fails to predict that raising verbs may exhibit inflectional restrictions of the sort pointed out in this section for Spanish. Similarly, it is mysterious that the subject of the lower clause crosses over the experiencer in English. This instance of movement should be in violation of Minimality. These issues can be reduced to the question of what kind of predicates raising verbs are. Some sort of reanalysis must be invoked in these structures.

In English, word order considerations suggest that the 'to'-phrase is lower than V, as verbs in English do not appear to raise overtly. Given this, the experiencer must either be in some inflectional category mediating between *seem* and the lower clause or adjoined to the lower clause:[7]

(11)

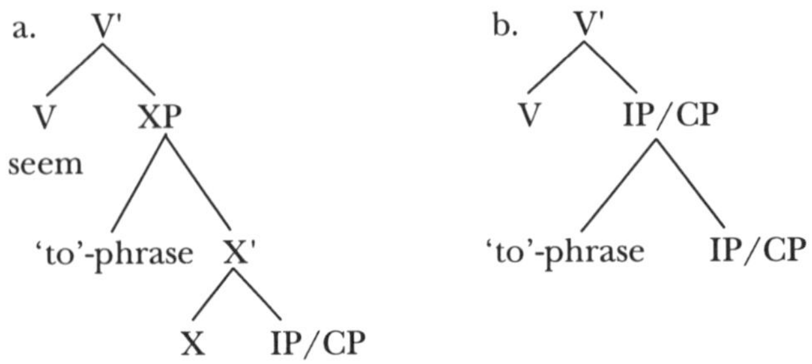

The tacit assumption underlying the configurations in (11) is that the experiencer is not a true argument of *seem*.[8] Rather, the experiencer is a participant of the entire predicate *seem*+V, as proposed by Napoli (1989).[9]

In spite of the Tense restrictions pointed out with respect to Spanish *parecer*, raising verbs in Romance appear to have a less transparent structure than restructuring verbs proper. Clitics cannot climb with either Italian *parere* or Spanish *parecer*.[10]

(12) a. *?Angela lo pareva aver riaccompagnato a casa.
b. Angela pareva averlo riaccompagnato a casa.
Angela seemed to have taken him home

(13) ???Lo parecia haber acompanado a casa.
S/he seems to have taken him home

Although the close Italian analogue *sembrare*, does allow clitic climbing (cf. *Giovanni lo sembrava vedere* 'Gianni it-seemed seen') there are enough indications that raising verbs may involve more structure than just a CP/IP.[11] Be this as it may, we must assume that the absence of an experiencer in Spanish induces restructuring obligatorily. Otherwise, there would be no reason for the inflectional restrictions shown to hold of *parecer* in this section.[12]

1.2. Parecer is a Raising Verb

Spanish *parecer* must be assumed to be a raising verb because it responds to standard diagnoses for raising. Consider idioms. The acceptability of (14) is a standard test for DP-trace: (*corria la sangre por las calles* (Lit. blood ran through the streets 'there was a lot of violence').

(14) La sangre parecia correr por las calles.
Blood seemed to run through the streets
'There seemed to be violence'

The impossibility of embedding "*parecer* XP" under causatives also suggests that raising has taken place (Kayne (1974))):

(15) *Su expresion hacia parecer sufrir a Juan.
His expression made seem Juan to suffer

Similarly, the scope ambiguities involving quantificational subjects are also a sign of raising (May (1977)):

(16) Poca gente parece [t leer mucho].
Few people seem to read a lot

As in English, the subject in Spanish (16) may have narrower scope or wider scope than *parecer*.

Note finally that when *parecer* is followed by a predicate NP or by an attributive adjective associated with *ser*, the results are different. Here the structure can be embedded under *hacer*:[13]

(17) Las canas hacen parecer viejo.
Grey hair makes (people) seem old

Also, as in English, a quantificational subject must have scope over *parecer*.

(18) Poca gente parece feliz.
Few people seem happy

I will return to both (17) and (18) in section 3.

We are now in a position to discuss the realization of the experiencer and its syntactic effects in the Romance languages that have the clitic-doubling phenomenon.

2. The Realization of the Experiencer

In this section I consider the surface realization of the experiencer of raising verbs in detail. I shall focus on one specific fact: in the Romance languages that can double 'to'-phrases with dative clitics (namely, Spanish,

Catalan, Galician and Romanian)[14] the experiencer of raising verbs requires a dative clitic obligatorily:

(19) a. *Parecio a mis amigos que Maria estaba cansada.
It seemed to my friends that Mary was tired
b. *A mis amigos parecio que Maria estaba cansada.
To my friends it seemed that Mary was tired
c. *Parecio que Maria estaba cansada a mis amigos.
It seemed that Mary was tired to my friends
d. Les parecio (a mis amigos) que Maria estaba cansada.
To them- seemed (to my friends) that Maria was tired

As illustrated in (19d), the lexical experiencer can be omitted; only the dative clitic is required. I assume that the dative clitic signals a null experiencer realized as 'pro'.

French and standard Italian do not behave in this manner. The following French example is from Rouveret and Vergnaud (1980)—their (174a):[15]

(20) Paul semble à Marie avoir résolu toutes les difficultés.
Paul seems to Marie to have solved all the difficulties

The Italian example (21) is from Rizzi (1982):

(21) A Piero, Gianni non sembra fare il suo devere.
To Piero, Gianni not seems do his duty
Gianni seems to Piero to not do his duty

The clitic strategy appears to be the preferred strategy in these languages too. This is problaby due to the fact that clitics favor restructuring perhaps because their trace can delete. Recall that I am assuming that raising verbs must undergo restructuring.

The next fact to be noticed is that in the Romance languages in which the dative clitic doubles the experiencer, subject-to-subject raising is impossible. To facilitate the presentation, I limit exemplification of this point to Spanish.

Consider the examples in (22) and (23):[16]

(22) a. *Este taxista me parece [t estar cansado].
This taxi driver seems to me to be tired
b. Este taxista parece [t estar cansado].
c. Me parece que este taxista esta cansado.
It seems to me that this taxi driver is tired

(23) a. *Juan me resulto [t estar sin un duro].
Juan me-turned out to be penniless

b. Juan resulto [t estar sin un duro].
   Juan turned out to be penniless
c. Resulto que Juan estaba sin un duro.
   It turned out that Juan was penniless

Whereas (22b) and (23b) are grammatical, their corresponding counterparts with an experiencer clitic (22a) and (22a) are impossible.[17]

As shown, French and Italian behave like English. The experiencer in these languages does not interfere with raising to subject. It does not matter that the experiencer be realized as a clitic. Still, the clitic does not bar raising to subject:[18]

(24) a. Molti studenti gli risultavano aver gia terminato l'esame.
   'Many students appeared to him to have already finished the exam'
b. Gianni non gli sembra fare il suo devere.
   'Gianni doesn't to him-seem to do his duty'

The same can be seen in French:

(25) Pierre me semble/parait être malade.
   'Peter to me-seems to be sick'

The following two descriptive generalizations hold, then, for clitic-doubling Romance:

(26) (i) The experiencer of raising verbs requires a dative clitic.
   (ii) The experiencer of raising verbs blocks subject-to-subject raising.

In the analysis I will propose (ii) is an effect of (i).

2.1. *Subject Raising and the Experiencer: Spanish vs English*

In this section I will attempt to account for the following three facts: (i) the experiencer in Spanish and the other clitic-doubling Romance languages requires a dative clitic; (ii) the experiencer bars subject-to-subject raising; (iii) the experiencer does not bar raising in English.

On standard assumptions, raising verbs do not have argumental subjects. The derived structure of a raising to subject sentence has the underlying structure (27):

(27) [e] seem to me [the man to be tired]

The subject of the infinitival clause must move to the matrix subject position [e] to acquire Case crossing the experiencer. Because the experiencer qualifies as a "closer" antecedent for the trace of the subject, this occurrence of movement should be disallowed by the grammar. Obviously, it is allowed. Therefore, some strategy must be making it possible.

Let us consider the configurations in (11) again. Much of the motivation for these structures is the idea that the experiencer is not a true argument of *seem*. The two possibilities I have offered are (a) that the experiencer be the Specifier of an inflectional category mediating between *seem* and the lower clause, or (b) that it be adjoined to the clause. I want to put forward the proposal that the experiencer of raising verbs is adjoined to the clause, and that the dative clitic that shows up in clitic-doubling Romance, heads an inflectional projection separating V from IP; roughly, as in (28):

(28)

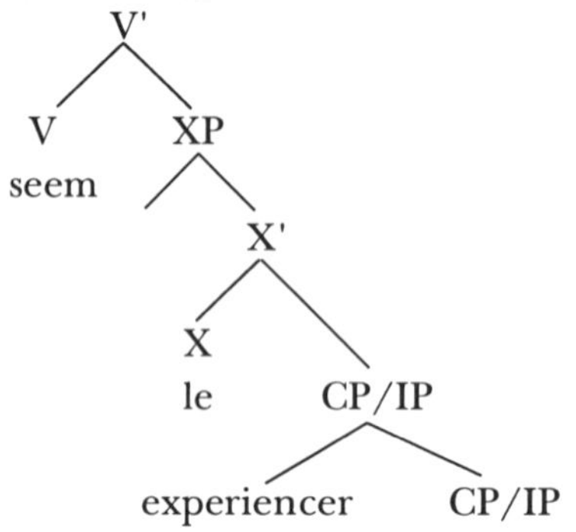

The experiencer and V are within two different projections. In clitic-doubling Romance, the dative clitic must be inserted as a Case-bearing head to accomplish Case-checking of the experiencer.

One characteristic property of 'to'-phrases (datives) in Romance is that they co-occur with a dative clitic. The dative clitic is optional in some cases and obligatory in others. With raising verb, there is no choice: the dative clitic has to be part of the structure. The reason for this 'is simply that 'raising' verbs do not have dative Case to license the Case of the experiencer. On the assumption that the experiencer is not licensed as an argument of the verb, this is entirely plausible. The dative clitic is required to license the Case of the experiencer. I claim that dative clitics have V-features and are the Case-checkers of 'to'-phrases in clitic-doubling Romance. I assume that the Case-licensing of dative Case takes place at LF. The dative clitic will head the matrix INFL. The experiencer will raise to "subject" position at LF and will satisfy Case-requirements in association to the clitic in a Spec-Head agreement relation.[19]

It is clear that the structure in (28) can create problems for movement of the infinitival subject to the matrix clause. There is, however, one fundamental aspect of the sketched proposal that will rule out subject-to-subject raising independently of any other consideration. Namely, the expletive nature of the dative clitic.

It is not new that some clitics in Romance have specific requirements to meet. For example, reflexive clitics have to be linked to arguments. I am now proposing that there are also clitics which must meet the opposite requirement; namely, to be linked to expletive pronouns.

Thus, the key to accounting for the blocking effects of the dative clitic for raising to subject in Spanish lies in the non-argumental character of the dative clitic. The expletive dative clitic will move to INFL, as clitics generally do in Romance. However, an expletive clitic will have to satisfy the requirement of being 'expletive'. The requirement in question will be its association to an expletive position prior to LF: the subject position of the raising verb 'seem'. Given that the matrix subject position is the position where the subject of the infinitival clause needs to move to acquire Case, only in contexts in which raising to subject does not occur raising verbs in clitic-doubling Romance can appear with 'to'-phrases.

By blaming the dative clitic for the blocking effects of subject-to-subject raising in clitic doubling Romance, we have left open the possibility that raising to subject proceeds over an experiencer in grammars in which the dative clitic is not required.[20] I want to suggest that NP-Movement over the experiencer is possible because the experiencer is in an adjoined position. The basic idea underlying this stipulation is that XPs in adjoined positions do not count as potential antecedents for an NP-trace. Although the exact formulation of this idea will depend on the specific theoretical framework of our assumptions, the intuition is clear enough.

One last comment regarding raising verbs. The INFL-incorporation analysis I have suggested for these verbs rules out the possibility that the CP-clause appears preposed:

(29) *That Mary is tired seems/appears

Although, in principle, the entire clause might move back to its original position at LF, presumably, economy considerations bar this instance of LF-Movement. Preposing the clause will prevent INFL from moving and adjoining to the matrix INFL; hence, (29) is impossible.

To sum up, we have seen that Spanish is not exceptional in disallowing subject-to-subject raising. All other Romance languages in which arguments are doubled by object clitics behave in this manner. I have argued that the impossibility of subject-raising is to be traced back to the obligatoriness of the dative clitic. The dative clitic is non-argumental and must be bound to an expletive. Since clitics raise to INFL, the clitic is bound to a (null) expletive in the matrix subject position.

3. Small Clauses

At a surface level of analysis, raising verbs also take AP and NP complements. If such complements are clausal, an experiencer clitic in Spanish ought to bar subject-to-subject raising. Although this prediction is borne out, certain distinctions must be made.

To begin, there are two major cases to be distinguished. Adjectives in Spanish can be associated with the verb *ser* or *estar*, both of which translate in English as 'be'. Adjectives associated with *ser* are individual level predicates, and those associated with *estar* are stage level predicates. The experiencer causes no problem for adjectives associated with *ser*:

(30) Ese chico me parece inteligente.
That boy to me-seems intelligent
(Cf. Ese chico es/*esta inteligente)
'That boy is intelligent'

By contrast, the experiencer causes ungrammaticality for adjectives associated with *estar*:

(31) a. Maria parece descalza.
Mary seems/looks barefoot
b. *Maria me parece descalza.
Mary to me-seems/look barefoot
(Cf. Maria esta/*es descalza)

Predicate NPs are also allowed with *parecer*, as in British English: 'John seems a fool' (Williams (1983)). The experiencer clitic causes no problems here either:[21]

(32) Clarin me parece un buen escritor.
Clarin to me-seems a good writer

According to the characterization of predicates proposed by Kratzer (1988), stage level but not individual level predicates involve a hidden davidsonian argument (i.e., an event argument). Assuming Kratzer's analysis, the data above suggest the following descriptive generalization:

(33) The possibility of predicate APs and NPs to appear with *parecer*+experiencer is restricted to semantic contexts in which the complement predicate has no eventiveargument.

Thus, predications involving *ser* yield well-formed sentences, while those involving *estar* yield ill-formed ones.

To draw the appropriate distinctions, I will argue that there is a small clause in cases like (31), which involves a stage predicate. I will claim though that in the context of (30), which involves an individual level predicate, there is no small clause. Instead, I will argue that the verb 'seem' and the ADJ form a complex predicate in this case.

In the small clause analysis, the ungrammaticality of (31b) follows directly from previous assumptions. As argued earlier, the contradictory requirements imposed, on the one hand, by the dative clitic, and, on the other, by the subject of the complement clause, cannot be satisfied by the grammar. Hence, (31b) is ill-formed.

To capture the grammaticality contrast between (31b) and (30), I will assume that adjectives associated with *ser* can assign their thematic role compositionally (together with V), but that those associated with *estar* cannot.

My intuition is that the motivation behind this difference should follow from a difference in the argument structure of these two classes of adjectives. In particular, from the idea that stage level adjectives, but no individual level adjectives, have an event argument. Raising Vs are non-eventive. If there is no eventive argument in the lexical entry of 'seem', but there is one in the adjective, it is plausible that this causes complex predicate formation to fail. Under this assumption, the adjective will have to be an independent predicate. This being the case, the predicate will have to be part of an independent clause.[22]

I will implement the idea that individual level predicates can assign a thematic argument in combination with *parecer* by using Higginbotham's (1985)/(1987) method of theta-identification. In Higginbotham's system, one of the modes of theta discharging is theta-identification. For a structure like (33):

(34) [seem, <1>] [intelligent <1>]]

the thematic positions in V and A are identified as shown, given rise to a single thematic grid for the predicate 'seem intelligent'. The resulting complex V will then discharge its <1> argument to the subject. We may now say that theta- identification fails when the thematic grid of the Verb lacks an e(vent)-position to identify the e-position of the other predicate.

Once a small clause analysis is ruled out for (30) the well-formedness of these Spanish sentences will be on a par with that of predicates taking a subject and a dative complement. Both the subject and the experiencer will be complements of the complex predicate. However, the underlying structure of (31b) is quite different. In this case, there will be a small clause embedded under 'seem'. Raising to subject will yield a structure identical in all relevant respects to the one we have ruled out for subject-raising from within complement IPs.

Let us test this approach in a few more cases. Consider the situation with adjectives such as *aburrido*, which is ambiguous between English 'boring' and 'bored'. In its active meaning, *aburrido* ('boring') is associated with *ser* (="Angel es aburrido"), and in its stative meaning, *aburrido* combines with *estar* (="Angel esta burrido"). Whereas the stative interpretation is impossible when *parecer* takes an experiencer, no problem arises with the causative interpretation:

(35) Angel me parece aburrido.
Angel to me-seems boring/*Angel to me-seems bored
'Angel seems boring to me'
The same results are obtained in cases of the following sort:

(36) a. Es/*esta cansado hablar con tanta gente.
it is tiresome to talk to so many people
(Cf. *esta cansado...)
b. Me parece cansado hablar con tanta gente.
it to me-seems tiresome to talk to so many people

As shown by (36a), 'tiresome' takes *ser* not *estar*. As predicted, the corresponding clause involving *parecer*+ADJ yields a well-formed sentence with the experiencer.

Let us look at one more class of cases. In Spanish, adjectives taking themes as complements require *estar*:

(37) a. Maria es orgullosa (*de su hija).
b. Maria esta orgullosa (de su hija).
'Mary is proud of her daughter'

As before, the experiencer causes ungrammaticality only when the adjective must combine with *estar*. Observe the following contrasts:

(38) a. Maria me parece orgullosa (*de su hija).
Mary me-seems proud (of her daughter)
c. Maria parece orgullosa (de su hija).
Mary seems proud (of her daughter)

In sum, the clitic realization of the experiencer with *parecer* prevents subject-to-subject raising in small clauses too.

4. Experiencer Subject Control

I want to turn now to a yet another context in which *parecer* and an experiencer can be found. Consider (38):

(39) Le parece haber resuelto todas las dificultades.
it to her-seems to have solved all the difficulties
'It seems to her that she has solved all the difficulties'
('her' and 'she' are correferential)

The example in (39) is well-formed. Under previous assumptions, (39) cannot be an instance of raising to subject.

There has been much discussion in the literature about the syntax of the French analogue to Spanish (39). Rouveret and Vergnaud (1980) put forward the hypothesis that this is an instance of subject-to-subject raising of the experiencer. They note that, in French, the experiencer argument of the verb 'seem' can be realized as a lexical NP (now DP) or as a clitic when raising to subject applies or when an expletive subject pronoun fills the subject position: (their (173)/(174)):

(40) a. Il semble a Marie que Paul a resolu toutes les difficultes.
b. Il lui semble que Paul a resolu toutes les difficultes.

(41) a. Paul semble a Marie avoir resolu toutes les difficultes.
b. Paul lui semble avoir resolu toutes les difficultes.

Yet, according to Rouveret and Vergnaud, when there is an expletive filling the matrix subject position and an infinitival clause, the experiencer must be realized as a clitic. A lexically realized DP is disallowed in this case: (their (171) and (175)):

(42) a. Il lui semble avoir resolu toutes les difficultes.
'It seems to him that he has solved all the difficulties'
b. *Il semble a Pierre avoir resolu toutes les difficultes.
'It seems to Pierre to have solved all the difficulties'

Rouveret and Vergnaud reason that the clitic realization of the experiencer in (42) favors a subject-to-subject raising analysis of the experiencer clitic, as there would be no other reason why the experiencer in (42a), unlike in (40a), must be a clitic.

Kayne (1980)/(1984), on the other hand, argues that (39) must be analyzed as an instance of subject control. Some of Kayne's arguments in defense of the control analysis relate to the possibility of having a complementizer preceding the infinitival clause in the Italian equivalent of (39). This complementizer, which introduces standard instances of subject control, also surfaces here, as shown by the Italian example below:

(43) Mi sembra/pare di aver capito (Kayne's (1984),chap. 5, (30)).

In what follows, I would like to provide some plausibility arguments in favor of a control approach to (39) on the basis of Spanish. The existence of contrasts like (44a)/(44b) favors the control over the raising analysis of (39):

(44) a. Le parece [PRO haber intentado [PRO comunicarse con ellos muchas veces]].
It seems to her (=I think/ believe) to have tried to communicate with them many times
b. *Ella le parece [t haber intentado [PRO comunicarse con ellos].
I seems to her to have tried to communicate with them many times
c. (*A ella) le parece haber intentado comunicarse con ellos.
(to her) to her-seems to have tried to communicate with them

The data in (44) strongly suggest that *parecer*+experiencer is functioning like a single verb with an epistemic meaning similar to *creer* (think/believe). Notice that (44a) is well-formed, but not (44b). The difference between the two lies in that in (44b) there is a nominative subject pronoun. Notice that the dative clitic in this case cannot be doubled by a pronoun (nor can it be doubled by a lexical DP either), as shown by (44c).

The desired result will follow if the experiencer has incorporated into the verb. The fact that the experiencer must be realized as a clitic in French, Italian and Spanish favors this approach. Incorporation is an instance of Head-Movement (Baker's (1987)). It is natural to assume that the clitic, rather than a lexical DP, must appear in this context because the clitic favors incorporation.

The semantic contribution of the experiencer argument to 'seem' can clearly be observed in Spanish adverbials.[23] Thus, *a mi parecer* (Lit. 'to my seeming') means "in my opinion". By contrast, their close analogues with no experiencer: *al parecer/ a lo que parece* or *segun parece*, mean 'apparently'.[24]

Finally, it is important to note that there are semantic restrictions to be met by the clausal complement of epistemic "cl+*parecer*". Namely, for structures like (43) to be well-formed, the semantics of the lower infinitival clause has to be that of a state. Where this is accomplished directly by the verb, as in (44), no further requirement is necessary. Otherwise, the clause requires aspectual manipulation to achieve this goal. Consider (45) and (46):

(45) a. *Me parece romper la ventana.
to me-seems to break the window
b. ?Me parece estar rompiendo la ventana.
to me-seems to be breaking the window
c. Me parece estar rompiendo la ventana sin querer.
to me-seems to be breaking the window inadvertently

(46) a. ??Me parece arrestar al ladron.
to me—seems to arrest the thief
b. Les parece haber arrestado al ladron mas sinverguenza del mundo.
to them-seems to have arrested the most shameless thief in the world

Let us examine (45) more closely. Thematically, *romper* ('break') takes an agent and a theme. Yet, although 'break' is the verb involved in the three examples of (45), (a) is strongly out, while (b) and (c) are fine.

Similar observations are valid for (46), which involves the verb *arrestar* ('arrest'). Thus, lexical elements with aspectual import such as auxiliaries and adverbs transform the event structure of the lower clause into a state. This is evidence that the matrix verb, as a lexical matter, requires that the infinitival clause is stative. These semantic restrictions point towards the correctness of the control approach.

NOTES

*This article is a revised version of a paper written in 1989. Since then, I have introduced some changes in the analysis of dative clitics. I thank R. Kayne for his comments on the oral presentation of this material in the Second Princeton Workshop on Comparative Grammar, and for his written comments on the previous version of this paper. I also thank an anonymous reviewer for comments on the previous version. Some portions of this material were presented at a Workshop on Syntax in Toledo (Spain) in the Spring of 1989, and at the 1990 International Summer Institute of Girona. I am grateful to N. Chomsky for comments and discussion over the ideas presented here, and also to S. Epstein, J. Grimshaw, I. Laka, E. McNulty, C. Otero, P. Pica, C. Piera, J. Uriagereka, K. Wexler, and K. Zagona. Thanks to those attending the class of Fall 1989 in the Instituto Universitario "Ortega y Gasset" in the University of Madrid for their questions and suggestions.

1 Although I gloss *parecer* as 'seem' and *resultar* as 'turn out', I should caution the reader that the English translations may not always be the exact equivalent of the Spanish sentences. Sometimes one and the same sentence has different interpretations when uttered in different situations. No doubt, the difficulty of translation is due to the aspectual modal-like semantic nature of raising predicates (Cf. Bresnan (1972)).

2 The use of the progressive with *resultar* is semantically restricted. It requires that the sentence can be interpreted as a qualified assertion concerning an individual or a situation:

(i) a. Juan esta resultando ser (*un excelente) cocinero.
Juan is turning out to be an excellent cook
b. *Esta resultando que Juan es un excelente cocinero.
It is turning out that Juan is an excellent cook

(ii) Esta resultando llover (*cada dia mas).
It is turning out to rain (more and more every day)

(iii) Las termitas estan resultando destruir la casa (*antes de lo que pensabamos).
The termites are turning out to destroy the house (in much less time than we thought)

[3] The form of the subjunctive licensed by *parecer* in this case is interpreted as the present progressive: "parece que lloviera= que estuviera lloviendo" ('it seems as if it would be raining'). This is presumably due to the "as if", non overt in Spanish.

[4] The subjunctive is also allowed when the experiencer argument of *parecer* is realized (I. Bosque, p.c.):

(i) No me parece que haga frio.
It does not seem to me that it is (SUBJ) cold

(ii) Te parece que vayamos al cine?
Do you want that we go (SUBJ) to the movies?

However, in this case, the negation or the question operator are the subjunctive "triggers", and not *parecer*, as shown by the impossiblity of (iii):

(iii) Me parece que hace/*haga frio.
It seems to me that it is cold

On the interaction between negation and the subjunctive, see Laka (1990).

[5] Since *parecer* <u>is</u> a raising verb (see the arguments in section 1.2), the lack of an epistemic reading in the second modal cannot be related to epistemic modals not being raising verbs, as hinted by Picallo (1990). It is possible that the epistemic interpretation of modals requires that the modal has scope over the entire sentence at LF. This would restrict the epistemic reading to just one modal. The fact that the epistemic interpretation is confined to the first occurrence of the verb in sequences of more than one modal (also brought about by Picallo (1990)) may follow from Chomsky's (1989) Principle of Economy. Given that, in principle, any of the modals involved could be first, for a modal in a second position to gain maximum scope in the sentence at LF, the second modal would have to move over the first. Such instance of movement will then be precluded by Economy. In Picallo's (1990) proposal, epistemic modals are base-generated in INFL and select VP rather than IP. A problem for this analysis is that *parecer*, which selects an IP, also blocks the epistemic interpretation. My hypothesis that epistemics must have scope over the entire sentence captures Picallo's insight without having to recur to INFL. See Burzio (1986) also.

[6] The fact that *deber* must be first might suggest that this verb occupies some higher position, or that is selected by some higher head.

[7] I label *parecer* as a V in (11), but this is more a notational issue than a conceptual one. I assume that when *parecer* is not the complement of a null verb, *parecer* is Modal.

[8] Both Jackendoff (1983)/(1990) and Emonds (1985) argue that some datives are not arguments of the verb.

[9] This claim amounts to suggesting that the experiencer mut c-command everything else in the structure at LF. An indication that this may be so is provided by the position where the experiencer surface in Italian with some raising verbs. See footnote 11.

[10] Example (a) is from Burzio (1986) (footnote 42 of chapter 5); (b) is from Rizzi (1978), his (9).

[11] It is worth noticing that in Italian a lexical experiencer with the verb *sembrare* must be clause initial or else the result is quite marginal (Rizzi (1982)):

(i) *?Gianni sembra <u>a Piero</u> non fare il suo devere.
Gianni seems to Piero to not do his duty this does not

This is probably due to the fact that *sembrare* and the lower V must join their INFLs before LF.

[12] The prohibition of auxiliary *haber* with Spanish *parecer* points toward restrictions having to do with Tense. There is a lot more to say about *haber* and *parecer*, though, and about *haber* and modals in general. For one thing, perfective *haber* can combine with an overt modal:

(i) Ha podido parecer que no nos interesaba la oferta.
'It may have seemed that we were not interested in the offer'

Also, *haber* can occur with *parecer* when *haber* is preceded by an overt modal:

(ii) Podria haber parecido que no queriamos decirlo.
'It could have seemed that we did not want to say it'

[13] Spanish *parecer* is homophonous with both 'appear' and 'look', as witnessed by semi-idiomatic expressions such as *ser bien parecido* (Lit. to be good seemed)ing'. Since 'look' in English does not take clauses, (see Chomsky (1981) for discussion), one may argue that there is no small clause when *parecer* is followed by a predicate adjective or by a predicate NP. If there is no small clause, there will be no subject-raising either. I think this analysis may well be valid for some cases, but not for all. The meaning of 'look' involves perceptions based on signs somewhat more physical than those entailed in 'seem' and 'appear'. See section 3 for discussion on small clauses.

[14] I have confirmed this with E. Bonet for Catalan; with J. Uriagereka for Galician; with C. Dobrovie-Sorin for Romanian; and with E. Raposo for Portuguese. A precautionary note for Portuguese is necessary. Portuguese and Spanish differ in regard to the position where clitics attach, and also in regard to restrictions on the clitic-doubling phenomena in general. How exactly Portuguese experiencer clitics interact with the syntax of raising to subject is left for further investigation.

[15] There is a preference in French for the clitic realization of the experiencer (P. Pica, p.c.). I believe this is due to the fact that clitics favor complex predicate formation, perhaps because their trace can delete. The realization of the experiencer also matters in French for a different, although related, class of cases, as observed by Rouveret and Vergnaud (1980); see Ruwet (1976). I return to discuss these cases at the end.

[16] For French, see Kayne (1984), chapter 5, footnote 7, who, in turn, cites Ruwet (1976), footnote 6.

[17] The experiencer yields ungrammaticality regardless whether the subject is preverbal or postverbal. Thus, the counterpart of (25a) with the subject postverbally is ill-formed:

(i) *me parece [t estar cansado] este taxista.
to me-seems to be tired this taxi driver

[18] The verb *resultar* cannot appear with an experiencer when the lower clause is finite:

(i) (*Me) resulto que...
to me-turned out that...

The experiencer can appear when this verb is associated with APs:

(ii) Me resulta desagradable\dificil dormir poco.
to me-turns out unpleasant\difficult to sleep litle

It is possible that *resultar* does not take an experiencer and that examples like (ii) are the result of some form of complex predicate formation, with the experiencer being an argument of the lower predicate. The following is evidence in support of the complex predicate approach:

(iii) (El) dormir poco me resulta desagradable\dificil.
(The) to sleep litle me-turns out unpleasant\difficult

In (iii), the infinitival clause has been preposed. This possibility suggests that the subject of this clause is PRO. This PRO can either be controlled by the experiencer (or its trace), or it can have an arbitrary reference (Cf. Epstein (1984)). The arbitrary interpretation is more salient in examples like (iv), for pragmatic reasons:

(iv) (El) tirar los papeles al suelo me resulta irresponsable.
(The) to litter papers to the floor me-turns out irresponsible
'I find it irresponsible to litter papers to the floor'

Obviously, if *resultar* does not take an experiencer argument, the ungrammaticality of (25a) would say nothing about experiencers barring subject raising.
[19] The Italian examples (23a) from Burzio (1986)—(his (100a) in chapter 5) and (23b) from Rizzi (1982) -his (22b).
[20] A discussion of the exact mechanism which accomplishes this is beyond the scope of this remark, and will require to take into consideration how exactly the experiencer eliminates the null expletive at LF, via substitution or via adjunction.
[21] My account of clitic-doubling Romance crucially realies on the assumption that there is subject-to-subject raising. This is incompatible with the proposal made in Williams (1980) concerning raising verbs.
[22] There are cases in which *parecer*+experiencer is followed by a prima facie PP. This, however, appears to be an instance of adjectival modification of the type which is associated with *ser*:

(i) Juan me parece de Madrid = Juan me parece madrileno.
Juan to me-seems of Madrid = Juan to me-seems "madrileno"
(ii) Juan es de Madrid/*Juan esta de Madrid.
Juan is from Madrid

(iii) Juan es madrileno/*Juan esta madrileno.
Juan is "madrileno"

[23] The question of what exactly goes wrong when the adjective cannot saturate its eventive argument depends on specific assumptions about e-arguments, about INFL in small clauses and so on. These issues all go beyond the scope of this work.
[24] The ability of the experiencer to occur with 'seem' in adverbials is evidence that

the experiencer is part of the lexical structure of 'seem'. The same point can be made for 'seem'-experiencer as a control verb.

[25] In some cases, *parecer*+clitic appears to be lexicalized:

(i) Yo me parece que no quiero ir.
I to me-seems that I do not want to go
'I think I do not want to go'

In (1), the nominative pronoun *yo* cannot be topicalized; there is no comma entonation between the nominative pronoun and the rest of the clause, as there is in cases such as (ii):

(ii) Los alumnos, me parece que no van a ir.
The students, to me-seems that they are not going to go
'The students, I think they are not going to go'

REFERENCES

Baker, M. (1987) *Incorporation: A Theory of Grammatical Functioning Changing.* Chicago: University of Chicago Press.

Bresnan, J (1972) *Theory of Complementation in English Syntax.* MIT PhD dissertation.

Burzio, L. (1986) *Italian Syntax: A Government and Binding Approach,* Reidel, Dordrecht.

Chomsky, N. (1981) *Lectures in Government and Binding,* Foris, Dordrecht.

Chomsky, N. (1989) Some notes on economy of derivation and representation. In Laka & Mahajan, eds., (1989), 43-74; also, edited, in Freidin, ed., (1991), 417-454.

Emonds, J. (1985) *A Unified Theory of Syntactic Categories,* Foris, Dordrecht.

Epstein, S. (1984) "Quantifier-pro and the LF Representation of PRO_{arb}," *Linguistic Inquiry* 15, 449-504.

Freidin, R., ed. (1991) *Principles and parameters of comparative grammar.* The MIT Press.

Higginbotham, J. (1985) "On Semantics," *Linguistic Inquiry,* 16, 547-593.

Higginbotham, J. (1987) "Elucidations of Meaning," *Lexicon Project Working Papers* 19, MIT.

Jackendoff, R. (1983) *Semantics and Cognition,* MIT Press, Cambridge, MA.

Jackendoff, R. (1990) *Semantic Structures,* MIT Press, Cambridge, MA.

Kayne, R.S. (1974) *French Syntax,* MIT Press, Cambridge, MA.

Kayne, R.S. (1984) *Connectedness and Binary Branching,* Foris, Dordrecht.

Kayne, R.S. (1987) "Null Subjects and Clitic Climbing," in O. Jaeggli and K. Safir (eds.), *The Null Subject Parameter,* Reidel, Dordrecht.

Kratzer, A. (1989) "Stage and Individual Level Predicates," in Papers on Quantification, NSF Grant Report, Department of Linguistics, University of Massachusetts, Amherst.

Laka, I. (1990) *Negation in Syntax: On the Nature of Functional Categories and Projections,* MIT PhD dissertation.

Laka, I., & Mahajan, A., eds. (1989) *MIT Working Papers in Linguistics 10: Functional Heads and Clause Structures.* Cambridge, MA: MIT.

May, R. (1985) *Logical Form,* MIT Press, Cambridge, MA.

Napoli, D.-J. (1989) *Predication Theory*, Cambridge University Press.

Picallo, C. (1990) "Modal Verbs in Catalan," *Natural Language and Linguistic Theory*, 8, 2, 285-312.

Rizzi, L. (1978) "A Restructuring Rule in Italian Syntax," in *Recent Transformational Studies in European Languages*, S.J. Keyser (ed.).

Rizzi, L. (1982) *Issues in Italian Syntax*, Foris, Dordrecht.

Rothstein, S. (1983) *The Syntactic Forms of Predication*. MIT PhD dissertation.

Rouveret, A. and J-R. Vergnaud (1980) "Specifying Reference to the Subject: French Causatives and Considitions on Representations," *Linguistic Inquiry* 11, 97-202.

Ruwet, N. (1976) "Subject-Raising and Extraposition," in M. Lujan and F. Hensey, (eds.) *Current Studies in Romance Linguistics*, Georgetown University Press, Washington, D. C.

Williams, E. (1980) "Predication." *Linguistic Inquiry* 11, 203-238.

Williams, E. (1983) "Against Small Clauses," *Linguistic Inquiry* 14,287-308.

JAKLIN KORNFILT

NP-MOVEMENT AND "RESTRUCTURING"*

INTRODUCTION:

In this paper, I shall describe a construction in Turkish which seems to involve a non-local application of an otherwise local process: NP-movement of an embedded object to matrix subject position. The construction in question involves a small number of subject control verbs and their infinitival complements.

A variety of phenomena taking place in similar syntactic contexts in other languages (e.g. Spanish, Italian, Czech, Hungarian) have been claimed to crucially involve Restructuring of the complex source into a monoclausal S-Structure. Restructuring is a problematic notion, since it violates the Projection Principle: a verb that takes a clausal complement at D-structure will end up taking one or more NP complements at S-structure; arguments that receive their q-roles from a given verb at D-structure will receive their q-roles from another verb (the newly formed verbal complex) at S-structure.

More recently, a number of proposals have been advanced to circumvent this problem: Base-generation of the "monoclausal" structure and the "verbal complex", in which the finite verb functions as a modal auxiliary (cf. Picallo (1990) for Catalan); simultaneous assignment of two distinct phrase structures to the same string, one monoclausal, the other biclausal (cf. Haegeman and van Riemsdijk 1986 for Dutch and Flemish and Kiss 1987 for Hungarian); movement of the lower Inflection to the higher Inflection, with resulting co-indexation of the two Infl positions (cf. Kayne 1989, mainly for Spanish and Italian).

It is not my aim here to evaluate any of this work. Rather, I shall focus here on a proposal for the Turkish construction at stake, thus inviting questions about possible extensions of the account to some other languages. That this is a realistic hope can be seen from studies like Rivero 1989 and related work for some of the Balkan languages, where explanations based on "CP-Transparency" are available for phenomena that look like Restructuring effects. More concretely, in spite of my title, I shall propose an extension of the familiar "S'-Deletion" (or "CP-Transparency") phenomenon to the (Turkish) instances in question, rather than a restructuring of the phrase marker. It might well be the case that there are different kinds of "Restructuring effects", with each type obviously requiring a different analysis. The aim of this paper is to propose that CP-Transparency is, indeed, one such type that is part of UG.[1]

CP-Transparency makes an embedded subject accessible to government (and Case marking) by the matrix verb in (essentially) factive contexts. In this paper, I claim that the same process makes accessible the same position to the corresponding matrix verb in (essentially) non-factive contexts, as well; in other words, we have "Exceptional Government" in both situations. However, we have (structural) "Exceptional Case Marking" in the factive type only. This is because some of the "Exceptional Government" matrix verbs that take non-factive complements are not structural Case markers; they assign only inherent Case. I assume here that such Case is assigned at D-structure (and thus cannot be assigned at some later stage of the derivation), the embedded subject position can only be "exceptionally" governed, but not "exceptionally" Case-marked by such verbs. While there is one matrix verb found with the construction under scrutiny that *is* otherwise a structural Case marker, it can be shown that its structural Case has to be assigned to the infinitival clause itself (which is nominal and hence needs Case) and thus becomes unavailable for the embedded subject.

The fact that the Case assigned to the infinitival clause stays on that clause and is still needed at S-structure strongly suggests that:

1. there was a bi-clausal structure at D-structure, hence the phenomenon we are dealing with is syntactic and not one of word-formation, and
2. that the S-structure of the construction is not monoclausal, hence there is no need to posit either Restructuring *or* two distinct (but simultaneous) phrase structures.

I should also mention that while the examples I shall be looking at involve just two verbs (and this is how the construction is most generally used), it is possible to construct examples involving three verbs, if the intermediate and the highest verb are both of the type that generally licenses the IDP construction. (Obviously, due to the length of the utterance and the general center-embedding nature of complementation in Turkish in general, these examples are awkward, but still grammatical. This is also why the construction seems to be impossible with more than three verbs, i.e. more than two embeddings.)

Given the possibility of iteration, a word-formation approach is quite improbable. (By itself, this last point would be a weak argument for a purely syntactic derivation, since compounding is a fairly productive process in Turkish. However, there are arguments to the effect that many compounds in Turkish are syntactic rather than purely morphological; cf. Kornfilt 1984 and Yükseker 1987; I shall not pursue this matter any further here.)

We shall also see that each verb in the Turkish construction under investigation retains its properties in assigning thematic roles, thus arguing against a unique complex verb at S-structure (whether such a verb would be base-generated *or* syntactically derived.)

Having thus introduced the general area of investigation and the main line of analysis, I now turn to the specifics of the construction.

1. The Construction: Infinitival Double Passives (IDPs) in Turkish

The construction in Turkish I shall focus on here is illustrated by (1) through (3) below:

(1) **üniversite-ler** (polis tarafından) kuşat-ıl-mak iste-n-di
university-pl. police by surround-Pass-Infin. want-Pass-past
'The universities were wanted to be surrounded by the police'

(2) **üniversite-ler** (polis tarafından) kuşat-ıl-mağ-a başla-n-dı
university-pl. policc by surround-Pass-Infin.-Dat. begin Pass past
'The universities were begun to be surrounded by the police'

(3) **üniversite-ler** (polis tarafından) kuşat-ıl-mağ-a çalış-ıl-dı
university-pl. police by surround-Pass-Infin.-Dat. try-Pass-past
'The universities were tried to be surrounded by the police'

The main properties of the construction are as follows:

1. The understood embedded direct object is the S-Structure matrix subject;
2. Whether an agent phrase shows up or not, the agent of the matrix and of the embedded
verb are understood as co-referential—just like in Control contexts in general;
3. The embedded verb is an infinitive (suffix -mAK)—a form found in Control contexts;
4. Both the embedded infinitive and the matrix verb have to carry Passive morphology (with one exception, to be discussed later);
5. Only 3 matrix verbs occur in this construction, exemplified above, all Subject-Control verbs;
6. Infinitives in Turkish bear no AGR morphology. This is true in Control contexts as well as in IDPs.

The related active sentences involving Control are (4) through (6):

(4) polis$_i$ [PRO$_i$ üniversite-ler-i kuşat-mak] iste-di
police university-pl.-Acc. surround-Infin. want-past
'The police wanted to surround the universities'

(5) polis$_i$ [PRO$_i$ üniversite-ler-i kuşat-mağ]-a başla-dı
police university -pl.-Acc. surround-Infin.-Dat. begin-past
'The police begun to surround the universities'

(6) polis$_i$ [PRO$_i$ üniversite-ler-i kuşat -mağ]-a çalış-tı
police university -pl. -Acc. surround-Infin. -Dat. try-past
'The police tried to surround the universities'

2. INTEREST OF THE CONSTRUCTION:

2.1. Limitations of Occurrence:

Note that the English equivalents of all IDPs are ungrammatical:

(7) a. *The universities were wanted/begun/tried to be surrounded (by the police)

Not surprisingly, attempts to construct IDPs in Turkish with verbs other than the three verbs listed in (1) through (3) fail, even where such verbs are "Subject Control" verbs, just like the three verbs in question:

(7) b. *üniversite-ler kuşat-ıl-mak unut-ul-du / planla-n-dı
university-pl. surround-Pass-Inf. forget-Pass-past/ plan -Pass-past
'The universities were forgotten/planned to be surrounded'

Crucially, the corresponding active Control structures are grammatical (and similar to those corresponding to the grammatical IDPs):

(7) c. ordu$_i$ [PRO$_i$ üniversite-ler-i kuşat-mağ]-ı unut-tu/planla-dı
army university-pl.-Acc. surround-Infin.]-Acc. forget-past/plan-past
'The army forgot/planned to surround the universities'

2.2. General Properties of Passive in Turkish, and Deriving its Boundedness:

NP-movement in Passive constructions is local in Turkish, just as it is in English. The examples in (8) through (10) illustrate that property.

(8) a. [Hasan-ın Zeyneb-i sev-diğ -in]-i duy-du-k
[H.-Gen. Z.-Acc. love-Gerund-3.sg.]-Acc. hear -past-1.pl.
'We heard that Hasan loves Zeynep'

b. [Zeyneb-in$_i$ (Hasan tarafından) t$_i$ sev-il-diğ -in]-i duy-du-k
[Z.-Gen. H.by love-Pass-Ger.-3.sg.]-Acc. hear-past-1.pl.
'We heard that Zeynep is loved by Hasan'

(9) a. *Zeynep$_i$ [t$_i$ (Hasan tarafından) t$_i$ sev-il-diğ -i] duy-ul-du
Z. H. by love-Pass-Ger-3.sg. hear-Pass-past
'Zeynep was heard [that (being) loved by Hasan]'

b. *Zeynep$_i$ [t$_i$ (Hasan tarafından) t$_i$ sev-il-mek] duy-ul-du
Z. H. by love-Pass-Inf. hear-Pass-past
'Zeynep was heard [to be loved by Hasan]'

c. *Zeynep$_i$ [t$_i$ (Hasan tarafından) t$_i$ sev-ıl-di] duy-ul-du
Z. H. by love-Pass-past hear-Pass-past
'Zeynep was heard [was loved by Hasan]'

(10) a. *Zeynep$_i$ [Hasan-ın t$_i$ sev-diğ-i] duy-ul-du
Z. Hasan -Gen. love-Ger.-3.sg. hear-Pass-past
'Zeynep was heard [that Hasan {loved / to love / loved}]'

b. *Zeynep$_i$ [Hasan t$_i$ sev-mek] duy-ul-du
Z. Hasan love-Inf. hear-Pass-past
'Zeynep was heard [Hasan to love] '

c. *Zeynep$_i$ [Hasan t$_i$ sev-di] duy-ul-du
Z. H. love-past hear-Pass-past
'Zeynep was heard [Hasan loved]'

In (8)b., "Passive" has applied within the embedded clause, and the output is fine. However, attempts to further apply Passive to the moved NP, "Zeynep", are unsuccessful, as shown by (9). Note, incidentally, that the complements in these Turkish examples are gerundives of sorts and hence, for all practical purposes, untensed (there is only a rough distinction between Future and non-Future in this particular complement type). (10) shows that it is not the (surface) subjecthood of the moved NP that matters—an embedded object cannot "passivize" and move to matrix subject position, just as little as an embedded subject can.

I assume that "Passive constructions" (at least those involving syntactic—as opposed to lexical—Passive) and NP-movement have the same properties in Turkish as in English (this is a controversial assumption within literature on Turkish, but I am not aware of any good argument to the effect that there might be any deep, significant differences):

Passive morphology (-Il -(I)n is suffixed onto the verbal root, with the first form as the basic allomorph, and the second form after root-final vowels and *l*) suppresses the structural (but not the inherent) Case of the verb, thus forcing movement of the Case-less complement to Spec of IP position, given the validity of the Case Filter in Turkish syntax (cf. Kornfilt 1984). The moved NP receives Nominative Case in its new position, assigned by (verbal) AGR (in "gerundive" complements, AGR is nominal and assigns Genitive Case to the Spec of IP position).

We also have to stipulate (again, just as in English) that a second property of Passive morphology is suppression of the verb's external θ-role. This stipulation is necessary in order to avoid a violation of the θ-Criterion by the moved NP, which inherits a θ-role from its trace.

Now, we have to turn to the locality of NP-movement. In what follows, I shall adopt an account based on Chomsky 1981, although the account can be transposed into the Barriers framework straightforwardly.

The trace of NP is an anaphor and has to obey Condition A of the Binding Theory. Moving the subject of a tensed (or, rather, "finite" in the sense of having AGR—cf. George & Kornfilt 1981) embedded clause out of that clause by NP-movement is prohibited, since the anaphoric NP-trace in embedded subject position will be free in its Governing Category. I take that Governing Category to be the embedded clause, since this is where that element is governed and where it has its Accessible SUBJECT, namely AGR) and will therefore violate Binding Condition A. (In addition, on might say that such a trace is also ruled out by virtue of the ECP, since it wouldn't be properly governed: AGR, the governor of the trace, isn't a proper governor, and the trace is not antecedent-governed, either, given that NP-movement doesn't go through Spec/CP. If so, we have a situation where we have two possible explanations for one and the same phenomenon—an undesirable state of affairs. However, given that Turkish is a "Pro-Drop" language, we might say that AGR *is* a proper governor. If so, the violation in question wouldn't be due to the ECP, but only to Binding Theory.

What about the trace left by NP-movement out of embedded subject position in infinitivals, however?

It's not clear that Binding Condition A achieves anything here—it simply doesn't say anything, since the embedded subject position of AGR-less clauses isn't governed and hence has no Governing Category.

In these instances, we can invoke the ECP, since, whether AGR counts as a proper governor or not, the subject position is ungoverned (given total lack of AGR). The general ungrammaticality of NP-movement out of embedded subject position of AGR-less complement clauses follows from this fact.

Such movement is licit, however, in certain instances: when the subject of an ECM-complement (whether itself derived by NP-movement within the clause, where the clause has a passive verb, or whether this subject is non-derived with an active verb) undergoes NP-movement; the same is true for Subject Raising. I shall not discuss the latter, since it is unclear whether SOV-languages exhibit this phenomenon productively—cf. Kuno 1976;

Turkish does have a few verbs which are arguably Raising verbs—cf. Kornfilt 1976, but I shall not pursue the matter here.

2.3. ECM in turkish:

Turkish does have some ECM verbs, but with properties slightly different from those of Control verbs. They don't take infinitival complements; crucially, they take fully finite complements (in addition to gerundives):

(Finite) S'-Complements:

(11) Hasan [biz üniversite-yi kuşat-tı-k] san-ıyor
H. we university-Acc. surround-past-1.pl. believe-pres.progr.
'Hasan believes (that) we surrounded the university'

Note that the subject of the constituent clause is in the Nominative, that the embedded verb is fully tensed, and that the verb agrees with the embedded subject.
When these verbs trigger CP-Transparency[2], they structurally Case-mark the embedded subject by assigning Accusative to it; the complement is still tensed (*not* an infinitival), but lacks AGR (at least for one dialect—cf. Kornfilt 1977):

(AGR-less) S-Complements:

(12) Hasan [biz-i üniversite-yi kuşat-tı] san-ıyor
H. we -Acc. university-Acc. surround-past believe-pres.progr.
'Hasan believes us to have surrounded the university'

The "ECM"-marked embedded subject can undergo movement with a passive "ECM"-verb, whether that subject is derived (as in (14) or not (as in (13)):

(13) Biz$_i$ [t$_i$ üniversite-yi kuşat-tı] san-ıl-ıyor-uz
we university-Acc. surround-past believe-Pass-pres.progr.-1.pl.
'We are believed to have surrounded the university'

(14) üniversite-ler [t$_i$ t$_i$ kuşat-ıl-dı] san-ıl-ıyor
university-pl. surround-Pass-past believe-Pass-pres.progr.
'The universities are believed to have been surrounded'

(14) is the more interesting example, since it looks very similar to IDPs. However, the morphology of the complement clause is different (tensed here, versus infinitival in IDPs); some basic properties of the main verb are different, as well (as can be shown independently—see below); and, the agents of the two verbs are not necessarily co-referent—typically, they are not.

3. BACK TO IDPs:

Remember that Infinitival Double Passives are ungrammatical in English:

(7) *The universities$_i$ were wanted/begun/tried [t_i to be surrounded t_i (by the police)]

Compare (7) with the grammatical (15):

(15) The universities$_i$ were believed [t_i to have been surrounded t_i]

While both traces are properly governed in (15), the trace in embedded subject position in (7) is not: The verbs in (7) are Control verbs, not ECM Verbs. (Actually, *want* in English can also be an ECM verb, but it does not passivize even then.) These verbs don't trigger CP-Transparency, and the trace in embedded subject position violates the ECP.

But then, the corresponding examples should be ungrammatical in Turkish as well, which they are not. The verbs in question are not Exceptional Case Markers in Turkish:

(16) a. Polis$_i$ [PRO$_i$ üniversite-yi kuşat-mak] iste-di
police university-Acc. surround-inf. want-past
'The police wanted to surround the university'

b. *Polis [ordu-yu üniversite-yi kuşat-mak] iste-di
police army-Acc. university-Acc. surround-inf. want-past
Attempted reading: 'The police wanted the army to surround the university'

Note that, even though the English translation of this example is grammatical, due to the possibility of "want" as an ECM-verb, the Turkish example is grossly ungrammatical—an NP in embedded subject position in such a context has no way of receiving Accusative Case, given that the matrix verb *iste* ('want') is not an ECM-verb in Turkish (although it does assign Accusative Case to its NP-objects).

The same facts obtain when the matrix verb is *çalış* ('try'):

(17) a. Polis$_i$ [PRO$_i$ üniversite-yi kuşat-mağ]-a çalış-tı
police university-Acc. surround-inf.]-Dat. try-past
'The police tried to surround the university'

b. *Polis [ordu-yu üniversite-yi kuşat-mak] (-a) çalış-tı
police army-Acc. university-Acc. surround-inf.] (-Dat.) try-past
Attempted reading: 'The police tried for the army to surround the university'

The semantics of (17)b. are OK and can be expressed in a "subjunctive" construction:

c. Polis [ordu-nun üniversite-yi kuşat-ma-sın]-a çalış-tı
police army-Gen. university-Acc. surround-mA-3.sg.]-Dat. try-past
'The police tried for the army to surround the university'

At this point, we should say a few words about general differences between Turkish Control verbs versus ECM verbs:

1. **Case:** ECM verbs are all structural Case assigners, i.e. it can be independently shown that, when they take an NP-object, they all assign Accusative Case; on the other hand, while there are also Control verbs that assign structural Case, there are many Control verbs that take oblique (i.e. Dative or Ablative) complements. Out of the three matrix Control verbs that enter the IDP construction, two (*çalış* 'try' and *başla* 'begin') take Dative complements; only the third one (*iste* 'want') is otherwise a structural Case assigner.

Note, incidentally, that *iste* can take Accusative objects, which, like any other objects of structural Case markers, can also "incorporate" if they are non-specific and lose their overt Case marking. Where *iste* takes an infinitival complement and is itself active, the complement can, but does not have to, be Accusative-marked. However, in the IDP construction, *iste* does not tolerate Accusative-marking on the infinitival verb of its complement clause, as can be ascertained by looking at all examples presented so far that involve that verb ((4') vs. (1')):

(4') polis$_i$ [PRO$_i$ üniversite-ler-i kuşat-mağ]-ı iste-di
police university-pl.-Acc. surround-Infin.]-Acc. want-past
'The police wanted to surround the universities'

(1') * [**üniversite-ler** (polis tarafından) kuşat-ıl-mağ]-ı iste-n-di
university-pl. police by surround-Pass-Infin-Acc. want-Pass-past
'The universities were wanted to be surrounded by the police'

2. **Morphology and category:** ECM verbs can take finite complements, where the embedded clauses have tense and Agreement. Under CP-Transparency, AGR disappears for one dialect; tense remains, however, in all instances (and the predicate appears in a morphology different from that of an infinitive). It therefore makes sense to assume that the fully finite complements in these instances have the status of CP, and, where ECM effects are to be seen, those complements would be bare IPs or "transparent" CPs).

On the other hand, Control verbs take only NP-complements; gerunds as well as infinitival clauses are NPs: these complements are marked with morphological Case, which is always the same Case as that found on simple, lexical NP complements of the respective verbs, if they do take such NPs otherwise. Further evidence for the NP-nature of gerundives comes from the Genitive (rather than Nominative) case on the embedded subject and the nominal (rather than verbal) AGR forms on the embedded predicate. (For more information on these points, cf. Kornfilt 1984.)

3. From a semantic point of view, ECM verbs are factives, while Control verbs are (essentially) non-factives.

4. Concurrent with this semantic grouping, we also find a dichotomy in the gerundive morphology that either group of matrix verbs can co-occur with. ECM verbs, if they don't take fully finite CP-complements or IP-complements, can take the more general gerundive complement. That gerundive is marked with the suffix -DIK on the verbal stem. That type of complement corresponds, roughly, to indicative complements in European languages.

Control verbs, on the other hand, where they don't take an infinitival complement, will take a gerundive complement clause, as well. However, the morphology found on those clauses is the -mA suffix, and the complement itself corresponds—again very roughly—to the subjunctive complements of European languages.

We conclude that the matrix verbs found in IDP constructions are bona fide Control verbs and do not belong to the group of ECM verbs. Rather, they are the kind of verb that takes an NP-complement, and does not co-occur with (overt) Accusative Case, as opposed to ECM verbs.

4. PROPOSAL

If IDPs are not explainable by ECM, why are they grammatical?

In order to turn to a discussion of the proposed derivation of IDPs, let us repeat the crucial examples:

(1) üniversite-ler$_i$ [$\mathbf{t}_i$ t_i kuşat-ıl-mak] iste-n-di
university-pl. surround-Pass-Infin. want-Pass-past
'The universities were wanted to be surrounded '

(2) üniversite-ler$_i$ [$\mathbf{t}_i$ t_i kuşat-ıl-mağ]-a başla-n-dı
university-pl. surround-Pass-Infin.-Dat. begin-Pass-past
'The universities were begun to be surrounded'

(3) üniversite-ler$_i$ [$\mathbf{t}_i$ t_i kuşat-ıl-mağ]-a çalış-ıl-dı
university-pl. surround-Pass-Infin.-Dat. try-Pass-past
'The universities were tried to be surrounded'

The boldfaced **t** in the previous examples is the "offending" trace—"offending" in the sense of violating the ECP.

If so, how come such "offence" doesn't lead to ungrammaticality?

We saw that CP-Deletion can "repair" such ECP-violation in the context of ECM-verbs; but we also saw that these Turkish Control verbs are not ECM verbs.

My proposal to solve this problem is as follows:

The three "IDP" verbs are triggers of another type of Transparency of maximal projection; purely descriptively speaking, instead of a CP that dominates a verbal IP), what becomes transparent is a CP that dominates a "nominal" IP rather than a "verbal" IP.

The effects of this type of "CP transparency" are similar to those of traditional "S'-Deletion": the "offending" trace in embedded subject position is now properly governed by the main verb and is saved from violating the ECP.

If this proposal is on the right track, CP-Transparency with "believe"-type verbs is not a unique phenomenon any longer. Furthermore, yet another parallel between nominal and verbal clauses is revealed.

5. DERIVATION OF IDPs ("REGULAR"):

The assumption of CP-Transparency solves the problem with the ECP, but, in itself, does not provide us with a derivation for IDPs. I assume the following derivation:

1. Passive morphology on the infinitive verb: Induces NP-movement to embedded subject position (since Passive morphology suppresses Case, the Case Filter would otherwise mark the embedded direct object as ungrammatical)
2. The embedded subject position lacks Case as well, given that the infinitive lacks Agreement, which would otherwise have assigned Case to that position; the original embedded direct object NP moves on to matrix subject position (again, that movement is motivated by the Case Filter)[3]
3. The matrix subject position receives Case from the matrix AGR—the Case Filter is satisfied.
4. However, now the matrix verb must have Passive morphology, in order to suppress external θ-role assignment to matrix subject position, since the derived matrix subject is in a θ-Chain with its traces and has the θ-role of the embedded object position. If the moved NP would, in addition, also receive the θ-role of the matrix subject, this would lead to a violation of the θ-Criterion.
5. "CP-Transparency" saves the trace in embedded subject position from violating the ECP.[4]

6. Derivation of IDPs ("impersonal"):
   We have presupposed that all IDPs exhibit a derived matrix subject (the understood embedded direct object).This is not the case, however. Where the embedded verb is intransitive (i.e. either lacks any object whatsoever or has only oblique objects), no NP-movement takes place; Passive morphology suppresses only structural Case, not oblique ("inherent") Case.

We assume that, in general, the subject position of an Intransitive Passive is occupied by an expletive—pro in a Pro-Drop language like Turkish (e.g. (20)), corresponding to an overt expletive in a language like German (cf. (18-19)): (English must be exceptional in not allowing intransitive Passives):

(18) a. Es wurde getanzt
it was danced

b. Es wurde der Frau geholfen
it was the (Dat.) woman helped

(19) a. Die Frau wurde gesehen
the woman (Nom.) was seen

b. *Die Frau wurde geholfen
the woman (Nom.) was helped

(20) a. **pro**$_{expl}$ dansed-il-di
dance-Pass-past
'it was danced'

b. **pro**$_{expl}$ kadın-a yardım ed-il-di
woman-Dat. help do-Pass-past
'The woman was helped'

c. *kadın yardım ed-il-di
woman (Nom.) help do-Pass-past
'The woman was helped'

Note that oblique (inherent) Case remains when the verb is Passive; structural (i.e. Accusative) Case doesn't—it gets suppressed by Passive morphology; the moved structural object receives the (structural) Case of its S-Structure position, i.e. of the subject position—which, in Turkish, is Nominative.

pro$_{expl}$ (like any **pro**), needs to be identified by morphological AGR (and perhaps also needs Case):

(21) a. [**pro**$_{exp}$ dansed-il-diğ -in]-i bil-iyor-um
dance-Pass-Ger.-3.sg.]-Acc. know-pres.progr.-1.sg.
'I know that it was danced'

b. [**pro**$_{expl}$ kadın-a yardım ed-il-diğ-in]-i bil-iyor-um
woman-Dat. help do-Pass-Ger.-3.sg.]-Acc know-pres. progr.-1.sg.
'I know that the woman was helped'

In the examples of (21), we have complement clauses that are marked with -DIK, a morpheme which signals (by and large) factive semantics. As mentioned earlier, the other general type of complement clause that has the semantics of "subjunctive" clauses is marked with -mA. When such a clause has a **pro**$_{expl}$ subject, it has to bear 3.sg. AGR morphology, as well:

(22) a. [**pro**$_{expl}$ dansed-il-me-sin]-i isti-yor-um
dance -Pass-mA-3.sg.]-Acc. want-Pres.Progr.-1.sg.
'I want for dancing to take place'
(Lit.: 'I want for there to be dancing')
b. [**pro**$_{expl}$ kadın-a yardım ed-il-me-sin]-i isti-yor-um
woman-Dat. help do-Pass-mA-3.sg.]-Acc. want-pr.prog-1.sg.
'I want for the woman to be helped'

Note that, since Control verbs are a subset of those that take subjunctive complements, the last set of examples is particularly interesting. Note also that in all of these examples, the embedded complement would be ungrammatical without the 3rd sg. AGR element—a fact which I take to be important in signalling that this AGR licenses an expletive pro. Without such AGR, the pro would be unlicensed, leading to the ungrammaticality just mentioned.

Note also that to have an infinitive instead of these gerunds (this should be possible in the last set of examples, since this particular matrix verb can be a Control verb) would still be ungrammatical, no matter what type of ec we assume to occupy the embedded subject position. If we assume it's expletive pro, it won't be licensed, due to lack of AGR, as mentioned in the previous paragraph for the gerundives. If we assume it's PRO, which is licensed in AGR-less structures (cf. the PRO-theorem), once again, ungrammaticality will result: PRO has to bear a thematic role and can't be an expletive in a position lacking a θ-role. (This last point is important, and we shall return to it presently.)

Let us look at the structure of "Intransitive" IDPs before CP-Deletion has applied (or CP transparency has been induced):

(23) a. e [**pro**$_{expl}$ üniversite-ler-e gir-il-meğ]-e çalış-ıl-dı
university-pl.-Dat. enter-Pass-Inf.]-Dat. try-Pass.-Past
'It was tried (for) the universities to be entered'

b. e [**pro**$_{exp}$ üniversite-ler-e gir-il-meğ]-e başla-n-dı
university-pl.-Dat. enter-Pass-Inf.]-Dat. begin-Pass-Past
'It was begun (for) the universities to be entered'

c. e [**pro**$_{exp}$ üniversite-ler-e gir-il-mek] iste-n-di
university-pl.-Dat. enter-Pass-Inf want-Pass-Past
'It was wanted (for) the universities to be entered'

pro$_{expl}$ can't remain in the subject position of an infinitival intransitive Passive, because there is no AGR to identify (and Case-mark) it—hence it moves up to matrix subject position; there, matrix AGR identifies (and Case-marks) it. But, being an expletive, **pro**$_{expl}$ can occupy only a position that lacks a thematic role; hence, the matrix verb must also carry Passive morphology. We now get:

(24) a. **pro**$_{expl}$ [$t_i$üniversite-ler-e gir-il-meğ]-e çalış-ıl-dı
university-pl.-Dat. enter-Pass-Inf.]-Dat. try-Pass-Past
'It was tried (for) the universities to be entered'

b. **pro**$_{expl}$ [$t_i$üniversite-ler-e gir-il-meğ]-e başla-n-dı
university-pl.-Dat. enter-Pass-Inf.]-Dat. begin-Pass-Past
'It was begun (for) the universities to be entered'

c. **pro**$_{expl}$ [$t_i$üniversite-ler-e gir-il-mek] iste-n-di
university-pl.-Dat. enter-Pass-Inf. want-Pass-Past
'It was wanted (for) the universities to be entered'

We now have explained Double Passive morphology by motivating CP-Transparency for Control verbs (via the ECP).

Why should we assume that the empty expletive subject is **pro**, rather than **PRO**? PRO is Case-less, hence wouldn't need to move up, and our account wouldn't go through. Also, PRO can have arbitrary reference; why shouldn't it qualify as an expletive (i.e. the expletive subject of an Intransitive Passive infinitive)?

It can't so qualify, because it can be shown that **PRO**, even where it is "PRO$_{arb}$", *needs a thematic role.*

(25) a. [**pro**$_{expl}$ havuz-da balık ol-ma-**sı**] güzel şey-dir
pool-Loc. fish be-Ger.-**3.sg.** nice thing-is
'It's nice that **there** are fish in the pool'

b. [**PRO** havuz-da balık ol-**mak**] güzel şey-dir
pool-Loc. fish be-**Inf.** nice thing-is
'It's nice **to be** a fish in the pool '

Hence, PRO cannot be an expletive element.

7. "RESTRUCTURING" CROSS-LINGUISTICALLY: MONOCLAUSAL S-STRUCTURE?

7.1. *Some Facts:*

Crucially, we have appealed here to the notion that CP-Transparency applies in a motivated way, namely in order to "repair" ECP violations. As mentioned in the introduction, there is a rich literature on similar phenomena in other languages, particularly in Romance. In the less recent work on that topic, a notion of "Restructuring" has been appealed to. However, typically, such "Restructuring" was assumed to be "triggered" lexically and not induced by any syntactic motivation. Further more, rich evidence was presented in those studies that such "Restructuring yields monoclausal S-Structures, thus explaining apparent locality violations of a host of syntactic processes; e.g. "Clitic Climbing" in Spanish (cf. Aissen and Perlmutter 1976) and in Italian (cf. Rizzi 1982/1978), as well as NP-movement and "long distance" Auxiliary selection in Italian (cf. Rizzi, op. cit.).

At least some of the properties of these constructions are different from those of Turkish IDPs, however. Note that in all of these examples, the "unbounded" application of the otherwise local operation is optional, which has been taken to mean that "Restructuring" is optional. Furthermore, the morphological reflex of whichever process in question (clitic, Aux) shows up only once; yet, in Turkish, the Passive morphology shows up twice—and this obligatorily.

Of course, one question that comes up is to what extent—if at all—the "restructured" construction is monoclausal. Another is, to what extent the so-called verbal complex is, indeed, one unit.

That these questions cannot be answered straightforwardly is shown by the fact that, in some instances, researchers have posited dual analyses: 2 distinct phrase markers are attributed to one and the same string, one of them monoclausal, the other one bi-clausal, since the string apparently exhibits syntactic behavior appropriate to either structure—such behavior would be contradictory under the more traditional view that a string has one phrase structure only at a time. (For discussions of such dual behavior—and dual analysis— see, for example, Kiss 1987 for Hungarian infinitivals, Zubizarretta 1982 for Romance infinitivals, and Haegeman and van Riemsdijk 1986 for Germanic infinitivals.)

Here, I shall not attempt a general assessment of these different approaches for these languages, but I will merely claim that in Turkish IDPs—a construction very reminiscent of those in the other languages mentioned, and also crucially involving Subject Control infinitivals and a subset of the same matrix verbs—no Restructuring need be assumed. As a matter of fact, Restructuring should not be assumed, since the S-Structure of IDPs is not monoclausal. I shall present arguments for this claim, and I shall further argue that the verb sequence in IDPs is not a real verbal complex.

7.2. Turkish IDPs are not Monoclausal:

First of all, IDPs do not exhibit clear-cut monoclausal behavior. I thus differ from George and Kornfilt 1977, where such behavior was posited. There, the main evidence came from three processes: 2 types of "Scrambling" processes (one involving pre-verbal, the other post-verbal positions), and one concerning placement of more than one adverb of the same type.

Since 1977, I myself seem to have become more permissive with respect to "Scrambling" constituents of any type of infinitivals out of their clause; I certainly have met more informants who are permissive in this way. Hence, I don't feel that possibility of "Scrambling" is a good test for clause constituenthood at this point in the development of the language.

As for adverbs, the situation is somewhat different. It is true that, say, two time adverbs in an IDP make the result awkward or worse:

(31) ?Daha bu sabah üniversite bina-lar-ı 27 Nisan-da işgal
only this morning university building-pl.-3.sg. 27 April-in
ed-il-mek iste-n-iyor-du, fakat şimdi durum değiş-ti
occupy-Pass-Inf. want-Pass-pres.progr-past but now situation change-past
'It's only this morning that the university buildings had been wanted to be occupied on April 27th—but the situation has changed now'

Crucially, such an example should be compared to one involving ECM, since we have claimed here that the same process of "exceptional government" is involved in the derivation of IDPs; I shall consider, for the sake of closest-possible resemblance, an ECM construction with an embedded object having undergone NP-movement in the embedded as well as matrix clause:

(32) bu sabah üniversite bina-lar-ı 27 Nisan-da işgal ed-il-di
this morning university building-pl.-3.sg. 27 April-in occupy-Pass-past
san-ıl-ıyor-du, fakat şimdi durum değiş-ti
want-Pass-pres.prog.-past but now situation change-past
'This morning the university buildings were believed to have been occupied on April 27th—but the situation has changed now'

Note that the IDP with two time adverbials is not completely ungrammatical, thus arguing that its potential monoclausal character is doubtful. While it is more awkward than the "Double Passive" example involving ECM, this might well be due to the fact that the complement clause of an ECM-verb is tensed, while that of a Control verb is, being an infinitival, tenseless and thus permits modification by an adverb less felicitously.

Another suggestive fact in the discussion about the mono- versus bi-clausal nature of Turkish IDPs consists of the observation that the infinitival in these constructions can be in the negative, while in Italian "restructuring" constructions, Neg cannot remain on the lower verb, but has to "climb" along with the clitic:

Turkish:

(33) a. ?(?) Hasan iş-e al-ın-ma-mak iste-n-iyor-du
H. work-Dat. take-Pass-Neg-Inf. want-Pass-pres.progr.-past
'Hasan was wanted not to be hired'
b. ? [Hasan iş-e al-ın-ma-mağ]-a çalış-ıl-dı
H. work-Dat. take-Pass-Neg-Inf.]-Dat. want-Pass-past
'Hasan was tried not to be hired'

Italian (from Kayne 1989):

(34) a. Gianni non li vuole vedere
G. Neg. them-wants to-see
b. Gianni vuole non vederli
c. *Gianni li vuole non vedere

While the Turkish examples are not perfect, they are nevertheless not ungrammatical; on the other hand, in Italian, examples like (34c), where Clitic Climbing has taken place while leaving Neg behind are ungrammatical. This strongly suggests that the phenomena in question in these two languages must be different, in spite of the similarities pointed out earlier. More specifically, the infinitival in Turkish seems to have preserved its nature as an independent clause more strongly than its Italian counterpart.

7.3. The Nature of the Verb Sequence in IDPs:

I now turn to the nature of the "verbal complex" found in IDPs.

Under the most general assumptions, a genuine verbal complex would assign one structural Case and one external θ-role; hence, it should have just one Passive morpheme when its object undergoes NP-movement. This is the case in genuine "complex verbs"; e.g.

(35) Bu kitap nihayet oku-n -abil-di
this book finally read-Pass-abilitative-past
'This book could finally be read'

While there is a dialect that "doubles" the Passive morpheme, placing the "double" on the abilitative morpheme, such constructions are not used in the standard dialect:

(36) (*) Bu kitap nihayet oku-n-abil-in-di
this book finally read-Pass-abilitative-Pass-past
'This book could finally be read'

Crucially, the standard dialect accepts and uses Infinitival Double Passives productively, thus providing evidence that the sequence of verbs in IDPs has to be treated differently from the complex single verb of the type illustrated in (35). Note also that these "ability-verbs" are not phonological words—the "ability" morpheme, essentially homophonous with the verb *bil* 'know', doesn't harmonize with the first part of the complex. Hence, we are dealing here with a genuine (verbal) compound.

Note that if we wanted to treat the sequence of two Passive verbs in IDPs as though they formed a compound like the one in (36), a morphological "doubling" of the Passive morpheme would have to be assumed, which

a. violates a constraint against "vacuous morphemes" (cf. Marantz 1984, Kornfilt 1984), and
b. is unmotivated within the language.

On the other hand, note that in our account, the two occurrences of the morpheme are accounted for straightforwardly.

To "take seriously" both occurrences of the Passive morpheme, especially that on the matrix verb, means that the matrix verbs of IDPs have always an external thematic role to assign. This is true in general for all three verbs that take IDPs; but the verb *başla,* just like its English equivalent 'begin', has a dual character between being a Control verb (and having an external thematic role) and as a "Raising" verb (where it has no external thematic role) (cf. Perlmutter 1970). If there are no vacuous morphemes and no purely morphological Passive morpheme reduplication (without any syntactic motivation and consequences), we might expect "Infinitival Single Passives" to occur with the "raising" type of *begin,* which, indeed, is possible:

(37) kapı çal-ın-mağ-a başla-dı (ISP)
door knock-Pass-Inf.-Dat. begin-past
'The door started to be knocked'

(38) kapı çal-ın-mağ-a başla-n-dı (IDP)
door knock-Pass-Inf.-Dat. begin-Pass-past
'The door was begun to be knocked'

Hatiboğlu (1972) notes an example like (37); her example is presented here as (39):

(39) kapı hızlı hızlı çal-ın-mağ-a başla-dı
door loud loud knock-Pass-Inf.-Dat. begin-past
'The door started to be knocked very loudly'
(Op. cit. p. 115, line 20 from top)

She points out that, while in the case of (38), a corresponding (ISP) construction like (39) is possible, there is no such option for other examples which are, at first glance, similar:

(40) kapı boya-n-mağ-a başla-n-dı (IDP)
door paint-Pass-Inf.-Dat. begin-Pass-past
'The door started to be painted'
(Op. cit. p. 115, line 21 from top)

She states that in such an example, the matrix verb has to carry overt Passive marking obligatorily; thus, the following ISP version of (40) would be ungrammatical:

(41) *kapı boya-n-mağ-a başla-dı (ISP)
door paint-Pass-Inf.-Dat. begin-past
'The door started to be painted'

I conjecture that the difference pointed out here is due to the following explanation:

Although, for all practical purposes (e.g. truth conditions) (37) and (38) are synonymous, there is a finely shaded difference: In the ISP, the "event"-reading is emphasized; no conscious, volitional "beginning" is expressed; in the IDP, in contrast, the agentive, volitional reading is clear. Note that this is exactly the contrast predicted under the approach taken and the assumptions made here.

With respect to the exmples discussed, it is certainly true that one can notice some loud knocking going on; as a matter of fact, one might translate (38) and (39) as something like: 'There is a (loud) knock at the door'. However, it is harder to imagine that one would similarly notice a door starting to get more and more paint on it, without also noticing—and reporting on—the instigator(s) of such an action. Thus, the only 'begin' which is possible in this case is the "Control-begin", i.e. the verb that marks its subject with a thematic role (i.e. "agent"). Hence, once the underlying embedded object moves up in the fashion outlined in this paper so far, the thematic role assigned to that matrix subject position will have to be suppressed (because of the θ-Criterion). Therefore, only the IDP construction is possible in that case, and not the ISP option.

On the other hand, with "knocking", one can view it as an event or an action. Depending on the choice, the particular "begin" verb is chosen that is compatible with either view. For the "event" reading, the Raising verb "begin" will be chosen; in that case, the original embedded object, having arrived in matrix subject position, can happily stay there without giving rise to a θ-Criterion violation, since its landing site is not assigned any thematic role, and the matrix verb does not need to (in fact, cannot) be marked with Passive morphology.

In contrast, for the "action" reading, the "Control-begin" is selected. Since this verb does mark its subject position with a thematic role, Passive morphology on the matrix verb is triggered, in order to prevent the original embedded object to violate the θ-Criterion after having landed in matrix subject position.

One implication is that the thematic properties of the individual verbs remain intact even with CP-Transparency.

Furthermore, the two verbs in IDPs can be separated under certain circumstances; note the following examples:

(42) [üniversite-ler-e gir-il-meğ]-e dün-den beri çalış-ıl-ıyor
university-pl.-Dat. enter-Pass-Inf]-Dat. yesterday-Abl. since try-Pass-pres.pr.
'(one) has been trying since yesterday (for) the universities to be entered'

(43) [yeni köprü-den geç-il-meğ]- yarın sabah başla-n-acak
[new bridge-Abl. pass-Pass-Inf]-Dat. tomorrow morning begin-Pass-Fut.
'It will be begun from tomorrow morning on (for) the new bridge to be passed'
(i.e. 'One will begin from tomorrow morning on to go over the new bridge')

This would pose a problem for a word-formation based approach to CP-Transparency (cf. Picallo 1990 where, based on Catalan, such an approach is advanced for the classical "Restructuring" cases in Romance), since genuine compounds cannot be separated at all:

(44) a. Hasan her sabah **dua** **ed-er**
H. every morning prayer do-Aorist
'Hasan prays every morning'
b. *Hasan **dua** her sabah **ed-er**

(45) a. Hasan her sabah **kahvaltı sofra-sın-ı** kur-ar
H. every morning breakfast table-3.sg.-Acc. set-Aorist
'Every morning, Hasan sets the breakfast table'
b. *Hasan **kahvaltı** her sabah **sofra-sın-ı** kur-ar

One might claim that in (44) and (45), the reason why the two conjuncts of the respective compounds cannot be separated is the Case Filter, rather than the inseparability of conjuncts per se; in (44), the nominal *dua* 'prayer' is not morphologically marked for Case and might therefore need Case assigned to it by the verb, under adjacency; in (45), the nominal *kahvaltı* 'breakfast' might need Case for similar reasons and would get it from the 3. person singular "Agreement" marker -sı(n) —again, under adjacency (cf. Kornfilt 1984).

But even if the Case Filter were the only explanation for the facts in (44) and (45), it couldn't explain the inseparability of single complex verbs of the type illustrated in (33), i.e. verbal compounds that behave like single verbs (at least with respect to Passive morphology):

(46) a. Hasan başvuru-sun-u dün **bitir-ebil**-di
H. application-3.sg.-Acc. yesterday finish-Abil-past
'Hasan could finish his application yesterday'
(i.e. Hasan was able to finish his application yesterday')
b. *Hasan başvuru -sun -u **bitir**-dün-**ebil**-di
c. *Hasan başvuru -sun -u **bitir-e**-dün-**bil**-di

The ungrammaticality of (46)c. is especially revealing, since a morpheme like -DA 'also' can show up there:

(46) d. Hasan başvuru -sun -u **bitir-me -ye**-de-**bil**-ir-di
H. application-3.sg.-Acc. finish-Neg.-Abil.1-also-Abil2-Aor.-past

I conclude, therefore, that the verbal complex in Turkish IDPs is not a verbal complex generated by word-formation.

It should be noted, incidentally, that in the Romance languages the "verbal complex" can be separated as well, as long as the intervening material is non-thematic (cf. Grimshaw 1988, Rizzi 1982). Having mentioned this fact, I will not pursue it further.

We have seen in this section that in Turkish IDPs, no genuine, inseparable verbal complex is formed, and that the two verbs retain their independent q-marking capabilities. We have thus concluded that Turkish IDPs don't have a monoclausal S-Structure, and that therefore no Reanalysis applies in their derivation.

8. CONCLUSIONS AND SOME FURTHER OBSERVATIONS:

This paper has presented a construction in Turkish that, at first glance, shares a basic property with so-called Reanalysis constructions in other languages: it exhibits apparent violations of locality. I have argued that the descriptive as well explanatorily best analysis for this construction is one that doesn't involve Reanalysis (in any of its guises) at all, but rather Exceptional Government without Exceptional Case Marking. Of course, Exceptional Government (but with Exceptional Case Marking) is needed independently elsewhere in the language. While this does seem to be a marked phenomenon and lexically restricted to a very small set of verbs, this is certainly a fact across languages for ECM and hence a fact of life we have to live with. Furthermore, the very fact that both the class of ECM verbs and that of "IDP verbs" in Turkish are much smaller than the class of ECM verbs and of "Restructuring" verbs, respectively, in many other languages (as a matter of fact, they are restricted to three verbs in each class in Turkish) is highly suggestive and in line with the proposal that essentially one and the same process is involved.

If this is so, then UG must allow for the phenomenon of Exceptional Government <u>without</u> Exceptional Case Marking, and languages other than Turkish should also exhibit its effects.

I am indebted to David Pesetsky (personal communication) for having pointed out to me that English—at least the British variety in its older stages—might be one such language.. For example:

(47) The book was tried to be read.

It appears that such constructions are grammatical in some British dialects and were actually grammatical in general at a former stage of English in general; if so, it would be interesting to find out further properties of the infinitival complements in Control structures and elsewhere in the language at that stage. Visser 1973 states that such constructions are first documented at the end of the fourteenth century and were found in British English until the recent past; some examples from Visser (op. cit.) follow:

(48) June 7 [the ship] was endeavoured to be fetched off by the Dutch.
(1666 Pepys's Diary, ed. Braybrooke; in Visser 1973, p. 2449)

(49) She talks of the house having been attempted to be broken open two or three times.
(1741 Richardson, Pamela I; in Visser, op. cit., p. 2449)

(50) A sensational atmosphere is being attempted to be created.
(1950 Daily Telegraph, 17 March 7/6; Visser, op. cit., p. 2449)

(51) Each station was planned to be worked by a small band of B.B.C. engineers.
(1945 Sunday Times, 8 July 5/3; in Visser, op. cit. p. 2449)

Interestingly enough, the verbs found with this English IDP construction are quite similar to their counterparts in Turkish. Questions worth investigating might be about the reasons that made modern stages of English lose the IDP, and about the differences between American and British English, since it appears that today's native speakers of the latter accept examples of the IDP somewhat more readily than speakers of the former.

I would like to conjecture that Exceptional Government without concomitant Case marking is a rather opaque phenomenon and thus unstable diachronically. What might make it possible—indeed quite stable—in Turkish is the fact that the infinitival clauses themselves are obviously NPs, thus exhibiting the Case properties of the matrix verbs on themselves. Indeed, this paper has suggested that the categorial nature of the complements lies behind the difference between ECM constructions and what we saw here: Since ECM verbs in Turkish can take fully verbal (rather than nominal) complements, their Case is not discharged to the complement, but rather to the exceptionally governed subject of that complement. But since Control verbs take only nominal complements, their Case is discharged to that complement and thus becomes unavailable for assignment under Exceptional Government.

My conjecture, then, is that in older stages of English, infinitivals were nominals, just as they still are in Turkish. Thus, Exceptional Government without Exceptional Case was possible. However, the infinitivals in modern English are not nominal any longer—at least not clarly so, thus making an opaque, unstable situation impossible. If this conjecture is on the right track, it should be possible to find some independent evidence for the change in the categorial status of English infinitives. I leave the nature of such evidence as an open question.

NOTES:

*Research for this paper has been funded in part by the American Council of Learned Societies and the National Endowment for the Humanities, in form of a "Fellowship for Recent PhDs" awarded by the ACLS, and a grant by the Institute of Turkish Studies. I would like to thank the members of the MIT Linguistics community for their hospitality during the period of my leave from Syracuse University, during which this paper was written, and to Syracuse University for granting me a research leave. I am grateful to Aslı Göksel, Sumru Özsoy, Engin Sezer, Gönül Alpay Tekin, şinasi Tekin, and Mehmet Yanılmaz for sharing their native judgements with me, to Noam Chomsky, Éva Csató Johanson, Gabriella Hermon, Susumu Kuno, Richard Larson, Beth Levin, David Pesetsky, and Luigi Rizzi for very helpful discussions, to Myron Lichtblau for his help with the Spanish data, and to Robert Freidin for giving me the opportunity to present this paper to the Princeton Workshop on Comparative Grammars 1989 as well as for his comments on a previous draft of this paper. All errors of fact and interpretation are my own.

[1] Since the original presentation of this material in 1989 and the writing of the original draft in 1990, I have been pursuing an alternative analysis, using the idea of syntactic verb raising, made possible by lack of INFL in these constructions. However, for the purposes of this volume, I viewed it as more appropriate to retain the original analysis.

[2] Another way to describe this complementation type is to say that verbs that take fully finite complement CPs can also license bare IPs. I shall not take a stand on this issue in this paper.

[3] There is a potential problem here: if CP-Transparency can "save" the trace in embedded subject position by enabling the matrix verb to govern that position, why couldn't it do so after stage 1 of our derivation? Then, the embedded subject of the infinitive might receive Case, and hence wouldn't need to move to matrix position. If this were possible, the matrix verb wouldn't have to be Passive, and the resulting ungrammatical construction with the passive infinitive and the active matrix would be predicted, incorrectly, to be good.

However, this is less of a problem than appears at first glance.

Note that of the three Control verbs that enter the IDP construction, two select the inherent oblique Case of Dative: *çalış* 'try' and *başla* 'begin'. It is a general assumption that such selectional requirements are satisfied at Deep Structure, as opposed to requirements of Structural Case, which are satisfied at S-Structure. Furthermore, inherent Case is "assigned" by a Case bearer only to those elements that Case bearer also theta-marks (i.e. assigns a theta role to). Structural Case, on the other hand, depends on structural configurations only; therefore, a structural Case marker can assign its (structural) Case to an element that it may, but doesn't have to, also assign a thematic role to—as long as the configuration permits such Case assignment.

Since, in an IDP construction, the two verbs in question "discharge" their (only) Case by selecting for Dative-marked infinitival clauses at D-Structure, they have no Case left to discharge at any later stage of the derivation. Furthermore, since it can be independently shown that they are not transitive verbs (i.e. have no structural Case to assign), we wouldn't expect them to be able to Case mark the embedded subject NP, since that NP does not receive any thematic role from the matrix verb.

It follows that, in spite of "CP-Transparency", the matrix verb would <u>not</u> be able to assign any Case to the embedded subject. As a result, that subject would have to move into the matrix subject position nevertheless, with the ultimate effect of making Passive morphology on the matrix verb necessary.

What about constructions with the matrix verb *iste* 'want', however? This verb is a structural Case-marker. Hence, it could— potentially— Case-mark at a level of derivation later than D-structure, especially in the constructions in question, via CP-Transparency.

I would like to suggest that, due to its nominal nature, the infinitival clause needs Case—and, being a complement of the transitive *iste*, this would be structural Case. Hence, there would be no Case left to assign to the embedded subject, which would thus have to move to matrix subject position.

This account presupposes the primacy of a θ-marked complement over a non-θ-marked element when both are candidates for <u>structural</u> Case marking by one and the same Case marker. While this makes intuitive sense, it is not necessarily expected under general assumptions.

Alternatively, one might say that the Case assigned to the complement is <u>inherent</u> objective Case—or, in the framework of Belletti 1988, Partitive Case; given that θ-marking seems to play a role in the assignment of this Case, this assumption is plausible. But then, the verb should have its <u>Structural</u> Case left to assign to the embedded subject, and apparently it does not—hence, this does not seem to be a viable alternative.

Yet another conceivable proposal may be some kind of "Superiority" effect— if a nominal phrase **N** dominates another nominal phrase **n**, and both need Case in any given syntactic representation, a Case assigner that could potentially Case mark either **N** or **n** will assign Case to **N**.

One other question arises with respect to CP-Transparency: what happens if, instead of a Passive infinitival, we have an active infinitival clause under one of the three matrix verbs in question? Here, a PRO subject would be governed by the matrix verb, leading to a violation of the PRO-theorem. I would therefore say that "CP-Transparency" doesn't apply when it would lead to a violation of a universal principle (as here in the case of the PRO-Theorem) (or, alternatively, it does apply optionally, and the resulting ungrammatical structure is discarded); it does apply when its non-application would lead to such a violation (here, of the Case Filter).

[4] Yet another derivation that we can rule out is the following: NP-movement of the embedded object to embedded subject position, and then "Passive" in the matrix. The second would, under usual circumstances, involve NP-movement of the whole infinitival clause, thus turning it into a Sentential Subject. But, first of all, we have to remember that two of the matrix verbs in question are inherent Case markers; their complement would not undergo NP-movement as a consequence, and the subject position would be occupied by an expletive **pro**. The third matrix verb, a structural Case marker, assigns "abstract" objective Case to the infinitival; such assignment requires adjacency to the verb (for discussion, see Kornfilt 1984 and 1990), and, once again, the subject position of the resulting S-Structure is occupied by an expletive **pro**.

Secondly, even if the infinitivals in question could become the subjects of the matrix clause in principle, this is not so in IDPs; we know this, because where the infinitive is transitive, its object becomes the subject of the matrix and exhibits all relevant subjecthood behavior (cf. George and Kornfilt 1977). Hence, this type of "Double Passive" is not a viable alternative derivation.

However, this alternative could be an intermediate step in the derivation of the correct S-structure: Passive within the infinitival, and (impersonal) Passive in the matrix, with the infinitival remaining in complement position. Now, the original embedded object violates the Case Filter in its derived position (i.e. subject of infinitive) and hence raises to matrix subject position.

This is a derivation almost identical to the one proposed in this paper, with the only difference that the derivation proposed in the text involves two steps, while the derivation just considered seems to involve three. Hence, one might assume that the principle of economy of derivation (cf. Chomsky 1989) would dictate the choice of the analysis proposed in the text. However, given that no genuine syntactic operation is involved in what I called the "intermediate step" in this alternative (i.e. the formation of "intransitive Passive"), nothing much is at stake here.

REFERENCES

Aissen, J. and D. Perlmutter. (1976). "Clause Reduction in Spanish," *BLS 2*. 1-30.

Baker, M., K. Johnson, and I. Roberts. (1989). "Passive Arguments Raised," *Linguistic Inquiry* 20, 219-251.

Bayer, J. and J. Kornfilt. (1990). "Restructuring Effects in German," In: E. Engdahl,

M. Reape, M. Mellor, and R. P. Cooper (eds.): *Parametric Variation in Germanic and Romance: Proceedings for a DYANA Workshop*, September 1989. Edinburgh Working Papers in Cognitive Science, Centre for Cognitive Science,University of Edinburgh. 21-42.

Belletti, A. (1988). "The Case of Unaccusatives," *Linguistic Inquiry* 19, 1-34.

Bordelois, I. (1988). "Causatives: From Lexicon to Syntax," *NLLT* 6, 57-93.

Chomsky, N. (1981). *Lectures on Government and Binding*. Dordrecht: Foris.

Chomsky, N. (1986). *Barriers*. Cambridge, MA: MIT Press.

Chomsky, N. (1989). "Some Notes on Economy of Derivation and Representation," In: I. Laka and A. K. Mahajan (eds.), *MIT Working Papers in Linguistics*, Vol. 10: *Functional Heads and Clause Structure*, MIT, Cambridge, Mass. 43-74.

George, L. & J. Kornfilt. (1977). "Infinitival Double Passives in Turkish," In: *NELS 7*. 65-79.

George, L. & J. Kornfilt. (1981). "Finiteness and Boundedness in Turkish," In: F. Heny (ed.), *Binding and Filtering*; Croom Helm, London, and MIT Press, Cambridge, Massachusetts. 105-127.

Grimshaw, J. (1988). "The Representation of Complex Predicates," Lecture and handout.

Haegeman, L. and H. v. Riemsdijk. (1986). " 'Verb Projection' Raising, Scope, and the Typology of Verb Movement Rules," *Linguistic Inquiry* 17, 417-466.

Hatiboğlu, V. (1972). *Türkçenin Sözdizimi*. (The Syntax of Turkish.) Ankara: Türk Dil Kurumu Yayınları (=Publications of the Turkish Language Organization), #353.

Kayne, R. S. (1989). "Null Subjects and Clitic Climbing," In: O. Jaeggli and K. Safir (eds.), *Approaches to the Null Subject Parameter*, Dordrecht: Reidel; 239-261.

Kiss, K. É. (1987). *Configurationality in Hungarian*. Dordrecht: Reidel.

Kornfilt, J. (1976). "Some Aspects of Turkish Subject Raising", ms., Harvard University.

Kornfilt, J. (1977). "A Note on Subject Raising," *Linguistic Inquiry* 8, 736-742.

Kornfilt, J. (1984). *Case Marking, Agreement, and Empty Categories in Turkish*. Harvard University Ph.D. dissertation. Cambridge, MA.

Kornfilt, J. (1990). "Remarks on Headless Partitives and Case in Turkish," In: M. Nespor and J. Mascaró (eds.), *Grammar in Progress: GLOW Essays for Henk van Riemsdijk*. Dordrecht: Foris Publications. 285-303.

Kuno, S. (1976). "Subject Raising," In: M Shibatani (ed.), *Syntax and Semantics*, Vol. 5: *Japanese Generative Grammar*. New York: Academic Press. 17-49.

Luján, M. (1980). "Clitic Promotion and Mood in Spanish Verbal Complements," *Linguistics* 18; 381-484.

Morin, Y. C. and M. St. Amour. (1977). "Description Historique des Constructions Infinitives du Français," In: *Montréal Working Papers in Linguistics* 9; 113-152.

Mahajan, A. K. (1989). "Agreement and Agreement Phrases," In: I. Laka and A. K. Mahajan (eds.), *MIT Working Papers in Linguistics*, Vol. 10: *Functional Heads and Clause Structure.*, MIT, Cambridge, Mass. 217-252.

Marantz, A. (1984). *On the Nature of Grammatical Relations*. Cambridge, MA: MIT Press.

Perlmutter, D. (1970). "The Two Verbs *Begin* ," In: R. A. Jacobs & P. S. Rosenbaum (eds.), *Readings in English Transformational Grammar*. Waltham, MA: Ginn & Company.

Picallo, M. C. (1990). "Restructuring and Modal Verbs in Catalan," *NLLT* 8, 285-311.

Rivero, M.-L. (1989) "Exceptional Case Marking Effects in Rumanian Subjunctive Complements," In: D. Wanner and D. A. Kibbee (eds.), *New Analyses in Romance Languages: Papers from the LSRL 18.* Amsterdam: Benjamins.

Rizzi, L. (1982). "A Restructuring Rule," *Issues in Italian Syntax.* Dordrecht: Foris. 1-48. (Originally published as "A Restructuring Rule in Italian Syntax", in: S. J. Keyser (ed.), *Recent Transformational Studies in European Languages.* (1978). Cambridge, MA: MIT Press.

Yükseker, H. (1987). "Turkish Nominal Compounds," In: P. Avery and H. Yükseker (eds.), *Toronto Working Papers in Linguistics,* Vol. 7. Department of Linguistics, University of Toronto. 83-102.

Zubizarreta, M.-L. (1982). *On the Relationship of the Lexicon to Syntax.* PhD dissertation, MIT, Cambridge, Mass.

WAYNE HARBERT

SOME OTHER POSSIBLE CASES OF NONLOCAL DEPENDENCIES: COMMENTS ON THE PAPER BY JAKLIN KORNFILT

Jaklin Kornfilt's contribution to this volume touches on a key problem in syntax—the question of what sorts of devices the theory of grammar should have at its disposal for explaining the fairly frequent instances in natural language in which typically local grammatical processes give the appearance of operating at a distance (as, for example, when a characteristically clause-bounded rule applies in a domain consisting of two clauses). The particular case she considers—the IDP construction of Turkish—results to be only an apparent, not a real instance of non-local application of NP movement, under the analysis she advances: the occurrence of passive morphology in both the main and the subordinate clause is not the result of any particular linkage between the INFL nodes of the two clauses (though she does explore an alternative possible analysis, under which the two are linked by head-raising). Rather, passive morphology in the main clause is simply forced when the embedded clause is passive by the fact that the failure of the passivized object to get case by moving to matrix subject position would result in ill-formedness. The analysis requires no special assumptions about locality conditions, aside from the claim that try-type verbs can in some languages exceptionally govern but not case-mark the subjects of their complements. In particular, a satisfactory account of IDP's does not require the assumption of restructuring/ reanalysis, and the consequent weakening of the Projection Principle. However, as Kornfilt suggests, the question of whether such devices can be wholly eliminated depends on the availability of alternative solutions to the numerous other putative "restructuring effects" reported in the literature. The larger question raised by the paper, therefore, is whether analysis of those other effects ever requires us to admit reanalysis as a possible grammatical process. In at least some of the cases, the availability of alternatives is less clear than it is in the case of IDP's. Rather than directly discussing Kornfilt's plausible and well-argued account of IDP's, therefore, I will confine my remarks to a survey of some other phenomena which appear relevant to the problem of restructuring and which will have to be taken into account in any general study of the phenomenon, excluding some of the more widely discussed ones, such as the case of clitic climbing in the Romance languages.

Approaches to apparent 'nonlocal' application of characteristically local processes fall, in the main, into three types. In the first, the relevant locality condition is relaxed to admit such application under specific circumstances.

In the second, it is assumed that the locality condition applies in its most restrictive form and that the requisite local relationship between the affected elements is established by (overt or abstract) movement. The third type of approach involves appeal to non-standard assumptions about structure which have the effect of minimizing the syntactic distance between the related elements without movement. Restructuring and the assumption of dual structural representations are instances of this last type. It is not at all unusual to find solutions of all three types proposed for individual phenomena. Consider, for example, the case of anaphor binding in the Russian and German sentences in (1). The anaphor is bound here to an antecedent, apparently across an intervening subject, in violation of the SSC effect of Principle A.

(1) a. On ne razresaet mne [PRO proizvodit' opyty nad soboj] (Rappaport 1982)
He not permitted me to-perform experiments on himself(/myself)
'He did not permit me to perform an experiment on him (/myself)

b. weil Hans [Peter für sich /(ihn) arbeiten] läßt/sah
because Hans Peter for self/him to-work lets/saw
'because Hans let/saw Peter work for him'

The first class of solutions to the problem of nonlocal binding in such cases, represented by Rappaport (1982), Yang (1984), among others, accounts for it through a relaxation of the relevant locality principle. The local domain for binding is parameterized, and Russian observes a less restricted version of it than English. A second possible account retains the assumption of the restrictive version of the locality condition and assumes only the apparent biclausal structure, but assumes that satisfaction of the locality requirement is assessed by reference to the abstract structure resulting from LF head-to-head movement of the anaphor into the main clause by way of the lower clause INFL. Such an account has been suggested for Russian by Bailyn (1991), following work by Cole et. al. (1990) on apparent long-distance binding in other languages. The third type of approach, the restructuring/clause union/dual structure approach was represented early on in the clause-union account of Reis (1976) for German facts like (1b), and more recently, in Harbert and Srivastav (1988), who follow Haegeman and van Riemsdijk (1986) and others in positing a dual structure representation for such sentences. Apparent nonlocal binding is possible because the sentence is monoclausal on one of the coexisting representations. I will return to this claim below.

A similarly wide range of accounts has been advanced for the apparently nonlocal assignment of nominative case to in situ objects, as in (2), from den Besten (1985).

(2) daß [dem Museum die Urne geschenkt worden] ist
that the museum-Dat the Urn-Nom given been perf-aux
'that the Urn was given to the museum'

Den Besten's account of these facts involves a partial relaxation of the government condition on case assignment; an NP governed by a non-case-assigning X^0 can, in some languages, receive case from the governor of the projection of that X^0, by 'Chain-Government'. (See also Sigurðsson (1989) for a similar idea about nominative objects in Icelandic, expressed in terms of government under relativized minimality.) In addition, however, there have been a number of attempts to account for such exceptional assignment of nominative case to objects of verbs by assuming that the requisite local relationship between INFL and the affected NP is established through movement. See Harbert and Toribio (1991) and the references cited there. Finally, other approaches to facts of this type have invoked nonstandard assumptions about structure. So, for example, Webelhuth (1985) claims that NP-movement is not required in order for objects of German passives to get nominative case because INFL originates in VP in German. Thus, in at least many instances solutions of all three types are available a priori. Moreover, we operate without clear guidelines concerning which is the most likely to succeed in individual instances, save that the burden of proof lies on those accounts which require us to add to our inventory of descriptive devices or to weaken/parameterize well-motivated conditions or principles (e.g., the Projection Principle, or locality conditions on binding and case assignment).

In the following, I will list some other cases of apparent crossclausal dependencies of the sort that may suggest reanalysis, some of which are quite curious, and which offer additional pieces to the puzzle posed by such dependencies. I will begin by mentioning a Norwegian construction which merits consideration in this discussion because it is, on the surface, at least, quite similar to the Turkish IDP. It is not entirely clear to me that the Turkish and Norwegian constructions do in fact represent the same syntactic phenomenon, though—there are, at least, some potentially significant differences. The construction is illustrated in the examples in (3) [The following Norwegian data are from Christen (1985), with the exception of 3c–e from Engh (1984).]:

(3) a. Boken ble anbefalt oversatt
book-the was recommended translated

b. Boken ble forsøkt anbefalt oversatt
book-the was attempted recommended translated.
c. Møtet ventes holdt
meeting-the is-expected held
d. oppgåver som er tenkt løyste i budsjettperioden
tasks which are thought carried out in budget-period-the
e. Journalisten ble forsøkt rapportert skutt
Journalist-the was attempted reported shot

It is, according to Engh, an increasingly frequent construction in legal and bureaucratic language. As in Turkish, the sentence is not well formed unless the main clause, as well as the embedded clause, is passive—that is, contains a passive/perfect participle, or a verb with the s-passive affix as in (3c). Interestingly, as (4) shows, the second participle need not be strictly passive, but may be a perfect participle of an unaccusative, though not of a basic intransitive verb.

(4) a. Fjellklatrerne ble meldt omkommet
the-mountain-climbers were reported perished
b. *Fjellklatrerne ble meldt jublet
the-mountain-climbers were reported rejoiced

So far as I can determine, the earliest discussion in the generative literature of this construction is that of Engh (1984), who gave it its by now standard label, the Complex Passive. Taraldsen (1984) and Christensen (1985) consider it an instance of reanalysis—"projection compounding"—, which produces derived structures of the form in (5), where the topmost V-bar is in effect doubly headed, subject to the requirement that the heads involved are not featurally distinct from each other. It is this requirement which insures that both verbs have passive form. (Conversely, Taraldsen uses this same requirement to insure the inadmissibility of passive and unaccusative verbs in causative constructions, which is illustrated in (6)):

(5) $[_S \text{NP}_k [_{V'} \text{V}_i [_{V'} \text{V}_j \; t_k]]]$

(6) a. Vi lot oversette boken
We let translate book-the
b. *Vi lot bli oversatt boken
We let be translated book-the
c. *Det ble latt oversette boken
it was let translate book-the
d. *Vi lot utkomme boken
We let appear book-the

Perhaps problematic for such an account is the fact that the verbs need not be adjacent; as (7) shows, matrix arguments may intervene between them, though Christensen claims that here the underscored string has itself undergone reanalysis, becoming a complex verb.

(7) ?Boken ble anbefalt oss forsøkt oversatt
book-the was recommended to-us attempted translated

A different analysis of these constructions is offered by Hellan (1984), who suggests that the Complex Passive constructions are derived by lexical rule. There isn't sufficient time to rehearse the details of these analyses, so I will attempt simply to point out some differences between this construction and the Turkish IDP construction. One difference—the realization of the embedded verb as a participle, rather than an infinitival form—I will presume has to do simply with the difference in the realization of passive in the two languages, though it is perhaps important that when the periphrastic passive is used, the passive auxiliary shows up only once—in the main clause.

More interesting is the fact that the Norwegian Complex Passive appears with a much wider range of main verbs that the Turkish IDP (Engh counts 84 different verbs in his sample of attestations) and that these are of a variety of semantic types. They include, apparently, all passivizable verbs taking clausal complements of any sort (control complements or finite complements), except for those whose complement clauses are obligatorily introduced by a preposition, as in (8).

(8) a. Det ble advart *(mot) å oversette boken
It was warned (against) to translate book-the
b. *Boken ble advart mot oversatt
book-the was warned against translated

Taraldsen proposes that this restriction is yet another consequence of the featural nondistinctness condition on Projection Compounding. Christensen devotes considerable discussion to reconciling such an account with the fact that Norwegian apparently does have Verb-Preposition reanalysis in other cases, such as pseudo-passives like (9):

(9) Boken ble advart mot
Book-the was warned against

The list of main verbs with which Complex Passives occur, according to Engh, includes factives, such as REPORT, as well as non-factives, such as TRY and BEGIN, as the examples in (3) show. Significantly, Engh reports that they also include such object control verbs as be 'ask', anbefale 'recommend', and tilby 'offer'. As (3b) and (3d) show, moreover, in Norwegian, unlike

Turkish, the matrix and embedded agents need not be understood as identical. This at least appears to suggest that there is nothing to gain from the extension of an INFL-to-INFL raising account to these Complex Passives, as Kornfilt has suggested is among the possibilities in Turkish, since the main empirical merit of such a move in Turkish and the Romance languages—insuring restriction of the phenomenon to subject control predicates—does not apply in Norwegian. Moreover, Norwegian clearly does not satisfy the strong INFL condition such an analysis would appear to require, since Norwegian has no person/number agreement morphology, and does not allow referential pro-drop.

I have nothing else to say about this construction except to note that it appears, on first consideration, to be amenable to a non-restructuring account of the sort proposed by Kornfilt for Turkish IDP's, and to remark that the literature on it, so far as I can determine, has failed to address many important questions, including whether there is evidence bearing on the monoclausality versus biclausality of the construction (e.g., from scrambling, adverb cooccurrence, scope and the like).

A second class of phenomena which come under consideration as potentially involving reanalysis, as Kornfilt has noted, involves object agreement between main verb and embedded object in Hindi and Hungarian infinitive constructions. Examples are given in (10) and (11). (I am grateful to Erika Mitchell for providing me with the Hungarian examples and for bringing these facts to my attention. They are treated at length in Kiss (1987).).

(10) raam-ne roTii khaanii caahii (Mahajan 1988)
Ram-Erg bread-Fem eat-Inf-Fem want-Perf. Pst-Fem

(11) (Examples from Erika Mitchell, p.c.)
a. (Én) (egy) könyvet akarok próbálni olvasni
I a book want-1sg.-INDEF try-Inf read
'I want to try to read a book'
b. (Én) a könyvet akarom próbálni olvasni
I the book want-1sg.-DEF try-Inf read-INF
'I want to try to read the book'
c. (Én) a könyvtárban akarok olvasni könyvet
I the library-in want-1sg.-INDEF read-INF book-Acc
'I want to read a book in the library'
d. (Én) a könyvtárban akarom olvasni a könyvet
I the library-in want-1sg.-DEF read-INF the book-Acc
'I want to read the book in the library'

In Hindi, when the lower participle agrees in gender with the object (which it does optionally), the main verb must agree with that object as well. This is illustrated in (10). Mahajan analyzes these constructions as biclausal at all levels. He considers the possibility, following Kayne, that agreement here is accomplished through AGR-to-INFL-to-INFL raising, but rejects this alternative (on what seem to me to be insufficient grounds[1]) in favor of an analysis under which it is the object itself which is raised, successive-cyclically, to the main clause Spec Agr position. In that position it controls the main clause agreement directly. This in turn is followed by LF raising of the verb to L-mark the relevant nodes, similar to clitic climbing in the Romance languages.

Such a movement could yield the observed order in (10) under the assumption of leftward Specs. It is less obvious that this analysis can be extended to the apparently similar cases in Hungarian in (11), however. Here, the matrix verb again agrees with the embedded object with respect to the definiteness feature. This is true whether that object is in the matrix clause focus position to the left of the matrix verb, as in (11a,b), <u>or</u> in the expected embedded clause object position, to the right of the embedded verb, as in (11c, d). In the latter case, it seems improbable that the object has been moved to the matrix Spec Agr, since Hungarian has leftward specifiers. Kiss argues for a dual representation approach to these constructions, taking object agreement with the matrix verb as one of the major arguments for the monoclausal dimension of the representation. Alternatively, however, it appears as if they are likely candidates for an INFL-to-INFL raising approach, under which the lower clause object agreement is carried along by head to head movement to the matrix clause; such an approach would seem to have the advantage of accounting for the fact that the class of matrix predicates involved is apparently restricted to subject control verbs. However, some means would still have to be found to account under such an analysis for the other major argument for monoclausality advanced by Kiss—the relatively free scambling between matrix and embedded clause constituents in these constructions.

Still further facts potentially bearing on the proper treatment of apparent reanalysis constructions, from Finnish, are illustrated in (12). Again, I am thankful to Erika Mitchell for bringing these facts to my attention. The phenomenon they represent could be remotely related to the one just discussed for Hungarian, given the genetic relationship between the two languages, though it is of a rather different sort. In Finnish, the unexpected relationship between the matrix verb and the embedded object is not one of agreement, but of case assignment.

The facts are as follows: Singular objects of verbs in Finnish normally take the ending -n, which is identical to the genitive case, as in (12a). However, in some contexts, including sentences containing modals of obligation, such as täytyy 'must', the object takes a zero ending nondistinct from the nominative case. In Karlsson's pedagogical grammar of Finnish (1983), these surface nominative and genitive cases on objects are treated as morphological variants of an abstract accusative case—an assumption reflected in my glosses. Evidence for this is provided by the fact that pronouns appear in distinct accusative forms in both contexts, and that in certain forms, including the plural, objects in both contexts take the same ending, t, which is again nondistinct from the nominative plural ending. This is illustrated in (12c, d).

(12) a. Irma avaa ikkuna-n (Karlsson 1983)
Irma opens door-Acc=Gen
b. Minun täytyy ostaa kirja
I-GSg. must buy book-Acc=Nom
c. Seija avasi ikkuna-t
Seija opened windows-Acc=Nom
d. Minun täytyy avata kirja-t
I-GSg. must open windows-Acc=Nom

Significantly, as (13b) shows, 'must' also triggers the appearance of surface nominative case on the object of a clausal complement of the verb with which it occurs, even when the verb in question is an object-control verb, such as käskeä 'order'. Thus, in (13b), both the matrix object and the embedded object appear in nominative case forms. As (13a) shows, in the absence of 'must', both the NP object of 'order' and the object of its clausal complement are in the genitive case. (In both cases, the verb also assigns lexical illative to its infinitival complement.)

(13) (Examples from Erika Mitchell, p.c.)
a. Minä haluan käskeä tuon miehen maalaamaan talon
I-Nom want-1sg. order that-A=G man-A=G paint-Ger-Ill house-A=Gen
'I want to order that man to paint the house.'
b. Minun täytyy käskeä tuo mies maalaamaan talo
I-G must order-1INF that-A=Nom man-A=N paint-Ger-Ill house A=Nom
c. Minä haluan käskeä hänet yrittämään maalata talon
I-Nom want order-1INF her-Acc try-Ger-Ill paint-INF house-A=Gen
d. Minun täytyy käskeä hänet yrittämään maalata talo
I-Gen must. order-1INF her -Acc try-Ger-Ill paint-INF house-A=Nom

That is, once again we see an apparently non-local dependency between a matrix clause INFL and an embedded clause object—of a sort that makes us think of reanalysis. This kind of extended assignment of nominative/ accusative case, apparently down into the embedded clause, occurs only in complement infinitive clauses. As the examples in (13e) and (f) show, the presence or absence of 'must' in the matrix clause has no effect on the case of an object contained in an infinitival adjunct clause.

e. Heitin poikaystäväni pois aloittakseni uuden elämän
   toss-P-1sg. boyfriend-A=G-1sg. away start-Inf-Trans-1sg. new life-A=G
   'I got rid of my boyfriend so I could start a new life.'
f. Minun täytyi heitää poikaystäväni pois aloittakseni uuden elämän
   I-Gen must toss boyfriend-A=G-1sg. away start-Inf-1sg. new lifeA=G
   'I had to get rid of my boyfriend so I could start a new life.'

Erika Mitchell is currently undertaking an extensive examination of the properties of these constructions, but I will venture a few possibly premature speculations about them. The primary question is why the object of the apparent complement clause should behave as if it were the object of the main clause for purposes of case determination. CP-transparency by itself will not provide a sufficient answer, since that would yield only external government of the embedded subject—not the embedded object. Object raising of the sort that Mahajan suggests for Hindi is counterindicated by the order of constituents. Alternatively, one could imagine that it remains an embedded clause object, but that its case is determined by the content of the matrix INFL by way of transmission of the relevant case feature from the main to the embedded clause INFL—mediated, possibly, by INFL to INFL raising and resultant coindexing. Problematic for such an account is the fact that these Finnish constructions (unlike those in Hungarian) are apparently not subject control constructions, as such an analysis would seem to predict given the assumption that I-to-I raising will result in coindexing of subjects (cf. (13d) . Another possibility, of course, is that the constructions in question involve a dual representation, and the embedded object is, at some level, in fact a main clause object. In conclusion, therefore, it appears that neither CP-transparency nor I-to-I raising can provide a sufficient account for all apparent restructuring phenomena.

I will conclude by examining one more possible instance of reanalysis, discussed in Harbert and Srivastav (1988). This involves the partial transparency of certain types of infinitival complements in Hindi and German to binding. For the sake of brevity, I will refer just to the facts of German. The Hindi facts, noted for the first time in our paper, are parallel in most relevant respects. In German causative constructions with lassen 'let', anaphors contained in adjunct phrases within the complement clause, as in (15a), but not in subcategorized object positions within that clause, as in (15b,c,d), may be bound to the higher subject. This was pointed out by Reis (1976) (whose examples we use here), and in much subsequent literature.

(14) a. ashok ne lalitaa se apne liye caay banaane ko kahaa
Ashok Erg Lalita-Obj self for tea to-make-prt said
b. siita ne raadhaa ko apnii bahan ke saath khelne ke liye kahaa
Sita Erg Radha Obj self's sister with to play asked
c. jon ne merii ko [PRO apne liye kamiiz laane ko] kahaa
John Erg Mary to self for shirt bring asked
d. *Ashok-ne Lalitaa-ko [PRO apnaa/uskaa vaadaa yaad karne] ko kahaa
Ashok-Erg Lalita-to self's/his promise remember-Inf said
e. *Ashok-ne Lalitaa-ko [PRO apnaa/uskaa khayaal rakhne] ko kahaa
Ashok-Erg Lalita-to self's/his thought keep-Inf said
'Ashok told Lalita to take care of self'
f. *Ashok-ne Lalitaa-ko [$_S$ PRO [apne baare] me bataane-ko] kahaa
Ashok ERG Lalita-to self about to-tell said

(15) a. weil Hans [Peter für sich /(ihn) arbeiten] läßt/sah
because Hans Peter for self/him to-work lets/saw
'because Hans let/saw Peter work for him'
b. *weil Hans [Maria sich töten] ließ
because Hans Maria self kill let
('because Hans let Maria kill him')
c. ? *Emma ließ Fritz lange und ungeduldig um sich werben...
Emma let Fritz long and impatiently for self sue
('Emma let Fritz court her long and impatiently')
d. *Nur mit Unbehagen ließ Fritz [den Reporter aus sich einen Helden machen]
Only with uneasiness let F. the reporter out-of self a hero make
('Only with uneasiness did Fritz let the reporter make a hero of him')

A CP-transparency/S'-Deletion account of a sort has been suggested here in work by Grewendorf (1983). The idea was, roughly, that adjuncts phrases like the one in (15a) are outside of VP in German, and therefore governed by the matrix verb by Exceptional Government. Having two governors, and therefore two Governing Categories, the anaphor has the option of being bound in the higher one. We argue against this account on two grounds. First, we believe that the claim that all such adjunct phrases are outside of VP is untenable, in view of the fact that these phrases can be moved along with the verb in VP topicalization. Second, we note that an account in terms of S'-Deletion and consequent Exceptional Government does not extend in a straightforward way to the apparently parallel Hindi facts. As the contrast between (14c) and (14f) shows, Hindi exhibits a similar asymmetry in binding between adjuncts and arguments. Here, however, the complement clauses are control complements. The matrix verb, therefore, cannot govern down into the embedded IP here, given the standard assumption that PRO must be ungoverned.

Other analyses suggested for these facts, we claim, have not been more successful. Such Verb Raising constructions do seem to be of a dual nature. In certain respects it appears as if they must be biclausal. The (accusative) apparent subject of the embedded clause, as well as the matrix subject, is a potential binder for anaphors occurring in the complement. Since binders of reflexives must be subjects in German, this fact supports a biclausal analysis, as does the fact that such NP's (in some cases) also trigger the SSC effect. On the other hand, certain other facts—including the availability of the main clause subject as an antecedent for embedded anaphors under certain circumstances—suggest a monoclausal analysis (cf. especially Evers (1975) for further arguments). This duality has traditionally been accounted for derivationally, by positing a syntactic rule of Verb Raising, Clause Union or Reanalysis to mediate between the two structures, by converting the biclausal structure into a monoclausal one. However, this seems to be insufficient, since the Hindi and German facts suggests that the duality exists at the single level at which Binding Theory applies. A derived monoclausal structure gives the wrong results for arguments, while a biclausal representation gives the wrong results for anaphors. An anaphor raising analysis would similarly seem to be counterindicated, since it is not clear why such raising should be possible from adjuncts but not from arguments. It has been suggested recently e.g., by Haegeman and van Riemsdijk (1986), that there may be advantages to assuming that the two representations are not ordered sequentially in a derivation, but exist 'simultaneously'. Our proposed alternative account is based on this idea of parallel structural representations.

In particular, we propose that each sentence containing a Verb Raising predicate like lassen is associated at S-structure with two phrase markers (dimensions). One of these—illustrated by the (simplified) structure in (16a)—is a full representation of the argument structure of the construction. We refer to this representation as Propositional Structure dimension. The other representation—illustrated by the stricture in (16b)—reflects the monoclausal 'surface constituent structure' identified by such processes as gapping (cf. Evers (1975)). We refer to this as the alpha-Structure dimension.

(16) a. $[_S$ $[_{NP}$ Hans] $[_{VP}$ $[_S$ $[_{NP}$ Maria] $[_{VP}$ sich töten] $[_V$ leiß]]]
b. $[_S$ $[_{NP}$ Hans] $[_{VP}$ $[_S$ $[_{NP}$ Peter] $[_{VP}$ $[_a$ für sich] $[_V$ arbeiten läßt]]]

We propose that Principle A of the Binding Theory can, in principle, be satisfied by reference to either dimension. For adjunct anaphors in German and Hindi constructions of the type in question, this makes the right prediction. If they are bound in the Propositional Structure representation, the only possible antecedent, given the SSC subcase of principle A, is the embedded clause subject. If they are bound in alpha-Structure, given the subject-antecedent requirement, only the matrix subject is a possible antecedent. This twofold possibility corresponds to the facts. It remains to be determined, however, why anaphors contained in argument phrases in the complement clause cannot have the higher subject as an antecedent. We can achieve this result by requiring that they be bound in the Propositional Structure dimension, where the SSC would preclude binding to the main clause subject. We believe that this requirement can be derived in turn from the Projection Principle. The Projection Principle requires that arguments be present at every level of structure. Let us assume that that means, in the present case, that they must be represented in both the Propositional Structure and alpha-Structure dimensions. We propose that an anaphor in a subject-antecedent language may be bound to an antecedent which is a subject in at least one dimension of an S-structure representation, so long as Principle A is not violated in any dimension in which it occurs. Consider the argument anaphor sich in the top example in (16). If it is bound to the embedded subject Maria, it satisfies both requirements of Binding Theory. It is subject-bound (bound to an NP which is a subject in at least one dimension), and the binding satisfies the domain restriction of Principle A in both dimensions. Thus, the lower-clause antecedent interpretation is possible. However, if it is bound to Hans, then the resultant indexing in Propositional Structure, [Hans_i...[Maria_k...sich_i...]] will violate Principle A.

A similar violation can be avoided in the case of anaphors in adjunct phrases if we assume, along lines suggested by Lasnik and Saito (1984), that the presence of adjuncts is not enforced by the Projection Principle. Thus, an adjunct phrase like für sich in the bottom example in (16) need not be present in both dimensions. It may be absent from Propositional Structure dimension, for example, and accordingly sich may be bound to the 'matrix' subject in the alpha-Structure dimension without producing an SSC violation in the Propositional Structure dimension.[2] (Of course, if the adjunct containing the anaphor were missing in both dimensions, it would have no phonological realization. Nor, assuming that indices are assigned to anaphors at S-structure, would the anaphor be assigned an interpretation.)

The phenomena listed here, of course, are just a few of the possible instances of restructuring that must be considered in deciding the question of the status of that process in the theory of grammar. In introducing and providing an alternative analysis for one such instance, with properties quite different from the others that have been observed, Kornfilt has made an important contribution toward that end.

NOTES

1. One of his arguments has to do with scope—in the example with main clause agreement, the object NP is understood to be outside of the intension of the main verb.
2. Compare Aoun (1982:271, note 45) for a similar suggestion. Aoun notes the apparent existence of an adjacency condition which is sensitive to intervening arguments but not intervening nonarguments, and argues for conditions for which adjuncts may be invisible.

REFERENCES

Aoun, Y. 1982. *The Formal Nature of Anaphoric Relations.* PhD. Dissertation, MIT.

Bailyn, J. (in prep) "LF Movement of Anaphors and Acquisition of Embedded Clauses in Russian," ms., Cornell University.

Cole, P., G. Hermon and L.-M. Sung. "Principles and Parameters of Long- Distance Reflexives," *Linguistic Inquiry* 21:1-22.

Christensen, Kirsti Koch. 1985. "Complex Passives and Conditions on Reanalysis," *Working Papers in Scandinavian Syntax* 19.

den Besten, H. 1985. "The Ergative Hypothesis and Free Word Order in Dutch and German," in J. Toman, (ed.), *Studies in German Grammar.* Foris.

Engh, Jan. 1984. "On the Development of the Complex Passive," *Working Papers in Scandinavian Syntax* 10.

Evers, M. 1975. *The Transformational Cycle in Dutch and German.* PhD. dissertation, University of Utrecht.

Grewendorf, G. 1984. "Reflexivierung in deutschen AcI Konstruktionen: Kein Transformationsgrammatisches Dilemma mehr," ms., Berlin.

Haegeman, L. and H. van Riemsdijk. 1986. Verb Projection Raising, Scope and the Typology of Rules Affecting Verbs. *Linguistic Inquiry* 17: 417- 466.

Harbert, W and V. Srivastav. 1988. A Complement/Adjunct Asymmetry in Hindi Anaphor Binding. *Cornell Working Papers in Linguistics* 8: 79- 105.

Harbert, W. and A. J. Toribio. 1991. Nominative Objects. *Cornell Working Papers in Linguistics* 9.

Hellan, Lars. 1984. A GB-Type Analysis of Complex Passives and Related Constructions. *Working Papers in Scandinavian Syntax* 10.

Karlsson, Fred. 1983. *Finnish Grammar.* Helsinki.

Kiss, K. 1987. *Configurationality in Hungarian.* Dordrecht.

Lasnik, H., and M. Saito. 1984. On the Nature of Proper Government. *Linguistic Inquiry* 15.

Mahajan, Anoop. 1989. Agreement and Agreement Phrases. in *MIT Working Papers in Linguistics* 10: Functional Heads and Clause Structure.

Rappaport, G. 1982. On Anaphor Binding in Russian. *NLLT* 4: 97-120.

Reis, M. 1976. Reflexivierung in deutschen A.c.I. Konstruktionen. Ein transformationsgrammatisches Dilemma. *Papiere zur Linguistik* 9.

Sigurðsson, H. A. 1989. *Verbal Syntax and Case in Icelandic.* PhD. dissertation, Lund University.

Taraldsen, K. T. 1984. Remarks on Complex Passives. in Brendemoen, B. and E. Hovdhaugen, (eds.), *Riepmocála. Essays in Honour of Knut Bergsland.* Novas Forlag, Oslo.

Webelhuth, G. 1985. German is Configurational. *The Linguistic Review* 4: 203-246.

Yang, D.-W. 1984. The Extended Binding Theory of Anaphors. *Theoretical Linguistic Research* 1:195-218.

HOWARD LASNIK

CASE AND EXPLETIVES: NOTES TOWARD A PARAMETRIC ACCOUNT*

It will be the purpose of this paper to explore a number of phenomena and problems revolving around the general issue of Case assignment, especially as concerns expletive NPs. The question of why expletives require Case, which has become a difficult one under several recent theories, will come under particular scrutiny. Recent proposals of Chomsky (1986) concerning expletives and of Belletti (1988) will (eventually) be considered in some detail. Evidence will be offered for Belletti's proposal that Case transmission does not exist, and, consequently, that even arguments associated with expletives must be directly Case-marked. Certain problems that this raises for the analysis of expletives of Chomsky (1986) will be examined and a refinement of Chomsky's expletive replacement will be offered.

In the time since the theory of abstract Case was first proposed by Jean-Roger Vergnaud, there have been two different instantiations of the basic idea. The original one, essentially Vergnaud's, is developed in Chomsky (1980). Basically for morphological reasons, every lexically realized NP must be assigned abstract Case. An example like (1) is straightforwardly ruled out as a violation of this morphological filter, as *seem* is not a Case assigner.

(1) *It seems [John to be here]

Under this approach, constructions involving WH-movement are treated in the same way: it is the lack of Case on *who* that is responsible for the ungrammaticality of (2).

(2) *Who does it seem [t to be here]

In Chomsky (1980), Case is assumed to be assigned prior to WH-movement (or as part of the movement operation), thus allowing (3), with nominative Case borne by *who.*

(3) Who does it seem [t is here]

Lasnik and Freidin (1981) point out a problem for this approach. Note first that, as one might expect, (4), with a relative operator, has just the status of (3), with its question operator, and that (5) has just the status of (2).

(4) The man who it seems [t is here]

(5) *The man who it seems [t to be here]

Now in general, a relative operator need not overtly appear. [Lasnik and Freidin assumed the COMP deletion rule of Chomsky and Lasnik (1977).]

But (5) is not improved by the elimination of *who*:

(6) *The man it seems [t to be here]

Apparently, no requirement on *who* can be relevant. Thus, Lasnik and Freidin concluded that along with lexical NPs, the trace of WH movement must be Case-marked.[1] While this correctly describes the facts, it strips the Case filter of its intuitive morphological motivation, since WH-trace presumably has no morphological realization.

Chomsky (1981), based on a proposal of Aoun (1979), suggests an alternative view of the Case filter which overcomes this difficulty. On this alternative, lexical realization is not the crucial property. Rather, argument-hood is. To be 'visible' for θ-marking at LF, an argument must have Case. A Caseless argument will then be in violation of the θ-criterion. This accounts for all of the examples considered thus far, including those involving WH-trace, which is, of course, an argument. Two new problems are created, however, as is well known. The first is evident in the contrast between (7) and (8):

(7) *I tried [[John to be here]]

(8) I tried [[PRO to be here]]

(7) is correctly excluded by the Case filter, on either interpretation of that constraint. A morphologically realized argument, *John*, is Caseless, since it is ungoverned, there being no S' deletion with *try*. But in the grammatical (8), PRO is also Caseless. Thus, on the visibility account, (8), like (7), should constitute a violation of the θ-criterion at LF. There are various stipulations in the literature aimed at this problem, none of them entirely satisfying. I will have little to contribute to this issue here, but see Lasnik (1992) for some speculations.

The second problem, which I will examine in some detail, involves the distribution of expletives. Expletives, like lexical arguments, must have Case, as seen in (9) and (10).

(9) *It seems [there to be a man here]

(10) *I tried [there to be a man here]

A simple visibility analysis would not predict this. Since *there* is not an argument, it should not have to be visible for θ-marking. The answer that has frequently been suggested is that in examples like (9) and (10), visibility ultimately imposes a requirement not on *there*, but rather, on *a man*. Since the latter NP is an argument, it must be visible for θ-marking, and this visibility must come via Case marking on the associated expletive. Following Safir

(1982), I will refer to this general approach as 'Case transmission'. Chomsky (1986, p.135) presents one recent version of this idea:

(11) A CHAIN is Case-marked if it contains exactly one Case-marked position; a position in a Case-marked CHAIN is visible for θ-marking.

The notion CHAIN encompasses standard (A-)chains, as well as expletive argument pairs. In (12), *There* and *a man* constitute a CHAIN, indicated here by co-superscripting.

(12) There^j is a man^j here.

Both (9) and (10) are excluded, as required. In both instances, according to this analysis, the CHAIN is not visible for θ-marking. Hence, in both instances, an argument, *a man*, winds up with no θ-role.

This account relies on an assumption which, to my knowledge, has not actually been justified in the literature. The assumption is that in the examples under consideration, *a man* could not be assigned Case by *be*, and therefore must receive Case via transmission.[2] In fact, a potential argument does exist. [A counter-argument does too, as will shortly become evident.] Note that in the existential constructions under consideration, *a man* need not be adjacent to *be*:

(13) There is usually a man here.

Yet there is generally an adjacency requirement on Case assignment in English, as discussed by Chomsky (1981) and Stowell (1981). The effects of this requirement are seen in (14).

(14) *I heard usually a car.
(cf. I usually heard a car)

Thus, the grammaticality of (13) provides some motivation for the Case transmission mechanism. *There* transmits nominative Case to the otherwise Caseless argument *a man*, which thereby becomes visible for θ-marking.

Consider now a slightly more complicated example:

(15) There is likely [$\underline{t}$ to be someone here]

Here, the CHAIN has three members, *There*, $\underline{t}$, and *someone*. Case is 'transmitted' from nominative *There* to *someone*, via $\underline{t}$. At this point, a difficulty emerges. Consider (16).

(16) *There is likely [someone to be here]

In (16), *There* and *someone* constitute a CHAIN (or a portion of a CHAIN; see below). Further, the positions in this CHAIN are a subset of those in the CHAIN in (15). Yet in (15), transmission succeeds, while in (16), it evidently fails. There is no obvious reason that this should be so.[3]

Chomsky (1986, p.92) points out a further problem, which I will argue is related to the one just noted. Even though *there* in (17) is clearly in a position to which Case can be assigned (by *consider*), the example is nonetheless ill-formed.

(17) *We consider [there a man in the room]

The question is why this does not have the status of (18).

(18) We consider [there to be a man in the room]

(19) is a similar construction.

(19) I want [there *(to be) someone here at 6:00]
cf. I want [someone (to be) here at 6:00]

Notice that there is no general prohibition against *there* as (surface) subject of a small clause:

(20) We consider [there_1 likely [t_1 to be a man in the room]]

All of these facts are mysterious under a transmission account. In each instance, Case ought to be transmitted via links of the CHAIN from the expletive to the argument. On the other hand, all of (16-20) would receive a simple explanation under a reactionary revision of Case theory, as in (21).

(21) Case is assigned only under government by a Case assigner.

Suppose, in accord with (21), that there is no Case transmission. (16) is then out because *someone* is not governed by any case assigner, hence is Caseless. Exactly the same is true of *a man* in (17). In both examples, *there* is Case-marked, but under (21), that is of no benefit to the argument NP. Finally, in (18), in the well-formed version of (19), and in (20) the argument NP is governed by *be*. If we reject the standard assumption and take *be* to be a Case assigner, this is just as expected.[4]

We are now left with two new (or very old) questions. Why do expletives need Case, if not for reasons of transmission? And why is (13) with its apparent violation of adjacency grammatical, given that (14) is not? I defer the first of these questions until a later section. The second question, which constituted the potential argument I offered <u>for</u> Case transmission, I turn to immediately. Consider in this connection another pair of examples that contrast in something like the way (13) and (14) do:

(22) A car is not here.

(23) *I heard not a car.

There are a number of accounts of this contrast in the literature, going back to Chomsky (1955).[5] For concreteness, let us examine a variant of the analysis in Lasnik (1981). There, it was proposed that the category Aux (INFL in recent work) in a finite clause consists of Tense (AGR in recent work) and, optionally, an auxiliary verb position. This position might be filled at D-structure, by a modal, as in (24).

(24) John $[_{Aux}$ Tense $[_{v}$ will]] $[_{VP}$ leave]

Or the position might be base-generated empty, and dummy verb *do* inserted:

(25) John $[_{Aux}$ Tense $[_{v}$ do]] $[_{VP}$ leave]

Note that these two possibilities are analogous to two possibilities for NP positions, with the first case similar to that of a base generated argument and the second similar to an expletive. The third possibility for an NP position, namely, as a target for movement, was also argued to exist for the auxiliary verb slot. In particular, a [+auxiliary] verb can 'raise' into an empty auxiliary verb position. This is what is involved in (22). Thus, the S-structure is as in (26).

(26) [[A car] [Tense be_1] [not $\underline{t}_1$ here]

This v-raising process is, essentially, the v-to-I of Chomsky (1986a). Note that, at least in overt syntax, the operation is limited to auxiliary verbs (for English), as shown by the ungrammaticality of (23) above. *Hear* is not [+aux], hence it cannot raise. Plausibly, this follows from some version of the structure preserving constraint.[6] In the traditional literature of generative grammar, again going back to Chomsky (1955), there is substantial further evidence for this dichotomy between auxiliary verbs and 'main' verbs. The contrast below is neatly accounted for in those terms.

(27) Is a car here

(28) *Heard I a car

The Aux in (27) contains *be*, via raising, but the one in (28) does not contain *hear*, since the latter is not [+aux], hence cannot raise.

We are now in a position to look more closely at the mysterious (13), repeated here as (29).

(29) There is usually a man here.

Recall that the difficulty is that *a man* appears to be in a position to which Case cannot be directly assigned (because of the adjacency requirement). However consider the S-structure of (29), under the v-raising analysis:

(30) There [Tense be_1] [usually $\underline{t}_1$ a man here]

As before, *a man* is not adjacent to *be*. However, that NP is adjacent to the trace of *be*. If we accept the null hypothesis that a trace has the syntactic properties of the moved item, then *a man* in (30) is in a configuration of Case assignment, with the trace of *be* the Case assigner. This answers the major empirical objection noted above to taking *be* as the Case assigner in existential constructions generally.

There is further evidence for the general approach advocated here. It is crucial to such analyses of the auxiliary that at most one auxiliary verb can raise to Infl. This restriction accounts for such contrasts as the following.

(31) Will a car be here

(32) *Will be a car here

(32) is excluded since *will* has raised to Infl thus preventing the raising of *be*. As a consequence, *be* cannot front to COMP along with Infl. (33-34) display the same effect.

(33) A car will not be here

(34) *A car will be not here

Structure (35) provides no target position for raising, so *be* must remain in the VP, to the right of *not*.

(35) [[A car] [Tense will] [not be here]]

Given this, a prediction emerges for existential constructions. If the right analysis of the lack of Case adjacency effects in (29) is to be provided by a derivation resulting in structure (30), then when raising is inapplicable, adjacency effects should emerge. This is just what we find. We have just seen that when there is a modal in Infl, raising is prevented. Consider, then, an example like (29), but with a modal:

(36) ?*There will be usually a man here

This is substantially degraded, having nearly the status of a classic Case adjacency violation as in (14), repeated as (37).

(37) *I heard usually a car

In both (36) and (37), the argument is separated from its nearest potential Case assigner, the overt verb in each case, by the intervening adverb. Further, there is no possibility of an adjacent verb-trace, since there is no possibility of raising. Thus, as predicted, while (29) is only an apparent adjacency violation, (36) is a true violation.

There is another property of raising that is relevant to the present discussion. It was argued in Lasnik (1981) that raising only takes place if the Aux contains Tense.[7] A contrast such as (38) v. (39) is elegantly explicable in these terms.

(38) a. John is not noisy
b. John [Tense be_1] [not t_1 noisy]

(39) a. *Be not noisy
b. [IMP e] [not be noisy] (-> Do not be noisy)

The Aux in (39) does not contain Tense, but rather, the Imperative affix. [That there is an affix here, rather than nothing at all, is argued for in some detail in Lasnik (1981).] Now note that infinitivals pattern with imperatives in this regard, which is to be expected if Tense is the required trigger for raising.

(40) ?*I believe John to be not here.
cf. I believe John is not here.

(41) ?*I believe John to be not singing.
cf. I believe John is not singing.

Without raising, (40) and (41) become completely acceptable:

(42) I believe John not to be here.

(43) I believe John not to be singing.

Consider now existential constructions in infinitival clauses. Since raising is blocked, in contrast to the situation with finite clauses, all apparent adjacency violations should be true violations, as there will be no possibility of a trace of *be* to serve as a Case assigner. Once again, the prediction of the theory is confirmed. In both (44) and (45), *a solution* fails to be adjacent to a Case assigner (or the trace of one), and the examples are bad.

(44) *I believe there to be not a solution.

(45) *I believe there to be usually a solution.

Compare (46-47), where the argument is adjacent to *be.*

(46) I believe there not to be a solution.

(47) ? I believe there usually to be a solution.

Also compare (48-49), where adjacency is superficially violated, but where the argument is actually adjacent to a Case assigner, namely, the trace of raised *be.*

(48) I believe there is not a solution
.............[Tense be_1] [not t_1 a solution]

(49) I believe there is usually a solution
.............[Tense be_1] [usually t_1 a solution]

It is important to note that not only do all of these facts fall out neatly from the hypothesis that *be* (or its trace) is the Case assigner, but also that Case transmission seems incapable of giving the right contrasts. If it is not *be* that is responsible for the Case on the argument, why should there be adjacency effects involving *be*?

In addition to existential constructions involving *be*, there are certain somewhat marginal 'unaccusative' constructions with *there*. (50) is such an example.

(50) ?There arrived a bus.

Just the same questions arise here as did in sentences with *be*. Is the Case on the argument assigned by the verb or is it transmitted from the expletive? Significantly, adjacency effects do obtain here:

(51) ?There usually arrives a bus (at this time)

(52) *There arrives usually a bus (at this time)

Once again, this would not be expected under Case transmission. Before concluding that this paradigm argues for direct Case assignment, however, it will be important to consider why the apparent adjacency violation in (52) is a real one, unlike that in (13), repeated as (53).

(53) There is usually a man here

Recall that the account of the well-formedness of (53) relied on the (independently motivated) process of verb raising. Thus, in (53), *a man* is adjacent to a Case assigner, the trace of *be*. Why could the same not be true of (52)? The answer is straightforward. Raising is limited to auxiliary verbs. *Arrive* displays none of the characteristic properties associated with raising. It can neither move to a position before *not*, as seen in (54), (55) nor can it undergo inversion with the subject, as seen in (56).[8]

(54) *There arrived not a bus [?There did not arrive a bus]

(55) *A bus arrived not [A bus did not arrive]

(56) *Arrived a bus [Did a bus arrive]

Thus, assuming the standard adjacency requirement on Case assignment, Case transmission is disconfirmed, and, correspondingly, (57) is supported.

(57) 'Unaccusatives' and *be* are Case assigners.

On the other hand, if there is no adjacency requirement as such, all of its seeming effects simply following from constraints on verb raising, Case transmission might still remain as a viable option. But shortly we will see that even when v-raising is not at issue, Case transmission gives incorrect results.

Given (57), the fact that expletives require Case cannot follow from Case transmission. Further, as hinted above, there is substantial evidence that Case transmission does not even exist. Thus, we must seek an alternative account of this Case requirement. Chomsky (1986) provides the basis for one possible solution to this problem. Noting the fact, reported by Burzio (1986), that expletive—argument pairs have the locality properties of NP movement chains, Chomsky proposes that at LF, they are such chains. For example, under this proposal S-structure (58) becomes LF (59), by what we might call expletive replacement (simply a special case of NP movement).

(58) There arrived a man

(59) A man_i arrived t_i

The S-structure position of an expletive thus becomes the LF position of the head of an argument chain. Then the following principle, from Chomsky (1986), might give the desired consequence.[9]

(60) If $C=(a_1,...,a_n)$ is a maximal CHAIN, then a_n occupies its unique θ-position and a_1 its unique Case-marked position.

This seems to guarantee that expletives are Case-marked. There are, however, certain difficulties with this. First, as we have seen, CHAINs do not have a unique Case-marked position. Both the expletive and the argument must be in Case-marked positions at S-structure. Further implications of this fact will be explored below. Second, even putting this question aside, (60) incorrectly predicts that a CHAIN could have a non-Case-marked intermediate expletive. But this is never possible. Thus, (61) is bad even though at LF, it should be identical to (62).

(61) *There is likely [there to be a man here]

(62) A man is likely [t to be t here]

We now have at least two related mysteries to deal with: 1) Why must expletives be Case-marked at S-structure? We have seen that this does not entirely follow from any independent property of chains. 2) Why must arguments (other than PRO) be Case-marked at S-structure, even when they are associated with Case-marked expletives which they will replace at LF? I will suggest an approach to these mysteries.

As noted earlier, Chomsky (1986) suggests a reduction of the Case requirement on arguments to a visibility requirement on LF θ-marking. Thus, Case filter violations are actually violations of the θ-criterion, hence, of the

Projection Principle. This approach raises certain empirical and conceptual questions. Empirically, we have seen that it does not suffice, even for arguments, since a non-Case-marked argument should then be able to move to the position of a Case-marked expletive at LF, and thus become visible for θ-marking. Conceptually, the question arises as to why LF should be the unique level that must satisfy a requirement that ultimately follows from the Projection Principle, a requirement on all syntactic levels. Both of these problems, the empirical one and the conceptual one, disappear if the visibility requirement is imposed upon S-structure as well as LF. An example such as (16) above, repeated here as (63), will run afoul of the visibility requirement at S-structure, hence will violate the Projection Principle at that level.

(63) *There is likely [someone to be here]

And, as far as S-structure is concerned, the conceptual problem straightforwardly disappears. Both S-structure and LF must conform to the requirement. Paradoxically, however, D-structure—the level that ought to be most closely associated with θ-marking—need not conform. As is well known, the D-structure position of an argument need not be one to which Case can be assigned. Simple passive or raising constructions illustrate this, as in (64)a, the D-structure of (64)b, or (65)a, the D-structure of (65)b:

(64) a. e was arrested John
b. John was arrested t

(65) a. e is likely [John to leave]
b. John is likely [t to leave]

It is not clear how these conform to the Projection Principle. A plausible answer lies in a consideration of the role that visibility plays in the system. Visibility distinguishes between NPs that lack a crucial licensing property, Case, and those that have this property. But at D-structure, there is no such distinction to be made, at least with respect to structural Case.[10] No NPs have this feature, given that Case is not assigned until S-structure. It would not be reasonable for a feature that doesn't exist at a level to be required at that level.

With this basis for limiting Case visibility to S-structure (and later) representations, I now suggest that visibility be extended in scope. Suppose that it is not merely a constraint on the operation of θ-marking, but on the operation of movement as well. Then, to be visible as the target of movement, an A-position must have Case, if, in principle, it could have Case. After S-structure, then, a Caseless A-position will not be a visible target. Consider again S-structure (61), repeated as (66).

(66) *There is likely [there to be a man here]

Since the lower *there* is Caseless, it will not be visible for LF expletive substitution. At the level of LF, this *there* will still remain, and Chomsky's principle of Full Interpretation, which demands that everything present at LF have semantic import, will be violated.[11] The S-structure Case requirement on expletives now follows completely.[12,13]

Having established that expletives must be assigned Case, and that their associated arguments must independently be assigned Case also, I turn next to a consideration of the nature of the Case assigned to those arguments. Belletti (1988) presents a detailed analysis of a variety of constructions that depends crucially on the assumption that there is no Case transmission and, hence, that unaccusatives assign Case. We have seen substantial evidence in support of this assumption above. Further, she argues that the Case assigned, which she calls 'partitive', "selects an indefinite meaning for the NP that carries it." This proposal, along with the assumption motivated above, makes possible Belletti's account of the 'definiteness effect' seen in a wide range of existential constructions, among others. If unaccusatives do not assign accusative, but do assign partitive, then, as Belletti shows, familiar contrasts such as those in (67) follow immediately:

(67) a. There arrived a man.
b. *There arrived the man.

The complement of *arrive* must have Case at S-structure (for reasons presented above), and that Case could not be assigned by transmission. Hence, *arrive* itself must be the Case assigner. Under Belletti's proposal, the partitive Case it assigns will be entirely compatible with the meaning of the indefinite *a man*, but will be incompatible with the meaning of *the man.*[14]

Belletti considers the properties of partitive Case and concludes that it is not a structural Case, like accusative or nominative, but rather, is an <u>inherent</u> Case, in the sense of Chomsky (1986). I believe that she has in mind three reasons for this conclusion. The first is that, as noted just above, this Case is associated with a semantic property, whereas accusative and nominative Case generally are not. Notice that while this is suggestive, it is not conclusive, given that the core characteristic of inherent Case in Chomsky's sense is that it be associated specifically with a <u>thematic</u> property. That is, it does not appear that anything excludes the possibility that a structural Case involve a <u>quantificational</u> property. The second reason involves the fairly widespread assumption that the trace of NP movement must not be in a Case-marked position. A constraint to this effect is a way of capturing half of 'Burzio's generalization', and it is discussed at length in Chomsky (1986).

As Belletti observes, the problem for this generalization and/or constraint is that the moved versions of unaccusative constructions seem to flagrantly contradict it, on her account. The trace in (68) is in a position to which partitive Case would be assigned.

(68) A man$_i$ arrived t$_i$

Belletti indicates that if partitive Case is inherent, then Burzio's generalization can be limited to structural Cases, and the contradiction disappears. Interestingly, however, as Belletti points out, it is necessary to make partitive Case assignment optional, even apart from these considerations. Inherent Case, for Belletti and for Chomsky, is assigned at D-structure. Consider, then, (69a), the D-structure of (69b):

(69) a. e arrived the man
b. The man$_i$ arrived t$_i$

Under the assumption that partitive Case is inherent, if it were obligatory, then at D-structure it would necessarily be assigned to *the man* in (69)a. As a result, (69b) would be incorrectly predicted to have the status of (70), with a definite expression receiving incompatible partitive Case.

(70) *There arrived the man

Belletti concludes that a special property of partitive Case is that it is assigned only optionally. But under this assumption, the prohibition on Case-marked trace can be maintained in full generality. Now note that one might conjecture that Case assignment more generally should be optional. After all, a stipulation of obligatoriness of Case assignment is almost entirely redundant with the Case filter (whether construed as a morphological filter, a licensing condition, or a visibility condition). And, in fact, it is difficult to find ill-formed examples excluded by the constraint on Case-marked trace (this constraint constituting the only reason for Case assignment to be obligatory) and by nothing else.[15] To the extent that this is true, this potential argument for treating partitive Case as inherent is mitigated.

The third reason for thinking that partitive Case is inherent is the most compelling. In fact, it seems to me decisive: First, Belletti shows that in Italian, passive verbs can assign partitive Case. That is, she shows that the object of a passive can receive Case, and that in such a circumstance, there is a definiteness effect. She gives the following examples, among many others.

(71) E stato messo un libro sul tavolo
has been put a book on the table

(72) *E stato messo il libro sul tavolo
has been put the book on the table

Next, she shows that certain verbs such as *considerare* 'consider' can exceptionally Case mark into a small clause:

(73) Ho sempre considerato [$_{SC}$Gianni intelligente]
I always have considered Gianni intelligent

This exceptional Case is presumably accusative here. There is no definiteness effect. Further, when pronominal, the subject of the small clause shows up as an accusative clitic:

(73') L'$_i$ ho sempre considerato [$_{SC}$ e$_i$ intelligente]

The conclusive fact is that when *considerare* is passivized, it can no longer take a small clause complement with an overt subject:

(74) *Sono considerati [alcuni studenti intelligenti]
are considered some students intelligent

Given that *considerare* can take a small clause, that structural Case marking is possible into a small clause, and that passive verbs can assign partitive Case, (74) should be perfect, if partitive Case is structural. If, on the other hand, partitive Case is inherent, Case assignment will be blocked in this construction, since *alcuni studenti* is not the complement of *considerati.* Inherent Case is, by definition, assignable only under θ-marking. Thus, *alcuni studenti* winds up Caseless and the example is correctly excluded.

While, as I indicated above, I find this argument compelling, there is contrary evidence that partitive Case is, structural. Consider again an English sentence such as (75).

(75) There is a man in the room

The standard definiteness effect obtains here:

(76) *There is the man in the room

Hence, the Case assigned must be partitive, given Belletti's account. Consistent with this, Belletti suggests that here, as in the Italian examples, the Case is assigned to a complement (rather than 'exceptionally' to the subject of a complement). That is, following Williams (1984), she suggests that everything after *is* is one NP, and that that NP receives (inherent) partitive Case. But there is reason to doubt this suggestion, and to favor the small clause analysis of Stowell (1981):

(77) There is [$_{SC}$ a man in the room]

Safir (1987) offers a number of arguments against the 'bare NP' analysis.[16] Some of these arguments involve extraction possibilities. Consider the following examples, which are of roughly the sort investigated by Safir.

(78) a. There are many fish in the lake.
b. In which lake are there many fish?

(79) a. I discussed many fish in the lake.
b. *In which lake did you discuss many fish?

In (79), where *many fish in which lake* is clearly an NP, extraction of the PP is blocked. This contrasts sharply with what is found in (78), suggesting that the structures should be differentiated. The small clause analysis provides just the right differentiation, in light of the fact that a small clause predicate is freely extractable:

(80) a. I want [$_{SC}$ some fish in the lake]
b. In which lake do you want some fish

But now there is a near contradiction: there is evidence (passive *considerare* constructions) that partitive Case is inherent; and there is evidence (existential *be* constructions) that it is structural.[17] Based on what we have seen so far, it might be imagined that we are dealing not with a contradiction, but with a parameter. Recall that there was no firm conceptual basis for demanding that partitive Case be inherent. Hence, theoretically, it need not be inherent. Suppose, then, that a language can choose whether to treat partitive Case as inherent or as structural, and that Italian chooses the former option. However, as Travis (1989) observes, this cannot be the answer. Italian existentials behave just like those in English, as shown in the following examples.

(81) Ci sono molti pesci nel lago
there are many fish in the lake

(82) In quale lago ci sono molti pesci
In which lake are there many fish

Further, also as in English, extraction of the PP is blocked out a clear instance of an NP:

(83) a. Ho discusso molti pesci nel lago
I have discussed many fish in the lake
b. *In quale lago hai discusso molti pesci
In which lake have you discussed many fish

In fact, Travis provides additional evidence that the sequence *molti pesci nel lago* does not constitute an NP in (81) even though it does in (83):

(84) a. *Quanti pesci nel lago ci sono
How many fish in the lake are there

b. Quanti pesci ci sono nel lago
How many fish are there in the lake

(85) a. Quanti pesci nel lago hai discusso
How many fish in the lake did you discuss
b. *Quanti pesci hai discusso nel lago
How many fish did you discuss in the lake

The sequence (or, more precisely, its interrogative version) must move as a unit in (85), but must not in (84). This follows immediately if the sequence is an NP in (85) but is not in (84). The small clause analysis of the existential construction gives this result. But then, the Case difference under examination here is not a difference between English and Italian. Rather, it appears to be a difference between 'be' on the one hand and contentful verbs on the other. The latter evidently assign partitive Case (if at all) only inherently, that is, only to their θ-marked complements, while the former can assign partitive structurally. As far as I know, *be* is, in fact, the only verb able to assign partitive Case 'exceptionally'. Configurations like (86) are uniformly prohibited:

(86) *There seems [someone to be here]

Plausibly, this Case assigning difference between 'be' and other verbs relates to θ-marking differences, under the assumption that 'be' has no θ-roles to assign. There are two reasonable ways to state the required property. First, for a purely 'grammatical' verb, a Case that is normally inherent is, instead, structural. Alternatively, the Case is always inherent, but the notion 'inherent Case' is defined in such a way that it demands θ-marking only when θ-marking is, in principle, available. For a Case assigner such as 'be', lacking lexical content, θ-marking could never be available, hence inherent Case marking could proceed in its absence. At this point, there is no basis for a choice between these two alternative views, though the second is neatly reminiscent of the earlier discussion of the absence of a Case visibility requirement at D-structure. Both phenomena instantiate a 'reasonableness' criterion: only if a requirement could, in principle, be fulfilled must it be.

There is one difference between Italian and English that must be considered now. We have seen that in Italian, passives can assign partitive Case. The construction exemplified in (71) above is evidently fully productive. In English, on the other hand, it is much less clear that passives have this capability. In fact, the very Italian example cited is bad in English:

(87) *There has been put a book on the table

Thus, in this instance, we are presumably dealing with a parametric property. How precisely to characterize this property is an interesting question. Belletti assumes that all verbs have the capacity to assign partitive Case, and some verbs additionally have the capacity to assign accusative Case. A passive verb loses its ability to assign accusative Case but retains its ability to assign partitive Case. Under this general approach, the relevant parametric property of English would be that the partitive Case assigning capacity is lost along with the accusative Case assigning capacity. An alternative, still consistent with the same general assumptions, might be that English differs from Italian in not allowing a verb to have two associated Cases. Recall that for Belletti, unaccusative verbs assign partitive Case and accusative verbs assign both accusative and partitive Case. Suppose that in English, a verb has (at most) just one associated Case. Unaccusative verbs will still behave just as they do in Italian: they will assign partitive Case and no other. English accusative verbs will differ from their Italian counterparts in assigning only accusative. Their passives will then have no Case at all to assign.

I would like to consider a second type of approach. Thus far, I have accepted Belletti's assumption that Italian accusative verbs also have the capacity to assign partitive Case (and, hence, that they retain that ability under passivization). But suppose that Italian verbs and English verbs both have at most one Case to assign. Then an accusative verb could not retain an ability to assign partitive Case under passivization, as it would not have the ability in the first place. On this point of view, in examples such as (71) above, making a verb passive gives it a capacity. The relevant difference between Italian and English would then be that in the former language, but not in the latter, the passive morpheme has a Case associated with it—partitive Case.

Interestingly, the two classes of approaches just outlined—one involving multiple Case assigning possibilities for individual verbs, the other involving an affix with the ability to assign a particular Case—both seem to have applicability in other (arguably related) phenomena. For example, there is evidence from Turkish and from Hebrew that verbs can assign both accusative and partitive Case. Enc, (1991) shows that in Turkish, the specific vs. non-specific distinction[18] among object NPs is marked by a Case distinction. In particular, specific objects are accusative while non-specifics have no overt Case marker. The following examples illustrate the general pattern discussed by Enc,:

(88) Ali bir piyano-yu kiralamak istiyor
Ali one piano-acc. to-rent wants
'A certain piano is such that Ali wants to rent it'

(89) Ali bir piyano kiralamak istiyor
Ali one piano to-rent wants
'Ali wants to rent a (nonspecific) piano'

(89) suggests that the absence of overt Case in Turkish should be assimilated to Belletti's abstract partitive Case. The interpretation of the direct object then follows immediately. Note that in (88), the very same verb in the very same form assigns accusative Case, thus confirming that a verb may have multiple Case assigning possibilities. (88) is interesting in an additional respect as well. According to Enc,, the direct object in (88), like accusative objects more generally, is <u>necessarily</u> specific. Apparently, just as partitive Case is associated with a semantic property (non-specificity), accusative is associated with the converse semantic property. Note that under the standard assumption that Accusative is a structural Case, we now have strong evidence that semantic properties are not limited to inherent Cases.

Hebrew displays a pattern very similar to that of Turkish, as observed by Chenausky (1990). As in Turkish, non-specific object NPs have no overt Case morphology:

(90) ani ro e sefer
I see a book

Specific objects, on the other hand, obligatorily show up with the morpheme *et*, often called a direct object marker, and analyzed by Rapoport (1987) as accusative:[19]

(91) ani ro e *(et) ha-sefer
I see acc. the book

On the second type of approach to passive, the partitive Case assigned by passive verbs is reminiscent of the Slavic 'genitive of negation'.[20] Russian verbs that normally assign accusative can assign genitive instead, when they are negated.[21]

(92) a. Ja polucal pis'ma
I received letters (acc. pl.)
'I got (the) letters'
b. Ja ne polucal pis'ma
I NEG received letters (acc. pl.)
'I didn't get the letters'
c. ja ne polucal pisem
I NEG received letters (gen. pl.)
'I got no letters'

Further, negated unaccusatives can assign genitive Case:

(93) a. ne pojavilis' studenty
NEG showed up (pl.) students (masc. nom. pl.)
'The students didn't show up'
b. ne pojavilos' studentov
NEG showed up (neut. sg.) students (masc. gen. pl.)
'No students showed up'

Thus, it is reasonable to conjecture that negation in Slavic and passive in Italian provide a verb with a special Case assigning feature. Indeed, the Case assigning feature might be the same one. Slavic genitive of negation is much like Belletti's partitive Case. In particular, it displays the definiteness effect:

> "In the traditional literature about this construction, it is usually said that genitive phrases under negation, unlike their non-genitive counterparts, are obligatorily <u>indefinite</u>." [emphasis in original] Pesetsky (1982, p.65)

Interestingly, the genitive of negation, even though it has semantic import similar (or perhaps identical) to that of Belletti's partitive, seems to be structural rather than inherent. Thus, Pesetsky notes that in addition to θ-marked complements, as in (92), non-θ-marked expressions of duration may also receive the genitive of negation, just as long as they are governed by the negated verb:

(94) a. ja ni odnu minutu ne spal
I not one minute (fem. acc. sg.) NEG slept
b. ja ni odnoj minuty ne spal
I not one minute (fem. gen. sg.) NEG slept

Neidle (1988) gives similar examples, noting that "...this type of case marking appears to be structural, and cannot be stated simply in terms of the function OBJ." The most directly relevant test for this turns out to be inconclusive. According to Pesetsky, Russian has small clause constructions. A negated verb with a small clause complement would be expected to assign genitive to the subject of that small clause, under the assumption that that Case is structural. This prediction is neither strongly confirmed nor strongly refuted, as Pesetsky indicates that the resulting configuration is marginal:

(95) ??ja ne scitaju inostrannyx fil'mov interesnymi
I NEG consider foreign films (masc. gen. pl.) interesting (masc. instr. pl.)

The fact that the example is not entirely out is at least suggestive of the hypothesis under consideration.

There is one further reason for thinking that the genitive of negation is structural. Pesetsky, following Babby (1980), notes that some verbs, instead of assigning accusative to their objects, assign particular oblique Cases to them. Such oblique objects never alternate with genitive under negation. For example, *pomogat'* ('help') requires a dative object, and *upravljat'* ('manage') demands an instrumental object. Neither verb allows its object to become genitive under negation:

(96) a. ja ne pomogaju nikakim devuskam
I NEG help no girls (fem. dat. pl.)
b. *ja ne pomogaju nikakix devusek
girls (fem. gen. pl.)

(97) a. ja ne upravljaju ni odnim zavodom
I NEG manage not one factory (masc. instr. sg.)
b. *ja ne upravljaju ni odnogo zavoda
factory (masc. gen. sg.)

As Pesetsky observes, this patterning is precisely what is expected under the assumption that these oblique Cases are inherent while normal accusative and genitive of negation are not. This follows from, for example, the Principle of Lexical Satisfaction of Freidin and Babby (1984), which demands that a lexical property (such as assignment of a particular θ-related Case) take precedence over a structural property.

Exactly why the genitive of negation is allowed to be structural is an interesting question. Certainly the negated verbs in the examples above are contentful, with θ-roles to assign. Thus, if it is the verb that is the Case assigner, we might expect the Case to be inherent, in accord with the discussion above. This difficulty disappears if, as already suggested, it is the negative morpheme itself, rather than the verb that it negates, that is the genitive Case assigner. Since, presumably, negation has no θ-roles to assign, any Case that it assigns will of necessity be assigned structurally.[22]

It is difficult to find facts internal to Italian (or to English) to determine which of the two general approaches discussed above provides the appropriate characterization of partitive Case assignment in those languages, particularly since neither language provides any overt morphological indication. There is, however, a theoretical consideration that provides a direction. Chomsky (1991) suggests that parametric properties are located exclusively in the functional portion of the lexicon, the substantive portion being invariant. Given that verbs in Turkish and Hebrew can assign both accusative and partitive, the same should be true of Italian and English as well, under Chomsky's speculation. The passive morpheme, being a functional element is available as the locus of parametric variation. The parametric difference between Italian and English should then be that in Italian, passive blocks only assignment of accusative, while in English, it blocks assignment of both accusative and partitive, roughly in accord with Belletti's proposal. How these blockage properties are to be instantiated is a difficult question, which I leave as a topic for future research.

To sum up: I have presented abundant evidence for Belletti's crucial underlying assumption that Case transmission does not exist and that, instead, the constructions that had been analyzed in those terms involve direct Case assignment. Further, I have shown how an extension of the visibility hypothesis might, in collaboration with Chomsky's expletive replacement, handle two apparent classes of exceptions to the original hypothesis, namely, ungrammatical constructions involving Caseless intermediate expletives and ungrammatical constructions involving truly Caseless arguments associated with Cased expletives. Finally, I have attempted to reconcile all of this with the small clause proposal for existentials by appealing to a plausible reconsideration of how inherent Case is assigned. To the extent that the resulting analysis is successful it provides support for the fundamental hypotheses (if not all of the details) of Belletti's and Chomsky's proposals.

APPENDIX: ON V-RAISING

Above, it was seen that in English finite clauses, auxiliary verbs raise to Infl while main verbs do not. Emonds (1978) argues that in French finite clauses, both types of verbs raise. Pollock (1989), developing these ideas further, gives minimal pairs such as (A1) vs. (A2).

(A1) *John likes not Mary

(A2) Jean (n')aime pas Marie

Pollock proposes that this difference between French and English follows from differences in Infl. Specifically, Pollock proposes that richness of inflection is the relevant distinguishing characteristic. This is instantiated in the following way: Verb raising to an affix creates a configuration headed by that affix, as in (A3).

(A3) $[_{\text{Aff}}$ [V [Aff]]

Auxiliary verbs are claimed to differ from main verbs in not assigning θ-roles. Then, the ill-formedness of (A1), or any other instance of main verb raising in English, follows from the θ-Criterion on the assumption that

"...AGR in English, unlike AGR in French, is not 'rich' enough morphologically to permit transmission of the verb's θ-role(s), i.e., is 'opaque' to θ-role assignment, unlike French AGR, which, being richer morphologically, is 'transparent' to θ-role assignment."

For an English main verb, then, the association of affix and verb will have to be via Affix Hopping, instead of verb raising (the conclusion of Emonds (1978)). This is an appealing analysis, though it is unclear why richness should correlate directly, rather than inversely, with transparency. There is one empirical difficulty that is of relevance to the analysis in the text. As Pollock discusses, given that the constraint on raising follows entirely from the θ-Criterion, and given that auxiliary verbs assign no θ-roles, there should be no constraint on the raising of such verbs. Even in infinitives, then, raising of auxiliaries should be possible, on these proposals. Pollock makes exactly this claim, though he does concede that the facts are murky. But we have seen a number of examples where aux raising was good in finite clauses but clearly bad in the corresponding non-finite ones. I repeat some of those examples below:

(A4) John is not noisy

(A5) *Be not noisy

Lasnik (1981) discusses (A4) vs. (A5) precisely in connection with the present concern: This pair suggests that verb raising is possible only in finite clauses. Further, under the analysis of Lasnik (1981), or that of Chomsky (1991), *do*-support is possible only when verb raising is not. Thus, the grammaticality of (A6) follows from the ungrammaticality of (A5).

(A6) Do not be noisy

As seen in the text, infinitivals pattern with imperatives in disallowing raising.

(A7) *I believe there to be not a solution
(A8) I believe there is not a solution

(A9) ?*I believe John to be not here

(A10) I believe John is not here

(A11) ?*I believe John to be not singing

(A12) I believe John is not singing

Thus, the patterning of data is somewhat different from what Pollock suggests. Putting aside the short raising cases Pollock presents for French, we find the following for verb raising to Infl:

(A13)

	English		French	
	finite	non-finite	finite	non-finite
main verb	*	*	ok	*
auxiliary verb	ok	*	ok	ok

There are three cases, evidently: 1) In English non-finite clauses, there is no raising at all; 2) in French finite clauses, any verb can raise; 3) French non-finite clauses are like English finite clauses—only aux verbs can raise. Suppose we classify affixes according to strength or richness, essentially following Pollock. Then French finite Infl could be classified as strong; English finite Infl and French non-finite Infl as moderate; and English non-finite Infl as weak. This third classification is plausible since there is no overt affixal morphology whatsoever in this case. Verbs too fall into categories, two in this case. Let us designate main verbs as strong and auxiliary verbs as moderate. Assuming, with Pollock, that verb raising involves adjunction of the verb to the affix, the generalization is that an affix cannot support as a dependant a verb that is stronger than it is. The following adjunction configurations are excluded:

(A14) * moderate (strong moderate)   *weak (strong weak)   *weak (moderate weak)

Strength of verbs apparently involves a number of factors. One of them is, perhaps, ability to assign a θ-role. But this cannot be all of it, if Pollock is right that auxiliary verbs assign no θ-roles. Another factor might be semantic content. Auxiliary verbs do, after all, contribute something to the meanings of the sentences in which they occur. In support of this conjecture, note that the imperative affix, which lacks any morphological realization, can still support pleonastic, contentless, *do*, as evidenced by (A6) above, even though it cannot support any other verb. One question remains. Why is infinitival Infl incapable of supporting even *do*?

(A15) *I believe there to do not be a solution

I offer the conjecture that while imperatives involve a morphologically impoverished affix (as argued in Lasnik (1981)), English infinitives involve no affix at all.

FOOTNOTES

*This article appeared in slightly different form in *Linguistic Inquiry*, Volume 23, Number 3. I am grateful to Maria Bittner, Noam Chomsky, Catherine Chvany, Samuel D. Epstein, David Pesetsky, Mamoru Saito, Lisa Travis, two *Linguistic Inquiry* reviewers, and a reviewer for this volume for valuable suggestions. In addition to presentation at the Second Princeton Workshop on Comparative Grammar, portions of this material were presented in seminars and/or colloquia at the following universities: University of Connecticut, University of Massachusetts, Massachusetts Institute of Technology, University of Tsukuba, International Christian University, University of Arizona, City University of New York, University of Toronto, University of Maryland, University of the Basque Country. The questions and suggestions of the audiences at those presentations have led to numerous improvements of the analysis.

[1] Throughout this discussion, 'WH-trace' will refer just to the trace of a WH-moved NP. Presumably, the trace of an AP, for example, need not be Case-marked.
[2] For example, Chomsky (1986, 95) claims that "*there* is linked only to non-Case-marked argument NP..."
[3] Safir (1982), while advocating a transmission approach, acknowledges the difficulty raised by such examples and considers various stipulations to address the difficulty.
[4] Safir (1982) briefly considers this possibility, rejecting it for reasons that will not be relevant under the account developed here.
[5] Emonds (1970;1976) and Jackendoff (1972) present analyses similar to the one I will discuss.
[6] See the Appendix below for further discussion of this limitation and its parametric properties.
[7] Emonds (1976) also gives a statement of v-raising with TENSE as a context term. However, as far as I can tell, he presents no explicit arguments for this detail of his rule.
[8] The two crucial properties of v-raising in English—that it is limited to auxiliary verbs and that it applies only in the presence of tense—will be briefly explored in the Appendix below.
[9] As noted earlier, CHAINs are expletive argument sets. At LF, they become chains via NP movement. Following Chomsky, in this discussion I limit this analysis to the expletive *there*. I leave open the possibility of extending it to *it*. Such an extension seems a priori plausible, on both empirical and conceptual grounds. Like *there*, *it* must be Case marked, and must be local to its associated argument, a clausal one in this instance. An S- structure like (i) would then become an LF like (ii).

(i) It surprised me [that Mary left]
(ii) [That Mary left] surprised me <u>t</u>

Potentially problematic is the example in (iii), since the predicted LF (iv), unlike the one in (ii), is not possible as an S-structure.

(iii) It seems [that Mary left]
(iv) (*) [That Mary left] seems <u>t</u>

However, note that just the same difficulty arises with *there*. S- structure (v) becomes LF (vi); but (vi) is ill-formed as an S-structure.

(v) There is a solution
(vi) (*) A solution is t

I assume that (vi) and (iv) instantiate the same problem. While the problem is a difficult one, it is quite limited in extent lexically: to the verb *be* in *there* constructions, and to the verbs *seem* and *appear* in *it* constructions, as far as I know.
[10] Chomsky (1986) proposes that one sort of Case —inherent Case—is assigned at D-structure. I put aside consideration of this proposal. See Lasnik and Saito (1992) for some discussion.
[11] It is possible that there would be other violations as well in this example. If the lower *there* is skipped, the resulting LF structure will be as in (i):

(i) A man_i is likely [there to be t_i here]

Since *a man* is rather far from its trace, Condition A or the ECP might be violated here. On the other hand, it is not clear that the lower clause constitutes either a governing category or a barrier. I leave these questions open.

A further example susceptible to the same line of analysis suggested in the text is as follows:

(ii) *There arrival of a man

This is reminiscent of a type of example considered by Chomsky (1986):

(iii) *There's arrival of a man

But while (iii) can be ruled out as a violation of Chomsky's Uniformity Condition (which entails that genitive Case, being inherent, can only be assigned under θ-marking), (ii) apparently cannot, since no inherent Case has been assigned to *there*. Under the proposals in the text, (ii) will violate the Full Interpretation requirement, since *there* will not be visible as a target for the movement of *a man*. Note that it could not be that *there* needs Case in order to satisfy a Case requirement of *a man*, since (iv) is grammatical even though *a man* is not associated with any other Case-marked position.

(iv) The arrival of a man

[12] As Samuel D. Epstein (personal communication) notes, if this requirement of 'movement visibility' covers not just the target of movement but the item to be moved as well, then the S-structure Case requirement on arguments follows completely. θ-visibility is apparently rendered redundant at S-structure.
[13] An alternative to 'movement visibility' might also be considered. Suppose that, at a given level, an NP must be licensed in an appropriate way. At S-structure, for an overt argument, or a chain headed by one, the licensing mechanism would be Case. Presumably, this is the relevant licensing mechanism for wh-trace as well, but see Epstein (1987) and Shlonsky (1987) for alternatives. Finally, since for PRO the mechanism could not possibly be Case, it is reasonable to assume that it is Control. If Case and Control are the only possibilities, then clearly an expletive will have to have Case, unless that expletive can be Controlled. See Lasnik (1992) for discussion of the non-existence of that latter possibility.
[14] Belletti's partitive Case proposal provides the basis for an answer to a puzzle raised by Chomsky's expletive replacement analysis, adopted above. As first noted by Lori Davis (personal communication), there is apparently an incorrect prediction con-

cerning scope in existential constructions. In (i), as is well known, both wide scope and narrow scope are available for *someone*, while in (ii), only narrow scope is.

(i) Someone is likely to be here
(ii) There is likely to be someone here

But under the expletive replacement hypothesis, the LFs of the two examples would appear to be identical. Assuming that LF determines scope, this is a paradox. However, there is a potentially relevant difference between the two examples. In (ii), *someone* must receive partitive Case at S-structure. In (i), on the other hand, *someone* receives nominative Case, and the trace of *someone* need not receive Case at all. The correct descriptive generalization is statable in terms of Belletti's partitive Case: Partitive Case marks the position of a variable. In (ii), then, the variable bound by the quantifier *someone* is necessarily in the lower clause. Given the general 'clause-boundedness' of quantifier raising, the quantifier too must be associated with the lower clause. Note that under this account, clause-boundedness becomes a condition on representation, which, in effect, forces quantifier lowering, in the sense of May (1977;1985), after *someone* has replaced *there* in the higher clause. See Barss and Lasnik (in preparation) for further discussion.

There is one further scope puzzle considered by Safir (1982) that falls under the same general account. Although, as seen above, (i) is ambiguous, (iii)) is not:

(iii) There is someone likely to be here

To describe the difference in usual terms, quantifier lowering is available in (i) but not in (iii). (iii) does not have a reading like that of (ii). This property of (iii) seems to fall neatly under the proposal of Williams (1984) that *there* is a 'scope marker'. However, that proposal does not handle the full range of relevant phenomena. In particular, it appears to be inconsistent with the interpretive properties of (ii), as observed by Safir (1987). In that example, as already discussed, the scope of *there* is crucially limited to the lower clause, even though the associated *there* occurs in the higher clause. No such problem arises on the account presented here. In (iii), *someone* is in the higher clause, and is necessarily marked partitive in that position. Correspondingly, the variable is in that position, and, to bind it, the quantifier must also be on the higher clause. Hence, there is no lowered reading. In (ii), on the other hand, the crucially partitive Case-marked position was in the embedded clause, so, correspondingly, the variable occurred in that position.

[15] The clearest instances I know of have the curious property that they are based on well-formed sentences that are themselves inconsistent with Burzio's generalization. Consider (i).

(i) It strikes me that Mary is peculiar

Here we have a verb that seems to assign Case to an object, *me*, but no θ-role to a subject. And now note that NP movement to that subject position is impossible:

(ii) *I_i strike $\underline{t}_i$ that Mary is peculiar

At present, I don't know an alternative to the ban on Case-marked trace for dealing with this phenomenon, but the fact that the phenomenon is so limited suggests that it should not be handled by such a broad and general constraint.

[16] Safir also presents counter-arguments, to which the interested reader is hereby referred, to Williams's criticisms of the small clause analysis.
[17] The prohibition on (structurally) Case-marked trace alluded to above is potentially problematic for (i) at S-structure and for (ii) at LF.

(i) Someone is [t here]
(ii) There is [someone here]

If Case marking is optional, the problem of (i) disappears, but that of (ii) remains. In (ii), even if Case-marking is optional, *someone* must be assigned Case at S-structure, or the Case filter/visibility requirement will be violated. The LF chain created by expletive replacement will then evidently terminate in a Case-marked trace. A potential solution to this problem relies on the fact that partitive Case assignment, even though structural here, does have semantic import. It is thus reasonable to conjecture that it is assigned not to the category NP, but to the contents of that category. Then, when the NP moves, it carries the Case along with it, just as it carries all other NP internal properties with it. The resulting trace is then without Case, just as it is without phonetic features. However, it is not clear that this conjecture can be reconciled with the analysis of scope presented in footnote 14. Below, the evidence for the structural nature of the partitive Case in (ii) will be reconsidered.
[18] Enc, argues that the standardly discussed definiteness distinction is more accurately analyzed in terms of specificity.
[19] Glinert (1989) vacillates between calling *et* a 'definite object marker' and calling it a preposition. In several respects, though, it has the behavior of accusative Case. Glinert notes that, in comparison with verbs taking other prepositions, "verbs taking *et* are much more likely to have a passive equivalent (by which *et* drops)." Needless to say, this is quite typical accusative behavior. Further, Glinert observes that nominalizations of verbs taking *et* introduce their object not with *et* but with *shel* 'of'. This is strikingly similar to the patterning of accusative in English.
[20] My remarks on the genitive of negation in Russian are based on the detailed discussion in Pesetsky (1982). See also Chvany (1975) for extensive discussion of existential constructions, and their negations, in Russian.
[21] See Willim (1988) for arguments that the negative element in Polish (which displays similar genitive of negation phenomena to those of Russian) is a clitic on the verb. Bar-Shalom (1986) presents related arguments for Russian. This strengthens the suggested parallel with passive, which also involves a verbal affix.
[22] This line of reasoning is, on the face of it, inconsistent with the conjecture above that it is the passive morpheme that is responsible for the assignment of partitive Case in Italian. This is so since partitive is, crucially, inherent in passive constructions, yet the passive morpheme, like the negative morpheme in Slavic, would seem to have no θ-roles to assign. Hence, we would expect Case assignment by the former to be structural, as it is for the latter. Perhaps the difference is that the passive morpheme, unlike the negative morpheme, is so closely related to the thematic structure of the verb it attaches to. Below, we will find further cause for reconsidering this approach to Italian passives.

REFERENCES

Aoun, J. (1979) "On Government, Case-marking, and Clitic Placement," ms. MIT.
Babby, L. (1980) *Existential Sentences and Negation in Russian* Karoma, Ann Arbor.
Bar-Shalom, E. (1986) "The Non-Theta Subject Position in Russian," ms., University of Connecticut.
Barss, A. and H. Lasnik (in preparation) "Quantifier Lowering".
Belletti, A. (1988) "The Case of Unaccusatives," *Linguistic Inquiry* 19, 1-34.
Burzio, L. (1986) *Italian Syntax*, Reidel, Dordrecht.
Chenausky, K. (1990) "Case in English Existential Sentences," ms. University of Connecticut.
Chomsky, N. (1955) *The Logical Structure of Linguistic Theory* [Published, in part, by Plenum, New York (1975)].
——— (1980) "On Binding," *Linguistic Inquiry* 11, 1-46.
——— (1981) *Lectures on Government and Binding* Foris, Dordrecht.
——— (1986) *Knowledge of Language* Praeger, New York.
——— (1986a) *Barriers* MIT Press, Cambridge, Mass.
——— (1991) "Some Notes on Economy of Derivation and Representation," in R. Freidin, ed., (1991) *Principles and Parameters in Comparative Grammar*, MIT Press, Cambridge, Massachusetts.
Chomsky, N. and H. Lasnik (1977) "Filters and Control," *Linguistic Inquiry* 11, 1-46. [Reprinted in Lasnik (1990).]
Chvany, C. (1975) *On the Syntax of BE-Sentences in Russian* Slavica, Cambridge, Massachusetts.
Emonds, J. (1970) *Root and Structure Preserving Transformations*, MIT Ph.D. diss.
——— (1976) *A Transformational Approach to English Syntax*, Academic Press, New York.
——— (1978) "The Verbal Complex V'-V" in French," *Linguistic Inquiry* 9, 151-175.
Enc,, M. (1991) "The Semantics of Specificity," *Linguistic Inquiry* 22, 1-25.
Epstein, S. D. (1987) *Empty Categories and their Antecedents*, University of Connecticut Ph.D. diss.
Freidin, R. and L. Babby (1984) "On the Interaction of Lexical and Structural Properties: Case Structure in Russian," *Cornell Working Papers in Linguistics* 6.
Glinert, L. (1989) *The Grammar of Modern Hebrew*, Cambridge University Press.
Jackendoff, R. (1972) *Semantic Interpretation in Generative Grammar*, MIT Press, Cambridge, Massachusetts.
Lasnik, H. (1981) "Restricting the Theory of Transformations," in N. Hornstein and D. Lightfoot (eds.) *Explanation in Linguistics*, Longmans, London. [Reprinted in Lasnik (1990).]
——— (1990) *Essays on Restrictiveness and Learnability*, Kluwer, Dordrecht.
——— (1992) "Two Notes on Control and Binding," ms. University of Connecticut. in R. Larson et. al., (eds.), *Control and Grammar*, Kluwer, Dordrecht.
Lasnik, H. and R. Freidin (1981) "Core Grammar, Case Theory, and Markedness," in A. Belletti et al, (eds.), *Theory of Markedness ion Generative Grammar* Pisa. [Reprinted in Lasnik (1990).]
Lasnik, H. and M. Saito (1992) *Move* α, MIT Press, Cambridge, Mass.
May, R. (1977) *The Grammar of Quantification*, MIT Ph.D. diss.

——— (1985) *Logical Form*, MIT Press, Cambridge, Mass.
Neidle, C. (1988) *The Role of Case in Russian Syntax*, Reidel, Dordrecht.
Pesetsky, D. (1982) *Paths and Categories*, MIT Ph.D. diss.
Pollock, J.-Y. (1989) "Verb Movement, UG and the Structure of IP," *Linguistic Inquiry* 20, 365-424.
Rapoport, T. (1987) *Copular, Nominal, and Small Clauses: A Study of Israeli Hebrew*, MIT Ph.D. diss.
Safir, K. (1982) *Syntactic Chains and the Definiteness Effect*, MIT Ph.D. diss.
——— (1987) "So There! A Reply to Williams' Analysis of There-Sentences," in M. A. Browning, E. Czaykowski- Higgins, and E. Ritter, eds., *MIT Working Papers in Linguistics* 9, Department of Linguistics and Philosophy, MIT.
Shlonsky, U. (1987) *Null and Displaced Subjects*, MIT Ph.D. diss.
Stowell, T. (1981) *Origins of Phrase Structure*, MIT Ph.D. diss.
Travis, L. (1989) "Notes on Case and Expletives," Presented at the Second Princeton Workshop on Comparative Grammar.
Williams, E. (1984) "*There*-Insertion," *Linguistic Inquiry* 15, 131- 153.
Willim, E. (1988) "On Case-marking in Polish," ms., Jagellonian University.

LISA TRAVIS

NOTES ON CASE AND EXPLETIVES: A DISCUSSION OF LASNIK'S PAPER*

INTRODUCTION

The main claim of Lasnik's paper is that in expletive NP chains, the postverbal NP as well as the expletive needs Case. This differs from many of the traditional analyses in the belief that the NP does not get its Case via CHAIN formation with the expletive, but rather needs to get its Case independently. In these comments, I focus my attention on the nature of this Case assignment. Lasnik, in order to account for intralanguage and interlanguage variation makes certain proposals. In order to account for the difference in behavior between *be* and other verbs that take small clause complements such as *consider*, he links inherent Case assignment to theta-role assignment only for theta-assigning verbs (such as *consider*), and not for non-theta-assigning verbs (such as *be*). To account for the ability of Italian passives to assign partitive Case, unlike their English counterparts, he proposes a parameter by which the passive morpheme itself assigns partitive Case in Italian but not in English (or alternatively, verbs in English can assign only one Case so that if they assign accusative Case they can never assign partitive). After a detour into the empirical arguments that Lasnik gives for assuming that existential *be* assigns Case to the following NP, I will turn to these two proposals. I argue that the difference in *be* falls out from a structural distinction that distinguishes *be* from verbs like *consider*. Then, in an effort to link the Italian/English difference to already attested variations between these two languages, I argue that partitive Case assignment in Italian passives is due to the availability of restructuring in this language.

1.0 DATA AND GENERALIZATIONS

Lasnik gives two empirical reasons to argue that existential *be* (which I will call eBE) assigns Case to the following NP (which I will call the existential NP or eNP). In this section I discuss each of these reasons in turn. The first argues that adjacency requirements on the eNP indicate that Case assignment is involved. To support this, Lasnik points to the following contrasts.

(1) a. There will be a man here.
b. There is usually a man here.
c. ?*There will be usually a man here. (HL: 36)
d. *I believe there to be usually a solution. (HL: 45)

His argument is that (1c) and (1d) are ungrammatical since the NPs *a man* and *a solution* must be adjacent to *be* to get Case. These strings are to be compared with (1a) where the NP is adjacent to *be* and to (1b) where the NP is adjacent to the trace of the raised verb. The link between an adjacency effect and Case assignment is made in parallel fashion to examples such as (2a) below. (I have added example (2b) which may be more appropriate since a VP-type manner adverb is used.)

(2) a. *I heard usually a car (HL: 37)
    b. *I heard clearly a car.

The second set of facts presented by Lasnik show that the existential *be* is obligatory in clauses containing an eNP. He argues that the presence of *be* is necessary in order to assign Case to this NP.

(3) a. I want someone (to be) here at 6:00.
    b. I want there to be someone here at 6:00. (HL: 19)
    c. *I want there someone here at 6:00.

As (3a) shows, *to be* is usually optional in a clause following a verb like *want* (*consider*, etc.). There is no such optionality, however, when the (small) clause has an expletive subject. *To be* must be present. Within Lasnik's analysis, this is due to the fact that *be* is needed to assign Case to the NP.[1] While Lasnik's account of this generalization appears at first problematic, I will conclude that, in fact, his claim is supported.

1.1 Case adjacency and predicate NPs

While there appears to be an adjacency effect in existential structures, it is not clear that all adjacency effects have to do with Case. To make the pattern complete, one must show that elements that do not require Case do not have to be adjacent to *be*. In this context, the following data raise interesting questions.

(4) a. They will be deliberately idiotic.
    b. I believe the children to have been deliberately idiotic.
    c. ?*They will be deliberately idiots.
    d. ?*I believe the children to have been deliberately idiots.

These data at first seem to uphold Lasnik's claim that NPs (and not APs) which follow *be* are assigned Case by the verb and, therefore, must be adjacent to the verb. It is important to note, however, that the post-verbal NPs in (4) bear a different relationship to *be* than do the NPs in (1). While the post-verbal NPs in (4) overtly follow the verb, they are, in fact, predicates of small clauses. The NP that follows the verb at D-structure has been raised to subject position. The relevant structure is given below.

(5) they$_i$ will be deliberately [$_{SC}$ t$_i$ idiots]

The question is why the predicate NP appears to have adjacency facts similar to those given by Lasnik for expletive NPs. If we were to say that *be* also assigns Case to an NP that is a predicate of a small clause (predicative Case), we would run into a problem with Lasnik's second set of examples. His argument that the obligatory presence of *be* in embedded infinitivals disappears if one requires predicate NPs of small clauses also to be assigned Case.

(6) a. I consider them **intellects**.
b. *I consider there **a man** in the room.

If *consider* assigns Case to *intellects* in (6a), we might also expect it to be able to assign Case to *a man* in (6b). In order to preserve the conclusions of Lasnik's obligatory *be* argument, therefore, I will assume that predicative NPs do not require Case and that the explanation for the adjacency facts falls outside of the domain of Case theory.[2]

1.2 Obligatory be

There is a further problem with Lasnik's second argument for his Case account of the variation shown in (3b,c), however. One might argue that Case is not needed to rule out the ungrammatical string since phrase structure will independently rule it out. Presumably *want* may select a small clause, and this small clause will consist of a subject position and a predicate position. Further, we may assume that the predicate position may consist of the normal predicate types such as AP, PP, etc. If this predicate assigns an external theta-role, the subject position must be filled by an argument. If this predicate assigns no external theta-role, the subject position must be filled by a pleonastic. The two cases are given below.[3]

(7) a. I consider [$_{SC}$ the children [$_{A*}$ intelligent]]
b. I consider [$_{SC}$ there [$_{A*}$ likely to be a storm tonight]]

In (7a), the subject position of *intelligent* is assigned a theta-role and requires an argument. In (7b), the subject position of *likely* is not assigned a theta-role, therefore a pleonastic is possible. Given these assumptions, it is not clear what the structure of (3c) would be. If there is no verb and no INFL, one could argue that there is no position to house the pleonastic *there*. Following the example given in (7b), in order to have a pleonastic *there* in (3c), *someone here* would have to be a predicate which assigns no external theta-role. But since *someone here* is already a small clause, the structure would be similar to that in (8) where the small clause has as its predicate another small clause. It is not obvious, however, that a small clause is a possible predicate and such a structure would require independent evidence.

(8) $[_{VP}$ $[_{V}$ want] $[_{SC}$ $[_{NP}$ there] $[_{SC}$ someone here]]]

One would argue that the reason why the addition of *to be* in (3b) makes the string grammatical is that an appropriate phrase structure is created. The verb *be* will select a small clause *someone here* and the addition of a functional category above the VP will create a specifier position which can house the pleonastic. In this view, the generalization is not whether or not there is a Case assigner for the eNP, but rather whether there is an appropriate specifier position for the pleonastic.

While this account of the facts presented in (3) looks appealing, Sportiche (1990) has introduced data which suggest that all small clauses involve movement of the subject. If there is such movement, then there must be a theta-bar position to act as a landing site. If there is such a theta-bar position, there should be a possible place for pleonastics. Sportiche's argument runs as follows. It has been shown that the fronting of constituents containing anaphors may extend the number of possible antecedents of the anaphor. This is shown in the examples below where in (9a) only *the boys* may be the antecedent of the reciprocal *each other*, while in (9b) either *the boys* or *the girls* may be the antecedent (examples taken from Sportiche, pp. 12-13).

(9) a. The girls$_i$ say that the boys$_k$ like the painting of each other$_{*i/k}$.
b. Which painting of each other$_{i/k}$ do the girls$_i$ say the boys$_k$ like?

The possibility of picking up an additional candidate for binding does not occur with all fronting. In (10), only *the boys* may act as an antecedent, and not *the girls.*

(10) Listen to each other$_{*i/k}$, the girls$_i$ say the boys$_k$ do.

One may account for this difference (see Barss 1985, Huang 1990) by supposing that the fronting of a VP carries with it the VP-internal trace of the moved subject. The anaphor must then refer to this trace as the closest subject. Fronting of an NP as in (9) carries with it no such trace and therefore no such restriction. A perhaps surprising result is pointed out by Sportiche. When an AP is fronted from a small clause, it behaves like the VP in (10) above, i.e. as if it contained a trace of a moved subject. This explains the ungrammaticality of (11a) below. *They* is not a possible antecedent for *each other* since the trace in the fronted AP will act as a closer antecedent.

(11) a. *How proud of each other do they consider John.

b. [t_k how proud of each other]$_i$ [do they consider John$_k$ t_i]

This implies, then, that the subject of a small clause must have moved from its base-generated position to some sort of derived object position. While it is a matter of debate what exactly the landing site is (see e.g. Johnson 1991, Mahajan 1990, Sportiche 1990, Travis 1991), if it is a possible landing site, one might presume that it is also a possible position for a pleonastic and that the string in (3c) cannot be ruled out by restrictions on phrase structure. A possible tree is given below, where F stands for some unnamed functional category.

(12) [$_{VP}$ V [$_{FP}$ [$_{NP}$ there] [$_{F'}$ F [$_{SC}$ [$_{NP}$ someone] [$_{PP}$ here]]]]]

The conclusion is, then, that we are back at the beginning, looking for an explanation for (3c). Why is it not possible to leave *a man* in the base-generated subject position of the small clause and put the pleonastic *there* in SPEC of FP? I will argue that Lasnik is, in fact, correct in assuming that Case must be assigned to the eNP and that this accounts for the ungrammaticality of (3c).

2.0 BE VS. CONSIDER

Given that Lasnik assumes that the Case assigned to the eNP is the partitive Case, an interesting problem arises. Belleti (1988) assumes that partitive Case is an inherent Case, and as such, cannot be assigned into a small clause. This is shown in the following examples.

(13) ho sempre considerato [$_{SC}$Gianni intelligente] (HL: 73)
I have always considered Gianni intelligent

(14) E stato messo un libro sul tavolo (HL: 71)
has been put a book on the table

(15) *Sono considerati [$_{SC}$alcuni studenti intelligenti] (HL: 74)
are considered some students intelligent

(13) shows that accusative Case may be assigned to the subject of a small clause, and (14) shows that passives may assign partitive Case. (15) shows, however, that these two mechanisms may not be combined. In other words, a passive may not assign partitive Case to the subject of a small clause. This, presumably, is due to the fact that partitive Case is inherent Case and therefore linked to the theta-assignment of the head. Since *consider* does not assign a theta-role to the subject of the small clause, it cannot assign it in-

herent partitive Case. The problem arises with the existential *be* constructions. Here it appears as if partitive Case is being assigned into a small clause.

(16) There will be $[_{SC}$ a man here]

Lasnik's solution is to say that partitive Case is only linked to theta-roles if the verb has theta-roles to assign as in the case of *consider*. If the verb has no theta-roles to assign, as in the case of *be*, the linking of Case assignment with theta-role assignment is not possible therefore not necessary.

I propose here, drawing on Ritter (1988) that the difference between *be* and *consider* is, in fact, a structural one. Ritter claims that *yeS*, the Hebrew counterpart to existential *be*, has the structure given in (17a) below using Larson's (1988) analysis of VPs. A rationale that might be given for such a structure is that, according to UTAH, Themes are generated as the external argument of VP2 (the label of VPs will be slightly changed later in the discussion). The structure of *be*, then, looks very similar to the structure of *put*, except that there is no external argument.

(17) a. Ritter (1988)
$[_{VP}\ [_{V'}\ [_{V}\ \text{is}_i\ ]\ [_{VP2}\ [_{NP}\ \text{a man}\ ]\ [_{V'}\ [_{V}\ t_i\ ]\ [_{PP}\ \text{in the room}\ ]]]]]$
b. Larson (1988)
$[_{VP}\ \text{she}\ [_{V'}\ [_{V}\ \text{put}_i\ ]\ [_{VP2}\ [_{NP}\ \text{the book}\ ]\ [_{V'}\ [_{V}\ t_i\ ]\ [_{PP}\ \text{on the table}\ ]]]]]$

Since the relation that holds between *put* and its object exhibits the core case of inherent Case assigment, it is not surprising that existential *be* is allowed to assign Case to the following NP. Further, the distinction between existential *be* and a verb such as *consider* is clear as shown in (18).

(18) a. $[_{VP}\ [_{V}\ \text{is}_i\ ]\ [_{VP}\ [_{NP}\ \text{someone}\ ]\ [_{V'}\ [_{V}\ t_i\ ]\ [_{PP}\ \text{in the room}\ ]]]]$
b. $[_{VP}\ [_{V}\ \text{consider}\ ]\ [_{FP}\ [_{NP_i}\ \text{some student}\ ]\ [_{F'}\ F\ [_{SC}\ t_i\ [_{AP}\ \text{intelligent}\ ]]]]]$

Whether the ability to have such Case assignment has to do with theta-role assignment or the complete transparency of VP_2 due to head movement, I leave open for further research. The important result, however, is that given the structure independently argued for in Ritter (1988), the difference between *be* and *consider* is due to a difference in structure. Now we may maintain Belletti's claim that partitive Case as an inherent Case may never be assigned to the subject of a small clause without weakening the restrictions on inherent Case assignment.

3.0 English passives vs. Italian passives

A second concern which is raised by Lasnik involves a parameter distinguishing Italian passives from English passives. As noted in (14) above, Italian passives may assign partitive Case allowing their direct objects to remain in D-structure position. This is not, however, true for English passives as shown in (19) below.

(19) *There has been put a book on the table. (HL: 87)

To account for this difference, Lasnik proposes two possibilities for a parameter. One possibility is that the passive morpheme in Italian but not in English can assign partitive Case. This, he argues, makes the Italian passive morpheme behave like NEG in Russian and Polish. The second possibility is that in English verbs may assign only one Case, so transitive verbs may only assign accusative Case. This means that when passivization absorbs this single Case, the passive verb has no Case left to assign. In Italian, verbs may assign more than one Case, like in Hebrew and Turkish, therefore transitive verbs may assign accusative and partitive. With passive morphology only accusative Case is lost.

3.1 Restructuring parameter

The problem with both of these parameters is that they solve only the problem at hand. If parameters truly capture a cluster of language specific phenomena, we would prefer an account which would link this Italian/English difference to some other distinguishing feature. Here I will argue that the ability of passive verbs in Italian to assign partitive Case to their objects is due to the availability of restructuring in this language. In particular, I would like to relate this to the *fare...da* constructions. The superficial similarities of these constructions are clear when we look at the following patterns.

(20) a. *There has been put a book on the table. (HL: 87)
b. E stato messo un libro sul tavolo (HL: 71)
c. *Maria makes intervene Giovanni.
d. Maria fa intervenire Giovanni. (Burzio 1986; pg. 236: 18b)

I argue that the similarities between these two structures are due to similarities between passive *be* (which I will call pBE) and *fare.* I claim that both s-select the "bottom VP", which I call VnP, in a Larson type structure, that both are restructuring verbs in Italian, and that both may have a Case that may be passed on to the object of the lower verb.[4] Note that VnP is s-selected by *fare* and passive *be.*

(21) $[_{VP}\ \text{AGT}\ [_{V'}\ \text{V}\ [_{VnP}\ \text{TH}\ [_{Vn'}\ \text{Vn XP}\ ]]]]$

To start this discussion, let us first look at the status of this "lower" VP. I claim that the top VP and the bottom VP are different in kind. First, the lower verb in this VP has no Case-assigning abilities.[5] Guilfoyle, Hung, and

Travis (in press) argue that this is true for Malagasy verbs and here I extend it to verbs in all languages. It is only through movement to the higher V that the verb may achieve Case-assigner status. A second property of this "lower" VP is that it has no position to which the external theta-role may be directly discharged. If it appears at all, it may only appear in an adjunct *by*-phrase. Since both of these properties are reminiscent of nominal heads, I call the "lower" VP a VnP; a verbal noun (or a nominal verb) similar to that in Irish (McCloskey 1983, Guilfoyle 1990).

Returning to the problem of *fare*, let us first look at the mechanism that allows *Giovanni* to be assigned Case in (20d). *Intervenire* is an unaccusative verb and therefore cannot be responsible for the accusative Case assigned to its object. It is clear that it is the presence of *fa* which allows this Case to be assigned. While there have been a variety of proposals concerning the details of Case assignment (e.g. Burzio 1986, Manzini 1983), I will assume an analysis involving S-structure coindexation and LF V-incorporation along the lines of Baker (1988).[6] If *intervenire* is coindexed with *fa*, together they may assign the accusative Case of *fa* to *Giovanni* in object position. The proposal outlined above takes an even stronger position. It predicts that no verb embedded in a *fare...da* construction will be able to assign accusative Case. This means that in (22) below, *la macchina* cannot be assigned Case directly by the verb *riparare*. Instead, it is assigned Case by the virtue of the fact that the verb *riparare* has combined with the accusative Case assigning verb *fare*.

(22) Maria fa riparare la macchina (da Giovanni) (Burzio: p.248: 44)
Maria has the car repaired (by Giovanni)

In both constructions, the passive and the causative, there will be an intermediary functional category. For the sake of this paper, I simply call this FP, though elsewhere (Travis 1991) I argue that it is an Aspect Phrase which can show agreement with the object.[7] The relevant structures are given in (23).

(23) a. $[_{VP}$ [V' $[_{V_i}$ fa [+acc]] $[_{FP}$ $[_{F'}$ $[_{F_i}$ intervenire$_k$] $[_{VnP}$ TH $[_{Vn'}$ $[_{Vn}$ t_k] XP]]]]]]
b. $[_{VP}$ [V' $[_{V_i}$ stato [+part]] $[_{FP}$ $[_{F'}$ $[_{F_i}$ messo$_k$] $[_{VnP}$ TH $[_{Vn'}$ $[_{Vn}$ t_k] XP]]]]]]

In both constructions, there will be coindexation of the higher V and the moved Vn. This is the formalization I assume for the traditional concept of restructuring. Through this coindexation, the lower Vn now takes on the Case assigning abilities of the top V. Note that the external argument will never be able to receive this Case as it is in an adjunct position and will never be governed by the verb. It is precisely the restructuring type of coindexation that allows *fare* to assign accusative Case to the embedded object, and that allows the pBE to assign partitive Case (optionally) to the embedded object.

Now it is clear what the difference is between Italian (and other Romance languages) and English. No new parameter need be proposed. English does not allow the passive participle to assign Case to its object since there is no restructuring in English. Since there is no restructuring, the partitive Case from pBE may not be passed on to the passive participle.

Note that this is in some ways similar to Lasnik's suggestion that it is the passive morphology on the verb that allows partitive Case to be assigned in Italian. In the present analysis, however, it is not the passive morphology as much as the presence of passive BE that is responsible for this Case assignment. More important is that this particular fact about Italian is tied to another particular fact about Italian. It is a language which allows restructuring.

3.2 Short passive movement: Existential BE vs. Passive BE

Above I have tried to answer the question of why Italian allows passive with no movement whereas English does not. A related question may be asked as to why English appears to allow passive with short movement while Italian does not. Sportiche (1990) raises this problem in discussing differences between French and English. The relevant data are given in (24) below. The examples in (25) show that Italian patterns with French.

(24) a. *There were killed three men. (Sportiche 1990: pg. 88)
b. There were three men killed.
c. Il a été tué trois hommes.
d. *Il a été trois hommes tués.

(25) a. There has been a book put on the table
b. *E stato un libro messo sul tavolo.

At first these facts look attractive for Lasnik's analysis. Sportiche states the generalization for English as follows: "I suggest that the classical approach to *there* insertion is correct : Insertion of *there* is licensed in the specifier of *be* when *be* governs an argument. Movement to the position governed by *be* is therefore necessary." (p.88) Lasnik easily accounts for this with his version of visibility. Since the eNP requires Case, and since passive cannot assign Case in English, movement to a position governed by *be* is required.

While these data appear to confirm Lasnik's proposal, they raise problems for the proposals sketched in this paper. I have adopted Ritter's structure for eBE in order to explain the assignment of inherent Case to the eNP. It is crucial that the eNP be an argument of eBE. What, then, would be the structure of a string such as (24b)? In order to have *three men* receive partitive Case, it must be the Theme of be+PRED. However, since *three men* originates as the object of *killed*, it already receives a theta-role in this position. The data below (developed from similar examples in Sportiche 1990) show even more clearly that the eNP is an argument of a lower predicate. Neither (26a) nor (26b) can be analyzed as an adjectival passive.

(26) a. There were two students given awards.
b. There were only two students considered intelligent enough to enter the competition.

In spite of this, I will argue that *given awards* and *considered intelligent enough to enter the competition* are predicates which assign a theta-role to *two students*. In other words, I claim that, in fact, the correct D-structure is as in (27), and that (26a,b) are not derived by short passive movement.

(27) a. [NP] BE [Pred]
b. [two students] BE [given awards]

I disagree, then, with Sportiche's analysis of (24b) as short passive movement. One argument for the analysis in (27a) is given in the example below.

(28) a. We met the two students [considered intelligent enough to enter the competition].
b. The two students [given the awards] were honored last night.

In each of these cases, one would not suggest that *the two students* moved from within the modifying phrase. Rather, the bracketed strings would be considered predicates.

Another argument against deriving these "partial movement" structures from a D-S passive construction comes from the Romance languages. It is not exactly true that these languages do not have structures as in (24b). In fact, they do, but the matrix verb must be the existential BE. The (a) examples below show how the structure would look if in fact the derivation began with the D-S passive. The (b) examples show the correct structure using the existential BE. The (c) examples show that the existential BE in these languages cannot be used as a restructuring verb, accounting for the fact that the partitive Case may not be passed through the participal to the following NP. Finally, the (d) examples show the effect of successful restructuring with the passive BE.

(29) French
a. *Il est **trois hommes** tués.
b. Il y a eu **trois hommes** tués. (existential BE)
c. *Il y a eu tués **trois hommes**. (existential BE)
d. Il est tués **trois hommes**.

(30) Spanish
  a. *Ha sido **un libro** puesto sobre la mesa
    have been a book put on the table
  b. Había **un libro** puesto sobre la mesa. (existential BE)
    was(imp) a book put on the table
  c. *Había puesto **un libro** sobre la mesa (existential BE)
  d. Ha sido puesto **un libro** sobre la mesa

(31) Italian
  a. *E stato un libro messo sul tavolo.
  b. C'erano due libri messi sul tavolo. (existential BE)
  c. *C'erano messi due libri sul tavolo. (existential BE)
  d. E stato messo un libro sul tavolo.

The conclusion here is that passive BE and existential BE are not the same. This comes as no surprise since in many languages the words are distinct (French: *être, avoir*; German: *wurden, geben*). Within the context of the analysis presented here, the former selects a VnP (contained in a functional category) while the latter has an external argument Theme and a complement PRED.

(32) a. $[_{V'}\ [_{V}\ \text{pBE}\ ]\ [_{FP}\ \text{NP}\ [_{F'}\ [_{F}\ \text{Vn}_{i}\ ]\ [_{VnP}\ \text{NP-theme}\ [_{Vn'}\ [_{Vn}\ t_{i}\ ]\ \text{XP}\ ]]]]]$
  b. $[_{V'}\ [_{V}\ \text{eBE}_{i}\ ]\ [_{VP}\ \text{NP-theme}\ [_{V'}\ [\text{V}\ t_{i}\ ]\ [_{XP}\ \text{Pred}\ ]]]]$

Partitive Case may only be assigned to one position in each structure. Where restructuring occurs (32a), partitive Case is passed from pBE to the Vn head of its complement. This Vn head may then assign partitive Case to its Theme argument in its theta-position. eBE may also assign partitive Case to its Theme argument in its theta-position as in (32b). In both structures, inherent partitive Case is assigned to an argument of the Case-assigning head.

4.0 Conclusion

In conclusion, I agree with Lasnik's main claim that an eNP requires Case at S-structure. Where I disagree concerns (i) the status of *be* in relation to other verbs, and (ii) the formulation of the parameter that distinguishes English from Italian.

To account for the different behavior of existential *be,* I adopt a proposal of Ritter's that the existential verb forms a two-part VP. This has the effect of giving an argument-like relationship between this verb and the eNP. Because of this, the verb is allowed to assign the eNP inherent partitive Case. I believe that this analysis of eBE is further supported by the "partial movement" facts of English and the Romance languages.

In fact, confirmation for Lasnik's proposal concerning Case can be found in the parameter which distinguishes Romance from English. In Romance languages, but not in English, there is a restructuring mechanism which allows for Case to be passed from a higher verb to the object of a lower verb. This has been shown to account for word order facts in Romance causatives. By assuming that eNPs need Case, the same Case account may be used to explain why objects of passive participles may appear after the particle in Romance languages but not in English. By strengthening the parameter, we, in fact, strengthen the original argument.

NOTES

*The work in this paper has benefited from discussions with Mark Baker, Lydia White, Máire Noonan and other members of the Syntax/Acquisition project at McGill and has been supported by FCAR grant #91-ER-0578 and SSHRCC grant #410-90-0523. I also thank Jon Bobaljik, Howard Lasnik and particularly Betsy Ritter for their input. Italian data was supplied by Jenn Wienstein and Spanish data by Joyce Garavito and Adriana Chamorro.

[1] *Want* may not be the best choice of verbs here since it does not take small clauses with NP predicates: **I want the children intellects.* vs. *I want the children intelligent.* However, the data can be replicated with *consider.* I consider there *(to be) too much crime in the US.

[2] As pointed out by K. Johnson (1991) certain facts that have been attributed to the adjacency requirement for Case assignment could just as easily be subsumed under restrictions on phrase structure.

[3] I am agnostic at this point as to whether the subject is in the SPEC of the XP or external to the XP.

[4] Maria Teresa Guasti (1990) has a very similar analysis for *Faire-Par* constructions, though she sees the difference between Italian and English as being whether or not infinitives have nominal characteristics.

[5] This idea draws on work done by Henrietta Hung on Malagasy morphology (see Guilfoyle, Hung, and Travis, 1992). A similar idea has been proposed by Sportiche (1990).

[6] Guasti (1991) argues that, at least in the *faire*-infinitive construction, verb incorporation in fact takes place at S-structure, but that this is syntactic incorporation rather than morphological incorporation.

[7] The existence of the functional category will not interfere with s-selection by the V since the Vn will still be the semantic head of the complement.

REFERENCES

Barss, A. (1985) *Chains and Anaphoric Dependence: on Reconstruction and its Implications*, unpublished PhD dissertation, MIT.

Belletti, A. (1988) "The Case of Unaccusatives" *Linguistic Inquiry* 19. 1-34.

Burzio, L. (1986) *Italian Syntax: A Government-Binding approach*, D. Reidel Publishing Company, Dordrecht, Holland.

Guasti, M.T. (1991) "Incorporation, Excorporation and Lexical Properties of Causative Heads" ms. University of Geneva.

Guasti, M.T. (1990) "The 'Faire-Par' Construction in Romance and in Germanic" in *The Proceedings of the Ninth West Coast Conference on Formal Linguistics*, ed. Aaron L. Halpern, pp. 205-218.

Guilfoyle, E. (1990) *Functional Categories and Phrase Structure Parameters*, unpublished PhD dissertation, McGill University.

Guilfoyle, E., H. Hung, and L. Travis (1992) "Spec of IP and Spec of VP: Two subjects in Austronesian languages" *Natural Language and Linguistic Theory* 10, 375–414.

Huang, J. (1990) "Reconstruction and the Structure of VP: some Theoretical Consequences" talk presented at NELS 21, Université de Québec à Montréal.

Johnson, K. (1991) "Object Positions" *Natural Language and Linguistic Theory* 9, 577-636.

Larson, R. (1988) "On the Double Object Construction", *Linguistic Inquiry* 19, 335-392.

Lasnik, H. (this volume) "Case and Expletives: Notes Towards a Parametric Account"

Mahajan, A. (1990) *The A/A-bar Distinction and Movement Theory*, unpublished PhD dissertation, MIT.

Manzini, R. (1983) *Restructuring and Reanalysis*, unpublished PhD dissertation, MIT.

McCloskey, J. (1983) "A VP in a VSO language" eds. G. Gazdar, E. Klein, and G.K. Pullum *Order, Concord, and Constituency*, Dordrecht, Foris Publications.

Ritter, B. (1988) "Existentials, Possessives, and Locatives in Hebrew" ms. Université de Québec à Montréal.

Sportiche, D. (1990) "Movement, Agreement, and Case", ms. UCLA

Travis, L. (1991) "Derived Objects, Inner Aspect and the Structure of VP" talk given at NELS 22, University of Delaware.

M. A. BROWNING

COMMENTS ON RELATIVIZED MINIMALITY

1. "RIGID" MINIMALITY

Minimality, the idea that government of an element can be blocked by an intervening governor, is simple and intuitively appealing; it is apparently of great utility in accounting for a wide variety of phenomena; and it has been very difficult to formulate in a manner that rules out all the relevant cases where government should be blocked while allowing government where necessary. The most influential version of minimality has been what Rizzi (1990) calls "rigid" minimality, by which an intervening head blocks government by any type of potential governor, regardless of category type. The central ECP-related proposal that Rizzi (1990) makes is to relativize minimality so that government is blocked only when competing governors match in some way, e.g., category level (X^0 vs. XP) or A/A' status. Before turning to Rizzi's proposals, I will review briefly three earlier versions of minimality and the core phenomena which they have been adduced to account for so as to highlight the similarities and differences between Rizzi's proposals and those which have come before. Two of these involve cases of heads blocking government by other heads, the other, Chomsky's "rigid" minimality, involves heads blocking government by any potential governor.

The idea that a head protects elements within its domain from external government is essential to the analysis of NP-*ing* constructions in Reuland (1983). (1) and (2) are Reuland's (47) and (48).

(1) *b* is in the governing domain of *a* iff
  a. $a = X^0$ (X = N, A, V, P, Comp, Infl);
  b. *a* and *b* are contained in X^i and *a* is the head of X^i;
  c. there is no *c* such that
    i. $c = Y^0$ and
    ii. *c* and *b* are contained in Y^i and *c* is the head of Y^i, unless Y^i contains *a*.

(2) *a* governs *b* if
  b is in the governing domain of *a* and
  a. *a* has a lexical feature or is coindexed with *b*, or
  b. *a* is subcategorized for *b*.

The definition of *governing domain* in (1) allows a head to protect all the elements contained in its projection, including specifiers. This is crucial to Reuland's account of the grammaticality of "PRO-*ing*" constructions, illustrated in (3a).

(3) a. The architects favored being placed on the investigations committee.
b. $[_{S*} \ldots [_{VP} V [_{S'} [_S NP^* [_{Infl} \text{-ing}] [_{VP} V \, NP]]]]]$
c. $[_{S*} \ldots [_{VP} V [_{S'} [_S NP^* e_i [_{VP} V\text{-}[_{Infl} \text{-ing}]_i \, NP]]]]]]$

If the inflectional morpheme *-ing* stays in its position as head of S, as illustrated in (3b), then NP*(=PRO) will be governed. Reuland assumes that *-ing* lowers to V in the mapping to SS so that Infl does not govern PRO. Although the trace of Infl is not a strong enough governor to violate the constraint against governed PRO, its presence protects NP* from government by V.

This result is problematic for ECM constructions. Reuland's solution for dealing with the latter is to adopt the proposal (essentially following Rouveret and Vergnaud (1980), Kayne (1981), Kayne (1981), and Hornstein and Weinberg (1981)) that verbs may be coindexed with prepositions heading their complements. Reuland assumes that infinitival *to* is a preposition susceptible to such coindexation and proposes that verbs can govern into the domains of prepositions with which they are coindexed. The embedded subject of an ECM complement is therefore accessible to external government and external Case-marking.[1]

While Reuland is mainly concerned with the ability of a head to protect its specifier from external government, the discussion of minimality in Chomsky (1986b) is directed towards solving the problem of *that-t* effects. The account of the ungrammaticality of (4) in Chomsky (1981) depends on the existence of only one COMP (base-generated pre-S) position. When this position is filled with the complementizer *that*, intervening maximal projections (VP and S') block antecedent government of the trace of *who*.

(4) a. *Who do you think that left?
b. $[_{S'} \text{who}_i [_S \text{you} [_{VP} \text{think} [_{S'} \text{that} [_S t_i \text{ left}]]]]]$

This account of (4a) is incompatible with the CP/IP clause structure and Chomsky (1986b) adopts the Minimality Condition, given in (5) (essentially Chomsky's (92)).[2]

(5) γ is a barrier for β if γ is the immediate projection of δ, a zero-level category distinct from β.[3]

(6) $[_{CP} \text{who}_i [_{IP} \text{you} [_{VP} \text{think} [_{CP} t_i' [_{C'} \text{that} [_{IP} t_i \text{ left}]]]]]]$

Thus, as illustrated in (6), the lexical complementizer blocks government of t_i by t_i', that is, C' is a minimality barrier.

Several questions immediately arise given the formulation of minimality in (5). For example, Chomsky notes that the grammaticality of (7a) presents two challenges, since (5) leads us to expect that V' (in parentheses) will act as a minimality barrier for the government of t_i' and both the embedded I' and the matrix I' (not shown) will act as minimality barriers for the relevant VP-adjoined traces.

(7) a. How do you want to fix the car?
b. $[_{CP}$ how$_i$ $[_{IP}$ you $[_{VP}$ t_i'' $[_{VP}$ $([_{V'})$ want $[_{CP}$ t_i' $[_{IP}$ PRO $[_{I'}$ to $[_{VP}$ t_i $[_{VP}$ fix ...

Chomsky proposes that I' never acts as a minimality barrier because the I projection is defective with respect to barrier creation; this is also true for the creation of non-minimality barriers. In addition, V' is assumed to be projected only when necessary, so there is necessarily no V' projection in (7b). Note that V' is also a potential minimality barrier for traces in complement position of V, which means that in every structure where a complement is allowably extracted, no V' may be present. (5) is therefore incompatible with any version of the VP-internal subject hypothesis which places the subject in the specifier position (daughter of VP, sister of V') and all V-related modifiers must be VP-adjoined. Another problem for (5) is the grammaticality of (8), which illustrates the well-known insensitivity of adjuncts to the presence of overt complementizers.

(8) How do you think that John will fix the car?

This can presumably be accounted for by allowing deletion of the complementizer at LF, thereby eliminating the intervening minimal governor.

Finally, additional difficulties for (5) arise with extraction from within NPs and PPs. Van Riemsdijk's (1978) analysis of extraction from PPs requires that the moved element stop off at a PP-internal landing site, as illustrated in (9b).

(9) a. Waar heeft zij vaak $[_{PP}$ over] gesproken
'What has she often spoken about?'
b. ...$[_{PP}$ t_i' $[_{P'}$ over t_i]]...

By (5), antecedent government of t_i will be blocked by P'. If P is not a proper governor (or if both lexical/head government and antecedent government are required) then all instances of preposition stranding will be incorrectly ruled out. Similar problems for extraction of adjuncts from within nominals in Spanish are pointed out by Torrego (1985). One might argue that the preposition in (9b) doesn't block government because both t_i' and t_i are directly related to it, whereas t_i in (6) is not directly related to the complementizer; however, it is unclear why the blocking effect of the head should be neutralized in this case. Alternatively, Chomsky (1986, class lectures) suggested that the presence of a maximal projection was necessary for the creation of a minimality barrier.

(10) γ is a minimality barrier for β wrt α iff
a) γ dominates β and excludes α;
b) γ is the immediate projection of an X^0 category which governs β;
c) γ dominates δ, an XP which dominates β and excludes α.
(γ and δ may be the same category.)

By (10), a head will block government only if its immediate projection is a maximal projection or if its immediate projection dominates a maximal projection which dominates the potentially governed element. In (9b) P' is not maximal and it does not dominate a maximal projection which dominates the trace t_i.

Taken one at a time, ad hoc solutions can be offered for these problems. Taken together, an odd apparent generalization emerges: the minimality condition in (5) goes into effect only when the two competing governors are far enough, but not too far, from the element to be governed. In (9) the two competing governors are sufficiently close to t_i that minimality is not triggered. In (7a) and (8), one could argue that the trace to be governed is sufficiently far from its potential governors that minimality again fails to be triggered. While the phenomena just reviewed suggest that some kind of minimality effect does exist, the difficulties in formulating a Minimality Condition that works and this odd generalization suggest that something is being missed. Relativized Minimality retains the basic idea (blockage of government by an intervening governor) while significantly shifting both the conceptual and the empirical motivation for the existence of a minimality condition.

Before turning to Rizzi's proposals, there is one other use for minimality that should be mentioned. Attempts to derive the Head Movement Constraint from the ECP, e.g., Baker (1988), seem to require a minimality condition to rule out the case of improper head movement shown in (11).

(11)

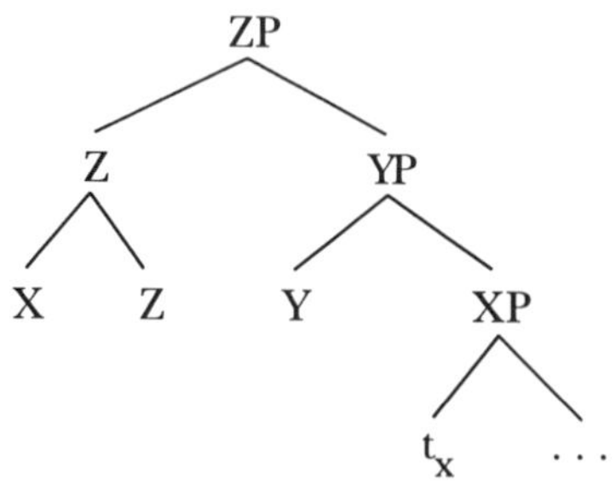

Even in cases where XP and YP are complements, direct movement from the head of XP to Z is generally blocked. All of the minimality proposals just reviewed will have this effect, as will relativized minimality.[4] See section 3 for remarks concerning the consequences of Rizzi's proposals for deriving the HMC from the ECP.

2. Rizzi's Proposals

Rizzi (1990) makes three basic proposals: that minimality should be relativized, that the ECP consists only of a proper head government requirement, and that empty categories must be identified. In this section I will give a brief summary of these proposals.

2.1 Relativized Minimality

Beginning with relativized minimality, the core proposal is to allow government to be blocked only when the two competing governors are of the same type. For example, heads can only block government by other heads, not government by XPs. The Minimality Condition is as in (12), with "potential α-governor" defined as in (13).[5]

(12) Relativized Minimality: X α-governs Y only if there is no Z such that
  (i) Z is a potential α-governor for Y, and
  (ii) Z c-commands Y and does not c-command X.

(13) a. Z is a potential head governor for Y = Z is a head m-commanding Y.
  b. Z is a potential antecedent governor for Y, Y in an A-chain = Z is an A specifier c-commanding Y.
  c. Z is a potential antecedent governor for Y, Y in an A'-chain = Z is an A'-specifier c-commanding Y.

The main argument in support of relativized minimality is that it allows a unified account of three phenomena: the impossibility of extracting adjuncts from wh-islands (as noted by Huang (1983)), Obenauer's (1983) "pseudo-opacity" effects, and Ross's (1983) "inner island" effects. These cases are illustrated in (14a,b,c), respectively.

(14) a. *How did you wonder <u>what</u> John fixed?
  b. *Combien a-t-il <u>beaucoup</u> consulte de livres?
    (cf. 'Combien de livres a-t-il beaucoup consultes?')
  c. *Bill is here, as they do<u>n't</u> know.
    (cf. 'Bill is here, as they know.')

In all three cases the intervention of an A'-specifier (underlined in the examples above) blocks antecedent government of the trace of an adjunct, resulting in ungrammaticality.[6] This approach to minimality makes it impossible to treat *that-t* violations as minimality effects since the potential antecedent governor of the subject trace is an XP in an A'-position, while the overt complementizer is a head.

2.2 Head Government

Rizzi reduces the ECP to the constraint in (15), with the definition of head government as in (16).

(15) A nonpronominal empty category must be properly head-governed.

(16) X head governs Y iff
  (i) a. X is a head
    b. X m-commands Y
  (ii) X = {[±V, ±N], AGR, T}
  (iii) a. no barrier intervenes
    b. Relativized Minimality is respected

'Proper head government' is head government within the immediate projection of the governing head.

Although the ungrammaticality of (17a) can no longer be traced to a minimality violation, the sentence is still ruled out by the ECP under this new formulation.

(17) a. *Who do you think that left?
  b. Who do you think left?

Rizzi argues that (17a), a partial representation of which is given in (18a), is ruled out because the trace of *who* is not head-governed. Infl cannot act as a head-governor for the trace because the trace is not within the immediate projection of Infl and the head of CP is by definition not a possible head governor.

(18) a. b.

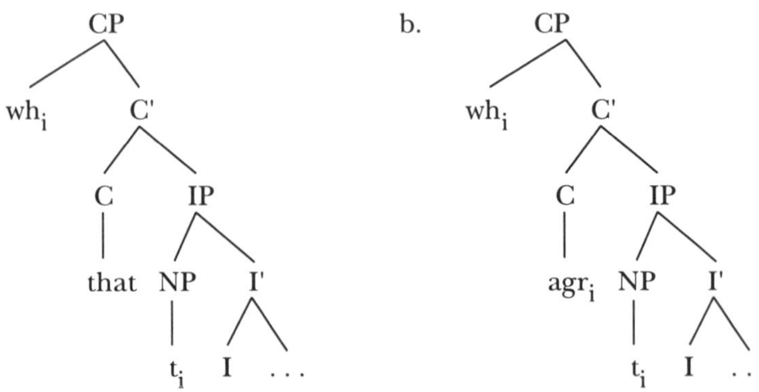

(17b) on the other hand is grammatical. Rizzi claims that this is because C may be generated as AGR, as illustrated in (18b). In this case it is capable of entering into an agreement relation with its specifier, as indicated by the coindexation in (18b). The fact that C and the trace in subject position are now coindexed allows the head of CP to act as a head governor for the trace in subject position.

Something additional must be said in order to rule out the ungrammatical (19a), with non-emphatic *do.*

(19) a.*Who did leave?

b.

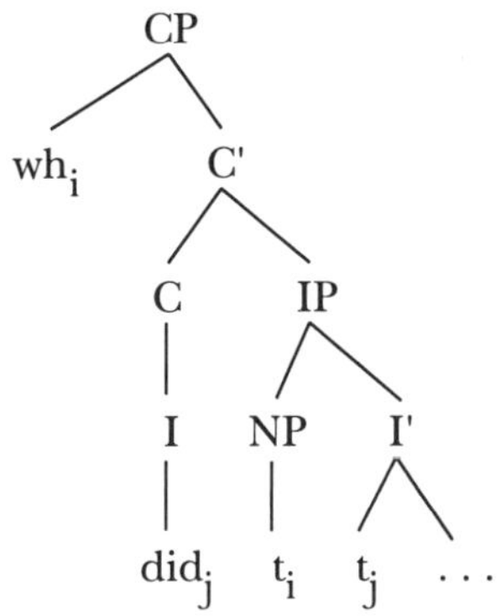

Assuming that i=j in (19b) via SPEC-HEAD agreement (in IP), it would seem that *did* should be able to act as a head governor for the trace in subject position, but this would incorrectly predict that (19a) is grammatical. Rizzi adopts two proposals made in Rizzi and Roberts (1989) to rule out (19): (i) substitution must be into a radically null head and (ii) substitution cannot turn a head which is not a possible head governor into a head governor. Thus, C in (19b) must be radically empty (i.e. it cannot contain AGR, as in (18b)) in order to receive Infl, but after substitution, C will still not be a head governor. Moreover, Infl cannot head govern the subject trace since head government can only occur within the immediate projection of the head governor and Infl is outside of its immediate projection in this structure. Therefore, the sentence is ruled out because t_i is not head-governed.

It has generally been assumed that traces of head movement (and empty heads in general) are subject to the ECP. However, as Baker (1988) showed, it is antecedent government of X^0 traces which seems to be crucial, not head government. A similar, though conceptually odder, result follows from Rizzi's system. If C in (19b) cannot head govern the subject trace, then it cannot head govern the trace left by movement of *did.*[7] So (19a) potentially violates the ECP at two points: the trace in subject position and the trace of *did* both fail to be head governed. This result is fine for (19a), since it is ungrammatical, but there are obviously sentences in which movement of V to C yields a grammatical result, such as (20a).

(20) a. What did John buy?

b.

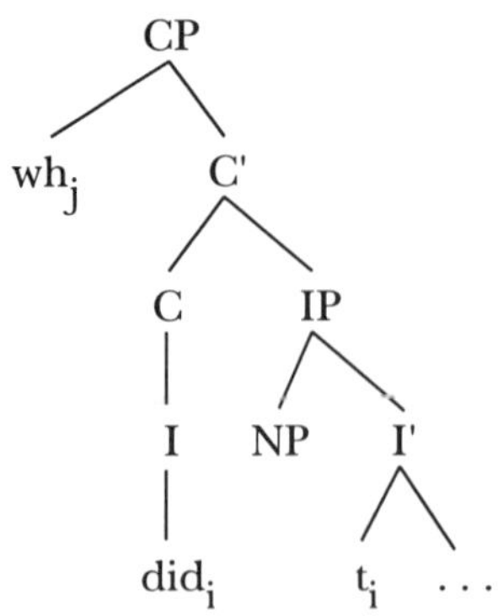

As has just been discussed, C in (20b) is not a licit head-governor (since it is not realized as AGR) and *did* cannot act as a head governor since it does not govern either NP or t_i within its projection. It follows that the trace of *did* has no head governor. However, since the representation is well-formed, Rizzi is forced to conclude that traces of heads are not subject to the head government requirement. In a preliminary reformulation of the ECP as a conjunction of conditions, Rizzi characterizes the head government clause as a Formal Licensing requirement and the antecedent government clause as an Identification requirement. The result that heads are not subject to the ECP (the head government requirement) means that, within Rizzi's system, traces of heads are not subject to the formal licensing requirement; an odd result if we take it to mean that heads need not be formally licensed. Rizzi suggests that the head government requirement is suspended for X^0 traces since the antecedents of these traces are themselves heads. There is another way of thinking about this property of X^0 traces that is more consistent with the idea that traces in general are subject to both formal licensing and identification requirements. Consider first that the canonical head government relation is that which exists between a head and its complement, that is, the formal licensing requirement is based on a substantive relation. One might argue that XPs in general are licensed by virtue of their relation to a head and attempt to derive the head government requirement from the set of substantive head-XP relations.[8] It might also be argued that heads are not licensed by virtue of their relation to other heads, but rather by their participation in a fully projected X' structure, for example. If this is true, then there is no reason to expect formal licensing for a head, if it exists, to take the form of a head government requirement.

2.3 Identification

Rizzi argues that there is no across-the-board antecedent government requirement for empty categories. Rather, empty categories must be licensed (or identified) in one of two ways: either by being part of a well-formed operator-variable pair or by being a member of a well-formed chain. The existence of these two distinct options explains the familiar argument/adjunct asymmetry in (21):

(21) a. ?Which problem do you wonder how to solve?
a'. $[_{CP}$ which problem$_i$ $[_{IP}$ ... $[_{VP}$ wonder $[_{CP}$ how$_j$ $[_{IP}$ PRO to solve t_i t_j]]]]]
b. *How do you wonder which problem to solve?
b'. $[_{CP}$ how$_j$ $[_{IP}$ ... $[_{VP}$ wonder $[_{CP}$ which problem$_i$ $[_{IP}$ PRO to solve t_i t_j]]]]]

Both traces in the embedded clauses of (21a',b') are properly head governed: the trace of *which problem*, t_i, by *solve* and the trace of *how*, t_j, by INFL. Neither trace is antecedent governed. Rizzi argues that, because *which problem* and its trace bear referential indices, the necessary operator-variable relation may be established via binding, which requires only coindexation and c-command. Notice that the binding relation cannot be subject to the minimality condition, since otherwise the intervening A'-binder *how* in (21a) would block the relation between *what* and its trace.[9]

The ability of an element to bear a referential index is crucial to Rizzi's account of the contrast in (21) and Rizzi argues that the distribution of referential indices is limited by the principle in (22) (Rizzi's (28), ch. 3).

(22) A referential index must be licensed by a referential theta role.

An index is assigned at DS to an element in a position which receives a referential θ-role. If the element moves, it carries the index along and leaves an indexed trace. No other elements may bear referential indices. The difference between a referential and non-referential θ-role is illustrated by the two types of complements possible with a verb like *weigh*.

(23) a. John weighed the potatoes last week.
b. John weighed 200 pounds last week.

Rizzi claims that the question in (24a) can be answered with either "the potatoes" or "200 pounds," but the (slightly marginal) question in (24b) can only be answered with the former.

(24) a. What did John weigh?
b. ?What did John wonder how to weigh?

Selected measure phrases thus pattern with adjuncts rather than complements. Rizzi demonstrates that the same is true of other quasi-arguments (e.g., idiom chunks).

Naturally adjuncts do not receive referential θ-roles; this is true even when they are selected by verbs such as *believe.* Therefore, *how* and its trace in (21) do not bear indices; (21a,b) are more correctly represented as in (25).

(25) a. $[_{CP}$ which problem$_i$ $[_{IP}$ ... $[_{VP}$ wonder $[_{CP}$ how $[_{IP}$ PRO to solve t_i t]]]]]
b. $[_{CP}$ how $[_{IP}$ ... $[_{VP}$ wonder $[_{CP}$ which problem$_i$ $[_{IP}$ PRO to solve t_i t]]]]]

A relation cannot be established between *how* and its trace by binding, since no indices are involved. Rizzi proposes that the only viable alternative relation is chain co-membership, with the definition of chain as in (26) and the definition of antecedent government as in (27).

(26) $(a_1, ..., a_n)$ is a chain only if, for $1 \leq i < n$, a_i antecedent-governs a_{i+1}.

(27) X antecedent governs Y iff
(i) X and Y are non-distinct
(ii) X c-commands Y
(iii) no barrier intervenes
(iv) Relativized Minimality is respected.

By specifying that the elements of a chain must be "non-distinct", instead of coindexed as is usually assumed, Rizzi allows for chains of non-indexed elements. The sharp ungrammaticality of (21b) is not the result of an ECP violation strictly speaking, but does follow from a failure of antecedent government. (Regardless of the definition of "barrier" one adopts, antecedent government of the trace by *how* will be blocked by Relativized Minimality.) Because of this failure, *how* and its trace cannot form a chain and the empty category is not licensed.

Turning finally to the licensing of NP-trace, the sharp ungrammaticality of super-raising cases such as (28) led Chomsky (1986b) to suggest that these should be ruled out by the ECP.

(28) *Bill$_i$ seems that it was told t_i that ...

Under Rizzi's system, the trace will be head-governed by *told.* Since the DS position of *Bill* receives a referential θ-role, the members of the chain will have referential indices. It will therefore be possible for the links to be related by binding. The prediction is that this sentence should be no worse than a subjacency condition violation. To account for the greater deviance of such cases, Rizzi appeals again to the definition of chain in (26) and to the θ-Criterion, as given in (29).

(29) (i) Each Theta position belongs to a chain containing exactly one argument.
(ii) Each argument belongs to a chain containing exactly one Theta position.

If an element in a θ-position is not a member of a chain as defined in (26), then the θ-role cannot be assigned and (29) will be violated. In (28), *Bill* and *t* must form a chain in order to receive the θ-role assigned by *told* to its object. This means that *Bill* must antecedent govern the trace—no barriers and no minimal governors may intervene between them. Under the definition of relativized minimality given above, *it* acts as a minimal governor and blocks the relation necessary for θ-role transmission.[10]

3. Observations

3.1 Unifying the Antecedent Government Requirement?

One way of characterizing the phenomena discussed in the preceding section is to say that chains which consist only of one type of element, (30a,b,c), are subject to stricter locality conditions than those chains which are "mixed," (30d). (See Chomsky (1991) and Browning (1991/1987) for discussion.)

(30) a. A' ... A' ... A' ... A'
b. A ... A ... A ... A
c. $X^0 ... X^0 ... X^0 ... X^0$
d. A' ... A

The operator and variable in (30d) need only be related via binding. Since binding is not subject to Relativized Minimality (nor is it sensitive to the intervention of barriers), operator-variable pairs will have a greater freedom of distribution than the other cases. Rizzi's system does have the result that all of the elements in each type of chain in (30a,b,c) must be related by government. However, for (30a) and (30c) this requirement is imposed by the identification requirement on empty categories, while in the case of (30b) the requirement is imposed by the θ-Criterion. The question which naturally arises is "could the locality conditions on (30a,b,c) be completely unified?" The answer may be yes, if we extend a proposal made in Barss (1986). Barss proposes that empty categories have no binding features (± pronominal, ± anaphor) and develops a compatible theory of their distribution. It could be argued that NP-traces lack not only binding features, but also referential indices. The idea would be that only the head of an A-chain bears a referential index, since only the head of an A-chain is referential, not the NP-traces associated with it. It would then be necessary, in Rizzi's system, for the links of an A-chain to be related by government, since the binding relation depends on the presence of a referential index on both participants in the relation. In this way, the locality conditions imposed on the three types of chains in (30a,b,c) would all arise from the same property: the absence of a referential index.

There is a phenomenon which seems to make this alternative account untenable, however. While the phenomenon supports Rizzi's distinction between referential and non-referential θ-roles, it also suggests that the locality constraint imposed on A-chains does not derive from the θ-Criterion. Consider first the contrast in (31), which Chomsky (1981) argued was to be accounted for by the ECP.

(31) a. *Dormire, Gianni sembra.
 b. Dormire, Gianni vorrebbe.

The subject of *dormire* in (31a), an NP-trace, is not properly governed when the complement of the raising verb *sembrare* is preposed. Preposing has no effect on the null subject of the complement of the control verb *volere*, which is PRO. In Browning (1989), I argue that the contrast between (31a) and grammatical sentences such as those in (32) indicates that the problem with (31) is a failure of head government. ((32b) is from Longobardi (1985).)

(32) a. How likely to win is John?
 a'. $[_{CP}$ $[_{AP}$ how likely $[_{IP}$ t_i to win]] is $[_{IP}$John$_i$ t_{infl} t_{ap}]]
 b. Tradito da sua moglie, credo che Mario non sia mai stato.
 'Betrayed by his wife, I believe that Mario has never been.'
 b'. $[_{CP}$ $[_{VP}$tradito t_i da sua moglie] $[_{IP}$... $[_{IP}$ Mario$_i$ non sia mai stato t_{VP}]]]

The ungrammaticality of (31a) also indicates that head government must be satisfied on the basis of the SS position of an empty category, a conclusion also reached by Rizzi.

Under Rizzi's system, head government is not the only requirement on the NP-traces shown in (32a',b'). In order for the θ-Criterion to be satisfied, the traces must form chains with the moved NPs and antecedent government must hold between the members of well-formed chain links. Consider again Rizzi's definition of antecedent government:

(33) X antecedent governs Y iff
 (i) X and Y are non-distinct
 (ii) X c-commands Y
 (iii) no barrier intervenes
 (iv) Relativized Minimality is respected.

Apparently, the antecedent governor of the trace need not literally c-command the trace at SS in order for antecedent government to hold. There appear to be three ways of expressing this. (1) C-command is only required to hold at some point in the derivation prior to SS; this would essentially be a modified gamma-marking approach whereby antecedent government *at some point* satisfies the requirement even if the relation ceases to hold later on. (2) A process of LF reconstruction replaces all or part of the wh-moved constituent in its DS position so that the trace is literally c-commanded, and therefore antecedent governed, at LF. (3) The c-command requirement is indirectly satisfied without literal reconstruction via an extended set of relations of the sort proposed by Barss (1986).[11] At present we have no evidence on which to base a choice between these three options.

Turning finally to the problematic phenomenon mentioned above, R. Kayne points out (personal communication), that the strong ungrammaticality of (34) is a problem for the claim that (32) involves raising.[12]

(34) a. *How likely to be taken of John is advantage?
b. *Kept on Jane Fonda, tabs have never been.

Such sentences are also discussed in Lasnik and Saito (1992), where it is suggested that the ungrammaticality of (34) indicates that the sentences in (32) must be cases of control, rather than raising. Rizzi's system offers another possible explanation for the contrast between (32) and (34), one which would not require the sort of modifications in the analysis of passives necessitated by a control approach. Compare (32a) and (34a): the salient difference between the two is that the raised subject is an idiom chunk in the latter and an argument in the former. In Rizzi's terms, the difference is that the subject in (32a) receives a referential θ-role, and therefore bears a referential index, while that in (34a) does not. In this respect, the contrast between (32) and (34) supports a fundamental aspect of Rizzi's approach.

In the discussion of wh-movement we saw a correlation between referential indices and locality: if an element bears a referential index, it can undergo "long" movement without incurring a severe violation. We seem to find a similar correlation in the data in (32)/(34): if an element has a referential index, its NP-trace can be pied-piped to a position in which it is not c-commanded/antecedent governed. Though the existence of this correlation is suggestive, it is not obvious how to account for the (32)/(34) contrast within the Relativized Minimality framework. The problem is the following: in the case of wh-movement, the presence of a referential index allows a relation to be established via binding, a looser requirement than that of antecedent government. With respect to NP-movement, Rizzi follows Chomsky (1981) in assuming that idiom chunks are quasi-arguments which receive a non-referential θ-role. So chain formation, with the necessary antecedent government requirement, is required for both (32) and (34) in spite of the referential nature of the θ-role being "transmitted" in the case of the former.

Consider the three mechanisms for establishing the antecedent government relation in (32) mentioned above. Literal LF reconstruction, option (2), will not differentiate between (32) and (34). If all or a portion of the wh-moved constituent is replaced at LF both referential and non-referential NP-moved elements will c-command, and therefore antecedent govern, their traces. A codicil could be added to option (1), the gamma-marking approach to antecedent government, which allows gamma-marking only when the elements involved bear referential indices. Since adjuncts, heads, and quasi-arguments do not bear referential indices but necessarily participate in antecedent government relations when moved, this would require that gamma-marking be an optional means of satisfying antecedent government, not the core indicator of the existence of the relation, as it is in the Lasnik and Saito (1984), (1992) system.

Option (3), establishing the antecedent government relation indirectly through a chain accessibility sequence (see footnote 11) without literal reconstruction, allows the appropriate distinction to be made if we argue that the related elements must bear referential indices. However, this last approach introduces an inconsistency into the Relativized Minimality system which is almost a contradiction. Within Rizzi's system, the two means of identifying an empty category could hardly be more dissimilar: binding requires the presence of a referential index and is not sensitive to barriers or Relativized Minimality; antecedent government does not require the presence of a referential index and is sensitive to barriers and Relativized Minimality. Now consider that Barss's chain accessibility proposals are a means of characterizing *binding* relations between antecedents and overt dependent elements such as anaphors. By allowing antecedent government to be satisfied via a chain accessibility sequence when the governed and governing elements bear referential indices, we are virtually saying that there are two kinds of antecedent government: one which is similar to binding and one which is not, an odd dichotomy.

Another way of approaching this problem is to say that NP-trace, in addition to being head governed to satisfy the ECP, must be both antecedent governed *and* bound in order to be licensed. This follows naturally if we maintain the "traditional" assumption that NP-traces are subject to Binding Condition A, contrary to recent proposals by Chomsky (1986a), Barss (1986) and others. The evidence for each requirement is as follows: The contrast between (31a) and (32) indicates that NP-trace must be head-governed and that head government must hold at SS (i.e., it cannot be satisfied in gamma-marking fashion). The ungrammaticality of super-raising cases such as (28) indicates that antecedent government is necessary. The grammaticality of (32) is not a problem for this if antecedent government can be satisfied in gamma-marking fashion and if gamma-marking is not ordered with respect to Move a (following Chomsky (class lectures, 1986)). This last point allows *John* in (32a) to raise to the SPEC of IP and gamma-mark its trace before the AP is wh-moved to the SPEC of CP. The ungrammaticality of (34) follows from Binding Condition A if we assume that the binding relation can be reconstructed via a chain accessibility sequence only when the anaphor and antecedent bear referential indices. Since quasi-arguments such as idiom chunks do not bear referential indices, the NP-traces in (34) violate Binding Condition A.

At this point, these proposals are in danger of incorrectly ruling out the grammatical (35):

(35) a. Advantage is likely to be taken of John.
 a'. [$_{IP}$ advantage is [$_{AP}$ likely [$_{IP}$ t to be taken t of John]]]
 b. Tabs have never been kept on Jane Fonda.
 b'. [$_{IP}$ tabs have never been kept t on Jane Fonda]

All of the traces in (35a',b') are head governed and antecedent governed, but do they satisfy Binding Condition A? According to Rizzi, binding can only occur when referential indices are involved. The account of (34) proposed above requires referential indices for the reconstruction of binding relations via a chain accessibility sequence. For Barss, *all* binding relations, even those involving direct c-command, are established via chain accessibility sequences. If the proposed account of (34) is to be maintained, we must depart from both Rizzi and Barss and claim that binding does not require referential indices when c-command is involved. While these proposals account for all of the data discussed in this section, they do not really eliminate the odd dichotomy mentioned above. Instead, the dichotomy is no longer between two types of antecedent government, one which looks like binding and one which does not, but between "direct" binding, which involves c-command at SS but no coindexation, and "indirect" binding, which requires something like chain accessibility and coindexation.[13] Moreover, the proposal that direct binding need not involve referential indices is in direct contradiction with Rizzi's account of the asymmetry between wh-movement of arguments and adjuncts. However, it is consistent with the proposals in Chomsky (1991), for example, which do not base their account of the argument/adjunct asymmetry on a distinction between binding and antecedent government. While this discussion is certainly not conclusive, I believe that the data discussed above offer support for Rizzi's claim concerning the distribution of referential indices, while casting doubt on the binding vs. antecedent government account of argument/adjunct asymmetries in wh-movement.

3.2 Head Movement

Rizzi's proposals force one to adopt a view of multiple head movement which makes it impossible to account for Mirror Principle Effects via the ECP. As the possibility of doing so has already been called into question on independent grounds (see Speas (1990)), it is unclear to me at this point whether this observation has serious consequences for the Relativized Minimality system. Consider a structure such as (36) in which X first moves to Y and the Y+X complex moves to Z.

(36)

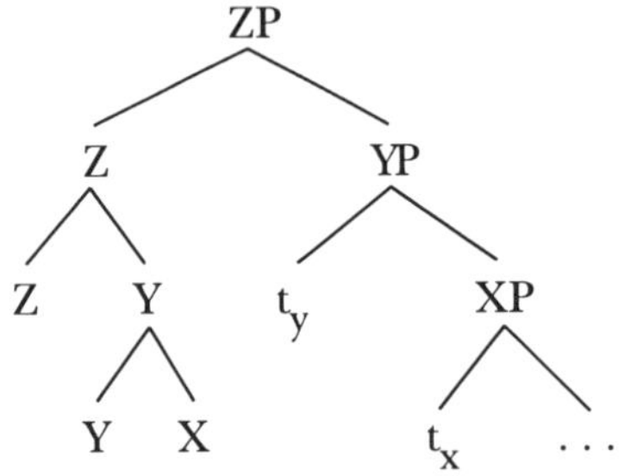

Since heads do not bear referential indices, both traces, t_y and t_x, must be antecedent governed. Recall that Rizzi defines antecedent government on the basis of c-command rather than m-command. However, his definition of c-command refers to the first *projection*, rather than the first *node*, dominating the potential c-commander[14], so Y and X will c-command their traces as is necessary. However, since antecedent government is subject to relativized minimality, antecedent government of t_x should be blocked by the intervention of t_y.[15] The only alternative is to assume that the antecedent governor of t_x is t_y. This is no problem if the moved elements and their traces form one chain with a complex head: (Z+Y+X, t_y, t_x). However, if (Z+Y+X, t_y, t_x) is to be considered a well-formed chain, then the members of the chain must satisfy the non-distinctness clause in the definition of antecedent government. This seems particularly problematic given that in most, perhaps all, cases, X, Y, and Z differ in categorial features. X^0 categories would thus appear to be non-distinct if they form a complex lexical item or if they are traces of elements which do so. This means that "successive cyclic" movement of heads cannot be enforced and the effects of the Mirror Principle (Baker (1988))

cannot be derived from ECP-related constraints on head movement. For example, take the case in (37) where X and Y move independently to Z.

(37)

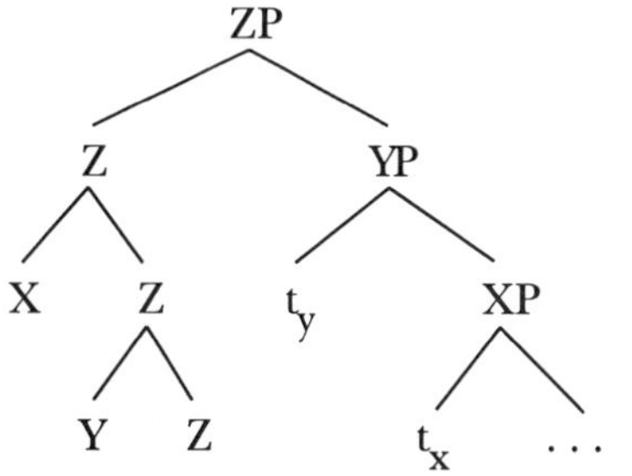

The heads X, Y, and Z are non-distinct as before; the chain (X+Y+Z, t_y, t_x) is well-formed. This would seem to be a seriously undesirable consequence; however, as noted above, recent work on head movement has called into question whether Mirror Principle effects exist and, if they do, whether they should be accounted for by a general principle such as the ECP or the identification requirement on empty categories. In addition, once morphological subcategorization frames are introduced, it becomes impossible to tell whether head-to-head movement is enforced by anything other than the morphological properties of the heads involved.

3.3 SPEC of VP

By the definition of "potential antecedent governor" given in (13c) in section 2, the quantifier in sentences such as (38) must be in an A'-specifier in order to block government of the trace of *combien* by its antecedent.

(38) a. Combien de livres a-t-il beaucoup consultes?
how many of books did he a lot consult
b. * Combien a-t-il beaucoup consulte de livres?
how many did he a lot consult of books

Thus, Rizzi's account of pseudo-opacity effects depends on the existence of an A'-specifier of VP. There are at least two other recent proposals which crucially involve the specifier of VP and both require that this position be an A-position. First, there are the proposals by Fukui and Speas (1986), Koopman and Sportiche (1988), and Kitagawa (1986), all of which involve generating external arguments within the maximal projection of the verb. Rizzi's proposals are incompatible with any of these which argue that the position in which external arguments are base-generated is the specifier of VP. However, as pointed out to me by L. Rizzi, Koopman and Sportiche (1988) actually propose that the subject originates in a VP-adjoined position, as illustrated in (39).

(39) ...$[_{VP}$ NP $[_{VP}$ SPEC $[_{V'}$ V ...]]...

In this structure NP is not in the specifier position of VP, but is rather the subject of a small clause headed by VP. This configuration is compatible with Rizzi's proposal that the specifier of VP is an A'-position. Moreover, combining Sportiche's (1988) analysis of "floated" quantifiers (which assumes the Koopman and Sportiche proposal in (39)) with Rizzi's proposal that adverbs such as *beaucoup* are in the specifier of VP yields the following prediction: when floated quantifiers and adverbs like *beaucoup* co-occur in a sentence, the word order will be floated Q-adverb, not adverb-floated Q. As illustrated in (40), the prediction is correct.

(40) a. Les enfants ont tous beaucoup vu ce film.
the children have all a lot seen the film
b. *Les enfants ont beaucoup tous vu ce film.

As Sportiche notes, "leftward Q-movement", illustrated in (41a), apparently places quantifiers in a position which is distinct from both the position of rightward floated quantifiers and adverbs.

(41) a. Elle a tout vu.
b. Les enfants ont tous tout lu.
the children have all everything read
c. *Les enfants ont tout tous lu.

The contrast between (41b) and (41c) indicates that the word order of left-floated and right-floated quantifiers is fixed. Sportiche argues that this word order is explained by his analysis, which assigns a structure such as that in (42) to the sentence in (41b).

(42) $[_{IP}$ les enfants$_i$ ont $[_{VP}$ $[_{NP}$ tous t_i] $[_{VP}$ tout$_j$ $[_{VP}$ V t_j]...

In this structure *tout* is adjoined to VP by the SS analog of QR. If Rizzi is correct about the location of adverbs such as *beaucoup*, the word order when such an adverb is added to (41b) should be as in (43).

(43) a. Les enfants ont tous tout beaucoup lu.
the children have all everything a lot read
b. $[_{IP}$ les enfants$_i$ ont $[_{VP}$ $[_{NP}$ tous t_i] $[_{VP}$ tout$_j$ $[_{VP}$ beaucoup $[_{V'}$ V t_j]...

L. Rizzi informs me that (43) is ungrammatical.[16] This would seem to be a problem for Rizzi's proposals since, although *tout* and *beaucoup* are both in A' positions and might be expected to interact, *tout* receives a referential θ-role. This should allow the necessary relation between *tout* and its trace to be established via binding, which is not subject to Relativized Minimality. Rizzi suggests that this fact can be accounted for by Cinque's (1989/forthcoming) revision of Relativized Minimality, which takes into account the referentiality of the head of the chain as well as the referentiality of the θ-role assigned. Because *tout* itself is not sufficiently referential, *beaucoup* would block its leftward movement, in spite of the fact that it receives a referential θ-role. So, while Rizzi's proposals are incompatible with some versions of the VP-internal subject hypothesis, they work well with the proposals in Koopman and Sportiche (1988) and Sportiche (1988).

There appears to be no way to combine Rizzi's system with Larson's (1988) analysis of double object constructions, however. Consider the structure Larson assigns to the sentence in (44a).

(44) a. John sent Mary a letter.
b. $\ldots[_{VP}\ [_{V'}\ \text{send}_j\ [_{VP}\ \text{Mary}_i\ [_{V'}\ [_{V}\ t_j\ t_i\ ]\ \text{a letter}\ ]]]]$

Mary moves from its DS position as sister of V to the specifier position of the lower VP. Since *Mary* receives Case in this position, it is difficult to see how it could be characterized as an A'-position. Moreover, placing *Mary* in a position similar to that shown in (39), as the subject of a VP-headed small clause, is conceptually at odds with Larson's X'-theory.

Another point of incompatibility between the two sets of proposals arises from the proliferation VP shells which Larson allows. Presumably every VP shell has its own specifier, each of which is positioned to block government by a c-commanding specifier. Consider Larson's direct derivation of the passive, illustrated in (45).

(45) a. Mary was sent a letter.
b. $[_{IP}\ \text{Mary}_i\ [_{I'}\ \text{was}\ [_{VP}\ [_{V'}\ \text{sent}_j\ [_{VP}\ \text{a letter}\ [_{V'}\ t_j\ t_i\ ]]]]]]$

In this derivation, *a letter* remains in its DS position: the specifier of VP. Since it c-commands t_i and does not c-command *Mary*, by Relativized Minimality *a letter* will block antecedent government of t_i by *Mary*.[17] It is difficult to see any way around the incompatibility between Larson's proposals and Rizzi's.

NOTES

* This is a revised version of comments made on a pre-publication draft of Rizzi (1990) at the Second Princeton Workshop on Comparative Grammar. My goal at the workshop was not to present an exhaustive analysis of Rizzi's proposals, a task which would have been far beyond the scope of the workshop format, but rather to point out some consequences and potential problems which I found interesting; I have not significantly expanded this version of my comments beyond the original.

[1] Reuland does not adopt an S' deletion analysis of ECM structures and seems to assume that verbs can in general govern into S', as long as C is null.
[2] Chomsky (1981) mentions (p. 163) the definition of government in (i), with the minimality clause in (b), as being "in the literature."

i) α governs β if and only if
(a) $\alpha = X^0$
(b) α c-commands β and if γ c-commands β then γ either c-commands α or is c-commanded by β

However, he rejects (i) in favor of a definition in which government is blocked only by the intervention of maximal projections dominating either the governor or governed element.
[3] Chomsky gives "a projection" as an alternative to "the immediate projection" in his (92), though he tends strongly in the discussion towards adopting the narrower formulation of the condition.
[4] Drawing on a pre-publication version of Rizzi (1990), Baker (1988) proposes a relativized version of minimality that takes into account other innovations in the ECP which he proposes. Discussion of Baker's proposals would take these comments too far afield.
[5] Rizzi's definitions of head government and antecedent government are discussed below.
[6] Note that, in order to function as minimal governors under the definitions in (13), *beaucoup* in (14b) and the negative morpheme in (14c) must be in specifier positions; see below for discussion.
[7] *Did* will be able to antecedent govern its trace.
[8] A potential conceptual problem for this approach to deriving the head government requirement of the ECP is that one would expect a specifier, in particular, a subject, to be licensed by the head of the projection. It is a basic property of all approaches to the ECP that subjects in general are not properly governed by Infl.
[9] In this respect Rizzi's proposals differ significantly from the proposals of Aoun and Li 1989, which, although they appeal to a kind of minimality condition, require that condition to apply to variable binding.
[10] A similar explanation is given for the contrast below involving the clitic-trace relation.

i) Jean essaie [de le faire t]
'Jean tries to do it.'

ii) *Jean l'essaie [de faire t]
'Jean tries to do it.'

[11] A discussion that does justice to the complex interrelated proposals in Barss (1986) is far beyond the scope of this paper. Instead I will give a radically simplified characterization of Barss's approach to reconstruction in cases such as (i).

i) Which picture of himself did John buy?

Barss's version of the binding theory basically requires the anaphor to be linked to an antecedent which is a sister of some member of the anaphor's *chain accessibility sequence*, defined as in (ii). ((ii), taken from Barss's chapter 3, is revised in later chapters, but the essence remains the same.)

ii) Chain Accessibility Sequence
S = (a_1, ..., a_n) is a well-formed chain accessibility sequence for an NP A only if:
a. A is a_1
b. some a_i is a projection of the governor of A
c. for every pair (a_1, a_{i+1}), either (1) or (2):
1) a_{i+1} immediately dominates a_i
2) (a_i, a_{i+1}) is a link of a well-formed (A' or A) chain

The structure of (i) is given in (iii) with the members of the anaphor's chain accessibility sequence in boldface with subscripts to indicate their position in the sequence. Clause (ii.a) stipulates that the anaphor is always a_1.

(iii)

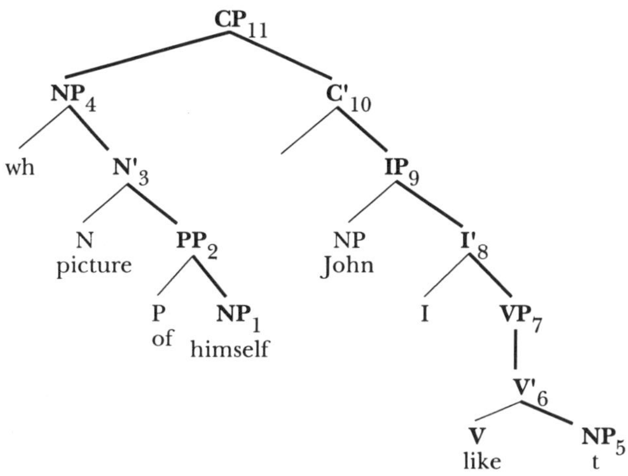

The sequence proceeds from 1 to 4 via clause (ii.c.1); PP_2 satisfies clause (ii.b). The link (a_4, a_5) is established via clause (ii.c.2). The rest of the sequence proceeds again on the basis of clause (ii.c.1). The antecedent *John* is sister to a member of the accessibility sequence, a_8 = I', and so the anaphor satisfies Binding Condition A.
It should be noted here that Barss (1986) argues that empty categories do not have binding features and are therefore not subject to the Binding Conditions.
[12] An anonymous reviewer points out that the same problem is raised by the ungrammaticality of "How likely to be a riot is there?" The comments which follow apply equally to these sorts of examples.
[13] I am using "indirect" binding informally here and do not intend to refer to the proposals in Haïk (1984)
[14] Rizzi's definitions of c-command and m-command, from his footnote 3, ch. 1, are given below.
i) X m-commands Y iff neither X dominates Y nor vice versa, and the first maximal projection dominating X dominates Y as well.
ii) X c-commands Y iff neither X dominates Y nor vice versa, and the first projection dominating X dominates Y as well.

[15] Rizzi assumes that even null heads can block government, *contra* Chomsky (1986). In particular, the two approaches differ in their analyses of sentences like (i).

i) John tried [$_{CP}$ C [$_{IP}$ PRO to leave]]

Rizzi argues that the empty C is a minimal governor for PRO, blocking government by the matrix verb. Chomsky argues that CP inherits barrierhood from IP, thereby blocking government of PRO.

[16] The simpler (i) should also be ungrammatical.

i) Les enfants ont tout beaucoup lu.
the children have everything a lot read

Rizzi's proposed solution for (43) would apply to (i) as well.

[17] Note that in (44) *a letter*, which is a V' adjunct, does not act as a minimal governor for the trace of *Mary* since it is not in an A-specifier. (See (13b) in section 2 above.)

REFERENCES

Aoun, J. and Y. A. Li (1989) "Scope and Constituency," *Linguistic Inquiry* 20, 141–172.

Baker, M. C. (1988), *Incorporation: A Theory of GrammaticalFunction Changing*, University of Chicago Press, Chicago.

Barss, A. (1986), *Chains and Anaphoric Dependence: On Reconstruction and Its Implications*, Doctoral dissertation, MIT, Cambridge, Massachusetts.

Browning, M. A. (1989), "ECP ≠ CED," *Linguistic Inquiry* 20, 481-491.

Browning, M. A. (1991/1987), *Null Operator Constructions*, Garland Publishing, NY.

Chomsky, N. (1981), *Lectures on Government and Binding*, Foris, Dordrecht.

Chomsky, N. (1986a), *Knowledge of Language*, Praeger, New York.

Chomsky, N. (1986b), *Barriers*, MIT Press, Cambridge, Massachusetts.

Chomsky, N. (1991), "Some Notes on the Economy of Derivation and Representation," in *Principles and Parameters in Comparative Grammar*, R. Freidin, ed., MIT Press, Cambridge, Massachusetts.

Cinque, G. (1989/forthcoming), "On the Scope of 'Long' and 'Successive Cyclic' Movement," in this volume.

Fukui, N. and M. Speas (1986), "Specifiers and Projection," ms.

Haïk, I. (1984), "Indirect Binding," *Linguistic Inquiry* 15, 185-223.

Hornstein, N. and A. Weinberg (1981), "Case Theory and Preposition Stranding," *Linguistic Inquiry* 12, 55-91.

Kayne, R. (1981), "ECP Extensions," *Linguistic Inquiry* 12, 93-133.

Kayne, R. S. (1981), "On Certain Differences between French and English," *Linguistic Inquiry* 12, 349-371.

Kitagawa, Y. (1986), *Subjects in Japanese and English*, Doctoral Dissertation, University of Massachusetts at Amherst.

Koopman, H. and D. Sportiche (1988), "Subjects," ms.

Lasnik, H. and M. Saito (1984), "On the Nature of Proper Government," *Linguistic Inquiry* 15, 235-290.

Lasnik, H. and M. Saito (1992), *Move α*, MIT Press, Cambridge, Massachusetts.

Reuland, E. (1983), "Governing *-ing*," *Linguistic Inquiry* 14, 101-36.

Rizzi, L. (1990), *Relativized Minimality*, MIT Press, Cambridge, Massachusetts.

Rizzi, L. and I. Roberts (1989), "Complex Inversion in French," *Probus* 1, 1-30.
Rouveret, A. and J.-R. Vergnaud (1980), "Specifying Reference to the Subject: French Causatives and Conditions on Representations," *Linguistic Inquiry* 11, 97-202.
Speas, M. (1990), "Incorporation Theory and the Mirror Principle," in *Proceedings of the Formal Linguistics Society of the Midwest.*
Sportiche, D. (1988), "A Theory of Floating Quantifiers and Its Corollaries for Constituent Structure," *Linguistic Inquiry* 19, 425-449.
Torrego, E. (1985), "untitled," ms.
van Riemsdijk, H. (1978), *A Case Study in Syntactic Markedness*, Foris, Dordrecht.

GUGLIELMO CINQUE

'LONG' WH-MOVEMENTS AND REFERENTIALITY

INTRODUCTION

In the recent literature on Bounding and Government, a certain consensus exists on the necessity of distinguishing two types of wh-movement : 'long' and 'successive cyclic'[1], even though many fundamental aspects of this analysis are still moot; among these, the questions in (1) and (2).

(1) a. What are the precise *classes of elements* that undergo 'long' and 'successive cyclic' wh-movement, respectively?
b. What are the principles that determine the existence of these and just these two types of wh-movement?

(2) What is the nature of the locality conditions on 'long' and 'successive cyclic' wh-movement?

Here, I shall be concerned primarily with question (1)a, and to a lesser extent with question (1b).[2] After briefly reviewing the influential position of *Barriers* on these points, and a recent alternative proposal, that of Rizzi (1988), I will discuss some new facts bearing on (1)a which seem to be more easily integrable in Rizzi's system than in the *Barriers*'s system, and which appear to suggest a particular refinement of the system proposed in Rizzi (1988) (See now Rizzi 1990).

The main point that will be made is that only those constituents can be 'long' wh-moved which are used *referentially* (in a sense to be made precise).

1. THE *BARRIERS* SYSTEM

In *Barriers*, Chomsky, building on work by Huang and Lasnik and Saito (see Huang (1982), Lasnik and Saito (1984)), suggests that the answer to (1)a and b is provided by (a particular formulation of) the ECP. Consider (3) to (7).[3]

(3) (Proper Government) a properly governs β iff a θ-governs or antecedent-governs β (p.17)

(4) (γ-marking) If β is properly governed it is assigned [$+\gamma$] indelibly. If β is not properly governed, it is assigned [$-\gamma$] indelibly (pp.17-18)

(5) Such γ-marking takes place at S-structure for A-positions, and at LF for A'-positions (p.18)

(6) Empty categories (ec's) not required by the Extended Projection Principle can delete between S-structure and LF (possibly after having properly governed and γ-marked other ec's) (p.21)

(7) (γ-checking, applying at LF) : * [-γ] (p.18)

This formulation of the ECP [4] has, among other consequences, that of forcing a strict successive cyclic derivation for all categories which (like adjuncts) are in A'-positions, and of permitting 'long' wh-movement of all categories which are in A-positions (*pace* the Subjacency condition). Consider briefly how. (8)a below is a case of extraction of a θ-governed category ; (8)b of a non-θ-governed category in A-position; (8)c-d cases of non-θ-governed categories in A'-position.

(8) a. ? Which particular problem were you wondering how to [t' [phrase t]]
b. ? Which student did he wonder whether to [t'[consider [t intelligent]]]
c. How have you [t'''[decided [t'' to [t'[phrase the problem t]]]]]
d. *How are you [t''wondering [which problem [to [t' [phrase t]]]]]

Let us start from (8)c. The trace there is non-θ-governed. Hence, to be properly governed, i.e. to be assigned [+γ], it must be antecedent-governed. It is if *how* moves successive cyclically adjoining first to the embedded VP. Given the *Barriers* definition of Government, t'' antecedent-governs t'. t'' cannot delete between S-structure and LF because, for ec's in A'-position like the trace of *how*, γ-marking applies only at LF. If it deleted, t' would not be γ-marked.

This also means that the trace left adjoined to the embedded VP must itself satisfy the ECP, i.e. be antecedent-governed, as must every higher ec needed to antecedent-govern a lower ec.

No one of the ec's represented in (8)c can thus be missing (whence the strict successive cyclic movement of *how*),nor can it delete prior to LF.

The reason why, within this system, (8)d is illformed is now transparent. It violates the ECP. If not t', t'' fails to be properly governed (antecedent-governed). As the SPEC of the embedded CP is filled by another wh-phrase, the closest antecedent is t'''. But this phrase does not antecedent-govern t''. A barrier (by inheritance), CP, intervenes between them.

Consider now (8)a and b. In (8)b, the trace is not θ-governed. Hence it must be antecedent-governed. This forces the phrase to adjoin to the higher VP, from where it can antecedent-govern the original trace and assign it [+γ] at S-structure since the latter is in an A-position. But once it has gamma-marked the original trace at S-structure, the VP-adjoined trace can delete, so that no other intermediate ec will be needed to antecedent-govern it. This has as an immediate effect that the phrase will be free to undergo 'long' wh-movement from the VP-adjoined position (I abstract again from the effects of Subjacency).

Finally, in (8)a, the trace is θ-governed by the verb, which thus assigns it [+γ] at S-structure. This marking, carried along to LF, by itself satisfies the ECP. No antecedent-government is required and 'long' wh-movement is again permitted by the ECP.[5]

2. AN ALTERNATIVE : THE REFERENTIAL θ-ROLE APPROACH OF RIZZI (1988)

Despite its remarkable success in deriving many important distinctions, the *Barriers* system raises a number of questions, both conceptual and empirical. Concerning the former, Rizzi (1988) notes the existence of a redundancy between the generalized requirement of head-government (cf. fn.4,here) and the θ-government requirement of 'proper government' (see (3) above). Every phrase which is θ-governed is, a fortiori, head-governed. So both clauses of the 'conjunctive' formulation of ECP turn out to require some sort of head government. A second problem inherent in the formulation of proper government is, as often remarked, the disjunction between θ-government and antecedent-government. To admit a disjunctive statement of this sort amounts to admitting that the nature of the relevant generalization is not understood.[6]

As to the empirical problems, they are inherent in the general prediction that phrases in A-positions should be able to undergo 'long' wh-movement. This does not seem always to be the case.

Consider, for example, measure object NPs and objects of idiomatic VPs. As pointed out by Rizzi (1988) and Koopman and Sportiche (1988)), among others, they fail to undergo 'long' wh-movement despite the fact that they are presumably θ-marked by the verb which selects them. See, for example, (9)-(10), which contain measure phrases, and (11)-(12), which contain the VP idioms *fare giustizia* 'do justice' and *prestare attenzione* 'pay attention'.

(9) *Quanti chili ti ha chiesto se pesavi?[7]
How many kilos has he asked you whether you weighed?

(10) *Quanti chilometri non sai se Venezia disti da Treviso?
How many kilometers don't you know whether V. is far from T.?

(11) *GIUSTIZIA, mi domando quando faranno finalmente!
Justice, I wonder when they will finally do!

(12) *L'attenzione che non ho ancora deciso a chi prestare è poca.[8]
The attention that I haven't decided yet to whom to pay is little.

These NPs can of course be wh-moved at an unbounded distance via the successive cyclic option, provided that no weak islands intervene. See (13) and (14):

(13) a. Quanti chili credi che riuscirà a pesare dopo questa dieta?
How many kilos do you think that he will be able to weigh after this diet?
b. Quanti chilometri credi che abbia detto che distava, Venezia?
How many kilometers do you think he said that V. was far?

(14) a. GIUSTIZIA, dice di voler fare!
Justice, he says he wants to do.
b. L'attenzione che ho deciso di prestare a Gianni è poca.
The attention that I decided to pay Gianni is little.

If we must conclude that 'long' wh-movement is not simply a prerogative of phrases in A-positions, of which class of elements is it a prerogative of?

On the basis of the contrast between ordinary objects which can be 'long' wh-moved and measure or idiomatic NPs, which can not, Rizzi (1988) suggests that it is the nature of the θ-role involved which matters, over and above the requirement that the target of 'long' wh-movement be in an A-position. He expresses this condition unitarily by requiring that the target of 'long' wh-movement be a phrase receiving a θ-role referring to the participants in the event described by the predicate (*agent, theme, goal*,etc.), but not *measure, manner*, or the role assigned to quasi-arguments such as idiom chunks. He calls the former referential, and the latter non-referential, θ-roles.

Concerning the deeper question of why 'long' wh-movement should be limited to phrases receiving a 'referential' θ-role, he proposes a solution in which the classical notion of *referential index* comes to play a crucial role.

The essence of Rizzi's proposal can be summarized as follows :

(15) a. The use of indices should be restricted, as in the classical theory of Chomsky (1965), to express referential dependences between different arguments.
b. Movement does not create indices, but can only carry (referential) indices which are "made legitimate by certain referential properties of the elements bearing it" (i.e. are assigned to phrases receiving a referential θ-role).
c. The Binding relation (X binds Y iff (i) X c-commands Y and (ii) X and Y have the same referential index) is defined in terms of the notion of *referential index*.

These assumptions have the effect of restricting Binding relations to phrases bearing a referential θ-role.

This restriction, as Rizzi notes, subsumes the essential effect of the identification clause of the ECP, capturing the fundamental argument/adjunct asymmetries. The A'-dependency between an operator phrase which receives a referential index at D-structure and its trace can be expressed through Binding. But the A'-dependency between an operator phrase which does not receive a referential index at D-structure and its trace cannot be so expressed. As the operator phrase must still be somehow connected to its trace, the system must resort to other available means. It is tempting to say that in the modular structure of the theory there are only two ways in which two elements can interconnect: through *Binding* or *(Antecedent-) Government.* Binding being unavailable except for elements bearing a referential index, only (antecedent-) government is left to A'-dependencies not involving referential indices.

As Binding is intrinsically non-local (*pace* Subjacency) and (antecedent-) government local, the option of 'long' wh-movement just for phrases bearing a referential θ-role follows; as follows the requirement that each link of the successive cyclic derivation (left for the other phrases) obey (antecedent-) government.

This is essentially the source for the observed asymmetries.

(8c), (13a-b) and (14a-b) are well-formed cases of successive cyclic wh-movement. The wh-phrases involved, not receiving a referential θ-role (hence, index) at D-structure, cannot connect to the original trace via Binding. But they can connect to it via a chain of antecedent-government relations since no government barriers intervene between any of the pairs of positions involved.

(8)d, (9)-(10) and (11)-(12) are illformed since the wh-phrase can connect to its original trace neither via Binding (it does not receive a referential index at D-structure), nor via (antecedent-) government (a barrier by inheritance, the interrogative CP node, intervenes between the embedded VP adjoined ec and the matrix VP adjoined ec).[9] (8a and b) are wellformed cases of 'long' wh-movement since here the wh-phrase receives a referential θ-role (hence a referential index) at D-structure and can thus connect to its trace via Binding, after movement.

The fact that a Government barrier (or a potential A'-antecedent) intervenes between them is thus unconsequential. The fact that wh-phrases not receiving a referential index at D-structure cannot cross other weak islands besides wh-islands also follows from the (antecedent-) government requirement on each link of the successive cyclic derivation. See, for example, (16)a-b through (18)a-b. The a-cases exemplify the behavior of measure phrases; the b-cases that of objects of VP idioms :

(16) a. Quanti chili (*non) pesi?
How many kilos do(n't) you weigh? (*negative island*- cf. Ross (1984))
b. Quanta attenzione (*non) ti ha prestato?
How much attention has(n't) she payed you?

(17) a. *Quanti chili ti rammarichi che lei pesi?
How many kilos do you regret that she weighs?
(*factive island* -cf. Erteshik (1973)
b. *Quanta attenzione ti rammarichi di avergli prestato?
How much attention do you regret you payed him?

(18) a. *Quanti chili ha certamente contato pesare per lei?
How many kilos was it certainly important to weigh for her?
(*Extraposition island*, cf. Kayne (1984))
b. *Quanta attenzione ha certamente contato prestargli?
How much attention was it certainly important to pay him?

In (17-18), a Government barrier, the non L-marked embedded CP, intervenes between two positions of the successive cyclic derivation. In (16), a potential A'-antecedent (the negation) intervenes (cf. Rizzi (1990)).[10]

Under this Binding/Government approach, the ECP can reduce to the formal licencing requirement (a non-pronominal ec must be properly head-governed), thus eliminating the redundancy observed above and simplifying the overall system. Even the second conceptual problem observed above dissolves. The irreducible disjunction between θ- and antecedent-government in the formulation of ECP has no primitive theoretical status, its effects having been subsumed by two independent principles, Binding and Government.

3. A REFINEMENT : THE ROLE OF REFERENTIALITY

Having thus reviewed two particular partitioning of the classes of elements undergoing 'long' and 'successive cyclic' wh-movement, that of *Barriers* and that of Rizzi (1988), I will now discuss some new facts bearing on this question, which in fact appear to suggest the necessity of further restricting the class of elements that undergo 'long' extraction. Since they point to the linguistic relevance of a particular notion of referentiality, they provide confirmation for the general approach of Rizzi (1988), while also suggesting an important refinement of that system.

To anticipate the main conclusions that will be reached, it appears that, of all the phrases that receive a referential θ-role, in Rizzi's sense, only those can be 'long' wh-moved which are used strictly referentially, i.e. which refer to specific members of a preestablished set. This characterization recalls Pesetsky's (1986) important notion of D(iscourse)-linking, to which I return later to subsume it under the relevant notion of referentiality utilized here. For the significance of (a somewhat different conception of) referentiality in the account of 'long' wh-movement, see also Aoun (1986), Aoun et al. (1987).

This result, within Rizzi's system, may be derived if, everything else held constant, we further restrict the assignment of referential indices just to (wh-)phrases which are used referentially (e.g., which are D-linked). Only these will be able to enter binding relations via the referential index mechanism (For a discussion on the notion of binding involved, also see Rizzi 1990,1991).

Whenever reference to members of a preestablished referential set is inherently impossible for some phrase, or hard to force, then, even if the phrase receives a referential θ-role, it will not be able to enter a binding relation with its trace, so that no 'long' wh-movement will appear to be open to it.

To check the relevance of referentiality for binding relations, we need some independent way to discriminate between the two classes of referential and non-referential elements. One phenomenon which discriminates between referential and non-referential constituents is *coreference.* Plainly, only referential elements can enter coreference relations. So, for example, R-expressions, pronominals and (lexical) anaphors can corefer with each other, but, as is well-known, certain types of quantifiers cannot freely corefer. They can be linked to a pronoun only if they c-command it; i.e., if they 'bind' it, in a sense of 'binding' that we might try to unify with that considered so far, but that I will treat as distinct here.

So, for example, it is possible for the pronoun *lo* 'him' in (19)a to be linked to the R-expression *il museo* 'the museum' even if the latter does not c-command the former. This is because they are both referential; hence, they can freely corefer. No link between *lo* and the quantified phrases *ogni museo* 'every museum', *nessun museo* 'no museum' is on the other hand possible in (19)b and c, respectively, as both possibilities fail here. The quantified phrases do not c-command the pronoun (at either S-structure or LF), nor can they corefer with it, being non-referential :

(19) a. [Gli alunni che dovevano vedere *il museo*] *lo* hanno visitato in fretta.
The pupils who had to visit the museum visited it hurriedly

b. *[Gli alunni che dovevano vedere *ogni museo*] hanno finito per visitar*lo* in fretta.
The pupils who had to visit every museum ended up visiting it hurriedly

c. *[Gli alunni che non volevano visitare *nessun museo*] *lo* hanno visitato in fretta.
The pupils who wanted to visit no museum, visited it in a hurry

Similarly, *ogni N'*, *nessun N'*, unlike ordinary R-expressions, show weak crossover effects. Cf. (20) vs. (21) :

(20) *Sua* madre ha presentato *Maria* ad un ragazzo.
Her mother introduced M. to a boy

(21) a. * *Sua* madre ha presentato *ogni figlia* ad un ragazzo
Her mother introduced every daughter to a boy

b. * *Sua* madre non ha presentato *nessuna figlia* ad un ragazzo.
Her mother introduced no daughter to a boy

Quite independently of the exact account of weak crossover one adopts[11], the contrast between (20) and (21) appears to be imputable to the same cause: namely, the availability in (20), and the unavailability in (21), of a coreference reading.

What we expect, then, quite generally, is that all those NPs that can be linked to a pronoun only if they c-command it (and which show weak crossover effects) will not undergo 'long' wh-movement, but only 'successive cyclic' wh-movement. This is so because they are not referential; hence do not receive a referential index; hence cannot enter a binding relation.[12] Since only the 'successive cyclic' option is open to them, we expect, then, that no such NP will extract from a 'weak' island.

3.1 Extraction from 'weak' islands

As a matter of fact,neither the universal distributive quantifier *ogni N'* nor the negative universal quantifers *nessun N'*, *niente* 'nothing', which we saw behave as non-referential elements (cf.(19)b-c), are extractable from weak islands. Cf. (22) and (23) :

(22) a. *OGNI DICHIARAZIONE, mi chiedo perché abbia ritrattato.
Every statement, I wonder why he retracted.

b. *OGNI MUSEO, non vuole visitare.
Every museum, he does not want to visit.

c. *OGNI DICHIARAZIONE, mi rammarico che abbia ritrattato.
Every statement, I regret that he retracted.

d. OGNI MUSEO, è uno scandalo che chiudano.
Every museum, it is a scandal that they shut.

(23) a. *{NESSUN LIBRO/NIENTE} mi domando perché abbia comprato![13]
{No book/nothing}, I wonder why he bought.

b. *{NESSUN LIBRO/NIENTE} non è vero che abbia comprato.
{No book/nothing}, it is not true that he bought.

c. *{NESSUN LIBRO/NIENTE} mi dispiace che abbia comprato.
{No book/nothing}, I regret that he bought.
d. *{NESSUN LIBRO/NIENTE} sarebbe disdicevole che avesse comprato.
{No book/nothing}, it would be unbecoming that he bought.

This implies, within the present analysis, that the quantifiers do not receive a referential index at D-structure as a consequence of their non-referential nature.

The distributive universal quantified phrase *Ogni N'* (and the similar *qualunque N'*, *qualsiasi N'* 'whatever N', *chiunque* 'whoever') contrast with the non distributive universal quantified phrase *tutti NP*, which apparently can be 'long' wh-moved (cf. (24) vs. (22)), and has consistently an interpretation (the 'collective' one) in which it is neither subject to the pronoun binding requirement (cf. (25) vs. (19b)), nor to weak crossover (cf. (26) vs. (21a)). See also Reinhart (1983).

(24) a. TUTTI I MUSEI, mi chiedo chi possa aver visitato.
All the museums, I wonder who can have visited.
b. TUTTI I MUSEI, non ha visitato.[14]
All the museums, he had not visited.
c. TUTTI I MUSEI, mi rammarico che abbiano fatto chiudere.
All the museums, I regret that they shut.
d. TUTTI I MUSEI, sarebbe necessario che chiudessero.
All the museums, it would be necessary that they shut.

(25) [Quelli di loro che hanno visitato *tutti i musei*] *li* hanno trovati uno piu' interessante dell'altro
Those of them who visited all the museums found them one more interesting than the other.

(26) [Le *loro* affermazioni incaute] hanno finito per rovinare *tutti i miei amici*.
Their uncautious statements ended up ruining all my friends.

3.2 Longobardi's scope Reconstruction facts

In Longobardi (1987b), the important observation is made that Reconstruction of the scope of an extracted quantifier is not only blocked by strong islands (cf. Longobardi (1986)) but also by weak islands.

Normally, the scope properties that a quantifier has on the basis of its D-structure position are preserved when it is moved to an A'-position (cf. Riemsdijk and Williams (1981), Cinque (1982), Haïk (1984) and references cited there), though new properties may arise as a consequence of its S-structure position (cf. Chomsky (1980)). For example, in (27)a, though not in (27)b, the quantifier phrase *quanti pazienti* 'how many patients' can be in the scope of the universal distributive quantifier *ognuno dei medici* 'everyone of the doctors'. That is, (27)a can be satisfied by a family of answers ("I think that dr. Rossi can visit 5 in one hour, dr. Bianchi 7, etc."). (27)b, on the other hand, admits only one answer (e.g. "7")[15]:

(27) a. Quanti pazienti pensi che ognuno dei medici riesca a visitare in un'ora?
How many patients do you think that everyone of the doctors can visit in one hour?
b. Quanti pazienti pensano che ognuno dei medici riesca a visitarli in un'ora?
How many patients think that everyone of the doctors can visit them in one hour?

As Longobardi noted, this scope Reconstruction is apparently blocked when the quantifier in question is extracted from a weak island, which otherwise normally allows extraction (and Reconstruction) of complements. See (28)a-d:

(28) a. ? Quanti pazienti ti chiedevi come ognuno dei medici riuscisse a visitare in un'ora?
How many patients did you wonder how everyone of the doctors could visit in one hour?
b. ? Quanti pazienti pensi che ognuno dei medici non riesca a visitare in un'ora?
How many patients do you think that everyone of the doctors can not visit in one hour?
c. ? Quanti pazienti ti lamenti che ognuno dei medici sia riuscito a visitare in un'ora?
How many patients do you regret that evryone of the doctors managed to visit in one hour?
d. ? Quanti pazienti sarebbe uno scandalo che ognuno dei medici visitasse in un'ora?
How many patients would it be a scandal that everyone of the doctors visited in one hour?

For each of (28), the family of answers which was possible in (27)a is excluded. (28)a-d are (in fact, only marginally) possible with an interpretation roughly paraphrasable as (cf. Longobardi (1987b)) "How many patients are such that you wondered how everyone of the doctors could visit them in one hour?", etc., in which the quantified phrase acquires a referential reading (cf. below for independent evidence to this effect).

Longobardi (1987b) and Rizzi (1988,fn.14) interpret this fact as suggesting that scope Reconstruction is only possible where the operator can be connected to its variable through a chain of antecedent-government relations ; hence not across the boundary of even one weak island. The question is why scope Recostruction should require such a chain whereas Reconstruction of other properties does not. See (29)a-c and (30), which exemplify Reconstruction of principles A, B, C of the Binding Theory and pronominal binding,respectively, across a wh-island :

(29) a. E' a *se stessa* che non so se *lei* pensi.
It's of herself that I don't know whether she thinks.
b. *E' a *lei* che non so se Maria pensi.
It's of her that I don't know whether M. thinks.
c. *E' a *Maria* che non so se *lei* pensi.
It's of Mary that I don't know whether she thinks.

(30) A chi *lo* ha aiutato, non so se *ognuno di loro* restituirà il favore.
To those who helped him, I don't know whether everyone of them will reciprocate

Given the preceding discussion, it appears that this curious property of scope Reconstruction need not be stipulated. In other words, no special condition need be imposed on this type of Reconstruction. Its properties as exemplified in (28) can rather be seen as simple effects of the non-referential nature of the extracted quantifier.When it interacts with another quantifer, *quanti N'* must be interpreted non-referentially. As a consequence of that, the wh-phrase will be able to connect to its trace only via a chain of antecedent-government relations, not via binding (whence the character of (28) noted by Longobardi). On the other hand, when *quanti N'* does not interact with another quantifier, it (marginally) admits of a referential reading. Hence the marginal possibility of extracting it from a weak island. Cf. (28) above and (31) :

(31) Quanti pazienti non ricordi se lui avesse visitato?
How many patients don't you remember whether he had visited?

It is apparently possible to check the correctness of this analysis by checking the twofold prediction that it makes. It was said that whenever *quanti N'* interacts with another quantifier it is non-referential. We should, then, expect no coindexation to be possible between it and a pronoun outside its c-command domain, since both coreference and pronominal binding are unavailable. Conversely, when it does not interact with another quantifier, such coindexation should be marginally possible, as reference (hence, coreference) is marginally available to it, as noted.

This is precisely what we find. Compare (32) with (33):

(32) * [*Quanti pazienti* ogni medico potesse visitare] non era chiaro neppure a *loro*?
How many patients every doctor could visit was not clear even to them?

(33) [*Quanti pazienti* fossero rimasti da visitare] non è chiaro neppure a *loro*?
How many patients were left still to be visited wasn't clear even to them?

Similar considerations apply to such quantifier phrases as *tanti N' ... quanti N'* 'as many N'...as', *cosi' tanti N'...che,* 'so many N' .. that', etc.

3.3 Clitic Left Dislocated bare quantifiers

The evidence discussed in this section presupposes an analysis of the Romance construction of Clitic Left Dislocation (CLLD) that cannot be given in full here. I refer to Cinque (1990, chapter 2) for a detailed justification of the main points of this analysis, which will be simply stated here.

CLLD, as opposed to Topicalization, does not involve (movement of) an empty operator. This entails, among other consequences, the following contrast :

(34) a. GIANNI, (*lo) ho visto.
G. (focus), I saw.
b. Gianni, *(lo) ho visto.
G., I saw him.

A 'resumptive' clitic is impossible with a Topicalized object (which in Italian is focalized and bears contrastive stress), but is obligatory with a CLLD object. The contrast follows under Chomsky's (1977) analysis of Topicalization and the above assumption concerning CLLD. (34)a-b receive the following analysis :

(35) a. [$_{TOP}$ GIANNI] [$_{CP}$ OP$_i$ [$_{IP}$ (*lo) ho visto e$_i$]]
b. [$_{TOP}$ Gianni] [$_{CP}$ [$_{IP}$ *(lo) ho visto e]]

(35)a, with a clitic locally binding the object ec, violates the principle barring vacuous quantification, and is thus parallel to (36)

(36) Chi (*lo) hai visto?
Whom have you seen him?

(35b), without the clitic, is not a well-formed structure, since the empty object qualifies as none of the various types of empty NPs : it can neither be an anaphor, nor pro, nor PRO, nor a variable, as no empty operator is permitted in CLLD.

Interestingly, if the object phrase in TOP (an A'-position) is a bare quantifier ($[_{NP}$ Q]) : *qualcosa* 'something', *qualcuno* 'someone', etc.), though not if it is a quantified NP (*qualche N' alcuni N'*, 'some N''', *molti N'*, 'many N''', etc.), the resumptive pronoun may be missing :

(37) a. Qualcuno, (lo) troveremo.
Someone, we (him) will find.
b. Qualcosa, di sicuro, io (la) farò.
Something, surely, (it) I'll do.

(38) a. Qualche errore, Carlo *(lo) ha fatto.
Some error, C. (it) has made.
b. Alcuni libri, *(li) ho comprati.
Some books, (them) I bought.
c. Molte lettere, lui *(le) butta via.
Many letters, he (them) throws away.

Presence or absence of the resumptive clitic in (37) is not, in fact, simply optional. It correlates with a difference in the referential properties of the quantifier. If the speaker has something or someone specific in mind (i.e. if the bare quantifier is used referentially), the clitic is required. If the interpretation is 'something or other' or 'someone unspecified', the clitic is impossible.

This suggests that bare quantifiers used non-referentially behave as intrinsic operators, able to identify an ec as a variable at S-structure, while bare quantifiers used referentially and quantified NPs cannot, so that the presence of a resumptive clitic is required (cf. Cinque (1986), Dobrovie-Sorin (1987)).[16]

Being non-referential when they identify an ec as a variable, left dislocated bare quantifiers should thus only be able to connect to the associated ec via a chain of antecedent-government links, and should accordingly be sensitive to weak islands. This is precisely what we find :[17]

(39) a. *Qualcuno, mi chiedo come troverai.
Someone, I wonder how you'll find.
b. *Qualcosa, mi chiedo chi farà per noi.
Something, I wonder who will do for us.

(40) a. *Qualcuno, non credo che trovi.
Someone, I don't think he'll find.
b. *Qualcosa, di sicuro, non farò.
Something, surely, I won't do.

(41) a. *Qualcuno, mi pento di aver aiutato.
Someone, I regret I helped.

b. *Qualcosa, mi pento di aver fatto per loro.
Something, I regret I did for them.

(42) a. *Qualcuno, è un vero scandalo che abbia schiaffeggiato.
Someone, it's a true scandal that he slapped in the face.
b. *Qualcosa, è un vero scandalo che abbia ottenuto.
Something, it's a true scandal that he obtained.

3.4 Pesetsky's D-linked and non-D-linked wh-phrases

As noted, the notion of 'referentiality', as the ability to refer to specific members of a set in the mind of the speaker or of one preestablished in discourse, recalls Pesetsky's (1987) important notion of D-linking. I think, in fact, that the two are one and the same notion, or perhaps, more accurately, that the notion of referentiality subsumes that of D-linking.[18]

In Pesetsky (1987), certain asymmetries existing between two types of wh-phrases in situ are interpreted as due to their different ability in relating to referential sets preestablished in discourse. *Which N'* phrases have the faculty (in fact, must) refer to members of a set that both speaker and hearer have in mind (as do the relevant answers). Bare wh-operators like *who,what* or *how many N'* phrases can do so only very marginally, and under very special contextual conditions forcing some linking to previous discourse. The simple addition of a phrase like *the hell* or *on earth,* which expresses surprise or ignorance of the possible answers, and is thus incompatible with the choice among the elements isolated in the previous discourse, suffices to exclude any such discourse linking. He calls the former *D-linked* and the latter *non-D-linked* wh-phrases.

By assuming a) that operators must occupy an A'-position at LF and b) that only non-D-linked wh-phrases are operators, he is able to account for a number of asymmetries between the two types of wh-in-situ. Only non-D-linked wh-phrases in situ (such as *who,what,how many N'* phrases) are expected to move in LF, and should thus show the usual diagnostics of movement (sensitivity to Subjacency, ECP and other conditions on movement like the Nested Dependency Constraint). D-linked wh-phrases in situ (such as *which N'*) are instead expected not to move at LF, since they do not qualify as operators. They are rather interpreted in situ via a different mechanism, of 'unselective binding' (cf. Pesetsky (1987) for more careful discussion).

The following relative contrasts are thus expected: (43a-b) vs. (44), and (45) vs. (46).

(43) a. *Mary asked what who read.
b. *I need to know whom how many people voted for.

(44) Mary asked what which man read.

(45) ??Tell me what proves that who is innocent.

(46) Tell me which piece of evidence proves that which person is innocent.

Pesetsky's conclusions about the behavior of wh-phrases at LF are consistent with the conclusions reached in the previous sections about the (movement of) quantifier phrases at S-structure. Only D-linked (in our terms, referential) phrases can indeed enter an (unselective) binding relation, whether at S-structure or LF. Non-D-linked (i.e., non-referential) phrases are instead forced to enter only chains of antecedent-government relations, both at S-structure and LF.

It is thus not unexpected that non-D-linked wh-phrases do not take scope over a wh-island, even in languages (such as French) that marginally allow for extractions out of wh-islands, since such LF movement is sensitive to antecedent-government relations, just as overt syntactic movement of non-D-linked phrases is:

(47) Qui sait quand Jean en a acheté combien?
Who knows when J. of them has bought how many

We shall in fact see in the next section that there is complete parallelism between wh-extraction from a wh-island in LF and in the syntax :

(48) *Combien te rappelles-tu quand Jean en a acheté?
How many do you remember when J. of them has bought?

That D-linking, in Pesetsky's sense, implies referentiality can be garnered by the fact that a D-linked wh-in-situ (but crucially no non-D-linked wh-in-situ) can enter *coreference* relations. See the contrast between (49) and (50) :[19]

(49) Which boy$_i$ started a fight with which girl$_j$ wasn't clear even to them$_{i+j}$

(50) *Who$_i$ started a fight with whom$_j$ wasn't clear even to them$_{i+j}$

3.5 (Non-)D-linked wh-phrases and the Wh-island constraint

As noted independently by various authors, extraction of interrogative phrases out of indirect questions depends on the character of the extracted wh-phrase. Both Rizzi (1982,Chapter 2,fn.5) and Engdahl (1980,1985) observe that only relatively 'heavy' wh-phrases can be extracted from wh-islands in Italian and Swedish, respectively. But, to judge from the examples, the relevant feature seems once again to be the D-linked vs. non-D-linked character of the extracted wh-phrase. Only the former can apparently be extracted ((51a) is in fact marginally acceptable if a pause follows *a chi*, and otherwise impossible):

(51) a. ??A chi non ti ricordi quanti soldi hai dato?
To whom don't you remember how much money you gave?
b. A quale dei tuoi figli non ti ricordi quanti soldi hai dato?
To which one of your children don't you remember how much money..?

(52) a. *Vad visste ingen vem som skrev?
'What does no one know who wrote'
b. Sven undrar vilken bok alla studenter minns vilken författare som skrev.
'S. wonders which book all students remember which author wrote'

See Comorovski (1985,1987), from which (52)a-b are drawn, and Bedzyk (1987) for the explicit claim that only D-linked wh-phrases can be extracted from wh-islands in Roumanian and Bulgarian, respectively.

As indeed remarked by Comorovski (1987), "the cross-linguistic generalization that emerges is that only D-linked wh-phrases can be questioned out of indirect questions". She proposes a solution for this contrast based on certain presupposition properties of D- and non-D-linked wh-phrases in interaction with the semantics of wh-islands. What we may note is that nothing at all is instead needed to account for the asymmetry in question, within the present analysis of 'long' wh-movement.

Only D-linked, hence referential, wh-phrases can enter a binding relation with their trace ; whence their insensitivity to wh-islands ('weak' islands, more generally). Non-D-linked (non-referential) wh-phrases instead can only move successive cyclically ; whence their sensitivity to 'weak' islands.

The other, often noted, asymmetry between questioning (impossible or marginal) and relativization (marginal or perfect) in extraction from wh-islands[20] appears to be amenable to the same account. If the relative clause head is referential, the relative wh-phrase can plausibly be taken to enter a coreferential relation with it via predication (also see Rizzi 1991). No such possibility is open to interrogative wh-phrases, which behave more typically as true operators.[21]

3.6 "Aggressively non-D-linked" wh-phrases : *Italian* che (diavolo) *and* (che) cos'altro di AP

Two phrases in Italian which appear to resist a D-linked interpretation are *che (diavolo)* 'what (the hell)' and *(che) cos'altro di AP* (lit.) 'what else of AP' (what else A). Not surprisingly, they give rise to quite sharp ungrammaticality when they are extracted from weak islands. See (53)a-d and (54)a-d :

(53) a. *Che ti chiedevi come fare?
What were you wondering how to do?

b. *Che pensi di non fare 'stasera? (vs. Che pensi di fare 'stasera?)
What do you think you won't do tonight?
c. *Che si è pentito di aver detto?
What did he regret saying?
d. *Che sarebbe uno scandalo fare?
What would it be a scandal to do?

(54) a. *Che cos'altro di interessante ti chiedevi chi avesse fatto?
What else interesting were you wondering who had done?
b. *Che cos'altro di buono non stai mangiando?
What else good are you not eating?
c. *Che cos'altro di stupido ti penti di aver fatto?
What else stupid do you repent doing?
d. *Che cos'altro di strano lo danneggerebbe fare?
What else strange would it harm him to do?

They contrast with bare *che (cosa)* 'what', which can apparently be extracted from 'weak' islands, albeit under very special conditions : namely, if the wh-phrase is heavily stressed and is followed by a pause, thus resulting in an echo-question rather than a literal wh-question, which possibly favors a referential reading of the phrase and allows it to enter a binding chain.

5. CONCLUDING REMARKS

To summarize, we have argued, following essentially Rizzi (1988), that A'-chains fall into two classes : government- and binding-chains, the latter being possible only where the head and the foot of the chain bear the same referential index. We have only slightly modified the conditions under which a referential index is assigned at D-structure by requiring that the phrase in question not only occupy an A-position and receive a referential θ-role, but also that it be referential, this, in turn, depending in part on the nature of the phrase in A'-position.

We have also assumed that a phrase entering a binding-chain can always enter the stricter government-chain, though, not conversely, of course (Cf. also Rizzi (1988,fn.14)). But, it is still possible (and perhaps desirable for parsing purposes, as Maria Teresa Guasti observed) that the two modes of connecting a phrase in A'-position and its trace be mutually exclusive, so that non referential phrases can enter only a government-chain and referential elements only a binding-chain.[22]

It appears that this may be right. If we abstract from the left dislocated bare quantifers considered in sect. 3.3 above, it turns out that phrases entering Clitic Left Dislocation in Romance, which involves no abstract operator—cf. Cinque (1990, chapter 2), for extensive discussion—can only enter binding-chains, not government-chains. This curious restriction can be explained if government-chains are only possible when a (non-referential) overt or null operator is present. Since the construction has no null operator, government-chains will be permitted just when there is an appropriate overt non-referential operator (I refer again to Cinque (1990, chapter 2) for more detailed discussion).

NOTES

*This is a revised version of the paper presented at the conference. I wish to thank Mark Baltin, Adriana Belletti, Paola Benincà, Richard Kayne, Giuseppe Longobardi, Luigi Rizzi and an anonymous reviewer for helpful comments and criticism. Material from this article has since appeared in chapter 1 of Cinque (1990).
Recently, it has been claimed that failure of certain elements to extract from weak islands follows from independent pragmatic (Kroch 1989) or semantic (Szabolcsi and Zwarts 1991) principles rather than from the fact that they fail to receive a particular θ-role (Rizzi 1988,1990) and be referential in the sense intended here (i.e. able to refer to specific individuals of a preestablished set—cf. Pesetsky 1987, hence to co-refer). Interesting arguments that such pragmatic and semantic principles cannot explain the full range of A'-dependencies across weak islands are given in Rizzi (1991) and Chung (1992). The latter also offers a particularly striking argument for the analysis presented here based on the phenomenon of Wh-agreement in Chamorro, which renders 'long' and 'successive cyclic' wh-movement morphologically visible, so to speak.

[1] This is true for the different systems of Bounding and Government proposed in Kayne (1981,1983), Huang (1982), Lasnik and Saito (1984), Aoun (1985,1986), Stowell (1985), Chomsky (1986), Koster (1987), Longobardi (1985,1988), Sportiche (1988), Rizzi (1988,1990), Cinque (1990), among others.
[2] I refer here to Cinque (1990,Chapter 1) for discussion of question (2).
[3] I omit here the further chain of definitions for the terms in (3) to (7). See Chomsky (1986).
[4] In the last section of *Barriers*, Chomsky suggests the possibility that 'proper government' satisfy a relation to a (lexical) head over and above antecedent-government (p.83). In this view, the ECP would consist of two separate clauses, which, in the terms of Rizzi (1990), we may refer to as : the 'formal licensing' requirement (a non-pronominal ec must be head-governed) and the 'identification requirement' (a non-pronominal ec must be θ-governed or antecedent-governed).

Stowell (1985), Koopman and Sportiche (1986), Aoun,Hornstein,Lightfoot amd Weinberg (1987), Longobardi (1987c), Rizzi (1990), among others, provide additional evidence for such a 'conjunctive' formulation of ECP.
[5] In the second half of *Barriers*, Chomsky briefly discusses the possibility of reducing the θ-government requirement of ECP to the antecedent-government requirement. Given that VP adjunction is always possible, the trace of a verb complement will always be properly governed via antecedent-government, independently of θ-mark-

ing. Thus, it seems that , at least for verb complements, θ-government could be eliminated from 'proper government' (p.79). Whether or not this reduction can actually be carried out (cf. Cinque (1990,chapter 2) for an analysis of Clitic Left Dislocation in Romance bearing on this question), it in no way affects the classes of elements that can undergo 'long' and 'successive cyclic' wh-movement, which will still be elements in A- vs. elements in A'-positions, respectively.

[6] Note that this problem is not resolved by the reduction of θ- to antecedent-government suggested in the second part of *Barriers*, since the reduction is only partial, limited as it is to verb complements.

[7] Note that this sentence is also impossible (or quite marginal) under the agentive reading of *pesare*, for reasons that will be discussed later.

[8] Measure phrases cannot ordinarily be resumed by object clitics in discourse. See (i)a-b :

(i) a. Speaker A: Io peso 70 chili.
'I weigh 70 kilos'
Speaker B: *Anch'io li peso.
'Even I weigh them'
b. Speaker A: Questo vestito costa 800 mila lire.
'This suit costs 800 thousands lire'
Speaker B: *Ma quello non le costa
'But that does not cost them'

But this has to do with the clash between their non-referential status and the referential status of object clitics. Where these are used non-referentially (as in Clitic Left Dislocation, in which they are simple place-holders of object positions - cf. Cinque (1990, chapter 2)), they are perfectly compatible with measure phrases (See , e.g., *70 chili, non li pesa di certo* '70 kilos, he does not weigh them certainly').

[9] In addition (or in alternative) to the barrierhood of the interrogative CP under the *Barriers* system, a potential A'-antecedent, the wh-phrase in the embedded SPEC of CP, intervenes, causing a violation of Relativized Minimality, in Rizzi's (1990) terms.

[10] As Giuseppe Longobardi suggested to me, if all decreasing monotones must move to SPEC-C at LF, such cases as (16) are excluded even if the negation, in its base position, does not count as a potential A'-antecedent.

[11] Cf. Reinhart (1983), Hornstein and Weinberg (1988), May (1988) for different views and further pertinent references.

[12] Indefinites are known to allow for both referential and non-referential readings (cf. Fodor and Sag (1982)). For example, in (i)a, the indefinite is used referentially, as it can be linked to the pronoun even if it does not c-command it. In (i)b, instead, it is used quantificationally (i.e. 'non-referentially', in the relevant sense) as it is under the scope of another quantifier :

(i) a. Carlo, se si innamora di una/qualche ragazza, non la lascia in pace.
C., if he falls in love with a/some girl, does not leave her alone
b. Ognuno di loro parla male di una/qualche ragazza.
Each of them speaks unrespectfully of a/some girl

As we should expect, indefinites are not extractable from a wh-island and display clear weak crossover effects only when they are used non-referentially (e.g. when they are under the scope of another quantifier). See (ii), which is compatible only with the wide scope (referential) reading of *una/qualche ragazza* , and (iii)a-b :

(ii) Di una/qualche ragazza non capisco perche' ognuno di loro parli male.
Of a/some girl, I do not understand why each of them speaks unrespectfully.

(iii) a. Se anche i *suoi* migliori amici tradiscono *un/qualche ragazzo,* questi puo' rimanerne irrimediabilmente scioccato.
If even his best friends betray a/some boy, he may be irremediably shocked.
b. *Di solito il *suo* autore vorrebbe presentare *un/qualche libro* ad ogni editore
Normally, his author would like to submit a/some book to every publisher. (under the interpretation in which the indefinite is under the scope of the universal quantifier)

I thank Giuseppe Longobardi for bringing the problem of indefinites to my attention.

[13] In Italian, when a negative element appears to the right of INFL, it is doubled by a sentential negation, which disappears when the element is to the left of INFL. See, e.g. :

(i) a. Dice che *(*non*) visitera' *nessun museo*
He says he will (not) visit no museum
b. *NESSUN MUSEO,* dice che (*non) visitera'
No museum, he says he will (not) visit.

See Rizzi (1982, Chapter 4), Longobardi (1987a), Zanuttini (1991) for different accounts of this asymmetry.

[14] Note that, as expected , this sentence has only one interpretation, the collective one, in which *tutti i musei* does not interact with the negation (∀- x, x ...he has not visited x). The (non collective) quantifier interpretation (NEG ∀ x...) available when *tutti i musei* is not fronted across a negation (*Non ha visitato tutti i musei*) is here filtered out by the weak island.

[15] The fact that *quanti pazienti* in (27)b is resumed by a referential object clitic appears to force an interpretation where a particular set of (n) people are involved.

[16] Recall that the construction is a non-wh-movement construction, or , more accurately, one not employing (movement of) an empty operator. It is thus interesting to observe that the only elements that can be clitic left dislocated are those which can enter a *binding* relation. In other words, every element which can only be moved via successive cyclic movement in wh-constructions cannot be clitic left dislocated (see Cinque (1990, Chapter 2)). The construction is thus a 'pure representation' of *binding* relations (also obtainable via 'long' wh-movement).

[17] Longobardi (1987b) noted the ungrammaticality of (i)

(i) *Qualcosa, ho mangiato di guasto.
Something, I ate spoilt.

taking it to follow from the fact that extraction of subparts of arguments must respect a successive cyclic derivation. The preceding discussion suggests that even under an analysis in which *qualcosa* and *di guasto* are reanalysed as two independent constituents, *qualcosa* must still connect to the appropriate ec via a chain of antecedent-government links, due to its strict non-referential interpretation (contributed by the presence of *di AP*). Cf. section 3.6 below.

[18] As noted, D-linking is only one way in which a phrase can become referential. Reference to specific members in the mind of the speaker is another (cf. the discussion on left dislocated bare quantifiers above).
[19] I thank Anthony Kroch for constructing these sentences for me.
[20] See Rizzi (1982,chapter 2) for Italian, Maling (1978) for Scandinavian, Rudin (1986) for Bulgarian, among others.
[21] Less clear is how to handle such cases as (i) below, pointed out to me by John Frampton :

(i) I know of nobody that I really know how to talk to.

Here, the (null) wh-phrase is connected to its trace via binding despite the non-referentiality of the relative clause head.
[22] It is of course still possible for a phrase to enter both, if it (like the case of *qualcuno/ qualcosa* in Italian discussed above) can qualify either as referential or non-referential.

REFERENCES

Aoun, J. (1985) *A Grammar of Anaphora*, MIT Press, Cambridge, Mass.

Aoun, J. (1986) *Generalized Binding*, Foris, Dordrecht.

Aoun, J., N. Hornstein, D. Lightfoot and A. Weinberg (1987) "Two Types of Locality," *Linguistic Inquiry*, 18.537-577.

Bedzyk, F. (1987) "Successive Cyclic Wh-movement in Bulgarian and Icelandic," ms. Cornell University.

Cardinaletti, A., G. Cinque and G. Giusti (eds.) (1988) *Constituent Structure Papers from the 1987 Glow Conference*, Venezia/Dordrecht.

Chomsky, N. (1965) *Aspects of the Theory of Syntax*, MIT Press, Cambridge, Mass.

Chomsky, N. (1977) "On Wh-movement," in P. Culicover, T.Wasow and A. Akmajian (eds.) *Formal Syntax*, Academic Press, New York, pp.71-132.

Chomsky, N. (1980) *Rules and Representations*, Blackwell, Oxford.

Chomsky, N. (1981) *Lectures on Government and Binding*, Dordrecht, Foris.

Chomsky, N. (1986) *Barriers* , MIT Press, Cambridge, Mass.

Chung, S. (1992) "Wh-Agreement and 'Referentiality' in Chamorro," ms., UCSC .

Cinque, G. (1982) "Constructions with Left Peripheral Phrases, 'Connectedness,' Move α and ECP," ms., Università di Venezia.

Cinque, G. (1986) "Bare Quantifiers, Quantified NPs and the Notion of Operator at S-structure," *Rivista di Grammatica Generativa*, 11.33-63.

Cinque, G. (1990) *Types of A'-Dependencies*, MIT Press, Cambridge, Mass. .

Comorovski, I. (1985) "Discourse-Linked Wh-Phrases," paper read at the Annual Meeting of the LSA, Seattle, Washington.

Comorovski, I. (1987) "Discourse-Linking and the Wh-Island Constraint," ms., University of Texas, Austin.

Dobrovie-Sorin, C. (1987) *Syntaxe du Roumain. Chaînes Thématiques*, Thèse de Doctorat d'Etat.

Engdahl, E. (1980) "Wh-constructions in Swedish and the Relevance of Subjacency," NELS 10.89-108.

Engdahl, E. (1985) *Constituent Questions : The Syntax and Semantics of Questions with Special Reference to Swedish*, Reidel, Dordrecht.
Erteshik, N. (1973) *On the Nature of Island Constraints*, Ph.D Dissertation, MIT.
Fodor, J. D. and I. Sag (1982) "Referential and Quantificational Indefinites," *Linguistics and Philosophy*, 5.355-398.
Haïk, I. (1984) "Indirect Binding," *Linguistic Inquiry*, 15.185-223.
Hornstein, N. and A. Weinberg (1988) "Logical Form. Its Existence and its Properties," in Cardinaletti, Cinque, Giusti (1988), pp. 143-156.
Huang, J. (1982) *Logical Relations in Chinese and the Theory of Grammar*, Ph.D. Dissertation, MIT.
Kayne, R. (1981) "ECP Extensions," *Linguistic Inquiry*, 12.93-133.
Kayne, R. (1983) "Connectedness," *Linguistic Inquiry*, 14.223-249.
Kayne, R. (1984) *Connectedness and Binary Branching*, Foris, Dordrecht.
Koopman. H. and D. Sportiche (1986) "A Note on Long Extraction in Vata and the ECP," *Natural Language and Linguistic Theory*, 4.367-374.
Koopman. H. and D. Sportiche (1988) "Subjects," ms., UCLA.
Koster, J. (1986) *Domains and Dynasties*, Dordrecht, Foris.
Kroch, A. (1989) "Amount Quantification, Referentiality and Long Wh-movement," ms., Univ. of Pennsylvania .
Lasnik, H. and M. Saito (1984) "On the Nature of Proper Government," *Linguistic Inquiry*, 15.235-289.
Longobardi, G. (1985) "The Theoretical Status of the Adjunct Condition," Scuola Normale Superiore, Pisa (now published in Longobardi (1988)).
Longobardi, G. (1986) "L'estrazione dalle 'isole' e lo *scope* dei sintagmi quantificati," in K.Lichem et al. (eds.) *Parallela II*, G. Narr Verlag .
Longobardi, G. (1987a) "Negation Parameters in Romance Languages and Dialects," paper presented at the GLOW Workshop on 'Dialect Variation and the Theory of Grammar', Venice. .
Longobardi, G. (1987b) "Extraction from NP and the Proper Notion of Head Government," Univ. di Venezia (published in A.Giorgi and G. Longobardi *The Syntax of Noun Phrases*, Cambridge University Press, (1991).
Longobardi, G. (1988) *Symmetry Principles in the Theory of Syntax*, Unipress, Padova.
Maling, J. (1978) "An Asymmetry with Respect to Wh-islands," *Linguistic Inquiry*, 9.75-89.
Pesetsky, D. (1987) "Wh-in-situ : Movement and Unselective Binding," in E.Reuland and A. ter Meulen (eds.) *The Representation of (In)definiteness*, MIT Press, Cambridge, Mass., pp.98-129.
Reinhart, T. (1983) "Coreference and Bound Anaphora : A Restatement of the Anaphora Questions," *Linguistics and Philosophy*, 6.47-88.
Riemsdijk, H. van and E. Williams (1981) "NP-Structure," *The Linguistic Review* 1.171-217.
Rizzi, L. (1982) *Issues in Italian Syntax*, Foris, Dordrecht.
Rizzi, L. (1988) "On the Status of Referential Indices," ms., Univ. de Genève (published in A.Kasher (ed.) *The Chomskyan Turn*, Blackwell, Oxford, 1991, pp.273-299.
Rizzi, L. (1990) *Relativized Minimality*, MIT Press, Cambridge, Mass.
Rizzi, L. (1991) "Argument/Adjunct (A)symmetries," ms., Univ. de Genève.
Ross, J. (1984) "Inner Islands," BLS, 10.258-265.

Rudin, C. (1986) *Aspects of Bulgarian Syntax : Complementizers and WH Constructions*, Slavica, Columbus, Ohio.
Sportiche, D. (1988) "Conditions on Silent Categories," ms., UCLA.
Stowell, T. (1985) "Null Operators and the Theory of Proper Government," ms., UCLA.
Szabolcsi, A. and F. Zwarts (1991) "Weak Islands and Algebraic Semantics," ms., UCLA and Univ. of Groningen.
Zanuttini, R. (1991) *Syntactic Properties of Sentential Negation. A Comparative Study of Romance*, Ph.D. Dissertation, Univ. of Pennsylvania.

MARK R. BALTIN

ON THE CHARACTERIZATION AND EFFECTS OF D-LINKING: COMMENTS ON CINQUE

Cinque's paper, "On the Scope of Long and Successive Cyclic Movement," is an important refinement of an approach to the Empty Category Principle developed by Rizzi (1990). It argues against the relevance of θ-government, a cornerstone of Chomsky (1986), to the notion of proper government, and views the ECP as requiring that traces meet two simultaneous conditions:

(1) a. head-government
b. identification

The requirement of head-government is a formal licensing requirement on traces, and requires that a trace be in some local relation with an appropriate X^0. The present paper concentrates on the identification requirement for traces, which deals with the nature of the anaphoric relation between the trace and its antecedent. Cinque proposes that a trace must be connected to its antecedent in one of two ways: either by being linked to a referential element, in which case the trace must simply be c-commanded by the element; or (ii) by being linked to a non-referential element, in which case it must be connected to the antecedent by a chain of antecedent-governed elements. Cinque characterizes Pesetsky's (1987) notion of D-linking as the relevant notion of referentiality, in which a phrase is D-linked if it assumes a small set of possible referents in the mind of the speaker. Thus, a wh-phrase such as *which man* is D-linked because it presupposes an answer from a small, pre-determined set of men, while a wh-element such as *who* is non-D-linked, because the answer to a question that includes interrogative *who* is not assumed to be limited to some small set of pre-determined individuals.

Cinque's arguments for this distinction tend to concentrate on demonstrating the insufficiency of θ-government in licensing traces across various barriers, showing that an element may be θ-governed in Chomsky's terms, and yet "long" extraction (extraction out of embedded questions, over sentential negatives, and out of factives) is impossible.

In these comments, I will demonstrate some additional areas in which θ-government seems to be too weak a condition for the licensing of an antecedent-trace relation across a barrier, but will suggest that Cinque's results, taken by him to support Pesetsky's (1987) account of the D-linked vs. non-D-linked distinction, in fact undermine Pesetsky's proposed correlation of D-linking with non-movement, and non-D-linking with movement.

I. THE INSUFFICIENCY OF θ-GOVERNMENT IN LICENSING LONG EXTRACTION

To the set of elements which would seem to be θ-governed, and yet cannot undergo long extraction, I would add adjective complements, which can be questioned, as in (2):

(2) How angry do you think that he became?

The verb *become* takes an AP complement, and thus the AP complement would appear to be θ-governed, and yet extraction over an embedded question, either by overt movement or LF movement is prohibited:

(3) *How despondent$_j$ do you wonder whether he became t_j?

(4) *Who$_i$ wonders whether John became how despondent$_j$?

Because wh-marked adjective phrases cannot remain in situ in yes-no questions, I assume that wh-APs cannot absorb with *whether*, in the sense of Higginbotham & May (1981). Therefore, the wh-phrase in (4) would have had to have moved to the spec of the matrix CP. The unacceptability of (3) and (4) is unexpected under an account that requires that traces must simply be either antecedent-governed or θ-governed.

On the other hand, we could say that it is precisely the fact that an AP with an interrogative specifier is not D-linked, in the sense that the answer to a question containing such an element does not come from a small predetermined set, that prevents such long movement.

However, note that if we ask a question such as (2), we are implying that the subject did become crazy to a certain extent. In this sense, a wh-specified AP would appear, on the face of it, to be D-linked, just as in the question in (5), the speaker is implying that John read books from a small set :

(5) Which books$_i$ did John read t_i?

The difference between an AP that is specified by *how* and an N' that is specified by *which* would seem to be the range of values that the two wh specifiers can take, in the sense that an A' that can be specified by *how*, being scalar, takes a set of values that fall along a continuum, while an N' that is specified by *which* is discrete. Thus, the set of values for the former constituent is infinite, while the set of values for the latter is discrete.Perhaps the notion of D-linking requires refinement along these lines.

In any event, the class of elements that Cinque claims requires antecedent government cuts across the complement/non-complement distinction which Chomsky claims is crucial. Most non-complements are non- D-linked, and hence long extraction is impossible.

II. THE CHARACTERIZATION OF D-LINKING

It is rather curious, however, that Cinque seems to be accepting Pesetsky's characterization of non-D-linked vs. D-linked wh-phrases in situ as a distinction between moved and unmoved wh-phrases respectively at LF. One of Pesetsky's main arguments related to the fact that D-linked wh-phrases could apparently take scope out of syntactic islands at LF, while non-D-linked wh-phrases could not, and Pesetsky attributed this difference in the behavior of the two types of wh-phrases to the movement character of non-D-linked wh-phrases, and the non-movement character of D-linked wh-phrases. Cinque comments (p. 20):

> "Pesetsky's conclusions about the behavior of wh-phrases at LF are consistent with the conclusions reached in the previous sections about the (movement of) quantifier phrases at S-structure. Only D-linked (in our terms, referential) phrases can indeed enter an (unselective) binding relation, whether at S-structure or LF. Non-D-linked (i.e., non-referential) phrases are instead forced to enter only chains of antecedent-government, both at S-structure and LF."

Cinque's acceptance of Pesetsky's proposal about the nature of the difference between the two types of wh-phrases mystifies me. Pesetsky proposed that D-linked wh-phrases do not move, and proposed a C.L. Baker (1970)-style Comp-indexing mechanism, in which the wh morpheme, or Q-morpheme, would be co-indexed with the D-linked wh-phrases in its domain. These wh-phrases would not move at all at LF. However, Cinque's paper contains numerous examples of overt syntactic movement of both non-D-linked and D-linked wh-phrases, as does Comorovski (1985, 1988) for Roumanian, and these authors demonstrate the lack of island effects for *syntactic* movement of D-linked wh-phrases. However, Comorovski (1988) points out that Pesetsky's mechanism of unselective binding fails for syntactic movement, since the D-linked phrases obviously move in the syntax, leaving a trace, and thus the difference in susceptibility to island constraints is not as simple as a distinction between movement and non-movement, since movement is involved in both types of constructions. Since there seems to be no distinction between overtly moved wh-phrases and non-overtly moved wh-phrases with respect to obedience to the island constraints in question, Occam's razor would suggest the same mechanism to account for the difference in both components—overt syntax and logical form.

The distinction that Cinque makes between the two types of antecedent-trace relations seems to be more on the right track, but notice that Cinque's mechanism doesn't rely on the distinction between movement and non-movement. In fact, it is incompatible with Pesetsky's distinction, assuming a uniform account of the D-linking phenomenon in both components. In short, as pointed out by Comorovski (1988) and Williams (1986), and reinforced by Cinque's observations, Pesetsky's account would require the following account:

(9)

	Wh in situ	**Overtly Moved Wh-Phrase**
D-Linked	Comp-Indexing	Non-Quantificational Antecedent-Trace Relation
Non-D-Linked	Quantificational Antecedent-Trace Relation	Quantificational Antecedent-Trace Relation

If we assumed Cinque's acccount, we could dispense with Comp-Indexing and posit the following account:

(9)

	Wh in situ	**Overtly Moved Wh-Phrase**
D-Linked	Non-Quantificational Antecedent-Trace Relation	Non-Quantificational Antecedent-Trace Relation
Non-D-Linked	Quantificational Antecedent-Trace Relation	Quantificational Antecedent-Trace Relation

Thus, general methodological considerations would posit LF-movement of D-linked wh-phrases as well. The question to ask, however, is whether we can find any independent evidence to support the idea that D-linked Wh-phrases move at LF. After all, the evidence for the distinction between D-linked wh-phrases and non-D-linked wh-phrases is the greater freedom of distribution of the former. In addition, Cinque cites the striking contrast discovered by Anthony Kroch to support the idea that D-linked wh-phrases are not quantificational, since pronouns linked to them cannot be viewed as variables—((11) = Cinque's (49) and (12) = Cinque's (50)):

(11) Which boy_i started a fight with which $girl_j$ wasn't clear even to $them_{i+j}$.

(12) *Who_i started a fight with $whom_j$ wasn't clear even to $them_j$.

Nevertheless, even D-linked wh-phrases exhibit quantificational behavior in the sense that they participate in scope interactions with other wh-phrases:

(13) Which man knows where which woman will live?

((13) = Pesetsky (1987), ex. (30)).

Pesetsky represents the ambiguity in (13) by two different indexed structures- one in which *which woman* is co-indexed with the Q in the embedded Comp, and the other in which *which woman* is co-indexed with the Q in the matrix Comp. Thus, the ambiguity is reflected by the location of the indexed Q, rather than by movement of the wh-phrase.

Consider the following subject-object asymmetry, however:

(14) a. Which books did every student read?
b. Which students read every book?

(14a) seems to be ambiguous between a reading in which one is asking for the identity of some particular set of books (wide-scope reading for the wh-phrase), and a reading in which one is asking, for each student, which books that student read (narrow-scope reading for the wh-phrase). (14b), however, is unambiguous, and asks for the identity of a particular set of students who had voracious literary appetites. This ambiguity is parallel to the one discovered by May (1985), who dealt with wh/quantifier interactions with non-D-linked wh-phrases:

(15) a. What did everyone buy for Max? (May's 2.12)
b. Who bought everything for Max? (May's 2.16)

May notes that the universally quantified NP can take either wide or narrow scope with respect to the wh-phrase in (15a), but can only take narrow scope with respect to the wh-phrase in (15b), and attributes this to a constraint against the intervention of a quantified NP between a wh-phrase and a trace bound by it in subject position, a reflex of Pesetsky's (1982) Path Containment Condition. Crucially, May's account relies on a movement analysis for these wh-phrases.

The contrast between (14a) and (14b) is the same as the contrast discovered by May, and would therefore most plausibly receive the same analysis. Of course, because the D-linked wh-phrases have had to move in the syntax, they would be subject to constraints that movement dependencies would have to obey, such as the Path Containment Condition. It is interesting to note, however, that the lack of a wide scope reading for the universally quantified noun phrase in (14b) would be inconsistent with a suggestion in *Barriers* that string vacuous movement of wh-phrases does not occur in the syntax , but does occur at LF for scopal reasons. If we accept Pesetsky's characterization of D-linking, then D-linked wh-phrases do not have to move at LF for scopal reasons, and, because the movement would be string vacuous from subject position, the LF for (14b) would be (16):

(16) $[Q_i [_{IP} [_{NP_j}$ every book$] [_{IP} [_{NP_i}$ which student$] [_{I'} [_I$ past$] [_{VP} [_V$ read$] [_{NP_j}$ t $]]]]]]$

There would be no trace in subject position for the wh-phrase, under this account, to call the Path Containment Condition into play, and so a wide scope reading should be possible. A real test case for the applicability of the Path Containment Condition to D-linked wh-phrases would come from a consideration of a language in which overt wh-movement doesn't occur, such as Japanese; in such a language, the only movement of wh-phrases would occur at LF, and thus Pesetsky's proposals would predict a wide scope reading for the universally quantified NP for the Japanese equivalent of (14b). Interestingly enough, Mamoru Saito (personal communication) informs me that the wh-phrases in the Japanese equivalents of (14b) and (15b) are all interpreted as taking wider scope than the universally quantified NPs.

Interestingly, Williams (1988) shows that May's analysis in terms of the Path Containment Condition can be re-formulated without assuming LF-movement of quantified phrases. However, Williams' re-formulation in terms of his notion of Q-superiority would require giving the two types of wh-phrases the same treatment, in view of the contrast between (14a) and (14b).

However, if D-linked wh-phrases are to be viewed as being quantificational, then how do we reconcile this view with the observations that, unlike non-D-linked wh-phrases, they can move out of embedded questions, and allow split control of pronouns linked to them,violating the Bijection Principle of Koopman & Sportiche (1982)?

I think that the answer is suggested by Cinque's account of the distinction between the two types of A'-bound traces. Furthermore, I would claim that D-linked wh-phrases are, in a sense, Janus-like, in allowing a referential interpretation *in addition to* a quantificational interpretation. The referential interpretation allows the D-linked antecedent of a trace to simply bind the trace without governing it, and to fail to be the unique antecedent of a pronoun, but the quantificational nature of the wh-phrase will cause it to behave like any other quantifier with respect to scope interactions. Thus, a D-linked wh-phrase will have the union of quantificational and referential properties, and the fact that there is a way of licensing their traces without viewing them as variables will enable them to bind their traces across barriers. Non-D-linked wh-phrases will not have this alternative way of licensing their traces, however, and could only be viewed as quantificational.

III. D-LINKING AND ISLAND CONSTRAINTS

Chomsky (1973) noted that, in general, subjects are extraction islands with respect to wh-movement:

(17) *[Of whom] did [pictures t] bother Fred?

Topicalization cannot extract parts of subjects, either:

(18) *[Of Sally], [pictures t] bothered Fred.

Chomsky (1973) has dubbed this constraint on extraction the Subject Condition, and there have been many proposals as to how to derive this constraint, including subjacency (Chomsky (1977)) and Kayne's connectedness condition (Kayne (1984)). Note, also, that subjects are considered to be ungoverned, not being L-marked, in terms of Chomsky (1986), and would therefore be barriers. The barrier status of subjects (apart from small clause subjects or subjects of ECM complements), would be relevant for subjacency. However, if it is the ungoverned nature of subjects that causes them to be islands, we would expect, given Cinque's proposals, that D-linked phrases could be extracted from subjects with less difficulty than non-D-linked phrases. Extraction of D-linked phrases should give rise to a subjacency violation, while extraction of non-D-linked phrases, which must be antecedent-governed, would violate the identification requirement for traces as well as subjacency. The degree of violation of (17) and (18) seems comparable, however. It seems that the subject condition is insensitive to whether or not the extracted phrase is D-linked. The unacceptability of sentences such as (17) and(18) is also unexplained under a disjunctive formulation of the ECP, such as that of Chomsky (1986), since the extracted phrase would be θ-governed by the head noun, *pictures*.

In conclusion, the paper goes a certain distance toward clarifying the notion of referentiality that is at play in natural language. There are some unanswered questions, however. In particular, it is thought that subjacency violations are weaker than ECP (or, in the present context, identification requirement) violations. This seems to be true only for Wh-island violations. Subject condition violations seem to be uniformly unacceptable, and this fact requires some explanation.

REFERENCES

Baker, C.L. (1970), "Notes on the Description of English Questions: The Role of an Abstract Question Morpheme," *Foundations of Language* 6, 197–219.

Chomsky, N. (1986), *Barriers*, MIT Press, Cambridge, Mass.

——— (1991) "Some Notes on the Economy of Derivation and Representation," in R. Freidin, ed., *Principles and Parameters in Comparative Grammar*, MIT Press, Cambridge, Mass.

Comorovski, I. (1985), "Discourse-Linked Wh-Phrases," paper presented at the Annual Meeting of the LSA, Seattle, Washington.

——— (1988), "Discourse-Linking and the Wh-Island Constraint," in J. Carter & R.-M. Dechaine, *NELS* 19, Graduate Linguistics Students Association, University of Massachusetts, Amherst.

Higginbotham, J. & R. May (1981), "Questions, Quantifiers, and Crossing," *The Linguistic Review*, vol. 1, 41–79.

Koopman, H. & D. Sportiche (1981), "Variables and the Bijection Principle," *The Linguistic Review* 2, 139–160.

Lasnik, H. & M. Saito, "On the Nature of Proper Government," *Linguistic Inquiry*, Vol. 15, 235–290.

May, R. (1985), *Logical Form*, MIT Press, Cambridge, Mass.

Pesetsky, D. (1987), "Wh-in-Situ: Movement and Unselective Binding," in E. Reuland & A. ter Meulen, *The Representation of (In)definiteness*, MIT Press, Cambridge, Mass.

Rizzi, L. (1990), *Relativized Minimality*, MIT Press, Cambridge, Mass.

Williams, E. (1986), "A Reassignment of the Functions of Logical Form," *Linguistic Inquiry*, Vol. 17, 265–299.

——— (1988), "Is LF Distinct from S-Structure: A Reply to May," *Linguistic Inquiry*, Vol. 19, 135–146.

JUAN URIAGEREKA

DETERMINER CLITIC PLACEMENT

1. INTRODUCTION: A SYNTACTIC OR A PHONOLOGICAL APPROACH?[1]

Some time in the High Middle Ages, the Romance languages created a determiner system from chunks of the demonstrative paradigm of Latin. This language did not have definite articles, nor did it have third person pronouns—it used demonstratives to refer to third persons. In fact, in many (though not in all)[2] Romance dialects, the Latin demonstratives used for the determiner paradigm are the same ones used for the pronominal paradigm; see Wanner (1988) for these matters. An empirical issue is then raised with respect to whether in some structural sense pronouns and determiners are of the same type. The intuition behind this idea goes back to Postal (1966), who specifically argued for "so-called pronouns" being nothing but a "determiner + one" (that is, he = the one).

Esther Torrego pursued this approach for the Romance languages, mainly in unpublished work reported in Uriagereka (1988). She placed Postal's insight into the DP analysis of Abney (1987), who in turn developed Brame's (1981) idea that determiners head their own phrases. For Torrego, third person Romance clitics are determiners (henceforth D's) heading a DP, whose complement is an NP and whose specifier is, in dialects which tolerate it, a DP "double".[3] For the Romance languages, the NP complement of D is pro, which makes her proposal almost identical to Postal's: where he had *one*, she has pro. This is coherent with the fact that English structures like *the one who left* come without *one*, and with a null category instead, in Romance variants. In turn, standard DPs differ from pronominal ones only in the fact that they realize the nominal complement overtly (*the man*, not *the pro*).

In Uriagereka (1988) I noted that this approach raises an interesting question: if determiners are heads, they should behave like heads with respect to such processes as head movement. I took clitic placement of the sort seen in Romance languages as head movement, in fact very specifically determiner head movement—thus covering what otherwise would have been a theoretical gap. Of course, we may be wrong in thinking that determiners are heads. The point is, though, if we are not, then movement should be an attested option. In Uriagereka (1988) I went a step further: I suggested that determiners raise not only when we see them as Romance clitics (by hypothesis associated to an NP pro), but more generally when they are standard determiners taking a regular NP complement, in the present terms.

I am fully aware of the fact that this was, and still is a controversial claim to make. I want to emphasize, though, that under my assumptions if standard determiner raising were not attested in any language, then we would have something to explain, not if it is attested. This is a point that Baker and Hale (1990) also raise, and in fact cite the work I am about to present as evidence for the position we all take. At this point, then, it becomes important to decide whether the evidence I adduced is in fact valid: do determiners really raise in some languages?

The first thing to note here is that determiners within the Romance languages, from the time we have available texts, cliticize either to the nominal to their right, or to the element to their left (which can be a verb, a preposition, and some other units). This much is uncontroversial, and separates languages like Italian, French, or the very extreme case of Rumanian where the determiner is wrapped around the head noun, from Galician, Leonese, older forms of Gascon and Provençal, and arguably also older forms of mainland Iberian dialects.[4] The second trait is archaic and in some instances substandard, and is perhaps associated to a "stronger" determiner system, in the sense discussed in Uriagereka (in progress, ch. 2).[5] Given this asymmetry, one of two issues is at stake: either we have a different phonological phrasing for each set of dialects, or else a different syntax.

I do not wish to create antagonism between these two positions, the syntactic and the phonological one. My own view is that although phonological principles may indeed have much to say about the right-ward placement, and may account for some instances of, and definitely all of the details of the left-ward placement, nevertheless the ultimate directive of the latter in many instances is purely syntactic—as a matter of fact is standard head movement. But I am willing to be persuaded otherwise, and for that I think that the evidence presented here is helpful: these are data that any analysis, syntactic or phonological, must account for. If both do, then we will have to decide among the competing theories on the basis of other criteria. All other things equal, and given the theoretical issues raised in the previous paragraphs, I would obviously prefer the syntactic account in as much as it would cover the gap of head movement for determiners. Only if it can be shown that the syntactic account cannot deal with certain facts which the alternative can deal with, would the latter be preferable.

It is my suspicion that three sorts of evidence favor a syntactic account: (i) the placement at issue is sensitive to government considerations in modern Galician: only determiners which are governed can move, and in fact they move to their governor; (ii) I shall construct some examples where determiners may and where they may not cliticize, which nevertheless appear to have identical phonological properties—and hence we should perhaps expect identical placements, which do not obtain; (iii) I shall argue that determiner cliticization interacts with syntactic processes such as the possibility of extracting from inside a DP, thus arguing for its taking place in a derivation early enough to affect the syntactic output. Needless to say, a rich theory of phonological phrasing, one for instance that is sensitive to government and to slight differences in syntactic structures may be able to deal with (i) and (ii). As for (iii), it could be argued that PF feeds LF, as many have, or that the exact sources for the cliticized and the non-cliticized determiners differ, and affect extraction. This would salvage a phonological account, and I can only insist that it is not my intention to prevent it—though sketching a concrete account is not within my abilities.[6]

Let me hasten to add that there are serious questions a phonological account can raise to a syntactic one. The position I take, for instance, will raise the issue of why determiner cliticization is not identical in all respects to standard cliticization of special clitics, in the sense of Zwicky (1977). I may not have a complete answer to this, but I shall present some arguments to the effect that standard principles of grammar predict a good deal of the observed differences between the two processes. In the present stage of our investigations into the nature of morphological processes from a syntactic perspective (as in Marantz (1989) and elsewhere, for instance), or the form of lexical units again from a syntactic perspective (as in Hale and Keyser (1992) and their references), to use existing principles to predict part of the actual facts may be all that one can get.

2. DETERMINER CLITICIZATION IN GALICIAN

In this paper I want to present the case of determiner cliticization in one of the languages where it can proceed to the left, namely Galician. The facts I am about to discuss are for the most part not exotic or even controversial, but paradigmatic instances of a phenomenon which is fully described in its essentials (see for instance Alvarez, Regueira, and Monteagudo (1986)), and totally robust within all three major dialects of Galician. Whenever a piece of evidence is controversial, I shall highlight it and present the necessary disclaimers.

2.1. *Some Phonological Cliticizations*

I want to start by emphasizing the well-known distinction between cliticization and clitic placement. Cliticization of regular clitics is a phonological phenomenon, and this paper will have little to say about it. In turn, clitic placement of special clitics involves syntactic movement. I will call the target the landing site of clitic placement, and the host the supporter of cliticization. I will be following Uriagereka (1988) in that clitic placement implies government by the target of the launching site of the clitic, being an instance of head movement.

Unfortunately, phonological cliticization is not even a reliable test for clitic placement, for there exist instances of cliticization onto non-heads, or onto elements which do not c- command the clitic source. Thus, consider (1):

(1) a. Van en cas'Basilio
go(they) in house-Basilio
'They went to Basilio's house'
b. estabanlle seus pais a dar un algo
were-DAT their parents to give a something
'his/her parents were giving him/her something'
c. disque /seica lles diron un algo
say(they)-that know(I)-that DAT gave(they) a something
'Reportedly / Apparently they gave them something'

In (1a), the head-noun *casa* appears cliticized onto its argument *Basilio.*[7] This cliticization would appear to have little to do with head-to-head movement, and looks instead like a standard phonological re-arrangement of words, with the light one becoming dependent on the heavy one. This sort of right-ward cliticization is rather common in the Romance languages, and typical for determiners in many. The pair (1b-c) is of interest because of the position of the special clitic in each instance.

If the traditional idea that verbal enclisis in matrix clauses of the type seen in (1b) is a result of verb movement to a sentence peripheral site, then it may well be that the target of the clitic is actually something like Infl—though see 4.4—while the phonological host ends up being the displaced verb. Conversely, in the embedded instance in (1c), the clitic placed in Infl can be shown to be hosted phonologically as a proclitic element in V, not raised in this instance. This needs some careful argumentation.

It is obviously the case that in some Romance dialects (very especially older ones, and in many current ones in colloquial speech) clitics can be hosted by a complementizer:[8]

(2) a. que.l siats fyl (Medieval Catalan)
that.DAT be-you son
'that you may be a son to her'

b. lo men frai que't volere parlar (Gascon)
the my brother that-you want.will talk
'That my brother will want to talk to you'

c. et si'l puede prouar... (Medieval Castillian)
and if-it can(he) prove
'And if he can prove it...'

However, this is not the case in Galician. Thus, Alvarez, Regueira, and Monteagudo (1986:164) explicitly note that in examples of the sort in (3), cliticization to the complementizer is unacceptable:[9]

(3) a. *non é cuestión do faceres de mala gana
not is question of-it do-you of bad desire
'It's not a matter of you doing it reluctantly'

b. *andei todo Lugo po-lo mercar
walked-I all Lugo for-it buy
'I walked the whole of Lugo in order to buy it'

c. *co-o er teño de abondo
with-it read have-I of enough
'Reading it is enough for me'

If they are correct, *lle* in (1c) is probably not enclitic in *que*, but proclitic in *diron*. This is of course different from what happens in (1b), where the clitic is obviously enclitic (see Uriagereka (1992) and (forthcoming) for these matters).

Let me add, also, that left-ward phonological cliticization was wide-spread in old Galician-Portuguese. Thus, we find examples like (4) (from Williams (1938), cited by Nunez (1992)):

(4) a. melho-la fezestes
better-it did.you
'You did it better'

b. Deu-lo sabe poi-la vi
God-it knows because-it saw.I
'God knows it because I saw it'

c. o bom rei en seu pode-la ten
the good king in his power-it has
'The good king has it in his power'

Save for a few instances of frozen expressions, like *Deu-lo tena na Gloria* 'May God have him in His Glory', left-ward cliticization onto a name, adjective, or noun is absolutely impossible in modern Galician dialects I am familiar with. I return to this matter.

2.2. *The Basic Instances*

Keeping these ideas in mind, consider now examples of determiner cliticization to the left:[10]

(5) a. comemos o caldo
   ate(we) the soup
   'we ate the soup'
  b. comemo-lo caldo
   ate(we)-the soup
   'we ate the soup'
  c. *comemo-lo o caldo
   ate(we)-it the soup
  d. comemo-lo
   ate(we) it
   'we ate it'
  e. *comemos o
   ate(we) it

Traditionally, it has been said that Galician has two article forms. One (5a) which is standard; the other (5b), which implies cliticization of the determiner onto elements such as verbs.

The first thing to note with respect to (5b) is that it is not an instance of clitic doubling. The latter involves a full nominal expression plus a clitic. In (5b) we have a determiner clitic, and the nominal expression (minus the determiner) in its base-generated site. In fact, clitic doubling of full nominal phrases is impossible in direct object (5c), as in other Iberian languages.

The second question to emphasize is that (5b) shows encliticization to the verb, instead of procliticization to the noun. This is the main difference with other Romance dialects.

The third important aspect of this process is that, as noted, many Romance standard clitics and determiners have the same origin, the Latin demonstrative. In fact, the similarity between special clitics and determiners in Galician is arguably more than a diachronical accident. Thus (i) morphologically, they are (mostly) identical; (ii) they invoke essentially the same semantic reading; (iii) they undergo very similar syntactic processes, one instance of which is the cliticization in (5d), identical to that in (5b). One of the few differences between structures as in (5b) and those of the sort in (5d) is that in the latter instance cliticization is obligatory (cf. (5e)). But in both cliticizations the underlying form of the article/clitic (lo) shows up (as opposed to the surface form *o*). Something in the phonological cliticization allows this form to surface, upon truncation of the last consonant of the host- -a matter I come back to.

The following is a list of elements which accept determiner cliticization in the modern language (from Alvarez Caccamo (1989)):

(6) Possible hosts:
  a. all verbs: comer+o = come-lo

b. most prepositions in preposition function (not as complementizers): por+a = po-la
c. special clitics: lles+as = lle-las
d. quantificational elements like *ambos* 'both', *todos* 'all': ambos+os = ambo-los
e. the conjunction *e mais* 'and': mais+a = mai-la

Together with these, Alvarez Caccamo notes a few frozen forms:

(7) *ulo* 'where (is) he/it'
pelo 'for it/he'

Ulo shows cliticization to *ub* 'where', which does not exist in the modern language, and *pelo* shows cliticization to *per*, which in the modern language is actually *por* (cliticization as in *polo* also exists). Essentially, these are all the relevant instances.

Of course, crucial to this list is (at least) the fact that (a) these elements can be analyzed as heads, and (b) elements of the [+N] type, like nouns and adjectives/adverbials are missing.

That (6a) and (6b) are heads needs no argument. Within the present framework, special clitics are also heads, hence (6c) is expected. Quantifiers have also been analyzed in many instances as heading a QP, and obviously we would have to take this route to make (6d) consistent with the generalization of attachment to heads. Finally, (6e) can be analyzed in one of two ways. First, it is possible that, as Ross (1967) argued, conjunction phrases have internal structure, where the operator is perhaps a head (for this specific position, see among others Munn (1991)). Second, strictly speaking *mais* is not a conjunction, but the element 'more' whatever this is. Expressions like *Xan e mais Pedro* 'John and Peter' literally stand for 'John and more Peter'. This cliticization can thus be aligned with those onto *ambos*, *todos* and quantificational elements of this sort, which may be heading their own QP.

If the generalization in point can be kept, the explanation for it would follow trivially from head movement: only heads are hosts of the relevant cliticization simply because only heads are the target of the syntactic process of head movement, which by hypothesis feeds the phonological cliticization.

The lack of attachment in the modern language to elements of category [+N] has to be evaluated in light of examples of the sort in (4), from the old language. The instances there involve special clitics, but the matter can be raised equally for determiner clitics. Thus, we can construct interesting minimal pairs on the basis of instances like (4c):

(8) a. en teu poder o tes
in your power it have.you
'You have it in your power'
b. *en teu pode-lo tes
in your power-it have.you

(9) a. *pra poder o facer,...
for be.able it do
b. pra podelo facer,...
for be.able-it do
'In order to be able to do it,'

(10) a. en teu poder a cousa está
in your power the thing is
b. *en teu pode-la cousa está
in your power-the thing is

(11) a. pra facer o caldo,...
for do the soup
b. pra face-lo caldo,...
for do-the soup
'In order to make the soup'

What we see in (8)/(11) is that, systematically, neither special nor determiner clitics can be hosted by the noun *poder* 'power', whereas they can, and in the case of special clitics must be cliticized onto the infinitival *poder* 'be able to'. I do not know how facts about determiner cliticization were in the old language—whether, in particular, (10b) was possible, just as (4c) was. What is clear is that in the modern one the process is restricted as described, and it is not obvious that we can prevent the left-ward cliticization where it does not occur solely on phonological grounds, for otherwise we would arguably also prevent the process in the older language.[11]

From a syntactic perspective, the distinction is again well behaved. Elements of type [-N] are known to be structural governors in a way which is not obvious for elements of type [+N] within this family of languages. Thus, for instance, nouns and adjectives do not assign structural Case, do not license complementizer deletion under government, and quite generally do not host special cliticization. If Grimshaw (1990) is correct, it is not even obvious that these elements take standard arguments, like verbs and prepositions do. If these ideas are on the right track, we may conclude not only that determiner cliticization targets heads, but furthermore that it targets structural governors, which again would follow rather naturally from an analysis in terms of head movement, assuming for instance the machinery I discussed in (1988) or (in progress), which I will return to below. In turn, we would have to assume that in the older language determiners in fact did not incorporate, perhaps because at the time they were still treated structurally (though not semantically) as demonstratives, and had not be reanalyzed as determiner heads—see fn. 22. The cliticization at the time was thus indeed phonological, and not sensitive to the matters discussed here.

2.3. The Phonological Marks of cliticization

Let us consider briefly the phonological contexts where cliticization onto verbs occurs:

(12) a. comemos o..., comemo-lo...
b. facer o..., face-lo...
c. viron os..., *viro-los...
d. viron-los —> viro-nos
e. comeu os, *comeu-los, comeu-nos
f. comeu o caldo, *comeu-lo caldo, *comeu-no caldo
g. comera o..., comera-o, *comera-lo

Galician words all end in either vowels/glides or the consonants [s], [r], [n], [l]. The clearest instances of the cliticization in question arise with words ending in [s] or [r] (12a-b). As for words ending in [n], the expected form does not surface (12c). However, Alvarez, Regueira, and Monteagudo (p.138) note that whereas the final [n] is always velarized at the end of words, in instances of what they argue is also determiner cliticization, the [n] that surfaces is fronted. If something along these lines is at stake, we can maintain the general hypothesis—that is, we can analyze (12c) as in (12d), with nasalization of the [l] in the determiner. We have no way of testing whether the relevant truncation (or assimilation) takes place in words finishing in [l], (a) because the underlying form of the clitic starts with [l] as well, and (b) because none of the targets of clitic placement happens to end in [l] anyway.

In words ending in glides, determiner cliticization and standard clitics differ in an interesting way (12e-f). First, it should be said that the underlying [l] never surfaces in these cases; instead, an [n] does—but only for the special clitic. This must surely have to do with some phonological rule triggered by glides, intuitively one which nasalizes [l], which I will not go into here. As for the fact that this does not extend to cliticized determiners, the reason is unclear.[12] This is the only morphological difference that I am aware of between standard and determiner clitics in Galician. Notice, however, that the more "conservative" form is that of the article; the special clitic seems to undergo a phonological operation. This has one possible consequence: we cannot obviously maintain that the determiner cliticization is "merely" phonological, for if it were, we should arguably expect the phonological process seen for the clitic. So this fact, though peculiar in itself, supports the view that what we are seeing is a form of clitic placement for the determiner, with or without "dramatic" phonological consequences.

Finally, when a word finishes in a vowel, no apparent difference exists between the cliticized and the non cliticized forms (12g). What is clear is that the underlying [l] does not surface here, at least not in most modern dialects. In Old Galician, and in some isolated areas of the interior, it does:[13]

(13)	En Lisboa sobre-lo mar	'In Lisbon, on the sea
	Barcas novas mandei labrar.	I sent new boats to work.
	En Lisboa sobre-lo ler	In Lisbon, on the beach
	Barcas novas mandei facer.	I ordered to make new boats.'

It must be noted that the [l] not showing up in the modern dialects might be signaling a general trend within Galician-Portuguese, which is apparently losing the phenomenon of determiner cliticization altogether.[14] I will stick to the position, though, that clitic placement of determiners is still possible even when we do not see any morpho-phonological correlates of a possible cliticization—the null hypothesis.

That is, I take it that in most contemporary dialects there are phonological rules operating on these determiners, roughly along the lines of (14) (in that order):

(14) a. $l \longrightarrow \underset{[+F]}{C} \;/\; \underset{[+F]}{C} + \_\_$ (e.g. sin+la —> sin-na)

b. $\underset{[+F]}{C} \longrightarrow \emptyset \;/\; \_\_ + \underset{[+F]}{C}V$ (e.g. sin-na —> si-na)

c. $l \longrightarrow \emptyset \;/ \left\{ \begin{matrix} \# \\ V \end{matrix} \right\} + \_\_$ (e.g. a-la —> a-a)

Innumerable details are left open here. For instance, the assimilation in (14a) is non-trivial—it does not spread an [r], but it spreads an [n]. The deletion of the first consonant (not the second) in (14b) can only be tested after a subsequent rule of velarization at the end of words applies, which doesn't apply in these instances.[15] Various rules bleed (14c) to break the hiatus—in some instances, stress does; in others, a iod is inserted. And not only readjustments of this sort are needed. Prepositions like *con* in many dialects reduce before merging, unlike *sin*, which merges first. Thus, we get *coa* and not *cona*. In turn, I noted that the process analogous to (14a) for word-final glides is not an obvious assimilation, but nasalization.

2.4. The Syntactic Pattern of Cliticization

To my mind, the most interesting and less understood aspect of determiner cliticization is where it can take place. I have already restricted the class of hosts, but I would like to show also some restrictions on the syntactic context where the process obtains.

Alvarez Caccamo (1989), in a socio-linguistic study, reports that cliticization from direct object is far more frequent than from subject or adjunct:

(15) a. para come-las patacas
in order to eat-the potatoes
b. %para fala-lo profesor
in order to talk-the professor
c. %queren vi-lo luns
want(they) to come-the monday

(% is supposed to express "infrequency".) It is also the case that most of the examples that Alvarez, Regueira, and Monteagudo report involve cliticization from direct object—although they themselves use scores of examples involving subject cliticization in their Galician text. Cliticizations of the sort in (15b) and (15c) are clearly grammatical—and I have nothing to say about their frequency. To see this, compare these instances to a number of completely impossible cliticizations that follow.

Consider first (16):

(16) a. din que vos chegastedes os fillos de Petra
say that you arrived the sons of Petra
'the sons of Petra say that you arrived'
b. *din que vos chegastede-los fillos de Petra

(16a) contains a post verbal matrix subject, *os fillos de Petra.* It is totally impossible for the determiner in this element to cliticize onto the embedded verb.

For many, another example where cliticization is out involves subjects of inflected infinitivals:[16]

(17) a. vimos os pallasos chegaren
saw(we) the clowns arrive
'we saw the clowns arrive'
b. (*)vimo-los pallasos chegaren

But a case parallel to (17b) with <u>un</u>inflected infinitivals is perfect for anyone who accepts the subject before the verb:

(18) a. vimos os pallasos chegar
saw(we) the clowns arrive
'we saw the clowns arrive'
b. vimo-los pallasos chegar

(19) is analogous to (16), except in this instance an infinitival complement clause is at issue:

(19) a. vimos o neno e mais ti chegardes os tres
saw(we) the child and more you arrive the three
'the three of us, we saw the child and you arrive'
b. *vimos o neno e mais ti chegarde-los tres

Here too we see a matrix post-posed subject trying to cliticize as in (16b), the result being equally impossible. The cliticization is still out in instances where the infinitival is uninflected:

(20) a. vimos ao neno e mais a ti chegar os tres
saw(we) to-the child and more to you arrive the three
'we saw the child and you arrive the three of us'
b. *vimos ao neno e mais a ti chega-los tres

Consider finally the contrasts in (21):

(21) a. fixonos mirar o home
made(he)-us see the man
'he made us see the man/the man made us see'
b. fixonos mira-lo home
made(he)-us see-the man
'he made us see the man/*the man made us see'
c. miramos os homes
saw(we) the men
'we saw the men/we the men saw'
d. miramo-los homes
saw(we)-the men
'We saw the men/we the men saw'

(21a) is ambiguous, with *o home* 'the man' being taken either as a direct object of *mirar* 'see' or the subject of *fixo* 'make'; the ambiguity disappears in (21b), where *o home* must be taken as direct object. A similar ambiguity in (21c), where *os homes* 'the men' is taken as either the subject or the object of *miramos* 'see(we)', is in fact kept in (21d), even after determiner cliticization.

Descriptively, we see that subjects and objects both allow determiner clititization. Problems start, though, when there is no grammatical relation between the determiner that incorporates and the host. Thus, in (16b) the subject trying to target the lower V is a subject of the higher V. (18b) contrasts with (17b) in that only in the former does the cliticized determiner come from a DP whose Case is assigned by the target of the cliticization; in (17b) what assigns Case to the DP is the inflected infinitival, so there is no relation, either Case- or Theta-theoretic between the determiner clitic and its would-be host. The examples in (19) and (20) pattern with those in

(16), in that the clitic is hosted by an element which bears no syntactic relation with it. The same is true about (21), though here another reading is possible in the ungrammatical instances. The intuition is clear enough from a syntactic point of view: the cliticization marks a syntactic relation, which possibly should be expressed via government.

I admit that phonologically there may be a correlate to all of this. To my ear, there is a slight break in intonation in examples with long-distance postverbal subjects, which is perhaps enough to signal that a phonological phrase with the consequence of determiner cliticization is impossible in those instances. I have a harder time seeing a real difference between (17) and (18) from a phonological view-point, though this is debatable. However, I believe there are some examples were it would be rather implausible to have real phonological differences—I for one cannot detect them. Consider some of these.

Take (22), from Alvarez, Regueira, and Monteagudo:

(22) a. lembrouvo-la súa dor
reminded(he)-DAT-the his pain
'he reminded you of his pain'

b. subiuno-lo sangue á cara
raised(it)-DAT-the blood to-the face
'Blood raised to our face'

c. gustalle-lo leite
appeals(it)-DAT-the milk
'milk appeals to them'

d. *recolleo-lo abó
picks(he)-them-the grandfather
(cf. recolleos o abo
'grandfather picks them up')

e. *falouno-lo abo
talked(he)-DAT-the grandfather
(cf. falounos o abo
'grandfather talked to us'

All of these examples have an interesting wrinkle: a special clitic has cliticized to the verb before the determiner. This does not prevent determiner cliticization in several instances. Thus, we see a direct object attached to the verb+dative in (22a), and the subjects of an unaccusative (22b) and a psych verb (22c) doing the same thing. However, when the subject of a transitive verb tries to cliticize onto a verb+accusative as in (22d) or a verb+dative, as in (22e), the result is impossible. Provided that subjects of unaccusatives and subjects of psych predicates are D-structure objects,[17] the descriptive generalization seems to be that cliticization to a verb+clitic is possible only from base objects.

I have a hard time seeing how exactly this fact can affect phonological phrasing. To see this clearly, we can construct a minimal pair following the same rule describing the examples reported by Alvarez, Regueira, and Monteagudo:

(23) a. asustou-lle-la curuxa
frightened(it)-them-the owl
'the (presence of the) owl frightened them'
b. *asustou-no-la curuxa
frightened-them-the owl
(cf. asustounos a curuxa
'the owl frightened them/caused them to be frightened')

The difference between (23a) and (23b) is structural: the first example is an instance of a dative-type psych construction, whereas the second one is an instance of an accusative-type psych construction.[18] Only in the former instance is *a curuxa* 'the owl' a D-structure direct object,[19] hence only there is the cliticization possible according to our generalization. It is hard to see, however, how the two sentences differ phonologically.

To insist on a point: I realize that a phonological theory of phrasal arrangements needs specific proposals about the input syntax. It may be that such a theory is atuned to distinctions such as whether a given dependent is a D-structure direct object, or whether a phrase is governed. The point is, though, that in light of the data adduced, such a phonological theory must contain such theoretical provisos if it itself is to deal with these paradigms. I have no idea whether these would be sound phonological provisos, and I won't venture any speculations in this respect. But I remain skeptical simply because the relevant provisos turn out to be sound syntactically.

3. A LARGER PERSPECTIVE

Let us now look at a wider variety of data bearing indirectly on the paradigms presented so far.

3.1. Cliticization Gates

Consider first the contrasts in (24):[20]

(24) a. *de quén liches os mellores poemas de amigo
of whom read(you) the best poems of friend

b. (?)de quén liche-los mellores poemas de amigo
of whom read(you)-the best poems of friend
'who did you read the best poems of friendship by'

Extraction of a subject from inside a DP is possible in Galician only if determiner incorporation has taken place. Similar facts can be seen when extracting an adjunct from the DP:

(25) a. *de que zonas liches os mellores poemas de amigo
of what areas read(you) the best poems of friend
b. (?)de que zonas liche-los mellores poemas de amigo
of what areas read(you)-the best poems of friend
'what areas did you read the best poems of friendship from'

But this rather dramatic contrast is reduced when extracting a complement from the NP:

(26) a. ??? de qué temas liches os mellores poemas
of what areas read(you) the best poems
b. de qué temas liche-los mellores poemas
of what areas read(you)-the best poems
'what themes did you read the best poems about'

These contrasts are identical to those in Torrego (1985, in progress) for extraction from DPs in Castillian Spanish—mostly:

(27) a. de qué autor has leido varios/*los/*esos libros t
of what author have(you) read several/the/those books
b. de qué país conoces muchas /*las/*esas ciudades t
of what country know(you) many / the those cities
c. de qué cantante salieron publicadas unas/ las/???esas fotos t
of what singer were published some/the/ those photos

Incorporated definite articles in Galician behave like indefinites in Castillian (allowing extraction), whereas non-incorporated articles are instead behaving like their Castillian counterparts, with one exception. The exception is DP-object extraction over a definite article, which seems fine in Castillian, but is still far from perfect in Galician. The difficulty with (26a) is comparable to that in the version of (27c) with a demonstrative.

Intuitively, there is a barrier in all extractions from DPs induced somehow by definite articles, and this barrier yields a violation of the Empty Category Principle (ECP) for subject/adjunct extraction, whereas the barrier allows movement across it for complements (which are "lexically governed"). This is the essence of Torrego's account, details aside. From this point of view, determiners in Galician act as "gates" when they cliticize.

For reasons of space, I shall not go here into what the precise explanation for these contrasts is—though see Uriagereka (in progress, ch. 2) for an account following Torrego. The intuition is clear: determiners are "stronger" in Galician than in Castillian. If they do not incorporate, they behave like the demonstratives they come from diachronically, preventing extraction.

In fact, other Romance languages present further differences in terms of extractions from DPs depending on the "strength" of their determiners. Thus, for instance:

(28) de qui as-tu vu [le portrait d'Aristote t]
of whom have-you seen the portrait of-Aristotle
'by whom have you seen the portrait of Aristotle?'

Within Western Romance, dialects of the French type are the most permissive ones for extraction across definite articles—vis-a-vis Castillian, and Galician. Thus, (28), a type of example discussed by Ruwet (1973), is extracting a subject over a definite article, which is impossible in Spanish and possible in Galician only with incorporation. There is a sense, though, in which the French determiner is the weakest within these languages, and thus for instance it systematically cliticizes downwards to the head noun.

Similar issues can be raised about Eastern Romance dialects like Rumanian. The most permissive ones, including Latin, allow even Left Branch extractions which are very ungrammatical elsewhere.[21] In Uriagereka (in progress) I argue there is a correlation between Left Branch extractions and weak determiners (or no determiners, as in Latin). In the opposite extreme of the spectrum, we probably have languages which allow no extraction from nominals whatsoever, not even direct objects which should be the easiest to move. I suspect this may have been the case of early Romance, at the time determiners were still demonstratives, albeit without the semantic import of deixis.[22] Galician and comparable archaic dialects may to some extent show a remanent of that, although with an interesting way of avoiding the barrierhood of DPs: incorporating the head of the category.

It is not my intention here to argue for why I think DPs can be barriers in certain circumstances, nor why I think head movement may have a consequence for turning these barriers transparent. My only concern is to show that if indeed incorporated determiners act as gates for extraction, it is plausible to assume that the cliticization takes place at a level that feeds the representations that go into the semantics, and not merely an output morpho- phonological level—at least within current assumptions about a T model.[23] And once again, this is all. I can see that in principle a phonological account can be amenable to these facts in various ways, including of course changing the T-model.

3.2. A Parallelism with Special Clitic Placement

In the hypothesis pursued here, special clitic placement and determiner cliticization are identical processes. I will show some differences that must be explained, but let me start by showing syntactic aspects in which the two processes look alike—apart from diachronical parallelisms or morpho-phonemic similarities. This is an important conceptual point: it is less controversial to assume special clitics are placed syntactically than to assume determiner clitics are. My point is that if we want to keep the parallelism, we can treat the two phenomena as one. Taking the prime directive for determiner clitic placement to be phonological, either we would have to discard the similarities I am about to discuss, or else we must treat special clitic placement as a phonological process. Consider clitic climbing first. This process is known to change the scope of a clitic from a downstairs predicate to an upstairs one. It is interesting that, among other things, the phenomenon occurs only in situations of restructuring and, occasionally, reanalysis (see Uriagereka (1988) for discussion and references):

(29) a. Pedroquere-o [facer __]
Pedro wants-it do
'Pedro wants to do it'
b. Pedro fixo-nos [__ saír]
Pedro made-us go
'Pedro made us go'
c. *Pedro di-os [que __ chegaron]
Pedro says-them that arrived
d. *Pedro di-os [que Maria comprou __]
Pedro says-them that Maria bought
e. (*)nos vimo-los [__ chegaren]
we saw-them arrive-AGR
f. *nos vimo-los [a Maria e Petra comprar(en) __]
we saw-them Mary and Petra buy(AGR)

In (1988) I argued, following recent treatments, that the principle responsible for the patterns here is the ECP. Given the particular instantiation I took, the movement of the clitic in (29a) and (29b) leaves behind a governed trace, but this is not obvious in the other instances—though see 4.3.[24]

Without going into an explanation for the facts above yet, I want to note that in some abstract sense at least the impossibility of the bad examples in (29) mimmicks the impossibility of such examples as (16b), (17b), (19b) and (20b). In all instances the clitic is hosted where it doesn't "belong". Further, the possibility of the good instances in (29) relates to the possibility of (18b), under similar structural circumstances. And in fact, the idiolectal variation over (29e) is also apparent in (17b), again under similar structural circumstances.

One last, important parallelism is shown by the contrasts below between examples of reanalysis (30b) and restructuring (30a):

(30) a. tentamos cantar os dous — tentamos canta-los dous
tried.we sing the two — tried.we sing the two
'The two of us tried to sing' — 'The two of us tried to sing'
b. fixemos cantar os dous (a Xan) — *fixemos canta-los dous (a Xan)
made.we sing the two to Xan — made.we sing-the two to Xan
'The two of us made (Xan/someone) sing'

I cannot go into the cumbersome nuisances of clitic climbing for reanalysis. Suffice it to say that, although clitic climbing of the subject of a complement clause is generally possible, the same is not true for the object.[25] In contrast, the object in a reconstruction situation can climb over the subject. Now, the examples in (30) add a further wrinkle. First, we are not incorporating a determiner from a downstairs object, but from the upstairs subject, after inversion. In fact, (30b) is fine if *os dous* 'the two' is interpreted as 'the two tangos', or whatever– that is, as the downstairs object. But when 'the two' is the subject in the matrix clause, then only in the restructuring case is the incorporation possible (30a). So obviously the problem is not just moving the clitic over the restructuring or reconstruction site in these instances, a matter I return to.

To conclude this section, I also want to note that the pattern of impossible placements seen in (22) may actually also correlate with facts this time about the sequential ordering of special clitics. I am thinking in particular of data as in (31):

(31) a. dixonolo
aid(he)-DAT-it
'he said it to us'
b. *dixolonos
said)he)-it-DAT
c. vimosllo roubar
saw(we)-DAT-it steal
d. *vimololle roubar
saw(we)-it-DAT steal

A direct object clitic can cliticize onto a verb+dative (31a), but an indirect object clitic cannot cliticize onto a verb+accusative (31b). A similar pattern occurs, for instance, in perception verb infinitival complements (31c,d): the object of the embedded clause (surfacing as *o*) can cliticize onto the perception verb which is already hosting the subject of the same embedded clause (surfacing as *ll-*); the converse is impossible. I also return to this.

4. A THEORETICAL ANALYSIS

As I said, thinking of determiner cliticization as head movement buys us, to begin with, the limited set of hosts allowed for the process in modern Galician (6). But now we have to see how exactly the process works, what structural notion it is sensitive to, and whether what the theory predicts accords with the facts.

4.1. Potential Difficulties for Head Movement

Descriptively, noun incorporation is usually from direct object position (see Baker (1988)). Prima facie, the phenomenon seen here is more extensive than that. In fact, not only can determiners from subjects cliticize, but also from some adjunct sites:

(32) a. con ela falamos o Luns da Feira
with her talked-we the Monday of-the Market
'With her, we talked the Monday which was a Market day'
b. con ela falamo-lo Luns da Feira

Then the question is: which one is more likely to be actual, syntactic incorporation, the one restricted to direct objects, or a more general process expressed perhaps in terms of government?

I actually suggested in Uriagereka (1988) that the sort of process I discussed is, all other things equal, a better candidate. In particular, if government is what is central for incorporation—and this is definitely Baker's view—then we should expect incorporation under government, and not incorporation of direct objects. The latter will of course always be governed, but other dependents may too, and we predict those should be able to incorporate as well.

This issue is complex, and is at the core of the debate between those who view noun-incorporation as compounding or a similar lexical phenomenon, and those who see it as head movement. I have nothing to add to that debate, but I will emphasize that the issue extends beyond the data here. Thus, for instance, Rosen (1989) questions Baker's analysis of incorporation in Iroquoian languages by arguing that what looks like an incorporated noun in these circumstances is best seen as a noun classifier. Furthermore, she notes that in instances that Baker took to be incorporation leaving a stranded possessor, the process can be observed for subjects and certain adjuncts in Tuscarora and Seneca, and not just for complements. She also notes that the languages in point can allow a null nominal head, and thus it is not obvious that they involve movement from the relevant null position.

In fact, I think it is good news for a Baker-type approach that syntactic incorporation extends beyond complements. If it were restricted to complements, an analysis in terms of internal arguments would always be an alternative—but obviously not when the process affects subjects and adjuncts, up to government. It is unclear to me also that Rosen's analysis can be extended to examples of the sort discussed here.

First, surely there may be a null nominal head in these instances; but if Torrego is correct, this head has nothing to do with the incorporation of the clitic: we need at D-structure both a determiner—which is what cliticizes—and either a full NP or a null NP pro. The former yields determiner cliticization; the latter special cliticization, by hypothesis. Second, for something like *comemo-lo* 'ate.we-it' to involve a classifier analysis, we would have to assume that the form denotes a subclass of eatings, namely "it-eatings". Usually, classifiers do not invoke deictics, but non- variable lexical notions. So in fact it would appear that Baker's syntax for incorporation is needed, although we may disagree on how many processes it encompasses—the ones in point, though, are about the strongest candidates one can imagine.

In all fairness, Baker himself showed some examples in (1988) that go well beyond the matter of direct objects. Thus, he pointed out instances where noun incorporation interacts with verb incorporation to yield results very much along the lines of (18b). The following example is from Southern Tiwa (p. 377)):

(33) Ti-seuan-p'akhu-kumwia-'am-ban wisi te-khaba-'i
1S:A-man-bread-sell-CAUS-PAST two 1S:C-bake-SUBORD
'I made the man sell the two breads that I baked'

In both (18b) above and (33), the subject of an infinitival complement incorporates upwards to the matrix verb.

Baker and Hale (1990) also discuss some examples that are identical to those seen here, and in fact are analyzed by them as determiner incorporation (data from Bresnan and Mchombo (1987)):

(34) a. Njuchi zi-na-lum-a alenje
bees SM-past-bit-ind hunters
'The bees bit the hunters'

b. Njuchi zi-na-wa-lum-a
bees SM-past-OM-bit-indic
'The bees bit them'

It is crucial for the Baker/Hale account that pronominals be analyzed as determiners, which they assume, as I do.

What is important is to admit two different processes—we may call them functional and lexical incorporation, to follow the terminology of Baker and Hale.[26] We need then to establish exactly which principles of grammar constrain each. Since I have nothing to add to the process of lexical incorporation, I leave it aside. For functional incorporation (for instance of determiners) of the sort seen here, I think government should be the prime directive.

This entails several things. First, instances of incorporation from adjuncts as in (32) have to be appropriately restricted. I think an important property of these examples is that they typically involve what Larson (1985) calls "bare-NP" adverbs, which can be seen as quasi-argumental and governed by some projection of the verb, or perhaps the verb itself after raising to Infl. That is, we don't expect determiner incorporation from most adjuncts, and these examples are clearly special.[27]

Second, we have to make sure that whenever incorporation from a subject takes place, the verb is high enough to govern the determiner. This is not hard to ensure in the Romance languages—particularly if we go with the current trend that has recast the old idea of Contreras (1976) or Westphal (1985) that subjects are within VP, and the verb raises as in Emonds (1978), Pollock (1989) and much current work.

Third, and this is the most delicate issue, we have to raise matters of minimality. The trickiest examples involve clitic placement, and have the format below:

(35) [...clitic...[V...t...]...]

The syntax I proposed in (1988) and elsewhere for the matter of special clitic placement involve movement of the determiner clitic over V—this is particularly obvious in instances of clitic climbing. How is this consistent with the Head Movement Constraint?

Much has happened since 1988; the good news is that several have looked into this sort of problem. The main purpose of Baker and Hale (1990) is precisely to address issues of this sort, which they generalize. Roberts (1991) and (1994) is also worried about matters of this sort, and after exploring the various domains where they occur, he proposes two different kinds of solutions.

One type of approach involves relativizing minimality to types of heads. Baker and Hale do it in terms of the lexical vs. functional distinction; Roberts, in terms of what he calls A heads vs. A'-heads. Baker and Hale's approach applies directly to the situation in (35), and Robert's does if we interpret the determiner as an A' head and the verb as an A head. In any case, the point is clear: (35) does not violate the Head Movement Constraint if minimal governors only interfere with heads of the same type, assuming verbs and clitics are elements of different type.

Another type of approach allows the possibility of "excorporation," that is, moving to a head and out of that head without carrying the head along. This was implicitly assumed in my (1988) work—without the name excorporation though, but simply as "movement through X". Roberts (1991) limits this idea to instances of head movement via adjunction. It is not implausible to see the cliticization in (35) as involving adjunction to V prior to the clitic moving upwards to wherever it lands, for clearly the clitic does not substitute the verb. Roberts has precisely instances of clitic climbing in mind for his excorporation, though instances of verb movement are also discussed.

Although this is ultimately a complex matter, I want to provide some evidence that may bear on deciding among these different approaches. I want to go into the matter because it bears on an important empirical aspect of cliticization.

4.2. Why don't Standard Determiners Climb?

Here's some serious ammunition for a phonological approach to the matters seen here. Whereas (36b) is possible (36a) is terrible:

(36) a. *fixemo-lo PRO cazar [t porco bravo]

made(we)-the hunt pig wild

b. fixemo-lo PRO cazar [t pro]

made(we)-it hunt

'we made (people) hunt it'

Descriptively, although determiners can be placed in a site adjacent to their source, they cannot climb (36a), like standard clitics do (36b). This happens even in structures as in (37):

(37) *fixemo-lo PRO comer [t pro que ti fixeches]

made(we)-the eat (one) that you made

(cf. fixemos PRO come-lo pro que ti fixeches)

But ignore (37) for the moment, and take the paradigm in (36) to be the standard problematic one.

These facts, no doubt, would appear to question extending the ECP analysis proposed for standard clitic placement to all instances of cliticization of determiners. However, I think there is a syntactic explanation for why placements as in (36a) (and arguably as in (37), but I return to this) are impossible. This is by distinguishing between pro and overt lexical NPs. In Raposo and Uriagereka (1990) we argued that an important difference exists between these two: although for the purposes of Visibility at LF, both elements need Case if they are arguments, for the purposes of the Case Filter at PF, only overt noun phrases do, not pro.

The intuition is that NPs need case for morphological reasons, whereas DPs need case for LF reasons, having to do with the visibility of argument substitution in the semantics. If NPs need Case, a natural question to ask is what assigns this Case to them. The standard answer that elements like V do has to be pondered in light of the DP hypothesis, for the Det structure intervenes. This, however, should be irrelevant in terms of a relativization of minimality (at least a-la Baker and Hale), for the verb governs both DP and NP in this structure:

(38) $[_V$ comer $[_D$ o $[_{NP}$ caldo]]
eat the soup

I want to show, though, that we do not want this relativization for some instances discussed in the literature.

At the very least, it is not clear that we can extend said relativization to government for the purposes of Case assignment. To see this, consider (39), a case discussed by Belletti (1988):

(39) All'improvviso è entrato un/*l' uomo dalla finestra
suddenly entered a the man from the window

Belletti shows a definiteness effect in unaccusative constructions like (39) in Italian. In her account, in the position of underlying direct object, an element like *un/l'uomo* 'a/the man' can only receive case from the unaccusative verb, and the Case this element assigns is incompatible with definites.

Her analysis would disappear if Infl, the assigner of nominative Case, would be able to assign Case to the underlying direct object. Nothing prevents Infl from assigning this Case, especially given that it can in other instances:

(40) All'improvviso è entrato dalla finestra un/l' uomo
suddenly entered from the window a the man

(40) is fine even with a definite subject precisely because Infl, and not necessarily the verb, can assign Case to the subject. The minimal difference between (39) and (40) is that, in the former, the verb governs *un/l'uomo* in the traditional sense. However, from the point of view of a would-be

relativization of minimality, Infl surely governs the post-verbal subject even in (39), and should thus be able to assign Case to this element, all other things equal.

At first sight, then, the relativization proposed by Baker and Hale seems incompatible with Belletti's analysis of the Case properties of Unaccusatives—and a similar conclusion can arguably be reached for some of the paradigms discussed in Raposo and Uriagereka (1990). Of course, the relativization of minimality is proposed for antecedent government, and it could be argued that it does not extend to traditional government for Case assignment.

This may be less unmotivated than it perhaps seems. Suppose Lebeaux (1988) is right in dramatically separating the lexical and the functional part of the phrase-marker. To make his idea more current, suppose in the spirit of Grimshaw (1990) and much work along these lines, that we have a tier for aspectual structure and a tier for predicate-argument structure. Somehow, these two tiers merge, to use Lebeaux's idea. It is not inconceivable, then, that the relevant notion for antecedent governance is expressed in the pre-D-structure tiers, whereas governance for Case assignment is expressed in D-structure. From this point of view, one would not view government as relativized, but instead as a unique notion, perhaps as in Raposo and Uriagereka (1990). What would differ in Case assignment vs. matters of antecedent governance is the level of representation at which each relation is expressed. However, for the remainder of this paper, I assume an analysis in terms of excorporation.

Returning to the issue of why climbing of standard determiners is impossible, note that the preceding discussion forces us to conclude that verbs, although capable of governing DPs, are not able to govern NPs, for D intervenes blocking government. (Regardless of which view of government we take.) However, following an analysis of inflected infinitivals in Raposo (1987), in Uriagereka (1988) I proposed that the verb assigns Case to Det, and this element then reassigns Case to its complement NP. Assuming this analysis, the verb can still (indirectly) Case mark the NP associated to it, even assuming strict government is at stake.

This may bear on the issue of determiner clitic climbing. To see this, note that the approach to Case Theory in Raposo and Uriagereka has a solution for a well-known puzzle (see also Shlonsky (1987) and Epstein (1988)):

(41) a. ?* I believed sincerely [John to be the best man]
b. who do you believe sincerely [t to be the best man]

Chomsky and Lasnik (1977) note the intriguing contrast in (41), noted by Paul Postal. This puzzle is not easy to solve in traditional terms: Freidin and

Lasnik (1981) show that a Wh-trace needs Case as much as an overt element like *John* does; then, why exactly is it that (41b) is good?

In a theory that separates morphological from visibility Case, an answer is possible. The trace in (41b) needs Case only at LF; *John* in (41a) needs Case already at S-structure.

Let the Case Filter be implemented as in (42) (where Case realization has roughly the sense in Chomsky (1986b)):

(42) Condition on Case Realization
Morphologically realized NPs are governed at S-structure by their Case assigner.

Assuming that the embedded clause in (41a) is extraposed over the adverb *sincerely, John* there is not governed by its Case assigner, *believed*, in violation of (42). The government facts are identical at S-structure for (41b), but since the trace is not subject to (42), this principle is not violated. Plausibly, the extraposed structures reconstruct to their D-structure sites at LF. If this is the case, the trace in (41b) can be governed by *believe* at this level, in satisfaction of Visibility.[28]

(42) provides a solution for why (36a) is impossible. *Porco bravo* 'hog' needs to be governed by its Case assigner, *lo* (which transmits Case from the verb), in order to satisfy (42). However, *lo* does not govern its complement, for the verb *cazar* 'hunt' does, and it is the closest governor.[29] In turn, (36b) is possible, for pro does not need morphological Case; indeed *lo* does not govern pro in (36b) anymore than it governs *porco bravo* in (36a), however, the former fact turns out to be irrelevant, given the nature of pro.

But we still have to account for the impossibility of (37). There, the element at stake is certainly pro, and yet the proposed climbing is out. However, we have to ask: does pro in (37) need Case? The question arises because of the associated predicative material (in (37) a relative clause, but it could have also been an adjective, and even a restricted class of prepositional expressions)—a material which is arguably specificational. Does this element turn pro morphological for the purposes of (42), perhaps upon agreement? If it does, then pro in this instance may be subject to the Case filter at PF.

This is not easy to test independently. We need a situation where Case is not realized morphologically at PF, though it may be at LF—for pro does need Case at LF if it is an argument. The analogue of (41) cannot be constructed, as far as I know, in Romance, for there are no obvious "adjacency" requirements in these languages for Case assignment—whatever those follow from. Another potential source of examples comes from the contrast between overt and null expletives. In Raposo and Uriagereka we argued, as have others, that whereas overt expletives need Case in as much as they are overt nominals, null expletives do not. This does not mean that at LF they do not get Case—that, if we were right, is a separate issue having to do with visibility. But in principle one can find a situation where at S-structure an overt expletive needs Case, and competes with another element for this Case.

The relevant format is clear:[30]

(43) $[_{IP}$overt expletive [[...] [overt subject]]]]

A paradigm along these lines is as follows—I am purposely leaving it without judgments (see fn. 30):

(44) esta e a proba de que...
this is the proof of that
'this is the proof that...
a. ... el mataron a Pedro
it killed.they to Pedro
... they killed Pedro'
b. ... el mataron a Pedro os guardia-civís
it killed.they to Pedro the guard-civic.pl
... the civil guard killed Pedro'
c. ... el mataron a Pedro os casteláns
it killed.they to Pedro the Castillian
... the Castillian killed Pedro'
d. ... el mataron a Pedro os de Castela
it killed.they to Pedro the from Castille
... the ones from Castille killed Pedro
e. ... el mataron a Pedro os que paga o goberno
it killed.they to Pedro the that pays.it the government
... the ones the government pays killed Pedro

To my ear (44a) sounds fine, slightly narrative perhaps. The rest, all of them, sound quite bad to me. If these are the correct judgments, then one expects them to follow from the theoretical issue at stake: only (44a) is acceptable because only there is a true pro, and nothing else, the semantic subject of the sentence—hence the expletive *el* can receive the only nominative Case there is, the one assigned by Infl.[31] The important point would be that (44c-e) be as bad as (44b), thus showing that [pro [predicate]] needs Case as much as an overt nominal does. But some may find (44a) unacceptable to begin with, and if so there is no argument here, one way or the other. Be that as it may, I think the theoretical issue is clear, even if hard to decide empirically.[32]

4.3. When Government is Not Enough

Given the previous facts and the position I took with respect to government in (1988), I was faced with the difficulty of constraining successive clitic movement across heads. The puzzling situation is this: if excorporation is allowed, how far can it proceed? Although there is quite a degree of linguistic variation here, it is also clear that something like clitic climbing tends to be fairly local.

The facts in (3) suggest a further variable is at stake. We must allow complementizers to govern the subject of the IP they take, at least given structures like *for him to go would be a pity*, where the complementizer *for* clearly assigns accusative Case to (hence governs) the subject *him*. But if this is the general case, it is unclear why the determiner in (3) should not be able to cliticize under government—unless government is a necessary, but not sufficient condition for the syntactic incorporation at issue.

In Uriagereka (1988) I suggested something else: incorporation (though not phonological cliticization) has a consequence for argument substitution. If you incorporate to something, you get integrated compositionally into that something. The idea was precisely to prevent clitic climbings which, given my assumptions, I could not bar. For instance, the way I was treating the phenomenon, nothing would prevent a clitic from excorporating all the way up to a matrix verb, even across a tensed sentence. This never happens. I said it did not because such a clitic would be forced to substitute as an argument in the wrong place, where it doesn't belong.

What is, though, the right place? For that, I introduced the idea of an "event matrix," which can be thought of in current terms as a unit of aspectual structure—see for instance Rosen (1990) or Parsons (1990). The intuition was simple: we have to allow units of aspectual structure to include standard verbs and instances of reconstruction and, to an extent, reanalysis—but not a series of temporally independent verbs. Various processes can happen within these event matrices: they are typically Exceptional Case Marking sites, allow Pasivization across them, Binding Domains extend over them, they are transparent scopally, and—I suggested—they allow argument substitution in a limited fashion; perhaps more limited for reanalysis than for reconstruction.

I did not define matters in (1988) beyond this intuitive level, but there are a couple of fairly obvious things one can say. For instance, given (3), we must say that an event matrix has to be defined within IP. More generally, we have to allow the head of IP to substitute an argument position in the head of Comp, the situation arising for Verb-second at S-structure, which I suggested in (1988) is universal by LF. But for dependents within IP, these cannot substitute argument positions in Comp (see fn. 34), or else we will not preclude the cliticizations in (3). Second, we must allow events to compose, perhaps under situations of temporal dependency.

Actually, there better be some degrees here to separate restructuring from reanalysis. My hunch is that in the first instance there is also aspectual dependency, while this is not obvious in the second. That is, intuitively, the connection between an event of trying or wanting and an event of, say, working may be stronger than that between an event of causing or seeing and the same event of working. To try/want to work you do something more directly involved with the actual working that to cause/see someone to work/working. A detailed exposition of these compositions, however, is entirely beyond my scope here. I mention this only because it bears on the data reported in (30).

For (30a), we must say that an event matrix is successfully formed, in such a way that there is a new predicate try-sing, and within this composite predicate, all dependents of each initial predicate can compose. Thus, it is possible for what was the subject of the matrix predicate to enter into a direct incorporation dependency with the downstairs predicate—after all, at LF all dependents will substitute an argument slot within try-sing. The situation must be different with make-sing. In fact, it must be the case that a unit make-sing is not formed in the syntax, and as a result if we try substituting the matrix subject into the downstairs predicate, we find a clash. To be concrete, if the mechanics proposed by Koopman (1994) for these issues are to be assumed, then the ungrammatical dependency in question would yield a Theta Criterion violation at LF.

But now the following objection can be raised: if you have a necessary condition on argument substitutability restricting certain incorporations under government, why do you need government to begin with? Wouldn't one get the same results without saying anything whatsoever about government?

That depends very much on what we are to do with dependencies which are not (fully) argumental, such as adjuncts, or the sort of arguments one sees in nominals and adjectives. The latter, as we saw, do not tolerate cliticizations in modern Galician, and it is not totally obvious that these could be prevented if we did not have a structural condition, such as government, to enter the picture. In fact, we need more than just government here: we need government by a head. That is, one can imagine situations where, say, a predicate phrase could govern a determiner; however, unless the predicate is verbal, the determiner does not incorporate in modern Galician. Now, of course, the fact that government by a head is at stake for us follows from an analysis in terms of head movement: government from the head is what counts because what is at issue is the licensing of a head trace. In turn, movement to a head and nothing else is constrained in terms of the Structure Preserving strategy of Chomsky (1986).

I think there is a further consequence of assuming government is at issue here. I devote the last section to showing this.

4.4. Structural Restrictions on The Ordering of Clitics

Recall the impossible examples as in (31). In Uriagereka (1988, forthcoming), I present an analysis of facts of this sort in ECP terms. The idea, which I won't go into here in any detail, is that the dative clitic does not need to antecedent govern its trace in the relevant configurations, whereas the accusative clitic does—in spite of appearances. I place this analysis within the proposals about dative shift in Larson (1988), whereby a shifted dative phrase is a direct argument of the verb that moves, whereas the accusative phrase is an indirect argument. I argue that in configurations of the sort in (31), the accusative element is structurally higher than the dative one, at least in dialects of the Spanish, Portuguese, and French sort. I assume that from this higher position, the accusative clitic can govern its trace, which it could not if it were buried inside the dative clitic—thus predicting the ungrammatical ordering violates the ECP.

I think that, abstractly, the ungrammatical examples in (22) pattern along the lines of the situation in (31). To show this, I need to make a couple of assumptions argued for in Uriagereka (in progress). First, special clitics in Galician are in a preverbal site at S-structure. This is so even in matrix clauses, where the verb appears before the clitics; I assume my (1988/1992) analysis that, in these instances, the verb has moved to a F(ocus) position, leaving the special clitics behind. This means that in all the examples in (22), the verb is higher than where it starts in the derivation—which is confirmed by embedding these sentences:

(45) di   que vos lembrou   a   sua dor
       says.he that DAT reminded(he)-DAT the his pain
       'he says that he reminded you of his pain'

In embedded clauses, the verb does not raise to F, and the order (special clitic, verb) is then clear.

The idea I want to pursue is that when the determiner in the examples in (22) cliticizes onto the verb, it is actually cliticizing onto a special clitic, and both determiners in turn eventually cliticize onto the verb. Consider the derivation of a grammatical (22d)—that is, without determiner cliticization:

(46) a. D-structure

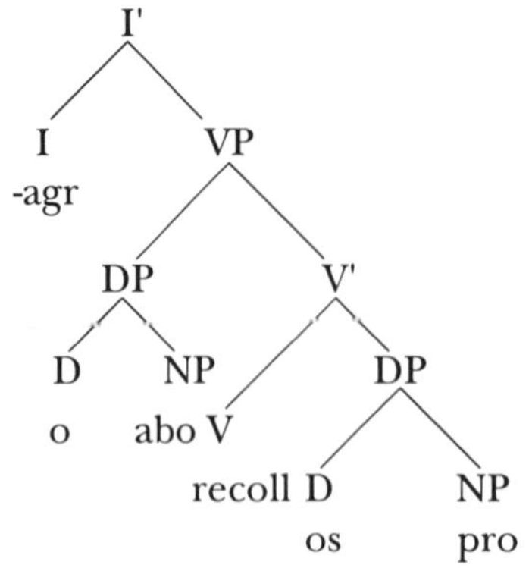

b. S-structure

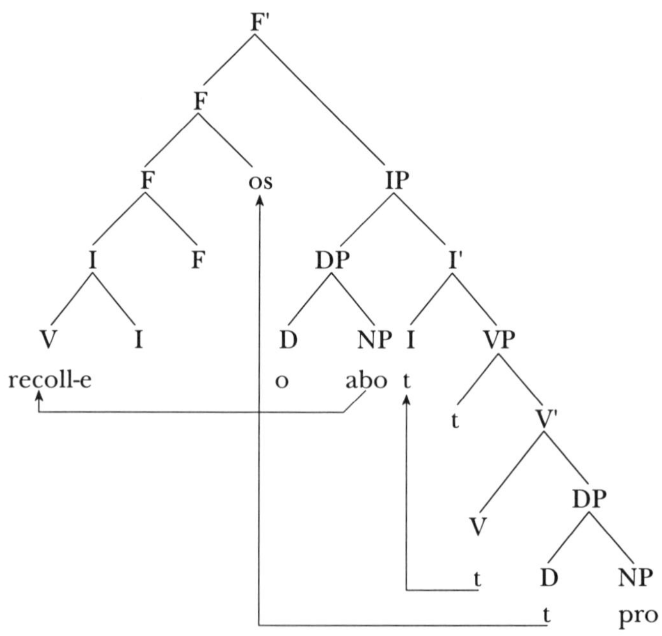

In D-structure, everything is in its usual place. In the mapping to S-structure, the verb raises to Infl and together with its morphological affixes, it raises to F in this language. In turn, the special clitic raises too, and if I am correct in my work (forthcoming), it functionally cliticizes onto F.[33] The important point is this: the only moment when the determiner clitic could have cliticized onto the special clitic *os* is when this element is outside IP—which reduces to the impossibility of examples as in (3), already discussed.[34] Elsewhere, the special clitic is structurally lower than the determiner clitic, hence the trace of the latter would not be governed if the relevant incorporation were to take place, and an ECP violation would ensue.

In the good examples in (22), the situation is different. The determiner cliticizes onto a special clitic which is structurally superior at some point in the derivation. For instance, consider the D-structure associated to (22a) in a Larson-type analysis:

(47) a. D-structure

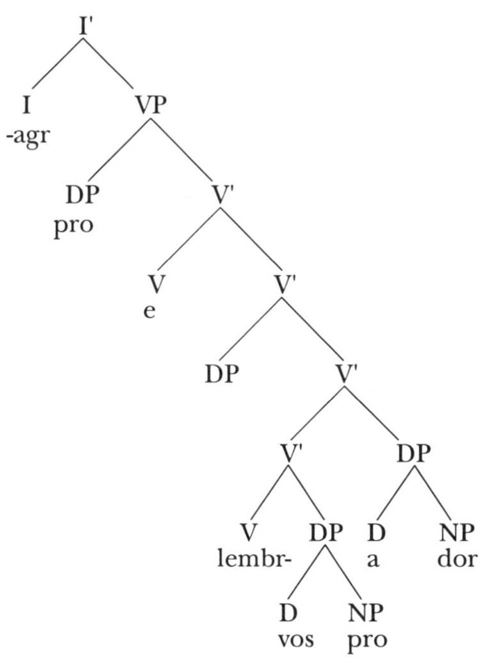

The determiner from *a dor* 'the pain' has the option of cliticizing onto *vos* in the following intermediate step (after A-movement):

(48)

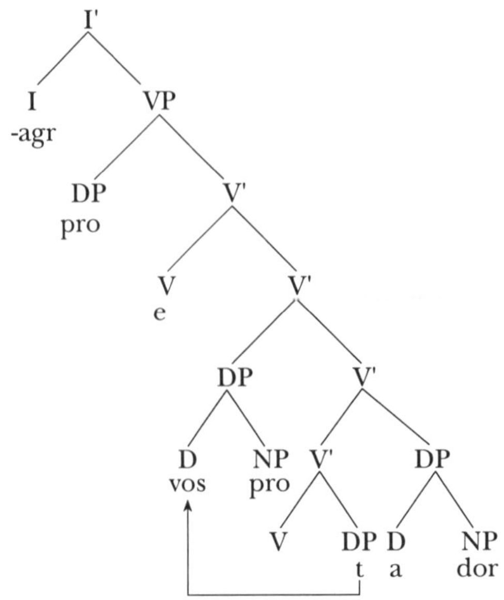

After the cliticization, the verb raises, and eventually the clitic unit *vos+a* (which yields *vola*) also raises, as in (46b). It is an intermediate step as in (48) that is missing in (46).[35]

Thus, we expect that only when a determiner cliticizes onto a superior special clitic will we have structures of multiple cliticizations—as a result of the ECP. In this way, we can deduce the descriptive generalization in 2.4, now a corollary of the ECP. Cliticization to a verb+clitic is possible only from base objects because only in this instance is the special clitic which is the target of cliticization by the determiner a superior element. The point is, this follows from sheer government, not from matters about argument substitution (see fn. 35 for an important instance of the opposite situation).

5. CONCLUSIONS

This paper shows a peculiar pattern of determiner cliticization seen in archaic Romance languages, such as Galician, which is lost in most other contemporary dialects. A syntactic analysis of the phenomenon is proposed, whereby the hosts of determiner cliticization are also targets of head movement. This may shed some light on matters of clitic placement in other Romance languages. The idea has the virtue of being sensitive to both diachronic and synchronic considerations, although admittedly it raises as many questions as it answers. Alternatives on non-syntactic grounds should be pursued and compared to the present approach. Finally, if the present analysis is to be rejected, we still must pursue the issue of whether determiners incorporate—if they do not, the DP hypothesis would be seriously questioned.

NOTES

[1] For several suggestions, criticisms, and discussions, I am indebted to Rosario Alvarez, Tom Ernst, Bob Freidin, Norbert Hornstein, Richard Kayne, Howard Lasnik, David Lebeaux, Ana Maria Martins, Alan Munn, Jairo Nunez, Carlos Otero, Eduardo Raposo, Cristina Schmitt, Esther Torrego, the participants on the Princeton Conference on Comparative Grammar in the spring of 1989, and my students and colleagues at the University of Maryland. I assume the errors.

[2] In Sardinian, for instance, Latin *ipse* is the source of the definite articles *su, sa, sos, sas* (m.s., f.s., m.p., f.p.). Instead, Latin *illi* is the source of the pronoun *lli*. Similar facts can be found in other dialects, some of which have died out.

[3] Raising the question of why only some dialects admit doubles. See Uriagereka (in progress, ch. 2/7) for a proposal.

[4] The phenomenon extends also to the Germanic languages, particularly within prepositional phrases (see Beerman (1990)), and to various others (see Anderson (1992)). Although Beerman proposes essentially the same analysis I did in (1988), Anderson invokes an entirely different approach. I should say also that cliticization of the determiner to a preposition is common even in Romance languages in which determiners do not otherwise cliticize onto verbs.

[5] This has several associated consequences, including the direct licensing of null NPs (which in French and Italian are only licensed either by a demonstrative proper or an article+adjective), a different pattern of extraction of elements from inside DPs, and perhaps the absence of *en/ne* cliticizations in the mainland Iberian dialects (not the Eastern ones), as opposed to its presence in other, particularly Western, Romance dialects.

[6] For recent theories of phonological phrasing and references, see Inkelas and Zec (1990).

[7] Constructions of this sort, without the cliticization (i.e., *casa Basilio*) were very common in Early Romance, particularly in those dialects that retained a genitive mark for NP arguments, like Provençal or Medieval French. The construction in question, for the most part, appears to demand cliticization in Galician, although it is still possible <u>without</u> the cliticization, for instance, in Aragonese (*la boca lo lobo* 'the mouth the wolf'). For these matters, see for instance Zamora Vicente (1974).

[8] For these and related data, see for instance Sampson (1980).

[9] Though they hedge a bit: "at least orthographically," they say. I admit that in careless speech some of the cliticizations in (2) do not seem terrible.

[10] Similar examples occur elsewhere. For instance:

(i) a. mata'l carneru (Leonese)
kill-the goat
'to kill the goat'

b. faill fogo de legna (Medieval Provencal)
makes-DAT-the fire of wood
'he makes the fire of wood for her'

The construction is also possible in sub-standard Iberian dialects, including Portuguese and Castillian, at least.

[11] Unless something affecting the formation of phrases, such as the placement of phrasal stress, changed in the course of the development of Galician, in such a way that it allowed a sort of attachment at one point, but not at the next. I really do not know whether this has been the case.

[12] The [n] in question is only apparent in modern Galician dialects, having emerged a couple of centuries ago. It should be said that expressions like *comeu no caldo* are well-formed, but mean something very different. Most direct objects in Galician can be either structurally Case marked, in which case they show no casemarker, or they can be associated to the preposition *en* 'in'. The difference in meaning is not unlike the one in English between *he is eating an apple* and *he is munching on an apple.* The preposition *en*, in Galician, obligatorily reduces in front of definite articles; thus: *en o caldo*, yields *no caldo.* It is imaginable that a functional issue is at stake for the unavailability of *comeu-no caldo*, which would be undistinguishable from *comeu no caldo.*

[13] For instance, Vasconcellos (1901), cited by Nunez (1992), reports examples from Tras-os-Montes, Portugal, such as *vejo-la* 'I see it', which in standard Galician would be *vexo-a.* There are also frozen forms in Galician, such as *a-lo menos* 'at least' that keep the *l* after a vowel.

[14] In standard Portuguese dialects and in at least the Ourensan variant of Central/Southern Galician, the [l] in question never shows up in instances of what may still be determiner cliticization (without the particular phonological correlate we have considered), though the phenomenon is still apparent in standard cliticization. The Brazilian instance also appears to be moving in this direction, although it is much more complex (see Nunez (1992)).

[15] Incidentally, as Alvarez Caccamo (1989) notes, the orthography, which is standardly *sin-a* and not *si-na* is arguably inaccurate, at least in as much as, say, *po-la* and not *pol-a* is the form to write the relevant cliticizations.

[16] Some do accept this example, though. My suspicion is that it is those who also accept clitic climbing out of inflected infinitivals—not everyone does.

[17] For discussion of unaccusatives, see Perlmutter (1978), Burzio (1986), and for psych predicates, Belletti and Rizzi (1989), Grimshaw (1990), Pesetsky (in progress), among several others.

[18] Incidentally, (12b) is possible with a different meaning, where the clitic is *nos* instead of *os* (with the n appearing after the glide). The interpretation in that instance is "the owl frightened us" (not them). I still think that even this example is an instance of the dative construction. Unfortunately, though, one does not have a direct way of telling, for the accusative and the dative form of the clitic *nos* are syncretized.

[19] Here I am following the analysis in Rosen and Uriagereka (in progress), which confirms the distinction between these two verb classes made in Pesetsky (in progress).

[20] The data I am about to report is not taken from grammars. I have consulted native speakers, and my own intuitions—but I have not conducted a systematic study. I think the data converge rather naturally with others from other languages, and in

that sense I feel confident that the analysis is solid. I know that a tradition within GB questions extraction from nominals altogether. I address this matter in Uriagereka (in progress, ch.2), where I provide arguments for the null hypothesis: extraction from nominals is possible in principle, with parametric variations ensuing as a result of factors that do not concern me here—but see below.

[21] For instance (i), from Ross (1967:131):

(i) cuius legis librum
whose read-you book
'whose book are you reading?'

[22] Within the DP hypothesis, one may conceive this intuitive idea in terms of two structurally different positions: the spec of DP and the head of DP. Arguably, elements that eventually occupy the head of DP start out diachronically as elements that occupy the spec of DP. This general trend is not peculiar to determiners, and can be seen elsewhere (see Uriagereka (in progress).

[23] As I said, I deal with a theoretical account in Uriagereka (in progress). In Uriagereka (1988) I tied up the process of determiner incorporation to Argument Substitution, an idea which has been currently pursued by Koopman (1994) in a different area. From this point of view, head movement occurs universally by LF, with parametric options appearing only for whether the movements take place before S-structure. In other contexts, I have also pursued the possibility that determiner incorporation and similar process (I-to-C, etc.) actually signal the merger of an aspectual and a predicate/argument tier, in the sense of Lebeaux (1988) and essentially with the mechanic import of Grimshaw (1990).

[24] See Quicoli (1976) for the classical analysis along conceptually similar lines, in terms in particular of the Tensed Sentence and Specified Subject conditions.

[25] Issues such as whether the subject has also cliticized, or is arbitrary, also ensue, as well as extreme dialectal variation. See Torrego (forthcoming) for extensive discussion and an analysis, and Manzini (1984) for an early proposal.

[26] Though of course this is loaded towards an incorporation analysis. For the purposes of this paper, I remain agnostic with respect to whether lexical incorporation is a syntactic or a lexical process. Incidentally, the terms I used in Uriagereka (1988) were morphological and syntactic incorporation.

[27] Though a very complex issue is raised by elements like *hi/ho* and *en* in languages like Catalan. These clitics are clearly adverbial, and if they are to be treated along the lines proposed here for other clitics, government must obtain. An analysis of these facts is entirely beyond my scope, but I must note that the issue raised relates, I think, to the impossibility in Galician of a sentence like (i) corresponding to (32b):

(i) (*)con ela falamo-lo
with her talked.we-it

That is, (i) can surely mean that we talked something or other with her, but not that we talked with her on such-and-such a date. I think this follows from the fact that Galician does not tolerate pro in adjunctal position, hence (i) can only invoke an argument of *falar* 'talk', not, say, a temporal adjunct. But this is precisely where Galician and Catalan do differ. Thus, consider something like (ii):

(ii) ves a casa, encara hi trobarás el meu germá
go to home still there find.will.you the my brother
'Go home; you'll still find my brother there'

(For data, see for instance Badia Margarit (1980).)

[28] Note that, in English, we cannot allow determiners to be Case assigners for the purposes of (42), or otherwise we would lose the analysis of an example like (i):
(i) *I believe sincerely the boss to be the worst man for the job
It is plausible that the determiner system in English does not have the necessary strength to realize Case, as in Romance. See Vergnaud and Zubizarreta (1992) for related discussion.

[29] And of course, for this idea to work, it cannot be enough for the trace of the determiner to realize Case. See also fn. 28, and note there may be a parallelism between the impossibility of a trace serving as a mark to realize Case and the unavailability of and expletive determiners as in English *the*.

[30] One needs a transitive structure along the lines of (43). In principle, these exist in Romance with null expletives, plausibly with direct Case assignment to the post-verbal subject. I used to think they did not exist with overt expletives simply because both the overt element and the post-verbal subject compete for nominative Case. In turn, the structures would be fine with overt expletives and null subjects, in the relevant languages. Unfortunately, there is an extra variable. If I am correct in my (1992) analysis of F(ocus) heads in archaic Romance, the languages that allow overt expletives do so largely in relation to an extra source of nominative Case assigned by F—in traditional terms, this is the source of nominativus pendens; see Zwart (1989). In such an instance, (43) should be able to surface for there are two, not just one, sources of Case in the relevant languages: F (which can assign Case to the expletive) and Infl (which can assign Case to the overt subject). One can control for this by placing the relevant examples in a situation where F does not occur, such as clauses which are the complement of a noun. This is why I embed the examples in (44) under *a proba de que* 'the proof that'.

[31] This is why it is crucial that there be no other source of Case, such as F in fn. 30.

[32] I should note two related matters. Determiners never appear before special clitics in a sequence; thus, one never finds verb+determiner+clitic. Although this issue is complex, and I return to it in the last section, let me note that assuming the inner position in this sort of sequence is not one of government to the outside, the determiner would always have to be exterior in order to realize case on its associated NP. Similarly, one never finds adverbials of any sort blocking the relation between a determiner and its associated NP—and once again, from the perspective taken here this would have to be explained in terms of government.

[33] I argue that lexical cliticization is to the left of heads (that is, leaving the head as a suffix), whereas functional cliticization respects the head parameter (leaving the dependent in the normal position of complements, in this instance, to the right of the head). Thus, the order of the heads attached to F.

[34] Though, admittedly, it adds a further wrinkle: why is F not part of the event matrix? A related difficulty that must be explored is how is argument substitution possible when the verb has raised past IP, given my approach to examples as in (3). Plausibly, the relevant readjustments occur in the mapping to LF, but obviously these are issues beyond the scope of this paper (see Koopman (1994) for a wider perspective).

[35] One could argue that the incorporation of a head into the head of the DP [vos pro] yields a configuration were c-command of the trace does not obtain, and hence the trace is not governed. However, since the clitic incorporates to the head of DP, and the index of the newly formed complex head percolates up the D projection, it

is DP that licenses the trace of the raised element. The reason I do not think this creates problems elsewhere is that, as noted, I want incorporation to bear on argument substitution. Thus, imagine that a verb were trying to incorporate onto the head of its subject. According to what I said, the maximal projection of the subject would indeed govern the verb trace, but at LF we would be forced to interpret the verb as an argument of the subject, in violation of the Theta Criterion.

REFERENCES

Abney, S. (1987), MIT Ph.D. dissertation.
Alvarez, R., X. L. Regueria, and H. Monteagudo (1986), Gramatica Galega, Galaxia.
Alvarez Caccamo, C. (1989), "Variacom Linguistica e o factor social na Galiza," *Hispanic Linguistics*, 2.
Anderson (1992), *A-morphous Morphology*, ms. Cambridge University Press.
Badia Margarit, A. (1980), *Gramatica Catalana*, Gredos.
Baker, M. (1988), *Incorporation*, Chicago University Press.
——— and K. Hale (1990) "Relativized Minimality and Pronoun Incorporation," *Linguistic Inquiry*, 21, 289-97.
Belletti, A. (1988), "The Case of Unaccusatives," *Linguistic Inquiry*, 19.
——— and L. Rizzi, (1988), "Psych Verbs and Theta Theory," NLLT 6,3.
Beerman, D. (1990), MA Thesis, UTexas, El Paso.
Brame, M. (1981), "The General Theory of Binding and Fusion," *Linguistic Analysis*, 7.
Bresnan, J. and S. Mchombo (1987), "Topic, Pronoun, and Agreement in Chichewa," *Language* 63.
Burzio, L. (1986), *Italian Syntax*, Reidel.
Chomsky, N. (1986), *Barriers*, MIT Press.
——— (1986), *Knowledge of Language*, Praeger.
——— and H. Lasnik (1977), "On Filters and Control," *Linguistic Inquiry* 8.
Contreras, H. (1976), *A Theory of Word Order with Special Reference to Spanish*, North Holland.
Emonds, J. (1978), "The Verbal Complex V'-V in French," *Linguistic Inquiry* , 9.
Epstein, S. (1988), UConn Ph.D. dissertation.
Freidin, R. and H. Lasnik (1981), "Core Grammar, Case Theory, and Markedness," in *Theory of Markedness in Generative Grammar*, Scuola Normale Superiore di Pisa.
Grimshaw, J. (1990), *Argument Structure*, MIT Press.
Hale, K. and S. Keyser (1992), "On Argument Structure and the Lexical Expression of Syntactic Relations," ms. MIT.
Inkelas, S. and D. Zec (eds.) (1990), *The Phonology-Syntax Connection*, University of Chicago Press.
Koopman, H. (1994), "Licensing Heads," in Hornstein and Lightfoot (eds.), *Verb Movement*, Cambridge University Press.
Larson, R. (1985), "Bare NP Adverbs," *Linguistic Inquiry* 16.
———(1988), "On The Double-Object Construction," *Linguistic Inquiry*, 19.
Lebeaux, D. (1988), Ph.D. dissertation, UMass.
Manzini, R. (1984), Ph.D. dissertation, MIT.

Marantz, A. (1989), "Clitics and Phrase Structure," in Baltin and Kroch (eds.) (1989).
Martins, A. (forthcoming), Ph.D dissertation, University of Lisbon.
Munn, A. (1991), Reply to Williams, forthcoming in *The Linguistic Review.*
Nunez, J. (1992), "The Position of Clitics in Brazilian Portuguese," paper presented at UNICAMP Conference.
Parsons, T. (1990), *Events in The Semantics of English,* MIT Press.
Perlmutter 1978, "Impersonal Passives and The Unaccusatives Hypothesis," in *Proceedings of the Berkeey Linguistics Society,* University of California at Berkeley.
Pesetsky (in progress), *Psych Predicates, Universal Alignment, and Lexical Decomposition,* MIT monograph.
Pollock, J.-Y. (1989), "Verb Movement, Universal Grammar, and The Structure of IP," *Linguistic Inquiry* 20.
Postal, P. (1966), "On So-Called "Pronouns" in English," in D. Reibel and S. Schane, eds., *Modern Studies in English,* Prentice-Hall.
Quicoli, C. (1976), "Conditions on Clitic Movement in Portuguese,"*Linguistics Analysis* 2.
Raposo, E. (1987), "Case Theory and Infl to Comp: The Inflected Infinitive in European Portuguese," *Linguistic Inquiry* 18.
——— and J. Uriagereka (1990), "Long Distance Case Assignment," *Linguistic Inquiry* 21.
Rizzi, L. (1982), *Issues in Italian Syntax,* Foris.
——— (1989), "On Chain Formation," in H. Borer (ed.), *The Syntax of Pronominal Clitics,* Academic Press.
Roberts, I. (1991) "Excorporation and Minimality," *Linguistic Inquiry* 22.
——— (1994) "Long Head Movement, Comp, and Agreement in Romance," in Hornstein and Lightfoot (eds.), *Verb Movement,* Cambridge University Press.
Rosen, S. (1989) "Two Types of Noun Incorporation: A Lexical Analysis," *Language* 65.
Rosen, S. (1990) Brandeis Ph.D. dissertation.
Rosen, S. and J. Uriagereka (in progress), "Psychological Predicates in Galician," ms. University of Maryland.
Ross, J. (1967), MIT Ph.D. dissertation.
Ruwet, N. (1972), *Theorié Syntaxique et Syntaxe du Français,* Editions du Soleil.
Sampson, R. (1980), *Early Romance Texts,* Cambridge University Press.
Shlonsky, U. (1987), MIT Ph.D. dissertation.
Torrego, E. (1985, in progress), "Pronouns and Determiners: A DP Analysis of Spanish Nominals," ms. UMass at Boston.
——— (forthcoming), *Internal Arguments in Spanish,* ms. UMass at Boston.
Uriagereka, J. (1988), UConn Ph.D. dissertation.
——— (1992), "A Focus Position in Western Romance," presented at GLOW, in K. Kiss (ed.) *Discourse Configurational Languages,* Oxford.
——— (in progress), *Extraction Parameters,* ms. UMD.
——— (1995), "Aspects of the Syntax of Clitic Placement in Western Romance," *Linguistic Inquiry* 26.
Vergnaud, J.R. and M.L. Zubizarreta (1992), "The Definite Determiner and the Inalienable Constructions in French and in English," *Linguistic Inquiry* 23.
Wanner, D. (1987), *The Development of Romance Clitic Pronouns,* Mouton de Gruyter.

Westphal, G. (1985), "On the Expansion of S in Spanish," ESCOL 85, Ohio State.
Zamora Vicente, A. (1974) *Dialectologia Espanola*, Gredos.
Zwart, J. (1989), Ma. Thesis, Groningen.
Zwicky, A. (1977), *On Clitics*, Indiana University Linguistics Club.

CARLOS P. OTERO

HEAD MOVEMENT, CLITICIZATION, PRECOMPILATION, AND WORD INSERTION* (COMMENTS ON URIAGEREKA'S PAPER)

These comments will be concerned only with Uriagereka's analysis, not (for reasons that will become obvious as we proceed) with the implications he claims that ensue from it.

The data that Uriagereka (U. henceforth) focuses on comes from Galegan ("galego" for its speakers), the westernmost Romance language and perhaps the most "conservative" variety of Western Romance, certainly of Hispanic Romance (I return to this topic in 3.1).[1] What U. finds of particular interest is a class of structures which, in his view, exhibits the effects of what he calls "determiner incorporation," a type of definite article leftward "cliticization" exemplified in expressions such as (1b) (the reason for the scare quotes, which will be dropped after the first occurrence, will become clear as we proceed):[2]

(1) a. Comemos o caldo (Cf. Spanish=Sp Comimos el caldo.)
b. Comemolo caldo (comemolo=comemos+o)
pro ate-1PL-the soup ('we ate the soup')

The (b) alternative provides an OPTIONAL way of saying (1a), this optionality raising an interesting question within the minimalist program, which does not include strictly syntactic optional operations. The crucial difference between the two alternatives is that in the former the host of the determiner clitic *o* is the following noun (the resulting word is *ocaldo*, readily analyzable as the noun *caldo* preceded by the article *o*—cf. Harris (1989)), while in (1b) the abstract form of the pronoun and the abstract verb form to its left are realized as a single word which is not readily analyzable as a verb form followed by the article *o*.

U.'s central claim, which will be the focus of my attention, is that there is a close parallelism between (1b) and (2a), where, in U.'s analysis, we have a non-overt noun instead of *caldo*, as shown in (2b):

(2) a. Comemolo (Cf. Sp lo comimos.)
b. Comemolo $[_{DP}$ t $[_{NP}$ e]]
pro ate-1PL-it ('we ate it')

It is easy to agree that there is some parallelism between surface forms such as those in (1b) and (2)—see 2.2 below—, but no persuasive evidence has ever been offered in support of the claim that whatever parallelism there is is due to the type of movement analysis U. appears to have in mind (something along the lines of syntactic "clitic movement" as understood in Kayne

(1989)—we return to this), and there are reasons to doubt such evidence will be forthcoming. This is because the disanalogy between article cliticization and unstressed pronoun "movement" (taken to be a special case of head movement) becomes immediately obvious when we turn our attention to the corresponding embedded structures:

(3) a. Dixo que comemolo caldo (Sp Dijo que comimos el caldo)
pro said that ate-1PL-the soup ('He/she said we ate the soup')
b. Dixo co comemos (co=que+o; Sp Dijo [que lo] comimos)
pro said that ate-1PL-it ('He/she said that we ate it')

A basic obvious difference between these two structures is that in (3a) the leftward cliticization does not affect the linear order (a necessary condition for phonological cliticization), while in (3b) the direct object of *comemos* does not occupy the post-verbal position of non-clitic direct objects, but rather a pre-verbal position, as is generally the case. This difference in position with respect to non-clitic arguments is the hallmark of so-called "special clitics," which in this respect contrast sharply with so-called "simple clitics" (see Zwicky 1977, 1985; Anderson 1992:200f.).

The main aim of this commentary is to try to show that article cliticization in Galegan is a different process than the one underlying pronominal clitic generation, henceforth PCG.

The outline of this paper is as follows. In Section 1, a discussion of the data that U. offers in support of his analysis, it is suggested that his first line of argumentation begs the question and his second line of argumentation overlooks a well- known alternative. In section 2 additional data are introduced and discussed which appear to lead to a very different analysis and to conclusions which are irreconcilable with U.'s conclusions. In section 3 some implications of the findings for the general theory of language are outlined which, if true, would lead to at least a refinement of the standard conception of a language system. A brief conclusion brings together the main points.

1. The case for article incorporation

The case for article incorporation that U. makes is based on two different lines of reasoning, which are examined in the next two subsections.

1.1 *"Determiner gates"*

The first line of argumentation is built on the assumption that the projection of an empty head cannot be a barrier. U. hypothesizes that the empty head left behind by the definite article in (4b), in his analysis, as shown in

(4c), provides a "gate" out of its projection, hence the contrast in the following two parallel instances of extraction:

(4) a. *De quen liches os mellores poemas de amigo?
b. (?)De quen lichelos mellores poemas de amigo
of whom read-2SG(-)the best "poems of friend"
'who did you read the best poems of friendship by'
c. ...lichelos $[_{DP}$ t $[_{NP}$ mellores poemas...

U. reports that for some speakers "the option with the incorporated determiner (38b) [=(4b)] seems at least possible," while he has "not found anyone allowing (38a) [=(4a)]" (Uriagereka 1991, n. 12). The claimed difference in acceptability would be relevant to U.'s analysis if it could be shown (i) that it is generally true and (ii) that such a difference could only follow from a process identical in nature to PCG (the complex dimensionality of acceptability judgements is uncontroversial). As for (i), the judgement of at least the speakers I put to the test is that there is no clear-cut difference in acceptability between the two alternatives. U. himself has shown some variation in his judgements along the way (see Uriagereka 1988, 1989a,b,c, 1990, 1991), allowing in particular the equivalent of (4a) at least in two examples (5a,c), contrary to what the last quote would lead us to expect, and finding the equivalent of (4b) "perfect" at least three times (5b,d,e):

(5) a. ???De quen viches [a foto t]
b. De quen viche-la [t foto t]
'Who did you see a picture of?'
c. ??Que posicion trasmitistedes a orden de atacar t
d. Que posicion trasmitistede-la orden de atacar t
'What position transmitted(you) the order to attack?'
e. * De quen vistedes o retrato t
f. De quen vistede-lo retrato t
'Of whom saw-you the portrait?'

This variation in judgement shows that the matter is rather subtle, which of course does not mean there is no point to be made; only that, if there is, it is not clear-cut and readily graspable, and requires more sophisticated (perhaps experimental) techniques (Noam Chomsky has recently suggested that inquiry has now gotten to a point in which such techniques may be necessary). In fact, speakers who accept the variant without cliticization to the verb form "could exist," as U. remarks, in which case he would be "forced to claim ... that they are indeed placing the determiner in a clitic site, even if the phonological assimilation did not occur" (we will see what he means by "clitic site" in 2.1, and what is behind his "phonological assimilation" in

3.1). As U. has noted (1991, n. 12), "this position would be unfalsifiable."[3]

As for (ii)—that the difference in acceptability could only follow from a process identical in nature to PCG—, the question is simply begged, given the lack of initial plausibility of U.'s analysis (to say nothing of some of U.'s theoretical assumptions—cf. Chomsky (1992), Kayne (1993b)), as will become clear as we proceed. The analysis rests on the unargued premise that the optional operation at issue is in fact a subcase of PCG. As we will see in the next section, there is strong evidence against this assumption. If the optional operation at issue is not PCG, as argued in section 2, the structures under consideration do not provide evidence for PGC.

1.2 Contexts

His second line of reasoning is based on an investigation of "the actual contexts where cliticization onto verbs occurs" (his (3)-(23)), which he sees as "the most interesting aspect" of the phenomenon. Among the pairs he considers is the "minimal contrast" between two infinitival constructions (uninflected and inflected), where the perception verb "permits the cliticization (8b) [(6a) below] so long as it is receiving Case from this verb" (Uriagereka 1991), which is not the case in (6b) (cf. (17b) in the current version of U.'s paper, with "(*)" instead of "*"):

(6) a. Vimolos (pallasos) chegar (U.'s (8b))
saw-1PL the clowns arrive
b. *Vimolos pallasos chegaren (U.'s (7b))
c. Vimos os pallasos chegaren
saw-1PL the clowns arrive (3PL)
'we saw the clowns arrive'

There is no denying that this and related paradigms demand an explanation. The question is whether the right explanation involves PCG. A reasonable alternative that appears to be preferable, as I suggested at the Workshop, is readily available. In fact, the contrast exemplified in (6) appears to be parallel (with respect to leftward cliticization) to the following Portuguese one, which has been analyzed by Rizzi (1984:47; 1990:33) in terms of subjacency (*por o* may surface as *pelo*, a highly idiosyncratic form not available in contemporary Galegan, only when subjacency is not violated, in Rizzi's analysis):[4]

(7) a. Estou contente pelo Manuel
'I am happy for Manuel'
b. *Estou contente pelo Manuel estar melhor
c. Estou contente por o Manuel estar melhor
'I am happy for the Manuel be-AGR better'

If current assumptions are on the right track, the two relevant structures, (6c) and (7c), differ only in one label, V versus P:

(8) a. [$_{VP}$ vimos [$_{CP}$ [$_{IP}$ [$_{DP}$ os pallasos] chegaren]]]
b. [$_{PP}$ por [$_{CP}$ [$_{IP}$ [$_{DP}$ o Manuel] estar melhor]]]

Under U.'s assumptions, *vimos/por* cannot possibly govern the definite article *os/o* in (8); on the other hand, *vimos* must govern the DP in (6a), since it assigns case to it. It is reasonable to assume, as U. does (cf. (34) in Uriagereka (1991)), that in (6a) there is no CP at the relevant level.[5] Now recall that the idea that "government plays a role in the PF component" (Chomsky (1985:162-164)) has been suggested independently by Aoun & Lightfoot (1984), Bouchard (1984), Schachter (1984), Saito (1985), and Sportiche (1987), among others.[6] For example, it has been shown that "the French liaison phenomenon is sensitive to government relations in that the final consonant of a word p can be transposed to the front of a vowel-initial word q only if p governs q," and that *wanna* is possible only when *want* governs *to* (Aoun & Lightfoot (1984), Chomsky (1985:162-4)—cf. now Zagona (1988) and Browning (1991), Appendix; more generally, contraction of Y on X requires government of Y by X (Sportiche (1988:438)).[7]

Given this alternative, the following is a reasonable hypothesis: A necessary PF condition for phonological cliticization, not being satisfied in the starred examples, is lexical government of the definite article by the head which could, if the condition were met, serve as an (adjacent) host. This most natural alternative to U.'s proposal appears to have a high degree of plausibility.[8] The least that could be said then is that it would have to be seriously considered before one comes to any conclusion (in particular, to a very radical conclusion).[9]

From this perspective it is of particular interest that Rizzi (1984:46, 1990:32) takes the impossibility of definite article leftward cliticization in (7) to be parallel to the one observed in the following Italian contrast, which is not unlike the failure of cliticization in U.'s (17b):[10]

(9) a. La stagione comincia con <u>Il postino suona sempre due volte</u>
'the season begins with "The . . ."'
b. *La stagione comincia col <u>Postino suona sempre due volte</u>

If the paradigms are indeed parallel, what U. calls "determiner incorporation" is a late operation not unlike the one giving rise to "articled prepositions" in Italian (we return to the topic in 3.1), and thus at odds with the assumption that "the determiners can incorporate in Italian, just as they do in [Galegan], only that this does not have any obvious morphological correlate" (Uriagereka 1988:410).

Other data offered as evidence in U.'s paper are no more persuasive. Consider one of the first three examples in his (22), say (22a) (any of the three will do), repeated here as (10a), and compare it with its negated counterpart, (10b):

(10) a. Lembrouvola sua dor
'he reminded you of his pain'
b. Non vos lembrou a sua dor (*...lembrouna...)
'he didn't remind you of his pain'

Under U.'s analysis, the failure of cliticization in (10b), in contrast with (10a), is entirely unexpected.

Consider now his (23), repeated below as (12). Let's assume, for the sake of the discussion, that the distinction between (a) and (b), found in Spanish (Strozer 1976:445f.; Parodi-Lewin 1991:46f.), as in

(11) a. Les asusta la lechuza
'the owl is frightening to them'
b. Los asusta la lechuza
'the owl frightens them'

obtains in Galegan, in which case U.'s (23b) would be fine in a sense parallel to (23a), as *nos asusta la lechuza* in the sense of (11a) is in Spanish, contrary to what his (23) (=(12) here) would lead us to believe:

(12) a. Asustoullela curuxa
'the (presence of the) owl frightened them'
b. *Asustounola curuxa
'the owl frightened them/caused them to be frightened'

Again, cliticization of the article is not possible in the negated counterpart of (12a), namely, *non lles asustou a curuxa*, a failure of cliticization which is again unexpected under U.'s analysis.

A not inconsiderable advantage of the alternative suggested in this subsection is that it avoids some of the difficulties with U.'s analysis. A sample illustration may suffice for our purposes. If "determiner incorporation instantiates argument substitution," the determiner being "really an index of the DP," as U. would have it, what are we to make of structures such as those exemplified in (13), where the article, in contrast with the pronoun (cf., e.g., (17d)), appears enclitic to hosts other than D, in particular *e* 'and' (a), *mais* 'more' (b), *a* 'to' and *e* 'and' (c), and *todos* 'all' and *mais* 'more' (d)?

(13) a. Comemolo caldo io pan
ate-1PL-the-SG soup and-the-SG bread
'we ate the soup and bread'

b. Comemos os teus e mailos meus
ate-1PL the-PL yours-PL and more-the-PL mine-PL
'we ate yours as well as mine'
c. Comemos alo menos os teus ios meus
ate-1PL to-the least the yours and-the mine
'we ate at least yours and mine'
d. Comemos todolos teus e mailos meus
ate-1PL all-the-PL yours and more-the mine
'we ate all of yours and (all of) mine'

In response to examples such as this, which I presented as counterevidence to Uriagereka (1989a,b,c) at the Workshop, U. writes that "*ambos, todos* and quantificational elements of this sort . . . are plausibly heads of QPs" and that "it is possible that, as Ross (1967) argued, conjunctions have in any case internal structure, where the operator is perhaps a head," as in Munn (1991) (see Pesetsky (1982), 3.1; Kayne (1993b)). But the fact is that all this, which is perfectly consistent with the alternative analysis just suggested, fails to show any kind of parallelism between this class of structures and clitic pronoun structures analyzed as involving syntactic movement by Kayne and others, and is certainly not evidence for a "determiner incorporation as argument substitution" proposal. Specifically, since the conjunction relation is not simply a relation between the conjunction and the last conjunct, the article in *comemolo* in (13a) cannot be taken to be the index of the larger DP (*o caldo io pan* 'the soup and bread'), and the articles in (13b,c,d) have nothing to do with argument substitution even within U.'s theory, argument substitution being at one point the basic motivation for his innovative analysis. It is particularly instructive in this context to compare (13d) with (13e), noticing that the host of cliticization, which always meets a strict string-adjacency requirement typical of non-hierarchical structure (cf. Marantz 1988, 1989), is contingent on the presence/absence of the quantifier:

(13) d. Comemos todolos teus e mailos meus
e. Comemolos teus e mailos meus
ate-1PL-the-PL yours and more-the mine
'we ate (all of) yours and mine'

The contrast between articles and pronouns in this respect is absolute, as shown in (14) in terms of U.'s analysis, where only pronouns exhibit the property of "special clitics" referred to above:

(14) a. Vimos todos [os nenos] (OPTIONALLY: Vimos todolos nenos)
saw-1PL all the children
'we saw all the children'

b. *Vimolos todos [$_{DP}$ t nenos]
c. *Vimos todos [$_{DP}$ os pro]
d. Vimolos todos [$_{DP}$ t pro] (*Vimos todolos [$_{DP}$ t pro])
saw-1PL-them all
'we saw them (all)'

Compare now the behavior of the coordinate structure (15a), analogous to (13a), with the parallel English structure (15b):

(15) a. Vimolos nenos ias nenas
saw-1PL-the boys and-the girls
b. We saw them and you (cf. We saw 'em)

In the English expression cliticization of them is not possible because it is part of a coordinate structure (see Solomon 1992:23, 32f.), whereas both articles may be optionally cliticized (onto the verb and onto the conjunction, respectively) in the Galegan expression. No less interesting is the following hitherto unnoticed contrast (cf. Chomsky 1985:159), a detailed analysis of which would take us too far afield (see Otero (1991)), where cliticization disambiguates the expression:

(16) a. Todos os vimos
'We all saw them'/ 'We saw them all'
b. Todolos vimos
'We saw them all'

Compare U.'s (21d).

Observe also that a contrast such as the following between pronoun cliticization and article cliticization structures (the pronoun cannot be the first element of a phonological phrase— "Wackernagel's law of enclisis" (Wackernagel (1892))—, but the article, even when followed by a non-overt noun, can) is left unexplained in U.'s proposal (I return to (17a) in 2.2):

(17) a. *O comemos (cf. Comémolo 'we ate it')
b. O *pro* que fixeches, comémolo
'the [e.g. caldo 'soup'] that you made, we ate it'
c. Comemolo *pro* que fixeches
d. Comprámolo *pro* e vendémolo *pro* (*o compramos io vendemos)
'(we) bought it and (we) sold it'
e. O *pro* que compramos io (=eo) *pro* que vendemos
'the one we bought and the one we sold'

As (17b), where the direct object has been "left-dislocated" (compare (17c)), and (17e) (compare (17d) show, it is also not the case that "the differences between [pronoun] cliticization and determiner cliticization reduce to independent properties of *pro* (only present in the former)" (Uriagereka 1991), since *pro* is present in all five examples in U.'s analysis. Compare 4.2 in the current version of U.'s paper.

To summarize this section: No persuasive evidence has been offered for the assimilation of what U. calls "determiner incorporation" to PCG. The data offered in support of the "gates" hypothesis provides no support for the thesis that optional article cliticization is a subcase of PCG. On the other hand, the data about the contexts of definite article cliticization may, and perhaps should (see below), be analyzed in terms of the idea that "government" (or whatever in the minimalist theory makes it possible to dispense with this notion) plays a role in the alternative outcomes of Spell Out under consideration; if so, we have no support for the assimilation of definite article cliticization to PCG, as understood by Kayne and others. Moreover, only the former is optional (a nontrivial matter for a syntactic analysis within the framework of a minimalist theory in which an operation is possible only when it is necessary). This could very well be the end of the story, at least until we have an argument that the alternative hypothesis suggested above will not do. However, for those willing to take a closer look and ready to go on, the next section offers additional reasons to be skeptical about U.'s proposal. It may also help the reader understand why Galegan cliticization (more generally, early Romance cliticization) can prove misleading even for the cautious.

2. Two types of grammatical operation

The first point that has to be made before going on is that there are two basic approaches in the literature to the grammatical analysis of structures containing "special clitics": Base generation and movement.[11] If a stressless pronominal of the Romance type requires a base-generated preverbal position, as repeatedly proposed in the last fifteen years, from Strozer (1976) to Roberge (1990), then the true analysis of the Galegan data has little in common with U.'s account.[12] However, for the purposes of this discussion it will be assumed that a variant of the movement aproach may be correct.

Of the two basic variants of the movement approach to structures surfacing with clitics, the recent attempt to subsume such structures under the (now superseded) theory of government appears to be, at the very least, no less plausible than the earlier attempt to subsume them under binding theory. We may then agree with U., for the sake of the argument if nothing else, that "a Head Movement account in terms of the ECP seems more promising," in the light of current understanding, than the earlier attempt to provide a binding theory account.[13]

Given this assumption, it is crucial, particularly in the case at issue, to keep apart two very different types of grammatical operation which are often confused: (i) Movement of a pronominal element to a usually non-adjacent position and (ii) "cliticization" of such element to a string-adjacent "host" (the reason for the scare quotes will be apparent directly). The first operation takes stressless pronouns from a "launching site" to a specific "landing site"; the second operation attaches stressless elements, in particular pronouns, to a string-adjacent host. The two operations can be neatly distinguished in Galegan (far more neatly than in other Romance languages). Only the latter operation can be properly referred to as "cliticization" in the narrow sense of the term. The two types of operation are discussed separately in the following two subsections.

2.1 Two different applications of V-movement

To see how misleading the observed similarity between (1b) and (2) can be, we must begin by looking into some basic features of a plausible derivation for a simple structure such as (18) (in this and the following two examples, the written representation differs from the conventional orthography in that it does not reflect the subsequent cliticization or the associated pronunciation of the resulting word—see 2.2—, and the abstract underlying pronoun, which is artificially separated from its eventual host for enhanced perspicuity, is capitalized):

(18) Non O comemos (Sp No LO comimos)
NEG it ate-1PL
'we did not eat it'

Since U. does not say anything about this class of structures (the one which presumably corresponds more closely to the underlying structure of pronominal clitic constructions in Galegan), we are left with the alternative of drawing from an explicit recent presentation of the "Head Movement" type of theory of Romance clitics he endorses and adopts elsewhere (Urigereka 1988, 1992b), namely that of Kayne (1989). In Kayne's view (see Kayne (1990), which is in fact not oblivious of Galegan, and now Kayne (1993a,b)), Romance clitics are heads available for syntactic head movement which have the (perhaps defining) property that they must left-adjoin to some functional head (either T or some other I-type head). Under this proposal, it seems reasonable to assume that at some level of the derivation the structure of (18) includes a substructure which is, in relevant respects, as follows (I stands for an I-type head):

(18') ...$[_I$ O comemos... $[_{VP}$ t_V t_D ...

What is crucial in this derivation, and to my knowledge hardly in doubt, is that the stressless pronoun is in preverbal position after the general type of V-movement (cf. Belletti (1990)) that we see in (18'), if not base-generated there. Surprisingly, this is not U.'s view. Perhaps the clearest hint of what he has in mind is the "structural analysis" diagrammed in (14') and (11') of Uriagereka (1991)—his two most explicit derivations—, which suggest that what he envisions is that a stressless pronoun is right-adjoined to I, and that the verb is moved to an unidentified position to the left of the I+pronoun(s) complex. Both of these operations appear to be at odds with what is known. The paper offers no justification for this drastic departure from standard assumptions, and I know of none.

The basic point I'm trying to make is that, under standard assumptions about head-movement generation of the syntactic elements which surface as pronominal clitics, a stressless pronoun is left-adjoined (not right-adjoined) to an I-type functional head in French, Catalan, Italian, and other Romance languages (Galegan among them), an operation not shared by definite articles even in U.'s proposal.

We turn next to a subsequent and very different syntactic operation that opens the way to the observed partial similarity between (obligatory) pronoun encliticization and (optional) definite article encliticization illustrated in (1)-(2). As in the infinitive-clitic languages of Kayne (1990), Galegan clitics may follow the infinitive with which they are associated.[14] The following paradigm, may serve as an illustration:[15]

(19) a. *Temos que O comer (Sp *tenemos que LO comer)
b. Temos que comer O (Sp tenemos que comer LO)
pro have-1PL that to eat it
'we have to eat it'

If Kayne (1990) is on the right track, a partial representation of such structures is the following (in Kayne's analysis, INFN stands for the functional head corresponding to the infinitival suffix, in line with Raposo (1987)):

(19') ...V+INFN...CL+T...$[_{INFN}$ e]...$[_{VP}$ $[_{V}$ e]...

Here "V has adjoined to INFN and V+INFN then adjoined to TP." Under this analysis, "there is <u>additional movement</u> of the infinitive which left-adjoins to TP" (emphasis supplied). The order verb-clitic is then a result of this additional movement; before this additional operation, the clitic is to the left of the infinitive (after being left-adjoined to T, in Kayne's terms, right-adjunction being excluded in general—see Kayne (1993b)). Moreover, if Kayne's proposal is adopted, a stressless pronoun NEVER incorporates into V, which by itself is enough to preempt the possibility of the operation falling together with a hypothetical incorporation of the article into V.

The last example illustrates one of the two contexts in which the stressless pronoun is to the right of the verb in Galegan, as in other infinitive-clitic languages. The other context, which we take up next, gives rise to a highly restricted class of structures, a class which is no longer found, in the modern period, in the more widely known Romance languages.

A hallmark of present-day Galegan is that it arguably retains basic properties of the stressless pronoun syntax of its 13th century ancestor (including 13th century "Portuguese," to use the customary term—I return to the topic) and 13th century Spanish, which appear to exhibit traits that may have once been shared by other Romance languages in a phase of their historical evolution, as Meyer-Lubke surmised a century ago.[16] Two basic features of Old Spanish and Galegan (including most varieties of modern Galegan) are that (i) the stressless pronoun cannot surface in the initial position of a phonological phrase (in my view), including the cases usually associated with "Wackernagel's law of enclisis" (Wackernagel 1892; cf. Spencer 1991:355, Anderson 1993), and (ii) the word embodying the abstract stressless pronoun (its host or rather "symbiotic" recipient—see below) need not be of the category verb; in particular, the object pronoun clitics appear in some finite structures (root or nonroot)[17] before the finite verb and in some after the finite verb, this being "un probleme classique de la grammaire portugaise" (Rouveret 1988, Sect. 6.2.3) and, more generally, "one of the most difficult problems that Galegan and Romance grammars have to face" (Alvarez Blanco 1980:402; cf. Spencer 1991:384).

These two properties (no stressless pronoun in the initial position of a phonological phrase, symbiotic recipients that not always are of the category verb) are not found in most contemporary varieties of Romance (cf. Kaisse 1985, ch. 4, esp. pp. 83-4; Renzi 1989). In the modern Romance systems, as in other languages, (i) a pronominal clitic may appear even in absolute sentence initial position, and (ii) the only type of host possible is a verb form. It is for this reason that the evidence provided by present-day Galegan is of unusual interest and value in the study of Romance (both diachronically and synchronically), hence in the investigation of language theory more generally.[18]

This is of course not the place to try to provide a detailed explanatory account of this remarkable and still poorly understood feature of Romance syntax (see Otero 1991 for an attempt at a first step in this direction).[19] The issues such an account raises are much too complex to be condensed into a few pages. What can be offered within the bounds of a commentary such as this is a representative data sample bearing directly on U.'s proposal and some hints about a way to approach what we might call Wackernagel-structures or simply W-structures—enough to (hopefully) shed some light on underlying properties of the observed similarity between (1b) and (2).

A good point of entry may be the following Spanish paradigm, where the clitic *lo* is separated from its host by a hyphen (a departure from conventional orthography):

(20) a. *Lo-come
Come-lo
'Eat it'
b. Lo-come
*Come-lo
'He/she eats it'
c. No lo-comas
*No comas-lo
'Don't eat it'

The position of the clitic in (20a) is unexpected in a language with rightward pronoun cliticization such as contemporary Spanish. Here is the corresponding paradigm in 13th century Spanish, a language with lefward pronominal cliticization (like Old and Modern Galegan):

(21) a. *Lo-com
Come-lo
'Eat it'
b. *Lo-come
Come-lo
'He/she eats it'
c. Non-lo comas
*Non lo-comas
*Non comas-lo
'Don't eat it'

Observe that in this paradigm, in sharp contrast with the preceding one, cliticization is uniformly leftward.[20] Reinterpreting a traditional insight (over a century old) we may say that in (21b) the clitic appears postverbally because there is no element (hence no stressed element that can serve as a host) to its left at the time (leftward) cliticization applies.[21] Thus, in (21a/b) the verb form serves, exceptionally (this exceptionality is crucial for our purposes), as the element required for leftward pronoun cliticization (an operation hard to confuse with syntactic left-adjunction). As a first approximation we may say that 13th century Spanish and present- day Spanish set Judith Klavans's third parameter for clitic systems (see Marantz (1988), Spencer (1991), 377f.) at opposite values, leftward/rightward, respectively. In the case of Galegan, encliticization (i.e., leftward cliticization) appears to be closely related to the character of its intonation (Otero 1971- 73, vol. 2, p. 166, and references therein), which seems to have more in common with the intonation of modern English than with that of modern Spanish or modern French.[22]

I know of only one account of the imperative-clitic order in contemporary Spanish that attempts to go beyond mere description. It is found in Laka (1990). Laka argues that, in contrast to what is standardly assumed for English, in Spanish and Basque the maximal projection that may be realized as the negation phrase (*inter alia*) immediately dominates the next highest IP-like phrase, a proposal for which there appears to be some evidence in Galegan also (see Otero 1991).[23] Then she goes on to propose that Spanish imperative verb-forms are base generated under the head of this highest phrase, that is, in the position occupied by the negation element no if there is one, as shown in (20'a) and (20'b), thus providing an elegant explanation for the paradigm (in part to facilitate typing and printing, E is substituted below for Laka's Σ as a designation for the head of this phrase, and EP for its maximal projection; IP stands for the next highest IP-type phrase):

(20') a.

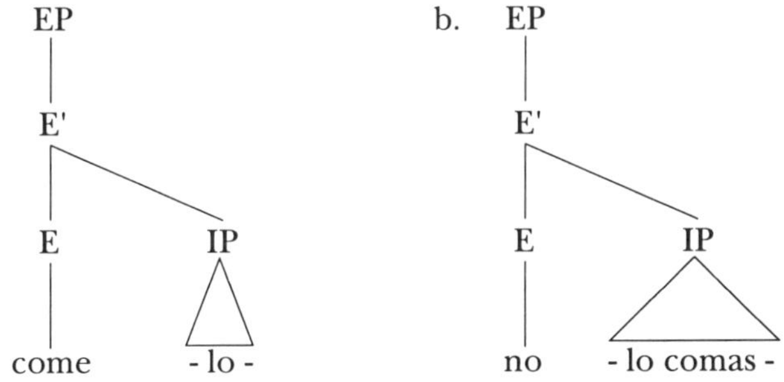

Whatever the merits of this analysis of contemporary Spanish, it does not appear to be directly applicable to the class of non- imperative Medieval Spanish structures exemplified by (21b) — or to their Galegan analogues. The reason is that the Medieval Spanish or Galegan (Medieval or Modern) imperative is not a vestigial oddity left behind by an ancestral grammatical system; rather, it is entirely expected. What is in need of explanation in the case of Galegan is the general phenomenon of leftward clitization peculiar to the language, of which the finite verb-clitic order is only a special case.

Consider now the corresponding Galegan paradigm (where, again, the pronoun is separated from its host and capitalized, and the star, again, indicates that the word order does not correspond to a viable PF structure):

(22) a. Non O comemos (Sp No LO comimos)
NEG it ate-1PL ('we did not eat it')
b. *O comemos (Sp LO comimos)
it ate-1PL
c. Comemos O (Sp *Comimos LO)
ate-1PL it ('we ate it')

The last two examples illustrate the ancestral feature at issue: The clitic cannot surface in (here absolute) phrase initial position.[24] To permit an output from the legitimate intermediate structure (22b), Galegan makes use of an additional operation that provides a host for leftward cliticization. At least for concreteness, we may tentatively assume that this operation is a further V-movement which places the verb in a position from which it can at least c-command the pronoun.[25] One possibility suggested by the foregoing considerations is that the landing site of this movement is analogous to the E of (20'); specifically, it is the position for affirmation/negation and other "elements of the same type" of Chomsky (1955:446f.), which, following Laka, will be assumed to be the head taking the highest IP-type phrase as its complement. For expository purposes I will refer to this operation giving rise to W-structures as I-to-E movement. In the case under consideration it yields (22c).[26]

As a result of I-to-E movement, the clitic appears after the finite verb in the highly restricted subclass of structures that undergo this operation. In other words, in Galegan there is a strategy that allows structures with stressless pronouns in initial position such as (22b) to overcome the lack of a host to their left at the particular point of the derivation in which enclitization takes place.

To sum up: The generation of either of the two classes of structures (finite and non-finite) with verb-clitic order involves two different instances of V-movement: The garden variety one, involved in the derivation of every pronominal clitic structure, and a special, additional operation which only a narrow subclass of those structures undergo. In the case of infinitive-clitic structures (and other nonfinite structures), the additional operation, which is found in other infinitive- clitic Romance languages (see Kayne (1990)), is not conditioned. In the case of finite verb-clitic structures (here called W-structures), the additional operation is highly conditioned; specifically, it is restricted to the class of structures in which there is no element within the relevant domain to the left of the stressless pronoun(s) when cliticization applies. Only the two classes of structures containing verb-clitic sequences (more accurately, verb-pronoun words—see Section 3) offer any similarity with structures containing verb-article words, as we will see in the next subsection.

2.2 *Encliticization*

In the foregoing discussion there has been no need to refer to definite article "cliticization." My claim is that this is because the observed partial similarity between (obligatory) pronoun "encliticization" and (optional) article "encliticization" is found at a later stage in the grammatical derivation than those considered so far, as will become clear directly. In particular, the unpacking of a class of examples I presented at the Workshop will allow us to see that the similarity on which U. bases his claim (involving only a narrow subclass of pronominal clitic structures) reduces to "encliticization" in this narrower sense, and that this process of "encliticization" has nothing in common with PCG.

Let us begin by stressing that only after the reordering brought about by I-to-E is it possible for pronominal "encliticization" to take place, as in (22'a,c) and in (19'b,d,e)—a fuller paradigm than (19)—, where the hyphen indicates "cliticization" and the string-adjacent abstract elements which will emerge as a single word when Spell-Out takes place are capitalized (we return to this in the final section):

(22') a. NON-O comemos (Sp No lo-comimos)
NEG it ate-1PL ('we did not eat it')
c. COMEMOS-O (Sp lo-comimos)
ate-1PL it ('we ate it')

(19') b. temos que COMER-O (Sp tenemos que comer-lo)
d. TEMOS-O que comer (Sp lo tenemos que comer)
have-1PL that to eat it
'we have to eat it'
c. NON-O temos que comer (Sp no lo tenemos que comer)
(NEG) PRONOUN have-1PL that to eat
'we (don't) have to eat it'

It is at this point that we can finally turn to what U. calls "determiner incorporation." The first thing to note is that even within the narrow subset of verb-clitic structures exemplified in (22') and (19'), the observed similarity of pronoun cliticization and determiner cliticization reduces to the two classes of verb- clitic structures exemplified in (23b,c), in contrast with other classes, for instance the one exemplified in (23a):

(23) a. COMERON O caldo; COMERONO (cf. *comerono caldo)
ate-3PL-the soup; ate-3PL-it
'they ate the soup; they ate it'
b. COMEMOS-O caldo
ate-1PL-the soup
'we ate the soup'
c. temos que COMER-O caldo
'we have to it the soup'

But even within these two classes there are notable differences, which become readily apparent when we embed the two members of U.'s "central contrast" and pair the resulting expressions with their structures (the words in capitals stand for abstract forms, irrelevant details omitted):

(24) a. Dixo que vimolos pallasos chegar (cf. U.'s (8b)=(6a) above)
[$_{CP}$ QUE [$_{IP}$ VIMOS [$_{IP}$ [OS PALLASOS CHEGAR]]]]
b. Dixo que OS vimos chegar (—> ... cos vimos ...)
[$_{CP}$ QUE [$_{IP}$ OS VIMOS [$_{IP}$ [t_{OS} CHEGAR]]]]
'he/she said that we saw the clowns (them) arrive'

The reason there is no longer any similarity between the two structures showing encliticization of article/pronoun is of course that in (24b) the verb has not moved to the left of the clitic. Since in (24b) the clitic-to-be is already syntactically in place, but it is not yet encliticized to *que*, it is clear that encliticization (amalgamation of an abstract head and a prosodic dependent to its right in the mapping to phonetic form before Spell Out) is not to be identified with PCG. For encliticization to proceed at least two requirements have to be met: (1) There must be a certain relation between the potential hosting head and the clitic-to-be (perhaps just c-command of the clitic-to-be by the host—see Kayne (1993b)), and (2) the clitic-to-be must be string-adjacent to the potential host. It goes without saying that the first requirement can only be met early in the mapping to phonetic form (at the latest) since at the level of PF conditions on syntax typically do not hold (cf. Chomsky (1989), n. 10).

Furthermore, there is a large class of clitic structures without any parallel at all with article encliticization, including the following, where the host-clitic(s) "sequences" (actually, "symbiotic" units, that is, single phonological words "precompiled" in the "morphological" component in a broad sense, each presumably inserted as a unit by Spell Out—cf. Otero (1976) and below) are within brackets:

(25) a. [NON-CHE-LLES] [COMiMOS-O] caldo
NEG 2-CL 3-CL ate-1PL-the caldo
'(roughly) between you and me,

we didn't eat the soup on them (their soup)'

b. [TEMOS-CHE-LLES] que [COMER-O] caldo
have-1PL 2CL 3CL that to-eat-the soup
'(roughly) between to and me,
we have to eat the soup on them (their soup)'

Observe that the verb meaning 'to eat', which is the host of the determiner clitic, is not the host of the second person and third person pronoun clitics (che and lles, the latter an indirect object, the former a sort of benefactive peculiar to Galegan).

These are some of the questions not addressed in U.'s paper. It is hardly necessary to repeat at this point that Galegan definite articles do not share the most characteristic property of Galegan stressless pronouns, namely, their inability to appear in "phonological phrase initial position" (see in particular (17)).

To sum up this section:

(1) Under Kayne's assumptions (adopted by U.), stressless pronouns NEVER incorporate into the verb, which appears to be true of Galegan, contrary to what U. concludes, and there is no reason to believe that Galegan determiners do; except in W- structures (in a broad sense) and non-finite structures, stressless pronouns NEVER surface right-adjacent to the verb.

(2) Whatever parallelism there is between Galegan structures with pronominal clitics and Galegan structures with article clitics, such as those exemplified in (1b) and (2), it is confined to a subset of the subset of structures which undergo I- to-E movement and meet a phonological requirement (the phoneme left-adjacent to the article must be /s/ or /r/ —we return to this), among other conditions. Typically, the host of the article clitic is not the host of the pronoun clitic(s) even when there is no Clitic Climbing (cf. (24).

(3) Galegan article clitics are inmune to the requirement(s) responsible for I-to-E movement, the most characteristic property of Galegan stressless pronouns.[27]

3. IMPLICATIONS

In the preceding section it has been shown that the Galegan evidence leaves little doubt that the process of encliticization (attachment of a prosodically dependent element to the end of a string-adjacent word), found also in English (Solomon (1992) and references therein), is not to be identified with the syntactic process which is sometimes misleadingly referred to as "clitic placement." In the next two subsections we turn to some of the implications of this and related findings.

3.1 Precompilation

It has recently been argued that phrasal PF rules, like rules that apply within words,

> originate phonetically, crystallize into categorial postlexical rules, acquire exceptions and irregularities, and at some crucial stage restructure as lexical rules—that is, as precompiled. Later, through leveling and other processes, they die out. The gradual death of precompiled rules can be seen in progress in the case of French liaison and the Celtic mutations. (Hayes (1990:105))

Or, we might add, in the case of Galegan article encliticization, as we will see next.

It is standardly assumed (Alvarez Blanco (1983), Alvarez et al. (1986), p. 136) that the regular forms of the definite article in Galegan are those in (26), where the /s/ within parentheses indicates plurality (the pronoun clitics happen to be each phonetically indistiguishable from the definite article with identical o-features, in contrast with their Spanish counterparts):

(26)	Masculine	Feminine
	o(s) 'the-MASC'	a(s) 'the-FEM'

The only question that may be still open to debate is whether this is the only paradigm within the core phonology of Galegan, as I'm going to suggest. It is true that in some contexts the articles seem to take a different shape, as some of the examples that we have seen show. It may be helpful to display in full here a representative verbal subparadigm (the preterite indicative forms, each in "symbiosis" with the masculine singular clitic— the infinitive is *comer* 'to eat'; the stem, *com-e*):

(27)		Singular	Plural	(Form without pronoun clitic)
	I	comino	comemolo	(=comin/comemos)
	II	comichelo	comestedelo	(=comiches/comestedes)
	III	comeuno	comerono	(=comeu/comeron)

Interestingly, in the case of definite article encliticization this subparadigm is narrowed down to half of the affixes (all and only those ending in /s/), another difference between pronouns and definite articles:

(28)		Sing.	Pl.	(Affix without clitic)	(Example)
	I	——	..molo	(=mos)	(comemolo caldo)
	II	...lo	..delo	(=s/des)	(comelo caldo)
	III	——	———		

Thus, *viunos*, for example, is the equivalent of either Spanish *nos vio* 'he/she/it saw us' or Spanish *los vio* 'he/she/it saw them(MASC)', but there is no **viunos nenos* as an optional alternative to *viu os nenos* 'he/she/it saw the children'.

To these verbal affix-clitic complexes we have to add the one for the infinitive, which again is ...*lo* (the affix by itself, i.e. without the clitic, is r), as in *comelo caldo* 'to eat the soup'.

A similar narrowing down is found in the pronominal paradigm (and for the same reasons):

(29)	Sing.	Dative Plural	(Left clitic alone)
I	———	nolo	nos
II	———	volo	vos
III	———	llelo	lles

Another difference between pronoun and definite article clitics is that only the latter have amalgamated with prepositions that end in /s/ or /r/:[28]

(30)	delo	des
	tralo	tras
	polo	por

Although the phonetic forms displayed in (27)-(30) are likely to have originally been generated by a phonological rule (responsible also for other forms), in present-day Galegan they are not derivable by synchronic rules of any generality. Synchronically, they are completely isolated. A rough diachronic derivation for those amalgamations that appear to have one is sketched in (31) (for a fuller account, see Otero (1971-73) and references therein; cf. 2.3 in U.'s paper):

(31) a. Diachronic rules (rough approximation, disregarding nasalization)

R1.	Forward spreading	l > n/n____
R2.	*l*-Deletion	l > 0/V___V
R3.	Backward spreading	C > l/____l
R4.	Degemination	CiCi > Ci (Ci={n,l})

b. Diachronic derivation of the regular forms

comolo	todolo	
comoo 'I eat it'	todoo 'all the'	(by R2)

c. Diachronic derivation of the two types of complex

Host ending in (i) /s/ (or /r/) (ii) /n/

comerlo	comenlo	
———	comenno	(by R1)
comello	———	(by R3)
comelo	comeno	(by R4)

It is immediately obvious that the regular forms of the definite article could not have been derived by rule in all the environments in which they now appear, for example in initial position, where there is no segment (hence no vowel) to the left of the article. On the other hand, in environments where the rule presumably could have applied (e.g. *alo menos* in (13c)—see his n. 13), it hasn't. A traditional account is that the regular forms developed in preverbal position in the appropriate environments and then "spread to other positions" (Williams (1938), 137.2; cf. Mussafia (1898)). This comes as no surprise under the assumptions of precompilation theory.

The diachronic processes just illustrated were synchronic ones eleven centuries ago at the very latest, that is, they appear to be just as old as the county of Portugal, the remotest ancestor of the kingdom of Portugal, which was to be established a quarter of a millennium later (Otero (1971-73), vol. 2, p. 75; cf. Torrego (1981:120)). What is the status of the amalgamated forms today? U. sees a "general trend" within Galegan and its sister languages toward the disappearance of these forms (in his words, the languages are "apparently losing the phenomenon of determiner cliticization altogether" (Uriagereka 1991), which is not literally true, but may be reinterpreted in light of n. 4 of that paper); we may add that the trend intensifies as we move away from the area of greatest historical depth of Galegan Romance, that is, from Galicia, to the north of Portugal, then to the south of Portugal, then to Brazil, for example. In short, "the gradual death of precompiled forms can be seen in progress" in the forms at issue, where the "moribund precompiled alternations" exemplified above, involving "rather haphazard environments that reflect [their] origins in true phrasal phonology," became "paradigmatic rules," as in the case of Irish mutation, French liaison, and Italian "articled" prepositions ("preposizioni articolate"). It is particularly important for our purposes that "precompiled phonology appears to be subject to a strict locality requirement: the triggering context for a precompiled allomorph must always lie in an adjacent word" (Hayes (1990:106); see also Marantz (1989)). The absence of any kind of "pied piping" in what U.'s calls "determiner incorporation" is consistent with this string-adjacency requirement.

The reference to Italian "articled prepositions" (single word spelling-outs of preposition-article amalgams) brings us back to the work by Rizzi referred to in 1.2 as an analog of Galegan article encliticization. One of the conditions these "articled prepositions" meet, beyond string-adjacency (see Rizzi (1988), 2.3), is that they are possible only in the case of monosyllabic prepositions, but typically not for all of them (other logical possibilities are not found, like *fral,...,tral,...*, or are now obsolete, like *pel/pella,...*), and when they are possible, the precompiled two-constituent-in-one allomorph (a ready-made spelling-out of the amalgam) can be either inescapable (*al,..., dal,...*, *del,..., nel,..., sul, ...*—cf. *a, da, di, in, su*) or just optional (*con il,...*, in addition to precompiled *col,...*).

The Galegan precompiled allomorphs are, if anything, "messier." Unsurprisingly, there is no "articled" equivalent of Italian *sul*, but there is a precompiled form identical to the missing Italian *tral,...* (with a very different meaning); there is a form, *ulo,...* (see n. 28), which is no less obsolete than Italian *pel,...*; there is a *del,...*, which has little in common with Italian *dal,...*, or Italian *del,...*; and there is *pro(s)/pra(s)* 'for the', a precompiled form without an Italian counterpart. The equivalents of Italian *del,...* (or French *du,...*, also inescapable), *nel,..., col,...*, and *pel,...*, are *do(s)/da(s), no,..., co, ...*, and *polo,...* (in some dialects, *pelo*, which alternates with *por* but derives from *per*, compounding the messiness). On the other hand, the equivalents of Italian *al,...* (or French *au,...*, again inescapable), are *ò(s)/à(s)*, where the accent mark stands for openness (i.e., [+low]), as in phonetic [*kò(s)/kà(s)*] 'than to (the-MASC/FEM)', which contrasts with [*ko(s)/ka(s)*] 'that the-MASC/FEM', where 'that' is the complementizer. (We return to this.) We see, then, that the range of Galegan encliticization is far broader and its character is far more haphazard than U.'s presentation (limited to a narrow subclass of exemplifications) would lead us to believe, as I emphasized at the Workshop.

It should perhaps be added that many of these forms depart sharply from regularity even in diachronic terms; in fact, even less irregular allomorphs than the ones just considered appear to lack phonological motivation. Moreover, this is also true of the diachronic process of "progressive" spreading responsible for the change from, e.g., unattested *nonlo* to unattested *nonno* (by R1 of (31)), later degeminated into *nono* (by R2)—cf. Italian *conla* —> *colla*).[29]

This random irregularity is not to be lost sight of. Recall that a defining property of standard "incorporation" is that it is "expressed by (reasonably) productive morphology" (Baker (1988:458)).[30] Interestingly, U. (n. 14 and related text) is quick to write off the problem, even if some of the linguistic material offered as evidence in the paper can be just as quickly dismissed once it is recognized that the appropriate precompiled spelling-out of the particular amalgam is not found in the Galegan system.

The departure from regularity also deprives U.'s assumption that *lo(s)/la(s)* is the underlying form of the definite article in Galegan of any conceivable motivation. It is abundantly clear that the Galegan "articled" allomorphs are not derivable by rules of core phonology. In particular, there is no justification anywhere else in the grammar of Galegan for a synchronic version of R2 of (31), which would now have to apply in environments other than V___V, that is, precisely the environment which is one of the hallmarks of Galegan (*pao, sair, voar*, and so on—cf. Spanish *palo, salir, volar*).[31] As we have seen, even some of the precompiled allomorphs do not exhibit the segment [l] in their surface forms.

A comparison with Spanish, which once showed a similar kind of encliticization (still found on occasion in Spanish folklore), immediately shows why the Galegan allomorphs may prove misleading. A systematic difference between the two languages is that in place of the degemination rule of Galegan (R4 above), in the historical evolution of Spanish we find a palatalization process (call it R4'). Compare, for example, Galegan *ela* 'she', *ano* 'year' with Spanish *eLa, ano* (where L stands for the Spanish lateral palatal), from Latin *illam, annum.* Here is a sample derivation, side by side with the Galegan one given above:

(32) a.	Galegan		b. Spanish	
	comerlo		comerlo	
	comello	(by R3)	comello	(by R3)
	comelo	(by R4)	comeLo	(by R4')

In a nutshell: It makes as much sense to say that in *comelo* the substring [*...lo*] is the form of the Galegan definite article (underlying or superficial) as it would to say that in *comeLo* the substring [*...Lo*], with a palatal lateral, is the form of the Spanish definite article. The fact is that either word is morphologically indivisible both for the native speaker and for the linguist (see Sapir (1921:33-4); cf. Di Sciullo & Williams (1987), Spencer (1991:11.1)). It cannot be broken up into a verb form and a clitic (contrasting even with, say, Gg *imonos*/Sp *vamonos* 'let's go', from underlying *imos+nos/vamos+nos* by *s*- truncation, where at least *-nos* may be taken to be a word of the language). We return to this indivisibility in the final subsection.

All these considerations suggest that we are not dealing here with core grammar. To this U. responds (in the "Conclusions" of Uriagereka (1991)) that "whenever we find an odd phenomenon like Determiner Cliticization, we face one of two options: either we throw it into the Periphery, or else we find a way of integrating it into the Core." My view is quite different. I believe we face only one option: To discover the truth (or rather, the best approximation to the truth available at the current level of understanding). It is also not the case that "peripheric analyses, though often elegant, are nevertheless not very illuminating," while "core analyses usually entail stretching either the data or the grammar, and tend not to be so elegant." I'm afraid U. has it backwards (cf. Baker 1991). The term "core grammar" was introduced to refer to the system determined "when the parameters of UG are fixed in one of the permitted ways," to be contrasted with an actual "language" incorporating "a periphery of borrowings, historical residues, inventions, and so on," that is, "a periphery of marked elements and constructions" (Chomsky (1981:8)). But perhaps the view of the originator of the distinction is clearer in this more recent statement:

My own feeling, maybe too much to expect people to accept at this point, is that there is no real notion of core and periphery. The things we call "languages" just aren't languages. The only "real" languages are core languages. The things in the phenomenal world deviate from anything permitted by the human language faculty, exactly as we would expect; this would not be true only if we could find some tribe that is a homogeneous speech community, and furthermore, has been so all the way back to Adam and Eve. Obviously, there is no such thing. Given the fact that the things we call "languages" do not truly merit the name, we try to patch things up by talking about core and periphery. But it is patchwork. With more scientific sophistication, we'd give it all up. (Letter of 3 Feb 1989)

To summarize: Galegan definite article encliticization is indeed "an odd phenomenon" and there appears to be no "way of integrating it into the core," let alone into the syntactic system in a narrow sense. There is little doubt that we are not dealing here with core phenomena (typically, with some elements the ready-made form is obligatory, with others optional, and with still others impossible). Rather, it seems reasonable to assume that the child who comes to master present-day Galegan learns the precompiled two-constituents-in-one allomorphs along with the rest of the vocabulary, a task not to be confused with the process of narrowing down the possibilities made available by the language faculty, that is to say, the process of constructing what from the linguist's viewpoint is a core grammar (cf. Borer (1984:29), Lightfoot (1991)).

3.2 Word insertion

It was mentioned above that words such as Galegan *comelo* or Old Spanish *comeLo* (Modern Sp *comerlo*, with *lo* a phonological clitic on *comer*) are morphologically indivisible for the native speaker and for the linguist (cf. Beninca & Cinque (1990)). They cannot be broken into *come* plus *lo/Lo* nor into *comel/comeL* plus *o*. The indivisibility is even more obvious in the case of Galegan *o,...*, for apparently nonexistent (in normal speech) *ao,...*, 'to the-MASC/FEM', *co,...*, for *cao,...*, 'than-to-(the-MASC/FEM)', and so on. No less indivisible are *vimolos* and *cos*, as in (24), repeated here as (24'):[32]

(24') a. Dixo que vimolos pallasos chegar (cf. U.'s (18b)=(6a) above)
$[_{CP}$ QUE $[_{IP}$ VIMOS $[_{IP}[$OS PALLASOS CHEGAR$]]]]$
b. Dixo cos vimos chegar
$[_{CP}$ QUE $[_{IP}$ OS VIMOS $[_{IP}[\ t_{OS}$ CHEGAR$]]]]$
'he/she said that we saw the clowns (them) arrive'

It is immediately obvious that the phonological Spelling Out of abstract complexes such as VIMOS+OS (in the case at hand, the morphologically indivisible phonological word *vimolos*) or QUE+OS (ultimately the indivisible word *cos*) cannot be inserted at the level of the derivation corresponding to the bracketed structures in (24') (a fortiori, at an earlier level), one of the claims of Otero (1976); see also den Besten (1976)). Such words can only be inserted after the prosodically dependent element lacking a metrical structure of its own becomes part of the string-adjacent head to its left. It is well known that such mismatches between phonological representations and initial syntactic representations are not confined to a small domain of morphology in Galegan; they are rampant in natural language. Phonological cliticization, which is typically characterized by just such a mismatch, is known to occur in many languages. The "articled" prepositions *du* and *au* in French, mentioned in 3.1, are just among the most widely known cases (cf. Marantz (1989)). A ready- made spelling-out of a sequence of underlying syntactic elements such as *du* or *au* is clearly a single phonological constituent, yet there is no reason to assume that the initial syntactic structure is any different from a case where the amalgamation has not taken place, such as *de la, a la*; both *de la* and *du*, like other "articled prepositions," presumably have the following initial syntactic structure:

(33) Initial syntactic structure of *du/au*: $[_{PP}$ P $[_{DP}$ Art ...

It is clear that in (24'), as in the case of *du/au*, the phonological structure is mismatched with the initial syntactic structure (cf. Chomsky & Halle 1968:8.6.2). It is not a startling conclusion that Galegan is one of the languages in which such mismatches occur. We have then additional evidence for the hypothesis that initial syntactic structure and phonological structure are not isomorphic. The obvious solution to this apparent "bracketing paradox" is that "there are two levels of representation for words, one level at which phonological considerations must be satisfied, and one at which syntactic considerations must be satisfied" (Sproat (1985a:186–7); cf. Spencer (1991: ch. 10), Cohn (1989), Berendsen (1986)).

From this it is a short step to a theoretical conclusion that is very different from the one drawn by U. from the Galegan evidence, namely, that "'lexical insertion' is actually two processes," the second one being "post-syntactic <u>phonological</u> <u>instantiation</u> of abstract markers..." (Hayes (1990:91)), a process which may involve the selection of the appropriate allomorph (possibly a ready-made spelling-out of a sequence of two initially non-immediate syntactic constituents). What is crucial is that these ready-made spelling-outs are precompiled in the "dictionary" or "paradigmatic system" (not to be identified with the "lexicon" in the sense of the system which specifies the abstract structure of each lexical item and is presumably essentially identical for all languages—Chomsky (1982:31); cf. Spencer (1991:47)).[33]

This is not only consistent with the framework of Chomsky (1989, 1992), but seemingly desirable. In an "economy" theory, some abstract complexes, instantiated in phonological words (possibly morphologically indivisible), may be formed by head movement from elements (including abstract elements sometimes referred to as (syntactic) "affixes") that originate far apart in underlying structure and often do not correspond to independently insertable elements (Chomsky (1965:4.2.2)—cf. Chomsky (1955, 47), Siegel (1974:13f.), Spencer (1991, ch. 2)); on the other hand, all that has to be in underlying structure in such a theory is enough to determine the phrase structure and such syntactically relevant features as f-features (the same set being found in all languages), a conclusion perhaps not uncongenial to U. (cf. Uriagereka (1991), n. 20). This move towards essentially universal underlying structure (cf. now Kayne (1993b), Chomsky (1994)) appears to be in line with the intuition that, abstracting away from language-particular vocabularies (which often include precompiled allomorphs), there is only one language—as the evolutionary biologist would expect.

If something along these lines is correct, there is little reason to suppose that the phonological instantiations of syntactic constituents (including precompiled one-word amalgams of sequences of two syntactic elements) are inserted in initial structures, as was generally assumed until 1992. This brings back the possibility of a theory in which "only abstract features are generated in the base (which is now limited to the categorial component [read: the X-bar module—see now Chomsky (1994)]) in positions to be filled by lexical items" (Chomsky & Lasnik (1977:n. 18)).[34] In this light it is quite astonishing to discover that the very data that first suggested the reduction of the "base" to an essentially universal categorial component defined by X-bar theory, in part because of the remoteness of the phenomena from underlying structure, came to suggest a major process of core grammar more than a decade later.

4. Conclusion

U. offers two kinds of evidence in support of his analysis of definite article encliticization in Galegan as "determiner incorporation," not to be confused with standard incorporation (Baker 1988). Both kinds are not compelling (under the widespread assumption that "government," or whatever takes its place in current theories, plays a role in the PF component).

U. himself recognizes three major differences between definite article encliticization and pronoun encliticization: (1) Only definite articles do not encliticize obligatorily, (2) only definite articles may never encliticize into a non-adjacent host (in particular, they never "climb"), and (3) only a definite article may encliticize from a certain type of "adjunct" phrase (cf. Larson (1990:591-2)) into a string-adjacent host. The three differences are consistent with the assumption that definite article encliticization is not to be identified with PCG or so-called "clitic placement." On the other hand, each raises serious difficulties for U.'s proposal.

There is much additional evidence against U.'s analysis, as argued in Sections 2 and 3:

(1) Under Kayne's assumptions (adopted by U.), stressless pronouns NEVER incorporate into a verb, which appears to be true of Galegan, contrary to what U. concludes, and there is no reason to believe that Galegan determiners do; except in non-finite V- clitic structures and W-structures (in a broad sense), stressless pronouns NEVER surface right-adjacent to the verb.

(2) Whatever parallelism there is between Galegan structures with pronominal clitics and structures with article clitics, such as those exemplified in (1b) and (2), it is confined to a subset of the subset of structures in which the verb moves past the clitic (including non-infinite structures and W-structures). Typically, the host of the determiner clitic is not the host of the pronoun clitic(s) even when there is no "Clitic Climbing" (cf. (24)).

(3) Galegan definite article clitics are inmune to the leftward cliticization restriction that triggers I-to-E movement ("Wackernagel's law of enclisis"), the most characteristic property of Galegan stressless (prosodically dependent) pronouns.

(4) The single word allomorph (realization of a sequence of two syntactic elements) that is part and parcel of structures with encliticized definite articles (characterized by U. as "an odd phenomenon") can be naturally subsumed under the theory of precompilation (Hayes 1990), which is definitely not part of the theory of core grammar. It seems reasonable to assume that the child who comes to master present-day Galegan learns the precompiled allomorphs (ready-made words) along with the rest of the vocabulary.

Finally, even though "the consequences [to be extracted] from this phenomenon for the larger picture" are not the ones suggested by U., we can extract consequences from it that do appear to have theoretical implications. If something along the lines sketched in 3.2 is correct, there is little reason to suppose that the phonological instantiations of lexical units (including precompiled allomorphs) are inserted in initial structures, which again leads to a theory in which "only abstract features are generated in the base (which is now limited to the categorial component) in positions to be filled by [phonological instantiations of] lexical items" (Chomsky & Lasnik (1977:n. 18)).

NOTES

*I am indebted to several participants of the Princeton Second Workshop on Comparative Grammar (April 1989) for their comments, in particular to Robert Freidin (who to begin with made it all possible), Joseph Aoun, Luigi Burzio, Richard Kayne, Howard Lasnik, Carlos Quicoli and Luigi Rizzi.

[Added in March 1993: This paper, which is essentially an expanded version of the one I presented (only in part, because of limitations of time) at the 1989 Workshop, was originally written in September 1991 as a commentary on the first four versions of Uriagereka's paper, with special attention to (what I took to be) the final version, completed in June 1991. The analysis he sketches in the fifth version (completed in May 1992), converges to some extent with the analysis sketched in my commentary, an encouraging sign. Since this convergence appears to be of interest in itself in the present context, I have refrained from introducing substantial changes in this updated revision. I did introduce some modifications and some additional examples to make things clearer or improve readability, added some footnotes relating my commentary to the fifth version of his paper, and included references to work unavailable to me in 1991. On the other hand, I deleted the opening (and a few other incidental remarks), which no longer seemed to me necessary and appropriate. I am indebted to Bruce Hayes and in particular to Robert Freidin for their comments on my first version. I am also indebted to Freidin for a copy of Pilar Barbosa's paper (and to Richard Kayne for bringing it to my attention), to María Luisa Zubizarreta for a handout of her recent lecture at UCLA and some related clarifications (and for a copy of the manuscript of Ian Roberts' book), to Guglielmo Cinque for copies of Paola Benincà's paper and of the paper they coauthored, to Steve Anderson for an electronic copy, sent in the nick of time, of his recent paper, to Claudia Parodi and to Tim Stowell for copies of four recent papers and a draft of a chapter of a dissertation, and to Chang Soo Lee for promptly sending me copies of several articles.]

[1] I may perhaps be forgiven for finding it difficult to give up the term "Galegan," which I have used for many years in lectures and publications, like other students of the language (the most recent example that comes to mind is Campos 1989). The term "Galician" is sometimes reserved (as below, note 16) for a hypothesized ancestor of both Galegan and Asturian or Astur-Leonese (possibly also Castilian, as distinct from the Romance spoken to the south of Old Castile). See Otero (1971-73), and references therein.

[2] For U. the process involved is not to be identified with the type of "incorporation" (X^0 movement) extensively studied in recent years (notably in Baker 1988 and references therein). In his 1988 dissertation he draws a distinction between two types of "incorporation," "morphological" and "syntactic" (cf. Sportiche (1993), 6.3.2), which

he now calls "lexical" and "functional" (adopting the terminology of Baker & Hale (1990)), and takes what he calls "determiner incorporation" to be an instance of the latter type (n. 26 and related text). As we will see, what he calls "determiner incorporation" crucially requires a string-adjacent host to the left (not a sufficient condition, however, as U.'s paper makes abundantly clear).

[3] Now he also notes (n. 20) that there is a tradition which "questions extraction from nominals altogether."

[4] Rizzi refers to two early studies "on the relevance of subjacency (or of an analogous principle of locality) for the morphological and phonological processes," Dell & Selkirk (1978) and Siegel (1978).

[5] Compare the parallel English example (i)

(i) I believe him to be crazy

where him optionally encliticizes onto the matrix verb, in contrast with (ii)

(ii) I believe he is crazy

where he cannot (Solomon 1992:24).

[6] Selkirk (1984) and Berendsen (1986) had proposed that English pronouns cliticize onto c-commanding verbs and prepositions; Solomon (1992) argues that the relevant condition is government.

[7] The questions raised by a reformulation in terms of the system without government of Chomsky (1992) are beyond the scope of this paper. Suffice it to say that it does not seem to pose unsurmountable difficulties in terms of an extension of the head-complement relation (or perhaps just c-command—cf. Kayne (1993b) and the preceding note) plus string-adjacency.

[8] As pointed out by Cinque and Kayne, structures of the form P-XP, where XP is a relativized phrase, as in (i), were problematic for Rizzi (1990:36, n.8), that is, possible subjacency violations, under the assumption that the structure for relative clauses is (ii):

(i) Na mesa que fixeches [<u>en a</u> —> <u>na</u>]
'in the table that you made'

(ii) en [$_{NP}$ [$_{NP}$ a mesa [$_{S'}$ que fixeches]]

However, they are not problematic for a structure such as (iii), an analysis which we may take to provide additional evidence for the DP hypothesis:

(iii) en [[$_{DP}$ a] [$_{NP}$ mesa [$_{CP}$ que fixeches]]

[9] It goes without saying that I'm not addressing the question of the existence of standard determiner incorporation as a grammatical process (cf. Baker & Hale (1990), Grimshaw (1991), Koopman (1991, 1992), Kayne (1993a)). My only concern here is U.'s claim that Galegan article cliticization and unstressed pronoun "movement" are special cases of PCG, that is, one and the same process.

[10] As in (6b) and (7b), a process is disallowed here: The preposition cannot be "articled" ("articolata"). There are apparently speakers who do not find the starred examples and similar ones ("...col <u>Trovatore</u>," "... col <u>Cavaliere della rosa</u>," "... colle <u>Nozze di Figaro</u>") "really terrible" (Pier Marco Bertinetto, p.c.).

[11] The desirability of a synthesis of the two approaches, usually taken to be incompatible, is at the root of Sportiche (1992a,b), a study of clitic constructions which can hardly be ignored (cf. Kayne (1993b), n. 58).

[12] In another paper of the same vintage (Uriagereka 1992c), U. specifically mentions (n. 2), "apart from Strozer's [1976] and Rivas's [1977]" dissertations, the base-gen-

eration analyses of Aoun (1981), Jaeggli (1982), Bouchard (1982), Borer (1984), Hurtado (1985), and Burzio (1986)"—to which at least Sportiche (1983) may be added—, and refers to Roberge (1990) as "a recent analysis which still keeps a base-generated approach." He also includes Sportiche (1992) among his references.
[13] Cf. Sportiche (1983:196f.), where it is argued that the relation between a clitic and its associated silent category can not be A-binding and that, at least in some cases, cannot be A'-binding either.
14 Kayne places Galegan in a class of "mixed languages" (note 59), without further elaboration.
[15] These are of course pre-PF forms. If the first were viable, it would emerge from the PF component as (i), which is ill-formed:

(i) *Temos co comer

In the (b) example, ... *comer O...* would emerge as ...*comelo.*
[16] Some (but only some) of the paradigmatic examples of this syntax are well known. The seminal observation within Romance scholarship goes back to at least Tobler (1875) on Old French, which is extended to Old Italian in Mussafia (1886). But Meyer-Lubke (1897), the first study of the equivalent constructions in Old Portuguese—see also Meyer-Lubke (1890-1902), vol. III—, written in the wake of Wackernagel (1892), sheds more light on the problem (cf. Mussaffia (1898)) than the much touted "Tobler-Mussafia law" (Schiaffini 1954, Ulleland 1960)—clearly a misnomer in more than one respect—, which is still invoked sometimes in recent generative work. Other relevant studies in this tradition are Staaff (1906) and Menendez Pidal (1944-46, first published in 1908) on Old Spanish, Sorrento (1950:139-201) on Italian and Sicilian, and Mariz de Padua (1960) and Ogando (1980) on Old Galegan. Perhaps the first book-length monograph is Ramsden (1963), which begins with an overview of "the most important attempts" in the "study of weak-pronoun position in the medieval Romance languages" from the first "serious" one in the early 19th century to the 1940s (cf. Wanner (1987)). More recent studies are Alvarez Blanco (1980)—closely followed by Alvarez et al. (1986); see also Carballo Calero (1979:283f.)—, Prieto (1986) and Campos (1989) on Galegan and Rouveret (1988, Sect. 6.2.3) on Portuguese, Rivero (1986, 1991), Granberg (1988) and Wanner (1991) on Old Spanish, Adams (1987, 1988) and Roberts (1993) on French, and Beninca (1992) on several Medieval Romance dialects, including Galegan, Catalan, Old French, and Northern and Southern Italian dialects. (Isolated illustrations of the "Tobler-Mussafia law," from a diversity of Romance languages, such as those included in Uriagereka (1991), (16) and n. 2, from Leonese—like Galegan, a dialect of Galician, diachronically—, Gascon, and Provencal, may be found in college anthologies.)
[17] It is a widespread belief (shared by Kayne (1990) and by Beninca (1992), among many others) that finite verb-clitic structures are possible only or mainly in root contexts. We return to the topic (see in particular note 24.)
[18] Such interest is not limited to the study of clitics (see Otero 1988 and references therein).
[19] A slightly more recent attempt is Barbosa (1991), written just a few months later, a very enlightening discussion which converges in part with Otero (1991) (in particular, both papers conclude that some preverbal subjects are outside the highest IP-like phrase), although the two papers differ in a number of important respects. Cf. below, note 24.

[20] This is hardly in doubt (see n. 32). In this case, it is not *lo-comas* (as in modern Spanish) but *non-lo comas*, as in the Galegan equivalent *nono comas*, *nono* being the residue of two phonological processes (nasal spreading and degemination) that were still part of the synchronic grammar of Galegan over a thousand years ago (see below).

[21] As is well known, a clitic is a prosodically dependent form, lacking its own metrical structure.

[22] It is noteworthy that the rising intonation of Spanish contrasts with the "reversed-S" falling intonation which is so characteristic of American English (Delattre 1965:23f.) and that Spanish speakers find Galegan intonation to differ sharply from theirs. Cf. Prieto (1971).

[23] And perhaps also in Italian (Kayne (1991), n. 3) and in French (Sportiche, p.c.). This is not a generally accepted view, however (cf., e.g., Zanuttini (1991)).

[24] It need not be an absolute sentence initial position, just the initial position of a phonological phrase, as the following examples show:

(i) a. Os nenos virono (cf. *...o viron)
b. Dixo que os nenos virono (cf. *...o viron)
'(he/she said that) the children saw him/it'

As is immediately obvious, there is no asymmetry between nonembedded and embedded structures. It would then appear that it is hopeless to try to assimilate or reduce W-structures to so-called V2-structures (i.e. I2-structures, in the analysis of Chomsky 1986), contrary to a widespread and widely shared belief (from Wackernagel (1892) to Beninca (1992) and Fontana (1993)), or to assimilate I2-structures to W-structures, as attempted in Anderson (1993). (As Anderson notes, Islandic and Yiddish are generally taken to be "SVO" languages; cf. Iatridou & Kroch (1992), Suñer (1993), and references therein.) Perhaps it should be added here for the record that when he was at MIT and about to finish his celebrated paper on what in current terms is I-to-C, first circulated in the early Spring of 1977 (a major attempt to improve on Emonds' theory of root transformations), Hans den Besten, after briefly examining a few relevant Galegan examples I provided, immediately dismissed the possibility of assimilating what I'm calling W-structures to I2-structures.

What the Galegan data suggest is that in Galegan (and perhaps other Romance languages, a theme beyond the scope of this paper—see Otero 1991) some preverbal subjects are outside the highest minimal IP-type phrase (cf. Koopman & Sportiche (1991)), that is, outside EP in terms of the proposal in this section (cf. Raposo & Uriagereka (1992)). The only preverbal subjects that are not outside of EP in Galegan (and perhaps Spanish and other Romance languages) are those which involve a focalization operator (see Chomsky (1980:166f.), Rochemont (1986), Kenesei (1993), and references therein; cf. Bolinger (1952, 1954a,b), Campos (1989), Campos & Zampini (1990), Bini et al. (1992)), as in (ii), where the relevant elements are capitalized (cf. Larson & Lujan (1992)):

(ii) a. (So) EU o vin (cf. (eu) vino)
'(Only) I saw him/it'
b. TODOS o viron (cf. *todos virono)
'All saw him/it'

Non-focalized preverbal subjects, on the other hand, appear to be outside the minimal EP, perhaps not unlike topics/themes (see Rochemont (1989), Rochemont &

Culicover (1990), Lasnik & Saito (1992); cf. Contreras (1991), Goodall (1991a,b), Uribe-Etxeberria (1991), Zubizarreta (1992, 1993a), Howard (1993) and other papers—among which Bordelois (1974) is perhaps the earliest in a generative framework—for Spanish). Hence the interest of the contrast in the following two embedded structures (indicative and subjunctive, respectively), first noted about ten years ago (cf. Granberg (1988:48-49)),

(iii) a. Dixo que os nenos divirtironse na festa (cf.*...se divirtiron)
said-3SG that the children amused themselves at the party
b. Dixo que os nenos se divirtan na festa (cf. *divirtanse)
said-3SG that the children amuse themselves at the party

together with the position of the clitics in relative clauses such as

(iv) Os libros cos nenos lles trouxeron (*trouxeronlles) son bos
'The books that-the children brought to them are good'
(cf. Dixo cos nenos trouxeronlles (*lles trouxeron) os libros)

It is because of these and related facts that the Galegan data under consideration are of the greatest interest in the investigation of language theory (in particular, theme-rheme PF and LF structures—cf. Meredith (1990), Zec & Inkelas (1990), Zubizarreta (1993b)), if Otero (1991) is on the right track.

[25] Note that this suggests that the verb and the clitic or clitic cluster are not yet part of the same head, something easier to accommodate in the analysis of Sportiche (1992a,b) or Kayne (1993b) than in alternative analyses.

[26] A striking difference between the current (May 1992) version of U.'s paper and the first three versions (Uriagereka (1989a,b,c), (1990), (1991)) is that now a functional phrase between CP and IP that he refers to as a "focus phrase" (FP)—an improved variant of the proposals in Prieto (1986) for Galegan and Campos (1986) for Spanish (see also Eguzkitza (1986)), traceable back to at least Kiss (1977, 1981a,b) and Horvath (1981, 1986)—plays an important role in the analysis (cf. Uriagereka (1992a,b)). The tree in (46), the only one including an FP, suggests that this FP differs in several crucial respects from Laka's ΣP, from which my EP derives. For one thing, it apparently is not meant as the position for afirmation/negation elements, a non-trivial matter (in afirmation/negation structures the surface parallelism at issue is never found—cf. Kayne (1993a), n. 36) which U. has never addressed. He also disregards preverbal focalization structures—where the surface parallelism is also disallowed—, which are just as crucial as affirmation/negation structures for a proper understanding of the syntax of Galegan clitic constructions (see note 24).

The new analysis, as the earlier ones, crucially does not provide for separate treatment of infinitive structures and of W-structures (recall that only in a subset of V-Clitic structures is the surface parallelism at issue sometimes possible), which require a longer derivation than Clitic-V structures. It also raises some questions already raised by the earlier analyses (for example, nothing is said about negated structures, which any true account of structures with clitics must address). Notice also that the indirect-object clitic is adjoined TO THE RIGHT of F directly, at one fell swoop (an unusual move, inconsistent both with Kayne's exclusion of syntactic right-adjunction as a matter of principle and with a minimalist program).

[27] In the light of these considerations, the closing of the current version of the paper comes as a surprise. U. writes that if his analysis "is to be rejected, we still must pursue the issue of whether determiners incorporate—if they do not, the DP hy-

pothesis would be seriously questioned." The logic of this conclusion is not immediately obvious. It is not that there are no alternatives to U.'s assumptions. One such alternative is found in Sportiche's recent work (1992a,b; 1993), first presented at GLOW in April 1992, clearly not in conflict with the DP hypothesis (cf. n. 12 above). Perhaps it should be added here that U.'s reference, in the first paragraph, to the intuition behind an idea that "goes back to Postal (1966), who specifically argued for so-called pronouns being nothing but a 'determiner + one' (that is, he = the one)," is somewhat misleading, as made clear in Koopman (1993), where it is argued that English pronouns (the only ones analyzed in Postal's paper) are NPs, in contrast with Norwegian pronouns (which she claims to be Ns) and French and other Romance pronouns (which she, like many other contemporary linguists, takes to be Ds). Recall that in his last paragraph Postal "conclude[s] by observing that an analysis like that proposed here for English is to me even more obvious for languages like German and Spanish..."

[28] The old form *ulo*, from *ub-lo*, is parallel in evolution to *fabla:re* > *fallare* > *falare* > *falar* 'to speak'.

[29] Cf. Williams (1938), a serious study of the topic, in particular §§137.4 and 143.4.

[30] This of course does not mean the same in, say, noun incorporation in the Iroquoian languages, in which the majority of nouns can incorporate, and antipassive in Chamorro, which has only one antipassive morpheme (Baker (1988:141)).

[31] A hallmark, incidentally, not unrelated to the origin of Galegan in the northwest of Roman Hispania, north of Lusitania. See Otero (1971-73), vol. 2, in particular p. 68, vol. 1, maps 1-8, and references therein; cf. Maia (1986). In light of this, taking Galegan to be "a dialect of European Portuguese" (Raposo & Uriagereka (1990), n. 2) is not unlike taking European Portuguese to be a dialect of Brazilian. One is reminded of the well-known quip that a language is a dialect with an army and a navy, which is often heard in introductory courses to linguistics.

[32] Surprisingly, for U. it is not obviously the case that in Galegan "clitics can be hosted by a complementizer" (1991, n. 2), as it is in "some (particularly older) Romance dialects." This is hardly open to question. Perhaps the clearest piece of evidence is that an apocopation rule that deletes word final [e] if preceded by a single consonant (a resonant or dental spirant) applies to the word that embodies the stressless pronoun. Thus, in (i) this rule applies twice, yielding the phonetic string corresponding to (ii):

(i) Dixole quele fablara

(ii) Dixol quel fablara
said-3sg-to-him/her that-to-him/her spoke-3sg
'he/she told him/her that he/she spoke to him/her'

This particular kind of evidence is not available in Galegan, for obvious reasons (see Otero (1984)), but the fact that Galegan does not differ on this from 13th century Spanish is a standard assumption, with which U.'s statement is at odds.

[33] The "objective conjugation" of traditional grammar (Llorente & Mondejar (1972)) may perhaps be reinterpreted as part of the "paradigmatic system" rather than as a substitute for the syntactic ("syntagmatic") derivation. Compare the "two parts" of a derivation in Chomsky (1955:73-4), "the first leading from Sentence to terminal strings, the second from string of words to strings of [phones]."

[34] See also Chomsky (1979:174), recorded in Jan 1976; Koster (1978:33, 1993); Chomsky (1980:277); Piera (1983). Cf. now Anderson (1992:90f.); Jackendoff (1994). Some recent ideas (e.g. the "mirror principle") and syntactic terms (e.g. "affix") would have to be reinterpreted accordingly.

The move in this direction of the new "minimalist program" outlined in Chomsky (1992), where post-syntactic Spell Out involves just feature checking, goes a step further than earlier proposals in that the point of Spell Out is parameterized, a substantial improvement, it would appear. It should be kept in mind that by "lexical item," Chomsky means "nothing more than a feature complex, and there are some feature complexes without much content, for example AGR" (p.c., Sep 1, 1993; cf. Chomsky & Lasnik (1991), section 2).

A natural interpretation of the system outlined in Chomsky (1992) appears to be that it consists of two interacting representational-computational systems (though of a quite different computational character): A "syntax" (including the "syntax" of LF and PF), possibly developed in terms of syntactic features (Chomsky (1965:79f.,164f.); cf. Wu (1993a,b, 1994)), which presumably is (virtually) the same for all languages, and a parameterized "morphology" (in the sense of a "syntagmatic (sub)grammar" and a "paradigmatic (sub)grammar," respectively—cf. Otero (1976, 1983), Bonet (1991), Harris (1993)). The present paper provides additional evidence that the "phonological words" generated by the "morphology" or "paradigmatic grammar" need not correspond one-to-one to the initial units of the "syntactic" or "syntagmatic" structure even in non-polysynthetic languages (cf. Chomsky (1982:97)).

REFERENCES

Abraham, W., ed. (1983). *On the formal syntax of the Westgermania: Papers from the "3rd Groningen Grammar Talks," Groningen, January 1981.* Amsterdam/Philadelphia: John Benjamins.

Adams, M. (1987) *Old French, Null Subjects and Verb Second phenomena.* UCLA doctoral dissertation.

Adams, M. (1988). Parametric change: Empty subjects in Old French. In Birdsong & Montreuil, eds.

Alvarez Blanco, M. R. (1980). *O pronome persoal en galego.* Universidade de Santiago de Compostela doctoral dissertation.

Alvarez Blanco, M. R. (1983). O artigo en galego: Morfoloxia, *Verba* 10, 169-82.

Alvarez, R., Regueira, X. L., & Monteagudo, H. (1986). *Gramatica galega.* Vigo: Galaxia.

Anderson, S. R. (1992). *A-morphous morphology.* Cambridge University Press.

Anderson, S. R. (1993). Wackernagel's revenge: Clitics, morphology and the syntax of second position, *Language* 69, 68-98.

Aoun, J., & D. Lightfoot (1984). Government and contraction, *Linguistic Inquiry* 15, 465-473.

Baltin, M. R., & Kroch, A., eds. (1989). *Alternative conceptions of phrase structure.* Chicago and London: The University of Chicago Press.

Baker, C.L. (1991). The syntax of English *not*: The limits of core grammar, *Linguistic Inquiry* 22, 387-429.

Baker, M. (1988). *Incorporation: A theory of grammatical function changing.* University of Chicago Press.
Baker, M., & Hale, K. (1990). Relativized minimality and pronoun incorporation, *Linguistic Inquiry* 21, 289-97.
Barbosa, P. (1991). Clitic Placement in EP [European Portuguese]. Syntax generals paper, MIT.
Belletti, A. (1990). *Generalized verb movement: Aspects of verb syntax.* Torino: Rosenberg & Sellier.
Belletti, A., Brandi, L., & Rizzi, L., eds. (1981). *Theory of markedness in generative grammar.* Pisa: Scuola Normale Superiore.
Beninca, P. (1992). Complement clitics in Medieval Romance: the Tobler-Mussafia law. Ms., Universita Statale di Milano.
Beninca, P., & Cinque, G. (1990). On certain differences between enclisis and proclisis. Ms., Universita di Padova/Universita di Venezia.
Berendsen, E. (1986). *The phonology of cliticization.* Dordrecht: Foris.
Besten, H. den. (1976). Surface lexicalization and trace theory. In Riemsdijk, ed., 4-28.
Besten, H. den. (1977). On the interaction of root transformations and lexical deletive rules. Included (with an additional appendix) in Abraham, ed. (1983), 47-131. Reprinted as chapter 1 in den Besten (1989), 14-60.
Besten, H. den (1989). *Studies in West Germanic syntax.* Amsterdam/Atlanta, GA: Rodopi.
Bini, M., Liceras, J., & Miguel, E. de. (1992). Operaciones sintacticas y estrategias de focalizacion. Paper presented at the VII Congreso de Lenguas Naturales y Formales, Girona, Spain.
Birdsong, D. & Montreuil, J.P., eds. (1988). *Advances in Romance linguistics.* Dordrecht: Foris.
Bolinger, D. (1952). Linear modification, *PMLA* 67, 1117-1144. (Reprinted in Bolinger 1962.)
Bolinger, D. (1954a). Meaningful sentence order in Spanish, *Boletin de Filologia* (Universidad de Chile) 8, 45-56. (Reprinted, with an author's note, in Bolinger 1991.)
Bolinger, D. (1954b). English prosodic stress and Spanish sentence order, *Hispania* 37, 152-6.
Bolinger, D. (1962). *Forms of English.* Harvard University Press.
Bolinger, D. (1991). *Essays on Spanish: Words and grammar.* Newark, Delaware: Juan de la Cuesta.
Bonet, E. (1991). *Morphology after syntax: Pronominal clitics in Romance.* MIT doctoral dissertation.
Bordelois, I. (1974). *The grammar of Spanish causative complements.* MIT doctoral dissertation.
Borer, H. (1984). *Parametric syntax: Case studies in Semitic and Romance languages.* Dordrecht: Foris.
Browning, M. (1991). Bounding conditions on representation. *Linguistic Inquiry* 22, 541-62.
Campos, H. (1986). *Inflectional elements in Romance.* UCLA doctoral dissertation.
Campos, H. (1989). Clitic position in modern Galegan, *Lingua* 77 (1989), 13-36.

Campos, H. & Martínez Gil, F., eds. (1991). *Current studies in Spanish linguistics.* Georgetown University Press.
Campos, H., & Zampini, M. (1990). Focalization strategies in Spanish, *Probus* 2.1, 47-64.
Carballo Calero, R. (1979). *Gramatica elemental del gallego comun.* 7a. ed. Vigo: Galaxia. (First version, 1973.)
Carstens, V. M. (1991). *The morphology and syntax of determiner phrases in Kiswahili.* UCLA doctoral dissertation.
Chomsky, N. (1955). *Logical structure of linguistic theory.* Chicago University Press, 1975.
Chomsky, N. (1965). *Aspects of the theory of syntax.* Cambridge, MA: The MIT Press.
Chomsky, N. (1979). *Language and responsibility.* New York: Pantheon.
Chomsky, N. (1980). *Rules and representations.* Columbia University Press.
Chomsky, N. (1981). *Lectures on government and binding.* Dordrecht: Foris.
Chomsky, N. (1982). On the representation of form and function, in Mehler et al., eds., 3-38.
Chomsky (1986a). *Knowledge of language.* New York: Praeger.
Chomsky (1986b). *Barriers.* The MIT Press.
Chomsky, N. (1989). Some notes on economy of derivation and representation. In Laka & Mahajan, eds., (1989), 43-74; also, edited, in Freidin, ed., (1991), 417-454.
Chomsky, N. (1992). A minimalist program for linguistic theory. Ms., MIT. (Reproduced by the MIT Working Papers in Linguistics as Occasional Paper 1.)
Chomsky, N. (1994). Bare Phrase Structure. MIT Occasional Papers in Linguistics, Number 5.
Chomsky, N., & Halle, M. (1968). *Sound pattern of English.* New York: Harper & Row.
Chomsky, N., & Lasnik, H. (1977). Filters and control, *Linguistic Inquiry* 8:3, 425-504. Reprinted in Lasnik (1990), 42-124.
Chomsky, N., & Lasnik, H. (1991). Principles and parameters theory. In Jacobs et al., 506-569.
Cohn, A. (1989). Stress in Indonesian and bracketing paradoxes, *NLLT* 7, 167-216.
Contreras, H. (1991). On the position of subjects, *Syntax and Semantics* 25, 63-79.
Delattre, P. (1965). *Comparing the phonetic features of English, French, German and Spanish: An interim report.* Philadelphia/New York: Chilton Books.
Dell, F. C., & Selkirk, E. O. (1978). On a morphologically governed alternation. In Keyser, ed., 1-51.
Di Sciullo, A. M., & Williams, E. (1987). *On the definition of word.* The MIT Press.
Duncan-Rose, C., & Vennemann, T., eds. (1988). *On language: Rhetorica, Phonologica, Syntactica. A Festschrift for Robert P. Stockwell from his friends and colleagues.* London/ New York, Routledge.
Eguzkitza, A. (1986). *Topics in the syntax of Basque and Romance.* UCLA doctoral dissertation. Distributed by IULC.
Fontana, J. M. (1993). *Phrase structure and the syntax of clitics in the history of Spanish.* University of Pennsylvania doctoral dissertation.
Freidin, R., ed. (1991). *Principles and parameters of comparative grammar.* The MIT Press.
Goodall, G. (1991a). Spec of IP and Spec of CP in Spanish wh-questions. Presented at LSRL XXI.
Goodall, G. (1991b). On the status of Spec of IP. Presented at WCCFL X. To appear in the proceedings.

Granberg, R. A. (1988). *Object pronoun position in medieval and early modern Spanish.* UCLA doctoral dissertation.

Grimshaw, J. (1991). Extended projection. Ms., Brandeis University.

Hammond, M., & Noonan, M., eds. (1988). *Theoretical morphology: Approaches in modern linguistics.* San Diego: Academic Press.

Harris, J. (1989). The stress erasure convention and cliticization in Spanish. *Linguistic Inquiry* 20, 339-363.

Harris, J. (1993). The morphology of Spanish clitics. Ms., MIT.

Hayes, B. (1990). Precompiled phrasal phonology. In Inkelas & Zec (1990), 85-108.

Horvath, J. (1981). *Aspects of Hungarian syntax and the theory of grammar.* UCLA doctoral dissertation.

Horvath, J. (1986). *FOCUS in the theory of grammar and the syntax of Hungarian.* Dordrecht: Foris.

Howard, H. (1993). Against topicalization as adjunction in Spanish. Paper presented at the XXIII Annual Linguistic Symposium on Romance Languages, Northern Illinois University, April 1-4.

Iatridou, S., & Kroch, A. (1992). The licensing and distribution of CP recursion, *GLOW Newsletter* 28, 26-27. (Abstract.)

Inkelas, S. (1989). *Prosodic constituency in the lexicon.* Ph.D. dissertation, Stanford University.

Inkelas, S., & Zec, D., eds. (1990). *The phonology-syntax connection.* The University of Chicago Press.

Jackendoff, R. (1994). Lexical insertion in a post-minimalist theory of grammar. Ms., Brandeis University. (To appear in *Language.*)

Jacobs, J., Stechow, A. von, Sternefeld, W., & Vennemann, T., eds. (1993). *Syntax: An International Handbook of Contemporary Research.* Berlin: Walter de Gruyter.

Jaeggli, O. & Safir, K., eds. (1989). *The Null Subject parameter.* Dordrecht: Kluwer Academic Publishers.

Kaisse, E. (1985). *Connected speech: The interaction of syntax and phonology.* Orlando: Academic Press.

Kayne, R. (1989). Null subjects and clitic climbing. In Jaeggli & Safir, eds.

Kayne, R. (1990). Romance clitics and PRO. CUNY ms. To appear in NELS 20. (Revised version in *Linguistic Inquiry* 22 (1991).)

Kayne, R. (1991). Italian negative infinitival imperatives and clitic climbing. Ms., CUNY.

Kayne, R. (1993a). Toward a modular theory of auxiliary selection, *Studia Linguistica* 47, 3-31.

Kayne, R. (1993b). The antisymmetry of syntax. Ms., CUNY.

Kenesei, I. (1993). On the syntax of focus. Ms., University of Delaware.

Keyser, S. J., ed. (1978). *Recent transformational studies in European languages.* The MIT Press.

King, L. D., & Maley, A., eds. (1985). *Selected papers from the XIIIth Linguistic Symposium on Romance Languages,* Chapel Hill, N.C., 24-26 March 1983. Amsterdam/Philadelphia: J. Benjamins Pub. Co.

Kiss, K. E. (1977). Topic and focus in Hungarian syntax, Montreal Working Papers in Linguistics 8, 1-42.

Kiss, K. E. (1981a). Focus and topic: The marked constituents of Hungarian sentence structure. In Belletti et al., 347-361.

Kiss, K. E. (1981b). Structural relations in Hungarian, a 'free' word order language, *Linguistic Inquiry* 12, 185-213.
Kiss, K. (1995). *Discourse configurational languages.* Oxford University Press.
Klavans, J. (1985). The independence of syntax and phonology in cliticization, *Language* 61, 95-120.
Koopman, H. (1991). The verb-particle construction and the syntax of PPs, ms., UCLA.
Koopman, H. (1992). Licensing heads. ms., UCLA.
Koopman, Hilda. (1993). The internal structure and distribution of DPs, ms., UCLA.
Koopman, H., & Sportiche, D. (1991). The position of subjects, *Lingua* 85, 211-258.
Koster, J. (1978). *Locality principles in syntax.* Dordrecht: Foris.
Koster, J. (1993). Structure-preservingness and the end of transformationalism. Ms., University of Groningen.
Laka, M. I. (1990). *Negation in syntax: On the nature of functional categories and projections.* Ph.D. dissertation, MIT.
Laka, I., & Mahajan, A., eds. (1989). *MIT Working Papers in Linguistics 10: Functional Heads and Clause Structures.* Cambridge, MA: MIT.
Larson, R. K. (1990). Double objects revisited: Reply to Jackendoff, *Linguistic Inquiry* 21, 589-632.
Larson, R. K., & Lujan, M. (1992). Focused pronouns. Ms., MIT.
Lasnik, H. (1990). *Essays on restrictiveness and learnability.* Dordrecht/Boston/London: Kluwer Academic Publishers.
Lasnik, H., & Saito, M. (1992). *Move a.* MIT Press.
Lightfoot, D. (1991), *How to set the parameters: Arguments from language change.* The MIT Press.
Llorente, A., & Mondéjar, J. (1972). La conjugación objetiva en las lenguas románicas, *Prohemio* 3:1, 5-27.
Maia, C. de A. (1986), *História do galego-português: Estado linguistico da Galiza e do Noroeste de Portugal desde o século XIII ao século XVI (com referência à situaçao do galego moderno).* Coimbra: Instituto Nacional de Investigaçao Cientifica.
Mariz de Pádua, M. da P. C. (1960). *A ordem das palavras no portugués arcaico (frases de verbo transitivo).* Coimbra: Instituto de Estudos Românicos.
Marantz, A. (1988). Clitics, morphological merger, and the mapping to phonological structure. In Hammond & Noonan (eds.), 253-270.
Marantz, A. (1989). Clitics and phrase structure. In Baltin & Kroch (eds.), 99-116.
Mehler, J., Walker, E. C. T., & Garrett, M., eds. (1982). *Perspectives on mental representation: Experimental and theoretical studies of cognitive processes and capacities.* London/ Hillsdale, N.J.: LEA.
Menendez Pidal, R. (1944-46). *Cantar de Mio Cid.* 2. ed. Madrid: Espasa-Calpe. (3 vols.)
Meredith, S. E. (1990). *Issues in the phonology of prominence.* MIT doctoral dissertation.
Meyer-Lubke, W. (1897). Zur Stellung der tonlosen Objektspronomina, *Zeitschrift fur romanische Philologie* 21, 313-334.
Meyer-Lubke, W. (1890-1902). *Grammatik der romanischen Sprachen.* Leipzig: Fues. 4 vols. (French translation, 1890-1906.)
Mussafia, A. (1886). Una particolarita sintattica della lingua dei primi secoli. In Ascoli et al., 255-61. Reprinted, with a note by the editors, in Mussafia (1983).

Mussafia, A. (1898). Enclisi o proclisi del pronome personale atono qual oggetto, *Romania* 27, 145-6.
Mussafia, A. (1983). *Scritti di filologia e di linguistica. A cura di A. Daniele e L. Renzi.* Padova: Antenore.
Neidle, C., & Nuñez-Cedeño, R., eds. (1987). *Studies in Romance languages.* Dordrecht: Foris.
Ogando, V. (1980). A colocación do pronome átono en relación co verbo no galego-portugués, *Verba* 7, 251-282.
Otero, C. P. (1971-73). *Evolución y revolución en romance.* Barcelona: Seix Barral, 1971, 1976. (2 vols.)
Otero, C. P. (1976). The dictionary in a generative grammar. Paper presented at the Language Theory Session of the MLA in New York.
Otero, C. P. (1983). Towards a model of paradigmatic grammar, *Quaderni di Semantica* 4, 134-144.
Otero, C. P. (1984). Sobre la pronunciación del romance hispano medieval, in *Homenaje al Prof. Dr. D. Alvaro Galmés de Fuentes,* Madrid: Gredos, volume 2, 140-153.
Otero, C. P. (1985). From Latin to Romance: The vowel systems. In Duncan-Rose & Vennemann, eds., 233-256.
Otero, C. P. (1991). Galegan and Romance word order. Ms., UCLA.
Parodi-Lewin, C. (1991). *Aspects in the syntax of Spanish psych-verbs.* UCLA doctoral dissertation.
Pesetsky, D. (1982). *Paths and categories.* MIT doctoral dissertation.
Piera, C. (1983). On the representation of higher order complex words. In King & Maley, eds., 287-313.
Prieto, D. (1971). *Description phonologique du galicien.* M.A. Thesis, Universite de Lille III.
Prieto, D. (1986). *Prosodie et syntaxe: La position des clitiques en galicien-portugais.* Ph.D. dissertation, University of Utrecht.
Ramsden, H. (1963). *Weak-pronoun position in the early Romance languages.* Manchester University Press.
Raposo, E. (1987). Romance infinitival clauses and case theory, in Neidle & Nuñez-Cedeño, eds., 237-49.
Raposo, E., & Uriagereka, J. (1990). Long-distance case assignment, *Linguistic Inquiry* 21, 505-537.
Raposo, E., & Uriagereka, J. (1992). Indefinite *se.* ms., University of California, Santa Barbara.
Renzi, L. (1989). Two types of clitics in natural languages, *Rivista di Linguistica* 1, 355-372.
Renzi, L., ed. (1988-). *Grande grammatica italiana di consultazione.* Bologna: Il Mulino.
Riemsdijk, H. C. van, ed. (1976). *Green ideas blown up: Papers from the Amesterdam Colloquium on trace theory.* University of Amsterdam. (=*Publikaties van het Instituut voor Algemene Taalwetenschap* 13.)
Rivero, M. L. (1986). Parameters in the typology of clitics in Romance and Old Spanish, *Language* 62, 774-807.
Rivero, M. L. (1991). Clitics and NP climbing in Old Spanish. In Campos & Martínez Gil, eds., 241-82.
Rizzi, L. (1984). *Spiegazione e teoria grammaticale.* Padova, Italy: CLESP.

Rizzi, L. (1988). Il sintagma preposizionale. Chapter 10 of Renzi, vol 1.
Rizzi, L. (1990). *Spiegazione e teoria grammaticale.* Padova, Italy: Unipress. (Revised and extended edition of Rizzi 1984.)
Roberge, Y. (1990). *The syntactic recoverability of null arguments.* Kingston: McGill-Queen's University Press.
Roberts, I. G. (1993). *Verbs and diachronic syntax: A comparative history of English and French.* Dordrecht: Kluwer Academic Publishers.
Rochemont, M. S. (1986). *Focus in generative grammar.* Amsterdam/Philadelphia: John Benjamins.
Rochemont, M. S. (1989). Topic islands and the subjacency parameter, *Canadian Journal of Linguistics* 34, 145-170.
Rochemont, M.S., & Culicover, P. (1990). *English focus constructions and the theory of grammar.* Cambridge University Press.
Ross, J. R. (1967). *Constraints on variables in syntax.* MIT doctoral dissertation. (Published as Ross 1986.)
Ross, J. R. (1986). *Infinite syntax!* Norwood, N.J.: Ablex.
Rouveret, A. (1988). *Syntaxe des dependances lexicales: Identiteéet identification dans la théorie syntaxique.* These de doctorat d'etat, Universite de Paris VII.
Saito, M. (1985). *Some asymmetries in Japanese and their theoretical implications.* MIT doctoral dissertation.
Sapir, E. (1921). *Language.* New York: Harcourt.
Selkirk, E. (1984). *Phonology and syntax: The relation between sound and structure.* The MIT Press.
Schachter, P. (1984). Auxiliary reduction: An argument for GPSG, *Linguistic Inquiry* 15, 514-23.
Schiaffini, A. (1954). Sulla legge Tobler-Mussafia. In Schiaffini, ed., 275-83.
Schiaffini, A., ed. (1954). *Testi fiorentini del dugento e dei primi del trecento.* Firenze: G. C. Sansoni.
Siegel, D. (1974). *Topics in English morphology.* MIT doctoral dissertation. (Published by Garland in 1979.)
Siegel, D. (1978). The adjacency constraint and the theory of morphology, in M. Stein (ed.), Proceedings of the VIII Annual Meeting of the NELS, Amherst, MA.
Solomon, S. L. (1992). *Clitics and phonological phrasing.* UCLA M.A. thesis.
Sorrento, L. (1950). *Sintassi romanza: Ricerche e prospettive.* II. edizione. Varese, Milano: Istituto Editorial Cisalpino.
Spencer, A. (1991). *Morphological theory.* Oxford: Basil Blackwell.
Sportiche, D. (1983). *Structural invariance and symmetry.* MIT doctoral dissertation.
Sportiche, D. (1987). Unifying movement theory. Ms., University of Southern California.
Sportiche, D. (1988). A theory of floating quantifiers and its corollaries for constituent structure, *Linguistic Inquiry* 19, 425-49.
Sportiche, D. (1990). Movement, agreement and Case. Ms., UCLA.
Sportiche, D. (1992a). Clitics, voice and spec/head licensing, *GLOW Newsletter* 28, 46-47. (Abstract.)
Sportiche, D. (1992b). Clitic constructions. Ms., UCLA.
Sportiche, D. (1993). Subject clitics in French and Romance: Complex inversion and clitic doubling. Ms., UCLA.
Sproat, R. (1985). *On deriving the lexicon.* MIT doctoral dissertation.

Sproat, R. (1985a). On deriving the lexicon, *The Linguistic Review* 5 (1985-1986), 185-96. (Abstract of Sproat 1985.)
Staaff, E. (1906). *Etude sur les pronoms abreges en ancien espagnol.* Uppsala: Lundstrom.
Strozer, J. R. (1976). *Clitics in Spanish.* UCLA doctoral dissertation.
Suñer, M. (1993). About indirect questions and semi-questions, *Linguistics and Philosophy* 16, 45-77.
Tobler, A. (1875). Review of J. Le Coultre's *De l'ordre des mots dans Crestien de Troyes,* Gottinger Gelehrte Anzeigen 75, 1057f. (Reprinted in Tobler 1912, 395-415.)
Tobler, A. (1912). *Der vermischten Beitrage zur franzosischen Grammatik.* Funfte Reihe. Leipzig: Verlag von S. Hirzel.
Torrego, E. (1981). Review of Otero (1971-73). In *Hispanic Review* 49, 119-121.
Ulleland, M. (1960). Alcune osservazioni sulla legge 'Tobler-Mussafia', *Studia Neophilologica* 32, 53-79.
Uriagereka, J. (1988). *On government.* University of Connecticut doctoral dissertation.
Uriagereka, J. (1989a). Head movement and syntactic transparency. Ms., UMass at Amherst.
Uriagereka, J. (1989b). Title. First draft [of the paper presented at the Workshop]. Ms., UMass.
Uriagereka, J. (1989c). Head movement and transparency. Handout distributed at the Workshop.
Uriagereka, J. (1990). Head movement and transparency. Ms., University of Maryland.
Uriagereka, J. (1991). Determiner clitic placement. Ms., University of Maryland.
Uriagereka, J. (1992a). Focus in Iberian languages. *GLOW Newsletter* 28, 52-53. (Abstract.)
Uriagereka, J. (1992b). An F position in Western Romance. In Kiss (1995).
Uriagereka, J. (1992c). Aspects of the syntax of clitic placement in Western Romance. Ms., University of Maryland. Submitted to *Linguistic Inquiry.*
Uribe-Etxeberria, M. (1991). On the structural positions of the subject in Spanish, their nature and their consequences for quantification. Ms., University of Connecticut.
Valois, D. (1991). *The internal syntax of DP.* UCLA doctoral dissertation.
Wackernagel, J. (1892). Über ein Gesetz der indogermanischen Wortstellung, *Indogermanische Forschungen* 1, 333-436. Reprinted in J. Wackernagel, *Kleinere Schriften.* Göttingen: Vandenhoek und Ruprecht, 1953, I, 1-104.
Wanner, D. (1987). *The development of Romance clitic pronouns: From Latin to Old Romance.* Berlin: Mouton de Gruyter.
Wanner, D. (1991). The Tobler-Mussafia law in Old Spanish. In Campos & Martinez-Gil, eds., 313-378.
Williams, E. (1938). *From Latin to Portuguese.* University of Pennsylvania Press. (Revised ed., 1962; reprinted, 1968.)
Wu, Andi (1993a). The S-parameter, *GLOW Newsletter* 30, 60-1. (Abstract.)
Wu, Andi (1993b). The Spell-Out of movement and features. Ms., UCLA.
Wu, Andi (1994). *The spell-out parameters: A minimalist approach to syntax.* UCLA doctoral dissertation.
Zagona, K. (1988). Proper government of antecedentless VP in Spanish and English, *NLLT* 6, 95-128.

Zanuttini, R. (1991). *Syntactic properties of sentential negation: A comparative study of Romance languages.* University of Pennsylvania doctoral dissertation.
Zec, D. & Inkelas, S. (1990). Prosodically constrained syntax. Chapter 18 in Inkelas & Zec, eds.
Zubizarreta, M. L. (1992). Word order in Spanish and the nature of nominative Case. Ms., University of Southern California.
Zubizarreta, M. L. (1993a). Fronting in Spanish. Lecture at UCLA (The Linguistics Colloquium Series), March 19.
Zubizarreta, M. L. (1993b). Some prosodically motivated syntactic operations. Ms., University of Southern California.
Zwicky, A. M. (1977). On clitics. Bloomington: Indiana University Linguistics Club.
Zwicky, A. M. (1985). Clitics and particles, *Language* 61, 283-305.

JUAN URIAGEREKA

A BRIEF RESPONSE[1]

It probably is uncontroversial that the determiner cliticization paradigm discussed in this chapter obeys some locality restriction in terms of government (or a similar notion). Whether the locality condition is syntactic or phonological in nature may be an open question, but I have nothing to say about the second possibility.

Uriagereka (1988, 1993) is concerned with local relations. In that context, it is interesting to look at the syntax of heads/dependents, and a natural question emerges: can we conceive the head/dependent relation—for instance, that between V and D—in terms of incorporation? Although the matter of determiner cliticization has potential consequences beyond or besides this question, it is this question that I have been concerned with. It is perfectly possible that the Galician (or Older Romance) paradigm is not a good exemplification of this process. In fact, it might even be even true that this is not a core phenomenon, and the Galician child does learn precompiled two-constituents-in-one allomorphs along with the rest of the vocabulary. If so, if we are interested in the matter of the relation between heads and dependents, we have to look elsewhere.[2]

But suppose (for the sake of argument) that one can clean the relevant evidence and that the phenomenon under discussion has standard syntactic properties. If this is the guiding intuition, we expect certain consequences. For instance, if determiner cliticization feeds other instances of Move α, it would not be surprising if certain opaque domains could become transparent as a result of moving their head upwards (see e.g. Chomsky (1986:70). The examples in 3.1 are then of theoretical relevance.[3] Likewise, we may expect determiner cliticization in a restricted set of syntactic environments (a matter discussed in 2.4), precisely those where, say, the ECP is satisfied.[4] Finally, we may expect differences with respect to standard phonological cliticizations. In this respect, for instance, it strikes me as significant that while the examples from the Old Galician-Portuguese dialect that I report in (4) are well-known from the texts, similar modern Galician examples involving incorporations to adjectives, nouns, names, and so forth, are entirely impossible.

We can first chose to be moved by these facts or not. Second, assuming that the facts lead to a syntactic interpretation, we can then chose to interpret them in terms of argument substitution (as in Uriagereka (1988, 1993); see 4.3 and fn. 23), or in other terms. In this chapter I did not take a strong position on this because I do not know what is the ultimate interpretation that one should give to the syntactic facts, nor do I think that it matters for present purposes.

But again for the sake of argument, suppose we interpreted the facts in terms of argument substitution at LF.[5] The intuition here is nothing but a syntactic instanciation of Stowell's (1981) co-indexation mechanism between roles and arguments, perhaps in the more explicit terms discussed in Jackendoff (1987). Suppose we assume (with Chomsky (1992)) that indices do not have a place in the grammar, for they merely mark relations. Then we have to reinterpret the dependency between, say, see and the man in some syntactic way. The determiner carries the phi features of the nominal expression, and possibly even the referential features—so it is in effect an indexical.[6] We may then think of determiner incorporation as setting the value of a thematic feature in a given way, where quite literally the incorporated determiner is the value for the thematic feature in the thematic bearer.

If things work this way, we have to consider a number of interesting questions. For instance: why is it that just one determiner incorporates overtly and not two or more? This must relate to why determiner cliticization is not analogous to clitic placement in all respects, a matter I addressed in 4.2. Suppose the solution I proposed is right: the reason the determiner does not move out of the immediate government domain of the associated NP is because it needs to transmit morphological Case when the NP is overt, but not when it is pro (as in special cliticization). Then we do not expect two or more determiners to cliticize onto a verb: all but one of these determiners will not be in the immediate government domain of the associated overt NP. This entails that we should never have the equivalent of clitic groups with determiner cliticization, just as we should never have standard determiner clitic climbing.

In this respect, each sort of cliticization does differ, as is natural: the model I am assuming has no place for construction-specific rules (such as a would-be rule of clitic placement), and whatever processes we happen to see patterning alike may cease to pattern alike when different principles of grammar are at stake. It is obvious that something is different between standard (special) cliticization and determiner cliticization, regardless of one's theory. In my view, whereas the former involves a determiner introducing a pro NP, the latter involves a determiner introducing a regular NP (see Corver and Delfitto (1993) for a recent justification of this analysis). And this should in principle have consequences, like perhaps the Case theoretic difference I mentioned. Or sensitivity to Wackernagel's Law.

Uriagereka (1992, 1995) suggests rethinking some aspects of Wackernagel's analysis in terms of V movement to a position outside IP, other than

Comp.[7] Special clitics themselves move outside IP, in order to license their associated pro—following the analysis in Corver and Delfitto (1993). From this perspective, as Corver and Delfitto point out, Chomsky's (1992) strategy of procrastination is enough for the standard determiner not to cliticize beyond its own independently needed site for cliticization. That is, suppose reason R forces the clitic to move to V. That alone will justify a strictly local cliticization. If clitic placement (or, in some instances, climbing) involve processes related to the fact that the special clitic introduces pro while the determiner clitic introduces a standard NP, then we expect the standard determiner not to be able to take the same route as the special clitic. Of course, a derivation where the determiner did take the route of the special clitic to its ultimate site would converge—it simply wouldn't be the most economic derivation.

It is easy to see that this alone takes care of any unjustified movement of the determiner clitic beyond reason R (under the assumption that there is always another reason for the special clitic to go on moving upwards, like Corver and Delfitto's licensing of pro). In other words, where special clitics and determiner clitics start to differ (triggering clitic placement vis-a-vis local cliticization) is where they should differ: special clitics have an extra reason to go 'higher' than determiner clitics do, assuming it is thus that pro licensing proceeds. If so, the fact that definite articles do not share characteristic properties of special clitics (their inability to appear in phrase initial position or their long-distance placement) is entirely expected.

Similar issues can be raised about the directionality of cliticization. Although one can assume Kayne's treatment of clitic placement (in terms of the ECP), I see no compelling reason why his stipulation that cliticization is always to the left of a head is necessary or even desirable. What is crucial for the details of Kayne's analysis to work is that cliticization be to some anchored position. This limits the class of potential analyses of enclisis and proclisis—which he specifically analyzes in terms of verb movement. It is consistent with this idea, however, that instead of clitics always adjoining to the left of heads, they actually adjoin to the right, or even that this matter is parametrized depending on values for the head parameter (cf. Uriagereka (1988, 1993)). This in languages which are head-first presupposes clitic-last attachments, if the clitic moves via functional incorporation. If on the other hand the clitic moves via lexical incorporation (as in instances of affixation), a clitic-first attachment will be possible. This may give us a way of distinguishing clitic placement in French and Spanish, among others. And from this point of view, I see no reason why the determiner clitic should not be able to cliticize to the right of the verb.[8]

The one difference between special clitics and determiner clitics that leaves me puzzled was noted in fn. 12. To make this point clearly, suppose that determiner cliticization were obligatory. In most instances we could not tell whether it has in fact happened, for the morphological changes in the shape of the determiner are not obvious. It is misleading to claim that just [s] or [r] ending words exhibit the relevant effects; as I said in 2.3, the change in the quality of the [n] that precedes a determiner indicates that it too involves cliticization of the determiner.[9] The only other consonant which Galician words end in is [l], and here too it is not easy to see an effect with a determiner which, underlyingly, starts with an [l]. So in fact all possible consonants behave as expected: they are truncated in front of a cliticized determiner. But there is a strange exception: special clitics get a (diachronically recent) [n] when they cliticize to a word ending in a glide, while determiner clitics do not.

This fact should be kept in mind when constructing impossible examples involving determiner cliticization. For instance, we don't find (1):

(1) a. *non vos lembrouna sua dor
   'he didn't remind you of his pain'
  b. *non lles asustouna curuxa
   'the owl didn't frighten them'

But these are irrelevant once we have established that the determiner (for some unknown reason) does not get the [n] that the special clitic does after a glide. The relevant examples we should consider are as in (2)—which are perfect:[10]

(2) a. non lles lembrache-la tua dor
   'you didn't remind them of your pain'
  b. non lles asustade-los anarquistas
   '(you) the anarquists don't frighten them'

In fact, when possible, determiner cliticization must be obligatory.[11] We are forced into this conclusion in a minimalist system, where different derivations which converge cancel one another, unless their cost is identical. I am very skeptical that the cliticized version of, say, (2a) is as costly as a (possible) non-cliticized version. The latter, obviously, involves one derivational step less. Then it must be the case that (2a) and a version without cliticization are entirely different derivations.

There are reasons to think this is the case. A non-cliticized determiner yields a focused reading on its associated NP:

(3) a. A: Bon, po-lo menos non perdemos os da casa...
   'Well, at least the home team didn't lose'

b. A: Bon, po-lo menos non perdemo-los da casa...
[Same, with cliticization]
B: E logo perderon os de fora? A: Non, empatamos.
So the visitors lost? No, we tied.

The discourse in (3) is well-formed only when (3b) is asked. A presupposition that someone else lost is involved in (3a), which does not appear in (3b). This is what we expect if the direct object is focused in (3a), but not in (3b). Assuming that focalization involves some kind of LF movement of the focalized constituent, we do not expect determiner cliticization in these instances, and clearly a different derivation is at stake.

Determiner cliticization yields a unique aspectual realization:

(4) a. Tocamos a gaita moitas veces
Played.we the bag-pipe many times
'We played the bag-pipe many times in the same occasion.'
b. Tocamo-la gaita moitas veces
Played.we-the bag-pipe many times
'We played the bag-pipe many times in different occasions.'

While (4a) allows (though does not force) multiple sub-events of playing within the same occasion, (4b) strongly favors a reading where multiple occasions for the main event are invoked.[12]

One context in which cliticization is clearly necessary is inalienable possession, as in (5):[13]

(5) a. Levantamo-la man
'We raised our hand'
b. Levantamos a man
'We raised the hand (someone's hand)'

Inalienably possessed elements cannot be focused in English:[14]

(6) AN ARM has the beast broken!
(cf. The beast has broken an arm)

The focused version of (6) disallows an inallienable reading. Whatever the impossibility of focusing an inallienable possessed element follows from, it aligns directly with the obligatoriness of (5a) in the relevant reading.

Finally, there is at least one other context in which cliticization is impossible, namely when the determiner is quantificational, as in (7):

(7) a. veremos os/veremo-los que chegaron
'We'll see the ones that have arrived'
b. veremo os/*veremo-los que cheguen
'We'll see whatever ones may arrive'

The impossibility of (7b) aligns with treating the direct object in this instance as an element that must undergo QR. This would make this example similar to (3a), in that a further LF operation is at stake in both instances.

I believe that a careful analysis of these matters can yield further contrasts, but I think that the ones shown are enough to suggest that the phenomenon at stake is not optional, and thus can be naturally explained in current syntactic terms.

NOTES

[1] I thank Carlos Otero, my commentator, for his reaction, and Robert Freidin, Elena Herburger, and Richard Kayne for their comments.
[2] Uriagereka (1988, 1993) does look elsewhere, as do others (see the forthcoming thesis of Peter Svenonius (UCSC) for a comprehensive presentation of these matters).
[3] As is standard, I give relative judgements only when necessary. Thus, the marks in 3.1 are relative to one another, but not across sections. Likewise, in any other article I may have written, a judgement (e.g. a star) is not meant to compare to a judgement here (e.g. question marks)—a point explicitly made in Uriagereka (1988) to avoid confusion. That is, anything short of a sentence without any mark is taken to be violating something. Parenthesized judgements mean that speakers disagree, which again is something I may have found in the course of an investigation (a clear instance of this is (17b), which I suggest correlates with variations in judgements about climbing out of inflected infinitivals (fn. 16)).
[4] However, recall from 4.3. that the ECP may not be enough. Thus, I take complementizers to be able to govern a determiner introducing an NP in the IP spec, but according to Alvarez, Regueira, and Monteagudo (1986), the relevant sort of cliticization is not acceptable. This makes the modern Galician examples in (3) contrast sharply with the sort of examples in (2), of the sort common in many archaic Romance dialects. (I must apologize to the philologist here, for I am using the word 'dialect' in the standard generative sense: every speaker in effect speaks a dialect of Universal Grammar; whether it is philologically proper to talk about Old Galician-Portuguese or similar notions is something I have no knowledge of.)
[5] In such a case, we of course have to be concerned with structures which do not have the obvious form of semantic arguments. A case in point is coordination, where only the determiner of the first conjunct incorporates. Interestingly, this is precisely what one would expect in a theory of the sort developed in Munn (1993). The issue is this: in instances of unlike-category coordination, a given head is sensitive in terms of selection to the first member of a conjunct, not the rest. Given this fact, Munn proposes that in a conjunction (for him a Boolean Phrase), the first member of the conjunct is the syntactic argument of whatever selects the phrase, while all other members of the conjunct are in effect adjuncts in the structure. At Logical Form, each of the members of the conjunct enters into an interpretive operation that makes it a semantic argument (though it was not the syntactic argument) of the relevant head. From this perspective, it is expected that the first determiner should incorporate. Following Herburger (1993), something similar can be said about generalized

quantifiers taking DPs as their first argument, or partitive phrases, and so on. These are not trivial from the point of view of Theta-theory, but a solution along these lines, looking at Logical Form instead of the overt syntax, seems straightforward.

[6] Maybe quite literally, for instance in terms of a theory like Heim (1982), where articles are free variables which get some discourse valuation.

[7] Whether that position is Laka's (1990) sigma or Uriagereka's (1988, 1992) F, or whether these two are one and the same is an interesting question that Ana Maria Martins addresses in her forthcoming dissertation (University of Lisbon).

[8] Richard Kayne notes that he has recently found generalized special cliticization to the right of verbs, in some Northern Italian dialects. He suggests that there may be a functional node the clitic attaches to (in his terms, leftwards) which is lower than the (standard) inflectional node the verb raises to, thereby yielding the observed order. Kayne also suggests that the Galician clitic may actually be targeting this functional node—which I think is compatible with everything I had to say here.

[9] For instance, in *comeron o caldo*, the final [n] of *comeron* is not velarized in normal speech, unless o caldo is focalized (in which case I would assume its determiner is not undergoing incorporation—see below). I take this to indicate that there is an [l] underlyingly in front of o, which assimilates to the [n], thus preventing the velarization which is otherwise standard in word-final [n] (see (14)).

[10] To insist, there is no reason why we should expect the determiner clitic to appear in the same group as the special clitics—in fact, if anything the opposite is the case, given procrastination. It should also be kept in mind that there is no obvious reason why the clitics should form a group either (and in fact they don't in many dialects, where 'split' cliticization is possible); see Uriagereka (1995) on these issues.

[11] I thank Richard Kayne for insisting on this point.

[12] Cristina Schmitt notes facts of this sort in her dissertation in progress (UMD), and proposes a minimalist analysis in terms of movement to an Aspect phrase.

[13] Thanks to Martin Hayden for raising this issue.

[14] We don't have to front the focused element, though there the judgments are clearer. Still, note that with an inallienable reading, it is possible to say John has broken an ARM (as opposed to a leg), but not John has broken AN ARM. The latter is possible only with a standard reading, as in 'John has broken someone's arm, not someone's leg'.

REFERENCES

Alvarez, R., X.L. Regueira, H. Monteagudo (1986) *Gramatica Galega*, Galaxia.

Chomsky, N. (1986) *Barriers*, MIT Press.

Chomsky, N. (1992) "A Minimalist Program for Linguistic Theory," MIT Occasional Papers in Linguistics.

Corver, N. and D. Delfitto (1993) "Feature Asymmetry and the Nature of Pronoun Movement," presented at GLOW, Lund.

Heim, I. (1982) *Semantics of Definite and Indefinite Noun Phrases*, UMass Ph.D. thesis.

Herburger, E. (1993) "Focus and NP Quantification," presented at SALT III, University of California at Irvine.

Jackendoff, R. (1987) "The Status of Thematic Relations in Linguistic Theory," *Linguistic Inquiry* 18.

Laka, I. (1990) *Negation in Syntax. On The Nature of Functional Categories and Projections*, Ph.D. thesis, MIT.

Munn, Alan (1993) *Topics in The Syntax and Semantics of Coordinate Structures*, Ph.D. thesis, UMD.

Stowell, T. (1981) *Origins of Phrase Structure*, MIT Ph.D. thesis.

Uriagereka, J. (1988) *On Government*, UConn Ph.D. thesis, distributed in (1993) through MITWPL.

Uriagereka, J. (1992) "A Focus Position in Western Romance," presented at GLOW, Lisbon, CAP In Kiss (ed.). (1995) *Discourse Configurational Languages*, Studies in Comparative Grammar, Oxford University Press.

Uriagereka, J. (1995) "Aspects of Clitic Placement in Western Romance," to appear in *Linguistic Inquiry* 26.

JOSEPH AOUN AND YEN-HUI AUDREY LI

TWO CASES OF LOGICAL RELATIONS: BOUND PRONOUNS AND ANAPHORIC RELATIONS

INTRODUCTION*

The Extended Standard Theory elaborated in Chomsky (1977) and Chomsky and Lasnik (1977) postulates the existence of an autonomous interpretive level: the Logical Form (LF) component. Representations at this level are derived from S-Structure representations via transformations (see May (1977)). These representations represent the structural meaning of a sentence and abstract away from other aspects of meaning such as word meaning or pragmatics:

I. D-Structure —<move α>→ S-Structure —<move α>→ LF-Structure

The organization of grammar illustrated in (I) has often been challenged. With respect to LF per se, alternative generative models have been devised, which challenge the existence of LF as an autonomous component or the transformational mapping between S-Structure and LF. In this paper, we discuss two cases of logical relations in so far as they bear on the existence of the putative level of LF. The first case of logical relation deals with bound pronouns in Mandarin Chinese. The study of pronouns used as bound variables undertaken in section 1 will indicate that these elements obey a specific (A'-) disjointness requirement: they have to be (non-argument) A'-free in a certain domain (D):

(1) *[$_D$... A'-antecedent$_i$ ... pronoun$_i$...]

Furthermore, this disjointness requirement is subject to a minimality effect. Essentially, pronouns have to be free in the relevant domain with respect to the first available A'-binder. That is, when a distinct A'-element intervenes between the pronoun and its antecedent in D, the relation between the pronoun and the antecedent becomes licit:

(2) [$_D$... A'-antecedent$_i$ ... A'-element$_k$ ... pronoun$_i$...]

Relevant to the status of Logical Form and to the transformational mapping between S-Structure and LF representations will be the proper characterization of this minimality effect. Modals, wh-operators, negation and negative polarity items, intermediate traces and quantificational elements will be shown to count as intervening A'-elements:

(3) $[_D$ ... A'-antecedent$_i$ ... modal$_k$ ... pronoun$_i$]
wh-operator$_k$
negation/neg polarity$_k$
intermediate trace$_k$
quantifier$_k$

It will appear that the minimality effect described in (3) cannot be captured at the levels where movement rules or linear order are encoded; namely, S-Structure and Surface Structure. Rather, the proper account for the minimality effect necessitates the postulation of a covert extraction process applying after S-Structure in the so-called Logical Form component. It is only at this level that the A'-elements will come to intervene between the pronoun and its antecedent in (3).

The necessity of a covert extraction process highlighted in the study of bound pronouns will reappear in the study of Chinese anaphoric expressions undertaken in section 2. Essentially, the distinction between long-distance and short-distance anaphors reveals that long-distance anaphors, but not short-distance anaphors, are subject to an obligatory covert movement rule applying at LF. As a consequence of this covert raising rule, long-distance anaphors end up in a non-argument position at the appropriate level (LF) and get locally identified with their antecedents. Since long-distance anaphors, but not short-distance anaphors, must be in an A'-position at LF, we expect the former, but not the latter, to enter into A'-disjointness with the pronoun in the context (4):

(4) a. * $[_D$ ... long-distance anaphor$_i$ ... pronoun$_i$ ...]
b. $[_D$ ... short-distance anaphor$_i$ ... pronoun$_i$ ...]

We also expect long-distance anaphors to play a role in the minimality effect described in (2-3). That is, we expect configurations where a long-distance anaphor intervenes between a pronoun and its antecedent to be well-formed in the same way that configurations like (3) are well-formed:

(5) $[_D$ ... A'-element$_i$ ... long-distance anaphor$_k$ ... pronoun$_i$]

We will see that these expectations are fulfilled only at the level where the covert extraction of long-distance anaphors is postulated to take place, namely, the Logical Form component. Thus, the interaction of pronouns and anaphors will provide further support for the transformational mapping between Syntax (S-Structure) and Logical Form (LF).

1. CASE 1: BOUND PRONOUNS

In Chinese, pronouns can be coindexed with a name (referential pronoun), as in (6):

(6) a. Zhang$_i$ shuo ta$_i$ de le jiang.
say he get ASP prize
'Zhang said that he got the prize.'
b. Zhang$_i$ shuo wo xihuan ta$_i$.
say I like him
'Zhang said that I liked him.'

The possibility of a pronoun coindexed with a quantificational expression (bound pronoun) varies with speakers. For instance, some speakers (speakers A) find both (7a) and (7b) unacceptable:[1]

(7) a. *Meiren$_i$ shuo ta$_i$ de le jiang.
nobody say he get ASP prize
'Nobody said that he got the prize.'
b. *Meiren$_i$ shuo wo xihuan ta$_i$.
nobody say I like him
'Nobody said that I liked him.'

There are, however, speakers (speakers B) who find both (8a) and (8b) acceptable.[2]

(8) a. Meiren$_i$ shuo ta$_i$ de le jiang.
nobody say he get ASP prize
'Nobody said that he got the prize.'
b. Meiren$_i$ shuo wo xihuan ta$_i$.
nobody say I like him
'Nobody said that I liked him.'

Finally, there exists a third set of speakers who find bound pronouns acceptable in certain contexts and yet unacceptable in other contexts. For instance, sentence (9a) is unacceptable, but (9b) is acceptable for thse speakers (speakers C).[3]

(9) a. *Meiren$_i$ shuo ta$_i$ de le jiang.[4]
nobody say he get ASP prize
'Nobody said that he got the prize.'
b. Meiren$_i$ shuo wo xihuan ta$_i$.
nobody say I like him
'Nobody said that I liked him.'

Contrasts similar to the one in (9a-b) are assumed in Huang (1988) (see also Aoun (1986)).

1.1. Locality requirements on pronouns

Concentrating on speakers C, sentences (9a-b) show that for these speakers bound pronouns can occur in object but not subject position of the embedded clause. This might suggest that there is a subject/object asymmetry in the distribution of bound pronouns (see Montalbetti 1984) for these speakers.[5] However, this cannot be the case. A bound pronoun in the subject position of a more deeply embedded clause is possible, as illustrated in (10):

(10) Meiren$_i$ yiwei ni shuo ta$_i$ de le jiang.
nobody think you say he get ASP prize
'Nobody thinks that you said that he got the prize.'

The distribution of bound and referential pronouns for speakers C are schematically represented in (11):[6]

(11)	CONTEXTS	RP	BP
a.	NP$_i$ V [$_{CP}$ NP$_i$ V NP]	√	*
b.	NP$_i$ V [$_{CP}$ NP V NP$_i$]	√	√
c.	NP$_i$ V [$_{CP}$ NP V [$_{CP}$ NP$_i$ V NP]]	√	√

The fact that bound pronouns can occur in (11b-c) but not in (11a) suggests that distance plays a role in the distribution of these bound pronouns. More precisely, it is indicated in Huang (1982) that AGR does not exist in Chinese. With this in mind, consider the paradigm in (11a-c). Let us discuss bound pronouns in (11) first. Assuming that bound pronouns must be free in the minimal domain of a subject, the opaque domain in which the bound pronoun must be free is the matrix clause in (11a) since AGR as indicated in Huang (1982) is missing in Chinese. In this opaque domain, the bound pronoun is not free; hence, the ungrammaticality of representation (11a). In representation (11b) and (11c), on the other hand, the bound pronoun is free in its opaque domain, the embedded clause which is the minimal domain containing a subject. Representations (11b-c) thus are grammatical.

Next we turn to referential pronouns. The grammaticality of referential pronouns in (11a-c) suggests that the notion of subject is not relevant for pronouns. Essentially, referential pronouns have to be free in the minimal clause in which they occur. This is the case for referential pronouns in (11a-c).

So far, we have discussed the behavior of pronominal elements on a sentential level for speakers C. The behavior of pronominal elements that occur within noun phrases supports the analysis assumed. The following contrast for speakers C highlights once more the different distribution of bound and referential pronouns:

(12) a. Zhang$_i$ xihuan ta$_i$de shu.
Zhang like his book
'Zhang likes his book.'
b. *Meiren$_i$ xihuan ta$_i$de shu.
Nobody like his book
'Nobody likes his book.'
c. *Meiren$_i$ xihuan ta$_i$ xie de shu.
Nobody like he write DE book
'Nobody likes the book that he wrote.'

Consider sentence (12b) first. The non-acceptability of this sentence comes as no surprise. Since bound pronouns have to be free in the domain of a subject, the clause in (12b) constitutes such a domain. The same analysis accounts for the unacceptability of (12c). On the other hand, since subjects are not relevant for referential pronouns, the domain in which the pronoun has to be free in (12a) is the noun phrase his book.

Before leaving the discussion of pronouns in NPs, one further clarification is necessary. We said so far that for speakers C, bound pronouns must be free in the minimal clause or NP containing a subject and that referential pronouns must be free in the minimal clause or NP in which they occur. However, we did not specify the type of disjointness requirements that each of these pronouns obey. Along the lines of Aoun and Hornstein (1986), we would like to suggest that the distinction between bound and referential pronouns may be understood in light of the following considerations: bound pronouns must seek a c-commanding antecedent. The antecedent is quantificational and at LF, after the application of Quantifier Raising, will be in an A'-position. Thus, bound pronouns seek an A'-binder. We would like to argue that for speakers C, bound pronouns must be A'-free in the minimal domain containing a subject and that referential pronouns must be free in the minimal clause or NP in which they occur. Notice that the A'-disjointness requirement for referential pronouns is trivially satisfied since they do not have an A'-binder. In brief, we are suggesting that for speakers C, pronouns, whether bound or referential, obey the following disjointness requirement:[7]

(13) a. The A-disjointness Requirement:
A pronoun must be A-free in the least Complete Functional Complex (CFC) in which it occurs (see Chomsky 1986b))
b. The A'-disjointness Requirement:
A pronoun must be A'-free in the least CFC containing a c-commanding subject and the pronoun.

The distinction between referential and bound pronouns for speakers C is accounted for by the existence of two distinct disjointness requirements. This distinction may also help us analyze the behavior of bound pronouns for speakers A and B. Recall that for speakers A, an overt pronominal expression such as ta can never be bound by a QP.[8] In other words, the locality condition on the A'-disjointness requirement for this type of speakers does not incorporate a locality effect. The two disjointness requirements for speakers A will then be (13c–d):

(13) c. The A-disjointness Requirement:
A pronoun must be A-free in the least Complete Functional Complex (CFC) in which it occurs.
d. The A'-disjointness Requirement:
A pronoun must be A'-free.

For speakers A and C, the domain where the pronoun has to be A and A'-free are distinct. This is not the case for speakers B. For these speakers, the domain where the pronoun has to be A'-free is the same as the domain where it has to be A-free. The two disjointness requirements for speakers B are given in (13e–f):[9]

(13) e. The A-disjointness Requirement:
A pronoun must be A-free in the least Complete Functional Complex (CFC) in which it occurs.
f. The A'-disjointness Requirement:
A pronoun must be A'-free in the least CFC in which it occurs.

1.2. Minimal disjointness

We have indicated so far that pronouns in Chinese obey two disjointness requirements. We would like to now to focus on the working of the A'-disjointness requirement for speakers C. Specifically, we would like to argue that for Speakers C, this A'-disjointness requirement incorporates a minimality effect formulated in (14):

(14) A pronoun must be free from the most local A'-binder in the smallest CFC containing the pronoun and a SUBJECT.

"The most local A'-binder" is defined as follows: A is the most local A'-binder of B iff there is no C such that C is an A'-binder and A c-commands C, C c-commands B. Illustrating the working of the minimality effect, the A'-disjointness requirement (13b) requires the pronoun to be A'-free in a certain domain D:

(15) a. *[$_D$ ... A'-element$_i$ ... pronoun$_i$ ...]

Reformulation (14) has the effect of making the relation in (15a) licit when a distinct A'-element intervenes the pronoun and its antecedent as in (15b):

(15) b. $[_D$ ... A'-antecedent$_i$ ... A'-element$_k$ ... pronoun$_i$ ...]

1.2.1. Modals

To substantiate the proposal in (14), we start by noting that sentences such as (9) improve when a modal occurs between the quantifier and the pronoun as in (16a):

(16) a. Meiren$_i$ yuangyi/keneng/hui shuo ta$_i$ dele jiang.
nobody will/might/will say he got prize
'Nobody might/will say that he got the prize.'

A similar improvement occurs when the modal occurs in the same clause as the pronoun:

(16) b. Meiren$_i$ shuo ta$_i$ yinggai/keneng/hui de jiang.
nobody say he should/might/will get prize
'Nobody said that he should/might/would get the prize.'

The contrast between the sentence in (9) on the one hand and (16a-b) on the other is not accounted for by the disjointness requirement formulated in (13). We show below that this contrast and other similar contrasts can be accounted for by incorporating the notion of minimality to the disjointness requirement, as in (14).[10]

Note that what is common to the sentences (16a-b), in contrast to the unacceptable sentence (9), is that these sentences contain a modal. Modals are assigned scope at the appropriate interpretive level. At this point, it is possible to assume that these elements are subject to a raising process at LF. After this raising process they will end up in an A'-position as illustrated in the LF representation of (16) in (17), for instance:

(17) Meiren$_i$ [x1$_i$ shuo [yingai/keneng/hui$_j$ [ta$_i$ x2$_j$ de jiang]]].
nobody say should/might/will he get prize
'Nobody said that he should/might/would get the prize.'

If we compare the LF representation in (17) with the LF representation of sentence (9) in (18), we notice that the difference may be traced back to the existence of an operator intervening between the QP and the bound pronoun: in (17), but not in (18), there is an operator intervening between the QP and the boud pronoun. This is why (17) is well-formed.[11]

(18) Meiren$_i$ [x1$_i$ shuo [ta$_i$ de jiang]]].
'Nobody said that he got the prize.'

The fact that the presence of a modal improves the acceptability of sentences involving bound pronouns, however, cannot be taken to provide evidence for an LF-Raising process. One may assume that modals are generated in INFL. In this position, which would have to be characterized as an A'-position, they would c-command (m-command) the subject position. If this were the case, the modal would be the most local A'-binder in (16) (or (15) for that matter). The minimality requirement on the pronoun could be satisfied with respect to this modal. This would account for sentences (16a-b) without necessarily postulating an LF-movement.

1.2.2. Wh-operators

The non-movement option, however, is not available when wh-operators are considered. We saw in the previous paragraphs that the existence of a modal intervening between the operator and the pronoun improves the acceptability of sentences like (9). Not only does a modal improve the acceptability of these sentences, but also wh-operators such as weishenme 'why', shei 'who', shenme 'what' and A-not-A questions have the same effect as illustrated in (19):

(19) a. Meiren$_i$ xiang-zhidao ta$_i$ weishenme de jiang.
nobody want-know he why get prize
'Nobody wonders why he got the prize.'
b. Meiren$_i$ xiang-zhidao ta$_i$ gen shei fen jiangpin.
nobody want-know he with whom share prize
'Nobody wonders with whom he shared the prize.'
c. Meiren$_i$ xiang-zhidao ta$_i$ de le shenme jiangpin.
nobody want-know he got what prize
'Nobody wonders what prize he got.'
d. Meiren$_i$ xiang-zhidao shi-bu-shi ta$_i$ de le jiang/
nobody want-know be-not-be he got prize
ta you-mei-you de jiang.
he have-not-have get prize
'Nobody wonders whether he got the prize.'

It is relevant to remind the reader that overt wh-movement does not occur in Mandarin Chinese. As argued in Huang (1982), wh-operators are raised to a (SPEC of) COMP position at LF. In other words, S-Structure cannot be taken as the level where the intervention effect of wh-elements is considered. It is only at LF that the wh-operator intervenes between the QP and the bound pronoun in sentences (19). We illustrate this in (20).[12]

(20) a. Meiren$_i$ [x1$_i$ xiang-zhidao [weisheme$_j$ [ta$_i$ x2$_j$ de jiang]]].
Nobody wonder why he get prize
'Nobody wonders why he got the prize.'
b. Meiren$_i$ [x1$_i$ xiang-zhidao [shei$_j$ [ta$_i$ gen x2$_j$ fen jiangpin]]].
nobody wonder who he with share prize
'Nobody wonders with whom he shared the prize.'
c. Meiren$_i$ [x1$_i$dou xiang-zhidao [shenme jiangpin$_j$ [ta$_i$ de le x2$_j$]]]
nobody wonder what prize he get ASP
'Nobody wonders what prize he got.'
d. Meiren$_i$ [x1$_i$ xiang-zhidao [shi-bu-shi/you-mei-you$_j$ [x2$_j$ ta$_i$ de jiang]]].
nobody wonder be-not-be/have-not-have he get prize
'Nobody wonders whether he got the prize.'

In brief, the paradigm involving wh-operators may be taken to provide support for the existence of the minimality effect postulated and of the process of LF-movement.[13]

1.2.3. Negation and Negative polarity items

A confirmation of this result is provided by negation and negative polarity items. Sentences with negation and negative polarity items pattern with sentences with modals and question words. Let us consider sentences involving negative polarity items first. The occurrence of negative polarity items between the quantificational element and the pronoun allows this pronoun to be bound to the quantificational element as illustrated in (21):[14]

(21) a. [Meigeren$_i$ dou mei dui renhe ren [ta$_i$ dele jiang]].
everyone all not tell any man he got prize
'Everyone did not tell anyone that he got the prize.'
b. [Meigeren$_i$ dou shuo [ta$_i$ mei kandao renhe ren]]
everyone all say he not see any man
'Everyone said that he did not see anyone.'

Assuming that the negative polarity item is raised at LF as suggested by Linebarger (1981), Kurata (1986) and Progovac (1988) or that the negative element mei 'not' is in an A'-position, an A'-binder will intervene between the pronoun and the QP in (21).

Similarly, the intervention of a negative element by itself between the quantifier and the pronoun allows the pronoun to be bound by the quantifier:[15]

(22) a. [Meigeren$_i$ dou mei shuo [ta$_i$ dele jiang]].
everyone all not say he got prize
'Everyone did not say that he got the prize.'

b. [Meigeren$_i$ dou shuo [ta$_i$ <u>mei</u> de jiang]]
everyone all say he not get prize
'Everyone said that he did not get the prize.'

Once again, if negation is assumed to be in an A'-position at the appropriate level, the acceptability of bound pronouns in (22) can be straightforwardly accounted for by the minimality effect.

It is possible to provide a rather strong argument for the existence of an LF raising process by contrasting the behavior of negative elements in (22) and sentences like (23):

(23) Meigeren dou mei kandao Zhang.
everyone all not see Zhang
'Everyone did not see Zhang.'

In (23), the negative element necessarily has narrow scope with respect to the quantificational subject. This straightforwardly follows from the Minimal Binding Requirement (MBR) discussed in Aoun and Li (1989) (see also Rizzi (1990)). The MBR requires variables to be bound by the first available A'-binder. This being the case, the only well-formed representation with respect to the MBR is the one where negation has narrow scope (namely (24b)). In (24a), the variable left by the raising of the negative element <u>x$_i$</u> is not bound by the first available A'-binder <u>everyone</u>:[16] (Representations (24a-b) are given in the English gloss)

(24) a. [not$_i$ [everyone$_j$ [x$_j$ [x$_i$ see Zhang]]]]
b. [everyone$_j$ [x$_j$ [not$_i$ [x$_i$ see Zhang]]]]

The unambiguity of (23), thus, indicates that the negative element does not c-command (m-command) the subject quantifier in the position in which it occurs at S-Structure. With this in mind, let us consider (22b). In (22b), the presence of the negative element allows the pronoun to be bound to the quantifier. That is to say that the negative element intervenes at the appropriate level between the pronoun and the quantifier. Since (23) indicated that the negative element does not c-command the subject in the position in which it occurs at S-Structure, the only way for the negative element to count as an intervening A'-binder will be after it undergoes raising at LF:[17]

(25) [Meigeren$_i$ dou shuo [mei$_j$ [ta$_i$ [x$_j$ de jiang]]
everyone all say not he get prize
'Everyone said that he did not get the prize.'

In brief, the intervention effect of the negation ought to be checked at a post S-Structure level after the negative element is raised.

We argued so far that in Chinese, pronouns obey an A'-disjointness requirement as well as an A-disjointness requirement. We furthermore suggested that the A'-disjointness requirement incorporates a minimality effect in (9): in case a distinct A'-binder intervenes between the pronoun and the quantificational antecedent at the appropriate level which we showed to be LF, the pronoun can be bound to this quantificational antecedent. Of course, we expect the occurrence of a modal, negation or wh-word not to facilitate the bound pronoun interpretation in case these elements do not intervene between a QP and its bound pronoun. This expectation can be tested in the contexts such as (26a-b) where the modal, negation, and wh-element do not intervene between the QP and the pronoun:

(26) a. modal/negation/wh-word ... QP$_i$ ... pronoun$_i$
b. QP$_i$ ... pronoun$_i$ ... modal/negation/wh-word

We expect sentences of the context in (26a-b) to be less acceptable than sentences of the context in (26c) if the minimal disjointness requirement just discussed is correct.

(26) c. QP$_i$ ... modal/negation/wh-word ... pronoun$_i$

Indeed, a contrast is found between sentences (27a-b) and (27c):

(27) a. * [Wo hui zhidao [meiren$_i$ shuo [ta$_i$ de le jiang]]].
I will know nobody say he get ASP prize
'I will know that nobody said that he got the prize.'
b. * [Meiren$_i$ shuo [ta$_i$ zhidao [wo hui de jiang]]].
nobody say he know I will get prize
'Nobody said that he knew that I would get the prize.'
c. [Meiren$_i$ shuo [ta$_i$ hui zhidao [wo de jiang]]].
nobody say he will know I get prize
'Nobody said that he would know that I got the prize.'
d. [Meiren$_i$ hui shuo [ta$_i$ zhidao [wo de jiang]]].
nobody will say he know I get prize
'Nobody said that he would know that I got the prize.'

A bound pronoun interpretation is possible in (27c-d) but not in (27a-b). This contrast is predicted by the minimal disjointness requirement on pronouns. Modals only have scope over the clause in which they occur. The modal intervenes between the the pronoun and the coindexed QP in (27c-d). That is, the most local A'-binder for the bound pronoun is the raised QP in (27a-b) but the modal is the most local A'-binder for the bound pronoun in (27c-d). The pronoun is A'-free from the most local A'-binder in (27c-d), but not (27a-b). The contrast between (27a-b) on the one hand and (27c-d) on the other, thus, supports the proposal according to which pronouns obey a disjointness requirement sensitive to minimality.

Wh-words behave in the same way as modals with respect to the intervention effect:

(28) a. * [Shei zhidao [meiren$_i$ shuo [ta$_i$ de le jiang]]]?
who know nobody say he get ASP prize
'Who knows that nobody said that he got the prize?'
b. *[Meiren$_i$ shuo [ta$_i$ xiang-zhidao [shi-bu-shi wo de le jiang]]].
nobody say he wonder be-not-be I get ASP prize
'Nobody said that he wondered whether I got the prize.'
c. [Meiren$_i$ xiang-zhidao [shi-bu-shi ta$_i$ de le jiang]].
nobody wonder be-not-be he get ASP prize
'Nobody wonders whether he got the prize.'

In (28a), shei is in the matrix clause. In (28b), the question word shi-bu-shi 'whether' cannot be raised beyond the clause subcategorized by 'wonder'. Only in (28c) does shi-bu-shi intervenes between the QP and the bound pronoun. The minimal disjointness requirement is satisfied in (28c) but not in (28a-b). The bound pronoun interpretation thus is more acceptable in (28c) than in (28a-b).

Similarly, the negation or the raised negative polarity item intervenes between the QP and the bound pronoun in (29c) but not in (29a-b). The contrast between (29a-b) on the one hand and (29c) on the other provides further support for the claim that pronouns obey the minimal disjointness requirement.

(29) a. *[Wo bu zhidao [meiren$_i$ shuo [ta$_i$ de le jiang]]].
I not know nobody say he get ASP prize
'I do not know that nobody said that he got the prize.'
b. * [Meiren$_i$ shuo [ta$_i$ zhidao [wo mei de jiang]]].
nobody say he know I not get prize
'Nobody said that he knew that I did not get the prize.'
c. [Wo zhidao [meiren$_i$ bu dui renhe ren shuo [ta$_i$ de le jiang]].
I know nobody not to any man say he get ASP prize
'I know that nobody did not tell anyone that he got the prize.'

1.2.4. Intermediate traces

We said so far that an A'-binder intervening between a pronoun and a quantificational element allows this pronoun to be bound by the quantificational element. Our analysis predicts that if a deeply embedded wh-word is raised at LF so as to intervene between a pronoun and an A'-antecedent, the pronoun can be bound by this quantificational antecedent. This prediction is born out, as shown by sentences (30a-b):

(30) a. *[Meiren$_i$ zhidao [ta$_i$ caidao [shei de le jiang]]].
nobody know he guess who get ASP prize
'Nobody knows that he guessed correctly who got prize.'

b. [Meiren$_i$ zhidao [ta$_i$ gen shei fen jiangpin]].
nobody know he with who share prize
'Nobody knows with whom he shared the prize.'

The contrast between (30a) and (30b) is not surprising. The wh-element shei intervenes between the QP and the pronoun at LF in (30b) but not in (30a), as shown in the LF representations of these two sentences:

(31) a. *[Meiren$_i$ [x1$_i$ zhidao [$_{CP1}$ ta$_i$ caidao [$_{CP2}$ shei$_j$ [x2$_j$ dele jiang]]]]].
nobody know he guess who got prize

b. [Meiren$_i$ [x1$_i$ zhidao [$_{CP1}$ shei$_j$ [ta$_i$ gen x2$_j$ fen jiangpin]]]].
nobody know this he with share prize

Contrasts such as the one illustrated in (30a-b) provide direct support for the assumption that wh-elements in situ are subject to raising at LF (see Huang (1982)).

In the examples discussed so far we saw that a wh-element intervening between a pronoun and a QP allows the pronoun to be bound by the QP. The analysis presented so far leads us to expect intermediate traces in the SPEC of COMP to play a role with respect to this intervention effect. This expectation is fulfilled as evidenced by the acceptability of sentence (30c) (see sentences (30a-b)) (see note 4):

(30) c. [Meigeren$_i$ dou shuo [ta$_i$ xiangxin [shei de le jiang ne]]]?
everyone all say he believe who get ASP prize Q-marker
'Who did everyone say that he believed got the prize?'

The wh-word shei in (30c) has matrix scope; i.e., it must be raised from its base position to the matrix SPEC of COMP, leaving traces in the intermediate SPEC of COMP position:

(31) c. [$_{CP1}$ shei$_j$ [$_{IP1}$ meigeren$_i$ [$_{IP1}$ x$_i$ dou shuo [$_{CP2}$ t1$_j$ [$_{IP2}$ ta$_i$ xiangxin [$_{CP3}$ t2$_j$
who everyone all say believe
[$_{IP3}$ x$_j$ dele jiang ne]]]?
got prize Q-marker

Since intermediate traces in the SPEC of COMP independently can function as A'-binders, the most local A'-binder for the pronoun in (30c) is the intermediate trace of shei in the COMP position of CP2, t1. The pronoun in this representation is free from its most local A'-binder and sentence (30c) is acceptable. Thus, the fact that (30c) patterns with (30b) rather than (30a) is accounted for by incorporating the minimality requirement in the formulation of the A'-disjointness requirement.

It is interesting to point out in this respect that the intermediate traces relevant for the working of the minimality effect are not only the one generated in the SPEC of COMP position. As argued in Chomsky (1986a), on its way to SPEC of COMP, a wh-element can be adjoined to a VP that dominates it. If the option of adjunction to VP is available, we expect the intermediate trace adjoined to VP to be relevant to the working of minimality. This expectation is fulfilled as illustrated in sentences (32), to be contrasted with sentence (9). Sentence (9) is repeated for convenience (for minimal contrast, meiren 'nobody' in (9) is changed to meigeren 'everyone' in this case, see note (4)) .

(9) Meigeren$_i$ dou shuo ta$_i$ de le jiang.
everyone all say he get ASP prize
'Everyone said that he got the prize.'

(32) Meigeren$_i$ dou dui shei shuo ta$_i$ de le jiang?
everyone all to whom say he get ASP prize
'To whom did everyone say that he got the prize?'

Assuming VP adjunction, the LF representation of sentence (32) will be (33) (in English gloss):

(33) $[_{CP}$ who$_i$ $[_{IP}$ nobody$_j$ $[_{VP}$ t_i $[_{VP}$ to x_i say $[_{CP}$ he$_i$ got prize]]]]].

In (33), the intermediate trace intervenes between the pronoun and the quantifier. This pronoun is free with respect to the first available A'-element and thus can be bound by the quantifier.

The discussion of wh-elements provides direct evidence for a successive cyclic application of wh-elements at LF as argued in Huang (1982) and for the existence of intermediate traces left by the LF raising of these wh-elements. The contrast between (30a) and (30b) and the acceptability of (30c) or (32) once more show that S-Structure cannot be retained as the level where the intervention of an A'-binder is to be considered. It is only after the LF-extraction of the wh-element that an A'-binder intervenes between the QP and the pronoun in (30c) and (32).

1.3.5. Quantifier

The previous discussion shows that the domain where modals, wh-elements and negation can be raised interacts with the interpretation of pronouns and that this interaction is accounted for by the minimal disjointness requirement on pronouns. This leads us to expect that QPs should behave the same as modals and wh-elements, since they are all subject to raising at LF. This expectation is generally born out: sentence (34b) is better than (34a).[18]

(34) a. Meiren$_i$ dui Zhang shuo ta$_i$ de le jiang.
nobody to Zhang say he get ASP prize
'Everyone said to Zhang that he got the prize.'
b. Meiren$_i$ dui meijia baoshe shuo ta$_i$ de le jiang.
nobody to every news-agency say he get ASP prize
'Nobody said to every news agency that he got the prize.'

This contrast can be accounted for by assuming Quantifier Raising and the minimal disjointness requirement.

Summarizing the discussion of bound pronouns, we saw that for speakers C, the A'-disjointness requirement is sensitive to a minimality effect: the relation between the pronoun and its antecedent within a certain domain D becomes licit when an A'-element intervenes between these elements. Modals, wh-operators, negation, negative polarity items, intermediate traces and quantificational elements count as intervening A'-elements.

(35) [$_D$ antecedent$_i$... modal$_k$ ... pronoun$_i$...]
wh-operator$_k$
negation/negative polarity$_k$
intermediate trace$_k$
QP$_k$

The working of the minimality effect revealed the existence of a covert process of raising applying after S-Structure. We took the existence of this covert process to provide evidence for LF and for a transformational mapping between S-Structure and LF representations. For the sake of completeness, we should point out that for Speakers A who do not allow the pronoun to be linked to a QP, the A'-disjointness requirement does not incorporate a minimality effect at all. For Speakers B for whom bound and referential pronouns have the same distribution, the minimality effect is trivially satisfied. The only context where minimality may have an effect is the following sentence:

(36) a. *Meiren$_i$ xihuan ta$_i$.
nobody like him
'Nobody likes him.'

We expect the intervention of an A'-element for these speakers to allow the bound pronoun interpretation in contexts such as (36a). This is not the case, however. Sentences such as (36b-c) do not allow a bound pronoun interpretation. The reason is that the A-disjointness requirement is violated in these sentences.

(36) b. *Meiren$_i$ bu xihuan ta$_i$
nobody not like him
'Nobody does not like him.'

c. *Meiren$_i$ hui xihuan ta$_i$
nobody will like him
'Nobody will like him.'

The unavailability of bound pronoun reading in sentences like (36b-c) clearly indicates that the A-disjointness requirement is not subject to a minimality effect.

We now turn to the study of anaphoric expressions and their interaction with bound pronouns.

2. CASE 2: LONG AND SHORT DISTANCE ANAPHORIC RELATIONS

2.1. Binding of anaphors by the first potential antecedent

In Chinese, there are two types of anaphors, the long-distance anaphor ziji and the short-distance anaphor taziji.

(37) a. Zhang$_i$ hen xihuan ziji$_i$/taziji$_i$.
Zhang very like self/himself
'Zhang likes self/himself.'

b. Zhang$_i$ hen xihuan ziji$_i$/taziji$_i$ de mama.
Zhang very like self/himself DE mother
'Zhang likes self/himself's mother.'

c. Zhang$_i$ shuo ziji$_i$/taziji$_i$ xihuan.
Zhang say self/himself like
'Zhang said that self/himself liked (it).'

d. Zhang$_i$ dui ziji$_i$/taziji$_i$ shuo tamen xihuan.
Zhang to self/himself say they like
'Zhang said to self/himself that they liked (it).'

e. Zhang$_i$ renwei Mali xihuan ziji$_i$/*taziji$_i$.
Zhang think Mali like self/himself
'Zhang thinks that Mary likes self/himself.'

f. Zhang$_i$ zhidao Mali renwei ziji$_i$/*taziji$_i$ xihuan.
Zhang know Mali think self/himself like
'Zhang knows that Mary thinks that self/himself likes (it).'

Although ziji and taziji differ with respect to the domain within which they must seek an antecedent, they share the property that they must be bound by the first potential antecedent. Consider sentence (38a) for instance.

(38) a. Zhang, $baba_i$ xihuan $ziji_i$/$taziji_i$.
Zhang father like self/himself
'Zhang, $father_i$ likes $himself_i$.'
b. *$Zhang_i$, baba xihuan $ziji_i$/$taziji_i$.
Zhang father like self/himself
'$Zhang_i$, father likes $himself_i$.'

In (38a), either the subject or the topic are possible antecedents for the anaphors. The anaphors, however, can only be coindexed with the closer NP, the subject (see Tang (1989)). In (39), on the other hand, the subject NP jiu 'alcohol' cannot serve as an antecedent for the anaphors, which in Chinese require a [+human] antecedent. As such the first potential antecedent must be the topic NP.

(39) $Zhang_i$, jiu haile $ziji_i$/$taziji_i$.
Zhang alcohol hurt self/himself
'$Zhang_i$, alcohol hurt $himself_i$.'

2.2. Raising of long-distance anaphors

The observation according to which anaphors in Chinese require to be bound by the first potential antecedent conflicts with the existence of long-distance anaphors in this language. In sentence (37f), for instance, the long-distance anaphor can be bound by either Mali or Zhang. Clearly, when it is bound by Zhang, it is not related to the first potential antecedent.

(37) f. $Zhang_i$ zhidao Mali renwei $ziji_i$/*$taziji_i$ xihuan.
Zhang know Mali think self/himself like
'Zhang knows that Mary thinks that self/himself likes (it).'

This conflict can be solved if it is assumed that long-distance anaphors raise at LF to an A'-position in order to get identified with their antecedents locally (see Lebeaux (1983), Chomsky (1986b), Battistella (1987), Cole et al. (1988), Huang and Tang (1988)). For the purpose of our discussion, we could assume that the anaphor raises at LF and adjoins to the predicate (VP) of the clause containing the subject antecedent. In sentence (40), for instance, the anaphor could be raised and adjoined to the VP of the embedded clause (41a) or the matrix clause (41b):

(40) [Zhang shuo [Mali renwei [ziji zui congming]]].
'Zhang said Mary thought self is most clever.'

(41) a. [Zhang shuo [Mali ziji$_i$ renwei [x$_i$ zui congming]]].
Zhang say Mali self think most clever
b. [Zhang ziji$_i$ shuo [Mali renwei [x$_i$ zui congming]]].
Zhang self say Mali think most clever

In (41a), the anaphor is bound by the first potential antecedent Mali and in (41b) by Zhang.[19]

The interaction between anaphors and pronouns provides direct support for the existence of this anaphor-raising process. Recall that for speakers C, pronouns must be A'-free within the least CFC containing a c-commanding subject. After ziji undergoes raising at LF, it ends up in an A'-position. As such, we expect the raised anaphor not to be able to bind the pronoun in case both elements occur within the domain D. This indeed is the case as ilustrated by the unacceptability of (42) for these speakers:

(42) *Zhang$_i$ dui ziji$_i$ shuo [ta$_i$ hen youqian].
Zhang to self say he very rich
'Zhang said to self that he was rich.'

After ziji raises at LF, (42) has the structure in (43):

(43) [$_{CP1}$ Zhang$_i$ ziji$_i$ dui x$_i$ shuo [$_{CP2}$ ta$_i$ hen youqian]].
Zhang self to say he very rich

In (43), the domain where the pronoun must be A'-free is the matrix clause since it is the least CFC containing a subject and the pronoun. In this domain, however, the pronoun is A'-bound by the raised ziji. Sentence (42) thus is unacceptable.

Raising of the anaphoric element also straightforwardly accounts for the unacceptability of sentences (44a-b) for these speakers:

(44) a. *Zhang$_i$ zhidao [ziji$_i$ xihuan [ta$_i$de nu pengyou]].
Zhang know self like his girl friend
'Zhang knows that self likes his girl friend.'
b. *Zhang$_i$ shuo [ziji$_i$ juede [ta$_i$ hen youqian]].
Zhang say self feel he very rich
'Zhang said that self felt he was rich.'

In this respect, it is worth noting that raising of anaphors at LF applies successive cyclically. Assuming that the anaphor raises successive cyclically, the unacceptability of (45a) for these speakers which have the LF representation in (45b), is expected:

(45) a. *Zhang$_i$ shuo Lisi dui ziji$_i$ shuo ta$_i$ hen hao.
Zhang say Lisi to self say he very good
'Zhang said that Lisi said to self that he was good.'

b. [$_{CP1}$ Zhang$_i$ [$_{VP}$ ziji$_i$ [$_{VP}$ shuo [$_{CP2}$ Lisi [$_{VP}$ t$_i$ [$_{VP}$ dui x$_i$ shuo [$_{CP3}$ ta$_i$ hen hao]]]]]]
Zhang self say Lisi to say he very good

In (45b), the pronoun is A'-bound by the intermediate trace t left by the raised anaphor in the relevant domain which is CP2. As such the A'-disjointness requirement is violated. This accounts for the unaccceptability of (45a). On the other hand, assuming that the anaphor raises in one swoop to the matrix clause, the unacceptability of (45a) would not be accounted for since the anaphor would be free in the relevant domain.

A confirmation of the successive cyclic application of the anaphor raising is provided by the unacceptability of sentence (46) for speakers C:

(46) *Zhang$_i$ shuo Lisi dui ziji$_i$de mama shuo ta$_i$ hen hao.
Zhang say Lisi to self mother say he very good
'Zhang said that Lisi said to self's mother that he was good.'

The unacceptability of (46) can be accounted for in case the anaphor is raised successive cyclically to the VP of CP2 first and then to VP of CP1 as in (47). The pronoun will be A'-bound by the intermediate trace in CP2.

(47) [$_{CP1}$ Zhang$_i$[$_{VP}$ ziji$_i$[$_{VP}$ shuo[$_{CP2}$ Lisi [$_{VP}$ t$_i$ [$_{VP}$ dui x$_i$ mama shuo [$_{CP3}$ ta$_i$
Zhang self say Lisi to mother say he
hen hao]]]]]]
very good

On the other hand, the one swoop movement of the anaphor would leave no intermediate trace in CP2. No violation would occur. Sentence (46) incorrectly would be expected to be acceptable.

Sentence (46) is interesting for one more reason. Since the anaphor does not c-command the pronoun at S-Structure, the unacceptability of this sentence cannot be accounted for by only considering its S-Structure representation. Its LF representation which encodes the successive raising of the anaphor ought to be taken into account. This provides another evidence for the application of movement at LF.

We indicated that a pronoun cannot be coindexed with a long-distance anaphor which occurs within the domain in which the pronoun ought to be A'-free. This account leads us to expect a pronoun to be bound by a long-distance anaphor which occurs outside this domain. This is the case. In sentences (48a-b), the domain where the pronoun must be A'-free is the embedded clause. The raising of ziji at LF occurs outside the embedded clause. Sentences (48a-b) therefore obey the A'-disjointness requirement and are acceptable for these speakers.[20]

(48) a. [Zhangsan$_i$ dui ziji$_i$ shuo [$_\alpha$Mali hen xihuan ta$_i$]].
Zhangsan to self say Mali very like him
'Zhangsan told himself that Mary likes him.'
b. [Zhangsan$_i$ dui ziji$_i$ shuo [$_\alpha$Mali zhidao [ta$_i$ hen ben]]].
Zhangsan to self say Mali know he very stupid
'Zhangsan told himself that Mary knew that he was stupid.'

2.2. Minimality and long-distance anaphors

We said so far that the A'-disjointness requirement regulates the interaction between pronouns and long-distance anaphors. Since the A'-disjointness requirement on pronouns displays a minimality effect, we expect that this minimality effect would also manifest itself in the interaction between pronouns and long-distance anaphors. In other words, we expect the binding of the pronoun by the anaphor to be more acceptable in case an A'-binder intervenes between the anaphor and the pronoun.

(49) [$_D$ ... long-distance anaphor$_i$ ... A'-element$_k$ ... pronoun$_i$ ...]

This expectation seems to be fulfilled. A modal intervening between the anaphor and the pronoun, for instance, makes it easier for the pronoun to be bound by the anaphor. This is illustrated in sentences (50a-c), which minimally contrast with sentences (42) and (44a-b), repeated as (51) for convenience.

(50) a. Zhang$_i$ zhidao ziji$_i$ <u>hui</u> xihuan ta$_i$de nu pengyou.
Zhang know self will like his girl friend
'Zhang knows that self will like his girl friend.'
b. Zhang$_i$ shuo ziji$_i$ juede ta$_i$ <u>hui</u> hen youqian.
Zhang say self feel he will very rich
'Zhang said that self felt he would be rich.'
c. Zhang$_i$ dui ziji$_i$ shuo ta$_i$ <u>hui</u> hen youqian.
Zhang to self say he will very rich
'Zhang said to self that he would be rich.'

(51) a. *Zhang$_i$ zhidao ziji$_i$ xihuan ta$_i$de nu pengyou.
Zhang know self like his girl friend
'Zhang knows that self likes his girl friend.'
b. *Zhang$_i$ shuo ziji$_i$ juede ta$_i$ hen youqian.
Zhang say self feel he very rich
'Zhang said that self felt he was rich.'
c. *Zhang$_i$ dui ziji$_i$ shuo ta$_i$ hen youqian.
Zhang to self say he very rich
'Zhang said to self that he was rich.'

We have shown in this section that an A'-binder intervening between an anaphor and the pronoun it binds salvages the relation betwen the two elements. This intervention effect may be accounted for by the minimality requirement which constrains A'-disjointness. This clearly supports raising of the long-distance anaphor at LF.

Furthermore, since long-distance anaphors are raised at LF, we expect them to affect the relation betwen a pronoun and its antecedent. That is, we expect an illicit relation between a pronoun and its antecedent to become licit in case a long-distance anaphor comes to intervene between these two elements (thanks to H. van Riemsdijk for pointing out this prediction to us):

(52) [$_D$ ... A'-antecedent$_i$ ... long-distance anaphor$_k$ ... pronoun$_i$ ...]

This expectation is also fulfilled. The non-licit relation between the pronoun and its quantificational antecedent in (53a) becomes licit when a long-distance anaphor intervenes between them as in (53b):

(53) a. *Zhang renwei meiren$_i$ shuo ta$_i$ zui hao.
Zhang think nobody say he most good
'Zhang thinks that nobody said that he was the best.'
b. Zhang$_j$ renwei meiren$_i$ dui ziji$_j$ shuo ta$_i$ zui hao.
Zhang think nobody to self say he most good
'Zhang thinks that nobody said to self that he was the best.'

Recall that the anaphor is raised successive cyclically. As such the anaphor in (53b) leaves an intermediate trace in the intermediate clause (see (53c)). This trace is the first A'-element with respect to which the pronoun must be A'-free. The minimality requirement thus is satisfied.

(53) c. [$_{CP1}$ Zhang$_j$ ziji$_i$ renwei [$_{CP2}$ meiren$_i$ t$_j$ dui x$_j$ shuo [$_{CP3}$ ta$_i$ zui hao]]].
Zhang self think nobody to say he most good

The same analysis accounts for the contrast between (54a) and (54b):

(54) a. *Zhang$_j$ renwei meiren$_i$ dui ta$_j$ mama shuo ta$_i$ zui hao.
Zhang think nobody to his mother say he most good
'Zhang thinks that nobody said to his mother that he was the best.'
b. Zhang$_j$ renwei meiren$_i$ dui ziji$_j$ mama shuo ta$_i$ zui hao.
Zhang think nobody to self mother say he most good
'Zhang thinks that nobody said to self's mother that he was the best.'

2.3. Non-obligatory raising of short-distance anaphors

The discussion of long-distance anaphors provided extensive evidence for the LF raising of these elements. This evidence can be used as direct testing grounds for whether or not short-distance anaphors have to raise at LF. If short-distance anaphors have to raise at LF like long-distance anaphors, we would expect them to enter into A'-disjointness with pronouns. On the other hand, if short distance anaphors do not have to raise at LF, we would not expect such an A'-disjointness effect. It turns out that replacing the long-distance anaphor with the short-distance anaphor in (52) makes the sentences acceptable:

(55) a. Zhang$_i$ zhidao taziji$_i$ xihuan ta$_i$de nu pengyou.
Zhang know himself like his girl friend
'Zhang knows that himself likes his girl friend.'
b. Zhang$_i$ shuo taziji$_i$ juede ta$_i$ hen youqian.
Zhang say himself feel he very rich
'Zhang said that himself felt he was rich.'
c. Zhang$_i$ dui taziji$_i$ shuo ta$_i$ hen youqian.
Zhang say himself say he very rich
'Zhang said to himself that he was rich.'

The contrast between the acceptability of (55) and the unacceptability of (52) clearly indicates that short-distance anaphors, contrary to long-distance anaphors, do not have to raise at LF.

The facts illustrated in (55) indicated that short-distance anaphors do not have to raise at LF. Notice that these facts are compatible with an optional raising of short-distance anaphors. If this is the case there will be two derivations corresponding to sentences (55). In the first derivation, raising of the short-distance anaphor applies. This derivation will not be well-formed since the relation between the pronoun and the short-distance anaphor would violate the A'-disjointness requirement. In the second derivation, raising of the short-distance anaphor does not apply. This derivation will be well-formed: no A'-disjointness requirement will be violated.

Unfortunately, due to the domain of the A'-disjointness requirement and the nature of short-distance anaphors, it is hard to construct an example to distinguish between the two possibilities. We thus leave open the issue of whether short-distance anaphors can be raised at LF.[21]

Recapitulating, the discussion of anaphoric expressions in Chinese indicated that long-distance anaphors are subject to an obligatory raising process at LF. Short-distance anaphors, on the other hand, need not undergo such a raising process. Evidence for this distinction was drawn from the interaction of these anaphors with respect to pronouns.[22] We saw that this interaction is constrained by the disjointness requirement and the minimality effect[23] and that it can only be accounted for at a post S-Structure level after anaphoric expressions undergo raising.

3. CONCLUSION

In this paper, we discussed two distinct interpretive relations: the relation between bound pronouns and their antecedent and the relation between anaphors and their binder. These interpretive relations share a certain number of characteristics:

i) They involve non-argument-positions (A'-positions): either the antecedent or the dependent is in an A'-position.

ii) They are sensitive to a minimality effect.

iii) They cannot be generated at the level where linear order is encoded (Surface Structure).

iv) They cannot be generated at the level where overt movement is encoded (S-Structure).

v) They cannot be generated at the level where thematic relations are encoded (D-Structure).

On the other hand, these relations can be captured by postulating a covert extraction process applying at a post-S-Structure level. We took the existence of such a covert extraction process to provide evidence for the characterization of LF component as an autonomous level of gramatical representations and for a transformational mapping between S-Structure and LF representations. This is what we set up to investigate at the onset of this work.

NOTES

*This paper is based on Aoun and Li (1988). We would like to thank James Huang and Edwin Williams for illuminating comments. We would like to thank Sylvia Chen, Yu-chin Chien, Grace Feng, Emily Huang, James Huang, Horng-yi Lee, Tim Shi, Yu-chin Tsai, Cathy Wei, Chong-ren Wu, You-wen Ye, Sheng-tai Zhang for their help with the data.

[1] Literature of this type is cited in Montalbetti (1984).

[2] According to the comments of some of the native speakers, (8a-b) "sound more like English." In this respect, it will be helpful to check with speakers of different ages.

[3] Such data is discussed in Aoun (1986) and Huang (1987).

[4] The contrasts that we illustrate in sentences (9a-b) and throughout this paper are the sharpest with quantifiers such as <u>meiren</u> 'no one'. The more "referential" the quantifier is, the less sharp the contrast is. Thus, the contrast between sentences (ia) and (ib) involving the quantifier <u>every child</u> is less sharp than the one between (9a) and (9b).

(i) a. Meige xiaohaizi$_i$ dou shuo ta$_i$ de le jiang.
every child all say he get ASP prize
'Every child said that he got the prize.'
b. Meige xiaohaizi$_i$ dou shuo wo xihuan ta$_i$
every child all say I like him
'Every child said that I liked him.'

Similarly, the contrast between (iia) and (iib) involving <u>who</u> is shaprter than the contrast between (iiia) and (iiib) involving <u>which child</u>.

(ii) a. Shei$_i$ shuo ta$_i$ de le jiang?
who say he get ASP prize
'Who said he got the prize?'
b. Shei$_i$ shuo wo xihuan ta$_i$?
who say I like him
'Who said that I like him?'

(iii) a. Nage xiaohaizi$_i$ shuo ta$_i$ de le jiang?
which child say he get ASP prize
'Which child said he got the prize?'
b. Nage xiaohaizi$_i$ shuo wo xihuan ta$_i$?
which child say I like him
'Which child said that I like him?'

Effects similar to the one discussed in this note are relevant for the interpretation of bound pronouns in other languages such as Spanish. See Montalbetti (1984).

[5] It is not possible to argue for Chinese that the pronoun <u>ta</u> cannot be bound by a quantificational element in the contexts where a non-overt element can be used as bound variables see (i) and (ii). It is not possible either to assume that a pronoun cannot be bound by a quantifier in contexts where an anaphor occurs (see (i) and (iii)). The reader is referred to Aoun (1986) for the discussion of (i-iii) and further relevant facts:

(i) Meigeren$_i$ dou shuo ta$_i$ baba you qian.
everyone all say he father have money
'Everyone said that his father is rich.'

(ii) Meigeren$_i$ dou shuo e$_i$ baba you qian.
everyone all say he father have money
'Everyone said that his father is rich.'

(iii) a. Meigeren$_i$ dou shuo ziji$_i$ baba you qian.
everyone all say he father have money
'Everyone said that his father is rich.'

b. Meigeren$_i$ dou shuo taziji$_i$ baba you qian.
everyone all say he father have money
'Everyone said that his father is rich.'

[6] It is clear that the choice of verbs affects the naturalness of a bound pronoun interpretation, in Chinese and English for that matter. Examples such as (ia-b) are pragmatically odd:

(i) a. Meigeren dou yiwei ta lai le.
everyone all think he come ASP
'Everyone thought that he came.'
b. Meigeren dou renwei ta mai le dongxi.
everyone all think he buy ASP thing
'Everyone thought he bought (some)thing.'

[7] The first cases of A'-disjointness applying to switch-reference is discussed in Finer (1985). In Borer (1984) and McCloskey (1989), the notion of A'-disjointness is used to account for the behavior of resumptive pronouns in Modern Hebrew and Irish.
[8] The behavior of overt pronominal expressions ta here is similar to kare in Japanese. As indicated by Hoji and Saito (19xx), kare can never be bound by a QP (see Hoji 1985, Aoun and Hornstein 1986).
[9] From what we said so far, it seems that the A-disjointness requirement is not subject to dialectal variation.
[10] For non-overt categories, the notion of minimality has been introduced in Chomsky (1986a) and reconsidered in Rizzi (1990).
[11] Note that a sentence such as (i) is ill-formed even though a modal intervenes between the pronoun and its antecedent (thanks to E. Williams for pointing out the relevance of this sentence):

(i) *[meigeren$_i$ x_i dou hui$_i$ xihuan ta$_i$]
everyone all will like him
'Everyone will like him.'

The reason is that it violates the A-disjointness requirement (13a): the pronoun is A-bound by the variable left by the raised quantifier.
[12] Following Huang (1982), we assume that A-not-A questions undergo raising at LF.
[13] For the reasons mentioned in Huang (1982), it is important to assume that wh-elements raise at LF. To mention some, the raising approach can distinguish between wh-arguments (who, what) and wh-adjuncts (why, how) with respect to the locality conditions. Furthermore, we will see in section 1.2.4. that these wh-operators leave intermediate traces relevant for the working of minimality. The same facts discussed here, however, can also be captured in an analysis that assumes the Question operator, rather than the wh-element, undergoes raising (see Aoun and Li 1990).
[14] Intervention by negation and negative polarity items seems to be better than intervention by negation alone in improving the acceptability of a bound pronoun.
[15] James Huang (personal communication) pointed out to us that the intervention effect of modals seems to be stronger than the intervention effect of negation. We have no account for this contrast.
[16] Note that in the English counterpart of (23), the negative element can have scope over the subject quantifier. For independent reasons we need not discuss here, Aoun and Li (to appear) argue that a bare quantifier can adjoin to a non-thematic position. Since subjects in English, contrary to subjects in Chinese, are in a non-thematic position (see Aoun and Li (1989)), the quantifier can adjoin to this subject NP, as in the representation (i):

(i) $[_{IP}\ \text{not}_i\ [_{NP}\ Q_j\ [_{NP}\ x_j \ldots]\ [_{I'}\ x_i\ VP]]]$

Representation (i), which does not violate the MBR, generates the wide scope reading of the negative element in English.

[17] It is useful to point out that the MBR is irrelevant in (25) since it is a constraint on variables derived by movement rules and not on pronouns.
[18] Some speakers, however, find that sentences (i-ii) are worse than (34b). In fact, for these speakers, these sentences seem to be treated on a par with (9):

(i) Meigeren$_i$ dou dui meigeren shuo ta$_i$ de le jiang.
'Everyone said to everyone that he got the prize.'

(ii) Meiren$_i$ dui meigeren shuo ta$_i$ de le jiang.
'Nobody said to everyone that he got the prize.'

The difference between (34b) and (i-ii) is that the intervening QP is a non-human NP in (34b) and a human NP in (i-ii). The pronoun he in Chinese can only be coindexed with a human NP. This suggests that pronouns used as bound variables seek to be bound by the first potential A'-binder, in the same way that lexical anaphors seek to be bound by the first potential antecedent as discussed in section 2.1. If this is the case, the intervening QP should bind the pronoun in (i-ii). However, the minimal disjointness requirement forces them to be disjoint from each other. In other words, in sentences (i-ii), there is a clash between the search for the first potential A'-binder and the disjointness requirement.
[19] Notice that after raising, the first potential antecedent for the raised anaphor is still baba in (40b):

(i) *[$_{IP}$Zhangsan$_i$ [$_{VP1}$ baba [$_{VP2}$ ziji$_i$ [$_{VP2}$ xihuan x$_i$]]]]
Zhangsan father self like

In Aoun and Li (1989), it is assumed, following Kuroda (1985), that in double subject constructions in Chinese, the internal subject is generated in the SPEC position of VP and the external subject in the SPEC of I'. The fact that anaphors have to be bound by the internal subject in double subject constructions follows from the assumption that the anaphor is raised and adjoined to the predicate of the clause containing the antecedent (VP2 in (i)). In the spirit of Koopman and Sportiche (1988), we are assuming that in (i), VP2 counts as the predicate and VP1 is the equivalent of a proposition since it dominates a predicate and a subject. See Katada (1988) for further relevant discussions concerning the LF raising of anaphoric expressions.
[20] See Katada (1988) for discussions of the relevant facts in Japanese.
[21] See Huang and Tang's (1988) account of anaphor-raising in terms of feature assignment, Pica (1987) and Katada (1988) in terms of the ECP.
[22] Modals, negation and other A'-elements are relevant to the A'-disjointness requirement applying to pronouns. These elements do not have an intervention effect on the binding of anaphors by their antecedents. Even though modals and negation intervene between the anaphor and its antecedent in (i-ii), the sentences are still acceptable:

(i) Ta hui hen xihuan ziji.
he will very like self
'He will like himself.'

(ii) Ta bu xihuan ziji.
he not like self
'He does not like himself.'

This discrepancy between pronouns and anaphors is not surprising. Anaphors, contrary to pronouns, require an antecedent in an A-position: they are sensitive to intervening A-elements as mentioned earlier. Another difference between pronouns and anaphors is the fact that the latter are sensitive to the kind of A-element intervening. As mentioned earlier, the first appropriate antecedent in sentence (39) (repeated here) is the topic Zhang and not the subject jiu 'alcohol' since anaphors in Chinese require a [+human] antecedent.

(39) Zhang$_i$, jiu haile ziji$_i$/taziji$_i$
Zhang alcohol hurt self/himself
'Zhang$_i$, alcohol hurt himself$_i$.'

Pronouns, on the other hand, are not sensitive to the kind of A'-element intervening. For the purpose of disjointness, any A'-element, even elements that cannot serve as appropriate antecedents for the pronouns (such as modals), seem to be relevant. Since the minimality effect between pronouns and A'-elements involves a disjointness effect, one may assume that the nature of intervening elements is taken into account only when a search for an antecedent is involved: anaphors, but not pronouns, need an antecedent. This speculation is reminicent of Huang's (1982) suggestion according to which the notion of accessibility plays a role in defining the binding domain for anaphors but not for pronouns.

Languages do differ, however, as to whether the contents of the A'-element should be considered in the application of the disjointness requirements. See Ouhalla (1990), Reinholtz (1991).

[23] Rizzi (1990) assumes that minimality applies only to government relations, not binding relations. In a forthcoming work, we will compare these two approaches.

REFERENCES

Aoun, J. (1986) "Bound Pronouns in Chinese," *NELS* 16.

Aoun, J. & N. Hornstein. (1986) "Bound and Referential Pronouns," ms., University of Southern California and University of Maryland.

Aoun, J. & Y.-H. A. Li. (1988) "Minimal Disjointness," *Proceedings of WCCFL VII*

Aoun, J. & Y.-H. A. Li (1989) "Constituency and Scope," *Linguistic Inquiry*, 20.2

Aoun, J. & Y.-H. A. Li (1990) "*Wh*-elements In-Situ: Syntax of LF," ms., University of Southern California, Los Angeles.

Aoun, J. & Y.-H. A. Li. (1993) *Syntax of Scope*, MIT Press.

Aoun, J. & D. Sportiche. (1983) "On the Formal Theory of Government," *The Linguistic Review* 2, 211-236.

Battistella, E. (1987) "Chinese Reflexivization," ms., University of Alabama at Birmingham.

Borer, H. (1984) "Restrictive Relatives in Modern Hebrew," *Natural Language & Linguistic Theory*, 2.2.

Chomsky, N. (1977) *Essays on Form and Interpretation*, North-Holland, Amsterdam.

Chomsky, N. (1986a) *Barriers*, MIT Press, Cambridge, Massachusetts.

Chomsky, N. (1986b) *Knowledge of Language*, Praeger, New York.

Chomsky, N. & H. Lasnik. (1977) "Filters and Control," *Linguistic Inquiry*, 8.3, 425-504.

Cole, P., Gabrilla Hermon and Li-may Sung. (1988) "Principles and Parameters of Long-distance Reflexives," paper presented at the 3rd Ohio State Conference on

Chinese Linguistics, Columbus, Ohio.
Finer, D. (1985) "The Syntax of Switch-Reference," *Linguistic Inquiry*, 16.1, 35-56.
Hoji, H. (1985) "Logical Form Constraints and Configurational Structures in Japanese," Doctoral dissertation, University of Massachusetts, Amherst.
Huang, C-T. James (1982) "Logical Relations in Chinese and the Theory of Grammar," Doctoral dissertation, MIT, Cambridge, Massachusetts.
Huang, C-T. James (1988) "Comments on Hasegawa's Paper," in *Proceedings of Japanese Syntax Workshop: Issues on Empty categories* edited by W. Tawa abd N. Nakayama, Japanese Program, Connecticut College, New London, Connecticut, pp.77-93.
Huang, C-T. & C-Z. Tang. (1988) "On the Local Nature of the Long-distance Reflexives in Chinese," *NELS* 19.
Katada, F. (1988) "What can Long-distance Anaphors Say about Operator Systems of Syntax," *NELS* 19.
Koopman, H. & D. Sportiche. (1982) "Variables and the Bijection Principle," *The Linguistic Review* 2.2. 139-160.
Koopman, H. & D. Sportiche. (1988) "Subjects," m.s., University of California, Los Angeles.
Kurata, J. (1986) "Asymmetries in Japanese," m.s., University of Massachusetts, Amherst.
Kuroda, S. Y. (1985) "Whether We Agree or Not," ms., University of California, San Diego. to appear in *Linguisticae Investigationes*
Lebeaux, D. (1983) "A Distributional Difference between Reciprocals and Reflexives," *Linguistic Inquiry*, 14.4, 723-729.
Linebarger, M. C. (1981) "Negative Polarity and Grammatical Representation," *Linguistics and Philosophy* 10, 325-387.
May, R. (1977) "The Grammar of Quantification," Doctoral dissertation, MIT, Cambridge, Massachusetts.
May, R. (1985) *Logical Form: Its Structure and Derivation*, MIT Press, Cambridge, Massachusetts.
McCloskey, James. (1989) "Resumptive Pronouns, A'-binding and Levels of Representation in Irish," to appear in *The Syntax of Modern Celtic Languages*, edited by Randall Hendrick, *Syntax and Semantics*, Vol. 23, Academic Press.
Montalbetti, M. (1984) "After Binding," Doctoral dissertation, MIT, Cambridge, Massachusetts.
Ouhalla, J. (1990) "Sentential Negation, Relativized Minimality and the Aspectual Status of Auxiliaries," *Linguistic Review*, 7.2, 183-231.
Pica, P. (1987) "On the Nature of the Reflexivization Cycle," *NELS* 17.
Progovac, L. "A Binding Approach to Polarity Sensitivity," Doctoral dissertation, University of Southern California, Los Angeles.
Reinholtz, Charlotte. (1992) "Verb Second, Negation and Minimality," paper presented at WCCFL 11, University of California, Los Angeles.
Rizzi, L. (1990) *Relativized Minimality*, MIT Press, Cambridge, MA.
Saito, M. & H. Hoji (1983) "Weak Crossover amd Move α in Japanese," *Natural Language and Linguistic Theory* 1, 245–259.
Tang, C-C. (1989) "Chinese Reflexives," *Natural Language and Linguistic Theory*, 7.1, 93-122.
Vergnaud, J. R. (1987) "Reformalization of Phrase Structures," paper presented at *GLOW*.

EDWIN WILLIAMS

REMARKS ON LINGUISTIC SCOPE COMMENTS ON AOUN AND LI'S PAPER

[Editor's note: Regrettably, Aoun and Li did not receive this commentary in time to reply.]

Aoun and Li's account of various facts of Chinese pronoun usage depends on a peculiar but widespread notion of linguistic scope. I will first address the general notion of scope in natural language, and then treat their analysis in the light of the conclusions drawn.

Aoun and Li use two features of the widespread notion of linguistic scope. The first is the notion that scope assignment is a transformational rule ("QR"), which derives the level of representation called LF, and their two principle claims about the analysis of Chinese are given as evidence for that rule and that representation. In addition, they crucially use a second feature of the widely held view of linguistic scope: they assume that QR is responsible for assigning scope to all elements that have scope: negation, quantified NPs, modals, and adverbs.

I think the first assumption is incorrect, and have given arguments against it elsewhere (see, for example, Williams (1986); but I think in fact that this assumption is not crucial to the A&L analysis, and that it would be straightforward to reconstruct it without it. But I think this second assumption, that QR applies wherever scope optains, is a grave mistake, and crucial to the analysis. I will first consider the notion of linguistic scope in general, and then turn to Aoun and Li's two principle claims about it.

1. QUANTIFICATION IN LANGUAGE

What is the evidence that things like modals, negation, and adverbs are assigned scope at all? To answer this, one must answer what it means to assign scope in the first place.

Quantified NPs in argument position can be assigned arbitrarily wide scope. For example, with some strain, it is possible to understand the following sentence as a statement involving multiple students and professors, indicating that the embedded subject has scope over the matrix subject:

(1) At one time or another, some student or other has claimed that each of those professors is incompetent.

The sentence requires a special intonation perhaps to get this reading, but the reading is possible.

But, consider the following:

(2) John thinks Bill must have left.

No amount of special intonation will render this the equivalent of:

(3) John must think Bill has left.

This is not simply a matter of a lexical variability in the scope potential; such certainly exists, and distinguishes, for example, the wide scope of *each* from the relatively narrow scopes of *every*. The failure of *must* to take matrix scope is categorical. The fact is, modals do not undergo QR; that is to say, they are not subject to a rule which assigns them some arbitrarily large containing phrase as their scope.

Now, modals do have scope, and their scope interacts with the scope of quantified NPs. How is that scope determined?

Modals get scope by the Head Scope Rule of Williams (1984) (see also Williams (1994). This rule says, a head of a phrase has scope over the whole phrase. Since a modal is the head of S, the modal has scope, for example, over the subject:

(4) No one must be there

This has a reading in which *no one* is subordinate in scope to *must*. In fact, (4) is ambiguous—it has in addition to the reading just indicated, a reading in which *no one* has wide scope. How can we distinguish the two readings, if the scope of the modal is fixed as the projection of S? By giving *No one* ambiguous scope:

(5) a. $[_S$ No one must leave]
b. $[_S$ No one $[_S$ t must leave]]

So, we now have two scope rules: a quantified NP argument is assigned some arbitrary containing phrase as its scope (Argument Scope) and a head of a phrase has its phrase as scope (Head Scope). There is one further type of scope, Adjunct Scope. An adjunct has as its scope what it is adjoined to. This is illustrated below:

(6) a. Quickly everyone arrived
b. Everyone will have quickly arrived

In (a), *quickly* is adjoined to S, and so has S as its scope, and is interpreted as superior to *everyone*. In (b) on the otherhand, *quickly* is adjoined to the VP, and so is strictly subordinate to *everyone*.

The Head Scope Rule and the Adjunct Scope Rule interact in an interesting way when an adjunct is adjoined to a head. The adjunct has the head in its scope, and the head has its phrase as its scope, so by transitivity of scope, the adjunct can have the phrase as its scope:

(7) Everyone [will quickly] arrive.

Here, quickly is adjoined to *will*, the projection of *will* (= S) contains *everyone*, and so *quickly* can have wider scope than *everyone*.

This view of scope is strongly supported by an analysis of ECP phenomena along the lines of Williams (1994). There it is argued the ECP is best understood as a licensing condition stated in terms of scope.

The relation between the ECP and scope has been acknowledged since Kayne (1981), who observed subject-object assymtries in scope assignment. The ECP has been understood as a syntactic constraint which applies by extension to the syntactic rule of QR. I would like to explore a different idea about the relation. First, I will understand the ECP not as a constraint, but as a licencing condition. And second, rather than using a constraint on movement to limit scope, I will rather understand the ECP to be a licensing condition on pure movement stated in terms of scope.

I think this view of scope can give insight into one of the empirical cornerstones of the ECP, the relative ability of adjuncts over arguments to move out of wh-islands and various other contexts ("long movement"):

(8) a. ? Which man did John wonder [which woman would like t]
b. *Why did John wonder [which woman would leave t]

This behavior has a straightforward explanation in terms of scope. Specifically, we have the following licencing condition;

(9) The Scope ECP (SECP):
An item can be licensed in displaced position if that item in its base position could have been assigned scope corresponding to that position.

Principle (9) is not a primitive principle, but will serve the present purpose; see Williams (1994) for a discussion of the status of (9), and of the principles from which it is derived.

Crucially, an adjunct, in its base position, can be assigned scope no higher than its sister; hence, it cannot be licensed in displaced position by scope assignment. Since an argument can be assigned indefinitely wide scope, it can be licensed in displaced position by scope assignment.

Of course, even an adjunct can be licensed in a moved position higher than it could be assigned scope:

(10) How slowly did you say [he sang t].

But here, the movement can be licensed by other means—specifically subjacent movement (or antecedent government). Hence, (9) is a licensing condition, not a covert prohibition: it does NOT say that a displaced item is ungrammatical if it is not licensed by scope assignment. (10) shows clearly that scope assignment and movement conditions cannot be identified; rather, scope assignment is one means of licensing movement.

A telling confirmation of this approach comes from the phenomena of "scope reconstruction":

(11) How many books do they think you published t.

a. They think $[_{S_i}$ you published $[_i$ QUANT books]] What is QUANT?
scope of QUANT

b. $[_{S_i}$ They think you published $[_i$ QUANT books]] What is QUANT?
scope of QUANT

This example is ambiguous in the way indicated in (a) and (b)—the quantifier *how many* can take matrix or embedded scope, giving two distinct readings; in one (a), there is no existing set of books except in their thoughts (narrow scope); in the other reading, there is an existing set of books (wide scope).

Longobardi (1985) observed that the narrow scope reading is blocked by weak islands:

(12) a. How many books do they think they will publish t.
b. How many books do they wonder whether they should publish t.
(adapted from Kroch (1989))

[QUANT books] (V (...))	a,b
V ([QUANT books] (...))	a,*b

Example (12b) is not ambigous, lacking the narrow scope reading. There is persuasive evidence against a process of scope reconstruction (see Williams (1994)); rather, we might understand (12b) in terms of the licensing effect of (9)—in displaced position, the phrase *how many books* can be licensed either by subjacent movement (impossible in the case of (12b)), or by scope assignment; but if it is licensed by scope assignment, then we will necessarily have wide scope.

The SECP then unites the complete ungrammaticality of adjuncts under long movement due to scope properties of adjuncts, with the limitations on the scope of arguments under long movement.

Likewise of course for modals and negation. The scope laws that govern these elements depend completely on their syntactic category, and not their meaning. So, we have "modal" meaning in many adverbs, like *necessarily*, and *probably*, but their scope is adjunct scope, not the head scope of such elements as *must* and *can*. Negation is a particularly interesting case, as it can be realized in all three sorts of categories: *never* is by adjunct scope, *no one* is by Quantified argument scope, and *not* (at least the contracted form) is by head scope.

2. THE TWO CLAIMS

In light of the view of scope just outlined I will now proceed to evaluate the two claims of Aoun and Li in support of the notion of LF.

Their first claim concerns quantifier bound pronouns. For speakers that allow bound pronouns, there must be an "A-bar intervener" between the quantifier and the pronoun. The class of A-bar interveners consists of the following;

(13) modals
wh operator
negation
intermediate trace
quantifier (scope boundary)
long distance anaphor

The idea is that the quantifier-bound pronouns are subject to a condition that they be "locally A-bar free", and if the closest A-bar binder is their own binder, then they will be forced to be free from their own binder:

(14) ... Q-Antecedent$_i$ ... Modal ... pronoun$_i$ ...
*... Q-Antecedent$_i$ ... pro$_i$ ...

The evidence for the existence of LF derives from the fact each of the A-bar interveners is forced to undergo LF movement for scope assignment.

I believe that the items in (13) do not form a coherent class. As I suggested earlier, it is unlikely that modals or negation undergo any sort of long scope assignment. It seems unlikely, then, that there is a class of "A-bar" elements that includes modals and negation, but excludes, for example, matrix verbs. On these grounds alone, Aoun and Li's claim is suspicious.

Given this theoretical incoherence, one must inquire next what the basis of evidence is for the claim. It turns out to be quite suspicious as well. Seven Chinese speakers were consulted, giving three different sets of judgments. Aoun and Li have restricted themselves to what they call "dialect C", which consists of 2 speakers. Are there really three dialects? It is impossible to tell, but since data concerns quantifier bound pronouns, notorious for giving linguists data-fits, it is likely that instead of three dialects, we simply have a delicacy of judgment, with different personalities, rather than different grammars, determing the constellation of the stars.

If this is so, then it is no wonder that an A-bar intervener has the effect that it does: since it further complicates the sentence in which it appears, it will tend to muddy judgments, and especially to obscure delicate hints of ungrammaticality. So, for example, the sentences that prove that the modals are in the class of A-bar interveners have not only the modal, but also a level of embedding; hence, from a semantic point of view, there are two levels of embedding, and no comparison is made with equally complex sentences but without modals.

Given these two problems—the questionability of the existence of dialects, and the lack of controls on the complexity of the data used—I think it would be foolish to consider any conclusions more than suggestive, however interesting they may be; and given the peculiar status of the notion of A-bar intervener in the context of a reasonable notion of scope, I think the conclusion is in fact not very interesting.

Aoun and Li's second claim is that long distance anaphors undergo LF movement, thus providing further evidence for the existence of LF. The long distance anaphor can take any appropriate c-commanding subject as its antecedent; in addition, if the subject is not appropriate, it can take the topic as its antecedent.

But if the subject is an appropriate antecedent, then the topic is not available (see Aoun and Li's (ex. 38)). On these grounds, Aoun and Li assert that the closest possible antecedent must always be taken:

(15) a. *NP-topic$_i$ NP<+human subject> ... anaphor$_{human}$
b. NP-topic$_i$ NP<–human subject> ... anaphor$_{human}$

The latter claim is inconsistent with the existence of the long distance anaphor, since it typically skips over many intervening subjects. Aoun and Li resolve this problem by supposing that the long distance anaphor is capable of moving, adjoining to higher VP nodes, and the computation of its closest antecedent is done with respect to this landing site.

This movement rule is a stipulation; in fact, it is necessary to stipulate that VP is precisely the only landing site of anaphor movement. For if they do not, it will be possible for the moved anaphor to adjoin to IP, where it will be able to take the topic as its antecedent even if the subject is an appropriate antecedent, since in IP adjoined position, the topic will be the only available antecedent:

(16) *NP-topic$_i$ [$_{IP}$ anaphor$_i$ [$_{IP}$ NP<+human subject> ...]]

Given that this stipulation derives nothing besides the observed facts, I think we must regard the observed facts as still in need of explanation, as interesting as they may be, and we must conclude that the further evidence for LF and LF-deriving movement is not found here.

REFERENCES

Kayne (1981) "ECP Extensions," *Linguistic Inquiry* 12, 93–133.
Kroch A. (1989) "Amount Quantification, Referentiality, and Long Wh-movement," ms. University of Pennsylvania.
Longobardi (1985) "The Theoretical Status of the Adjunct Condition," ms. University of Venice.
Williams, E. (1986) "A Reassignment of the Functions of LF," *Linguistic Inquiry* 17, 265–299.
Williams, E. (1984) "There Insertion," *Linguistic Inquiry* 15, 13–153.
Williams, E. (1994) *Thematic Structure in Syntax*, MIT Press.

INDEX

Studies in Natural Language and Linguistic Theory

Managing Editors

Liliane Haegeman, *University of Geneva*
Joan Maling, *Brandeis University*
James McCloskey, *University of California, Santa Cruz*

Publications

1. L. Burzio: *Italian Syntax.* A Government-binding Approach. 1986.
ISBN Hb 90-277-2014-2; Pb 90-277-2015-0
2. W.D. Davies: *Choctaw Verb Agreement and Universal Grammar.* 1986.
ISBN Hb 90-277-2065-7; Pb 90-277-2142-4
3. K. É. Kiss: *Configurationality in Hungarian.* 1987.
ISBN Hb 90-277-1907-1; Pb 90-277-2456-3
4. D. Pulleyblank: *Tone in Lexical Phonology.* 1986.
ISBN Hb 90-277-2123-8; Pb 90-277-2124-6
5. L. Hellan and K. K. Christensen: *Topics in Scandinavian Syntax.* 1986.
ISBN Hb 90-277-2166-1; Pb 90-277-2167-X
6. K. P. Mohanan: *The Theory of Lexical Phonology.* 1986.
ISBN Hb 90-277-2226-9; Pb 90-277-2227-7
7. J. L. Aissen: *Tzotzil Clause Structure.* 1987.
ISBN Hb 90-277-2365-6; Pb 90-277-2441-5
8. T. Gunji: *Japanese Phrase Structure Grammar.* A Unification-based Approach. 1987. ISBN 1-55608-020-4
9. W. U. Wurzel: *Inflectional Morphology and Naturalness.* 1989
ISBN Hb 1-55608-025-5; Pb 1-55608-026-3
10. C. Neidle: *The Role of Case in Russian Syntax.* 1988 ISBN 1-55608-042-5
11. C. Lefebvre and P. Muysken: *Mixed Categories.* Nominalizations in Quechua. 1988. ISBN Hb 1-55608-050-6; Pb 1-55608-051-4
12. K. Michelson: *A Comparative Study of Lake-Iroquoian Accent.* 1988
ISBN 1-55608-054-9
13. K. Zagona: *Verb Phrase Syntax.* A Parametric Study of English and Spanish. 1988 ISBN Hb 1-55608-064-6; Pb 1-55608-065-4
14. R. Hendrick: *Anaphora in Celtic and Universal Grammar.* 1988
ISBN 1-55608-066-2
15. O. Jaeggli and K.J. Safir (eds.): *The Null Subject Parameter.* 1989
ISBN Hb 1-55608-086-7; Pb 1-55608-087-5
16. H. Lasnik: *Essays on Anaphora.* 1989
ISBN Hb 1-55608-090-5; Pb 1-55608-091-3
17. S. Steele: *Agreement and Anti-Agreement.* A Syntax of Luiseño. 1990
ISBN 0-7923-0260-5

Studies in Natural Language and Linguistic Theory

18. E. Pearce: *Parameters in Old French Syntax.* Infinitival Complements. 1990
ISBN Hb 0-7923-0432-2; Pb 0-7923-0433-0
19. Y.A. Li: *Order and Constituency in Mandarin Chinese.* 1990
ISBN 0-7923-0500-0
20. H. Lasnik: *Essays on Restrictiveness and Learnability.* 1990
ISBN 0-7923-0628-7; Pb 0-7923-0629-5
21. M.J. Speas: *Phrase Structure in Natural Language.* 1990
ISBN 0-7923-0755-0; Pb 0-7923-0866-2
22. H. Haider and K. Netter (eds.): *Representation and Derivation in the Theory of Grammar.* 1991 ISBN 0-7923-1150-7
23. J. Simpson: *Warlpiri Morpho-Syntax.* A Lexicalist Approach. 1991
ISBN 0-7923-1292-9
24. C. Georgopoulos: *Syntactic Variables.* Resumptive Pronouns and A' Binding in Palauan. 1991 ISBN 0-7923-1293-7
25. K. Leffel and D. Bouchard (eds.): *Views on Phrase Structure.* 1991
ISBN 0-7923-1295-3
26. C. Tellier: *Licensing Theory and French Parasitic Gaps.* 1991
ISBN 0-7923-1311-9; Pb 0-7923-1323-2
27. S.-Y. Kuroda: *Japanese Syntax and Semantics.* Collected Papers. 1992
ISBN 0-7923-1390-9; Pb 0-7923-1391-7
28. I. Roberts: *Verbs and Diachronic Syntax.* A Comparative History of English and French. 1992 ISBN 0-7923-1705-X
29. A. Fassi Fehri: *Issues in the Structure of Arabic Clauses and Words.* 1993
ISBN 0-7923-2082-4
30. M. Bittner: *Case, Scope, and Binding.* 1994 ISBN 0-7923-2649-0
31. H. Haider, S. Olsen and S. Vikner (eds.): *Studies in Comparative Germanic Syntax.* 1995 ISBN 0-7923-3280-6
32. N. Duffield: *Particles and Projections in Irish Syntax.* 1995
ISBN 0-7923-3550-3; Pb 0-7923-3674-7
33. J. Rooryck and L. Zaring (eds.): *Phrase Structure and the Lexicon.* 1996
ISBN 0-7923-3745-X
34. J. Bayer: *Directionality and Logical Form.* On the Scope of Focusing Particles and Wh-in-situ. 1996 ISBN 0-7923-3752-2
35. R. Freidin (ed.): *Current Issues in Comparative Grammar.* 1996
ISBN 0-7923-3778-6; Pb 0-7923-3779-4

Kluwer Academic Publishers – Dordrecht / Boston / London